For the principal, staff and students at Wycliffe Hall, Oxford

N. T. Wright, a native of Northumberland, took a 'double first' in Classics and Theology at Oxford and went on to complete his doctorate there on Pauline theology. He taught New Testament in Cambridge, McGill and Oxford universities, and worked in chaplaincy and other church contexts, before becoming Bishop of Durham in 2003 and then Professor of New Testament and Early Christianity in St Andrews in 2010. He is now Senior Research Fellow at Wycliffe Hall in Oxford. He has written more than eighty books and hundreds of articles, and has broadcast frequently on radio, TV and in podcasts. His online courses at www.ntwrightonline.org now have an audience of over 40,000 in over 180 countries.

Professor Wright is married to Maggie, with four adult children and five grandchildren. He lists golf, poetry and the Isle of Harris among his keen interests.

INTERPRETING SCRIPTURE

Essays on the Bible and Hermeneutics

N.T. Wright

ZONDERVAN
ACADEMIC

ZONDERVAN ACADEMIC

Interpreting Scripture
Copyright © 2020 by N. T. Wright

Requests for information should be addressed to:
Zondervan, *3900 Sparks Dr. SE, Grand Rapids, Michigan 49546*

Also published in Great Britain in 2020
Society for Promoting Christian Knowledge
36 Causton Street
London SW1P 4ST
www.spck.org.uk

ISBN 978-0-310-09836-2 (hardcover)

ISBN 978-0-310-09861-4 (ebook)

Cover Design: Brand Navigation

Printed in the United States of America

20 21 22 23 24 25 26 27 28 29 30 /LSC/ 20 19 18 17 16 15 14 13 12 11 10 9 8 7 6 5 4 3 2 1

For the principal, staff and students at Wycliffe Hall, Oxford

Contents

Contents

Preface

When I first began to read the Bible seriously for myself, around the age of twelve, I little thought just what a central place in my life it was going to occupy. Nor did I realize just how challenging it would be to try, over the years, both to think my way into the minds of the biblical writers and to explain and expound their work in many different contexts. Several of my books have, of course, drawn together my reflections on particular biblical themes (perhaps the best-known being *Surprised by Hope* (2007), on the resurrection and its relation to traditional teaching on 'heaven and hell'), but I have also given many lectures, and published many papers, on particular topics of scriptural interpretation, and this volume collects together what seem to me to have been some of the key ones.

I am grateful to the many publishers and editors who have given permission for these pieces to be made available in this way, and to my friends and publishers at SPCK and Zondervan for their work behind the scenes. I am greatly indebted to my research assistants Simon Dürr and Ethan Johnson for their painstaking work in scanning the original documents, inserting pagination with relevant page numbers in square brackets, lightly editing where typographical mistakes had crept in, and inserting occasional references to relevant material published subsequently. No attempt has been made, of course, to smooth out any internal contradictions or indeed repetitions. My views on various subjects displayed here have undergone a mostly gentle development, though not without some sudden leaps, and anyone interested in observing such changes will find plenty of material here.

Throughout the present volume, unless otherwise stated, quotations in English from the New Testament are either my own translation or taken from my published translation *The New Testament for Everyone* (SPCK, 2019), known in the USA as *The Kingdom New Testament* (Zondervan HarperCollins, 2012). As in that work, I always use lower-case 's' for 'spirit', not because I hold a 'low' view of the third person of the Trinity but because, in the first century, the early Christian use of the common and polysemous word *pneuma* had to make its own way without such help. Quotations from the Old Testament are either my own translation or taken from the New Revised Standard Version with Apocrypha, Anglicized (1995 edition). When quoting from the NRSV, I have replaced the term 'the LORD' with the name YHWH.

N. T. Wright
St Mary's College, St Andrews
Trinity 2019

Abbreviations

1 Stylistic Shorthands

cf.	confer
ch(s).	chapter(s)
ed(s).	edited by
edn.	edition
e.g.	for example
esp.	especially
et al.	and others
etc.	et cetera
f.	and the following
i.e.	that is
lit.	literally
n.	(foot/end)note
par.	parallel (in the synoptic tradition)
para.	paragraph
repr.	reprinted
tr.	translation/translated by
v(v).	verse(s)
vol(s).	volume(s)

2 Primary Sources

1 Esdr.	1 Esdras
2 Esdr.	2 Esdras
4 Ez.	*4 Ezra*
bYom.	Babylonian Talmud, Yoma
Jos.	Josephus (*Ant.*=*Jewish Antiquities*; *War*=*The Jewish War*)
Jub.	*Jubilees*
LXX	Septuagint version of the Old Testament
Philo	Philo of Alexandria (*Somn.*=*De Somniis*; *Vit. Mos.*=*De Vita Mosis*)
Suet.	Suetonius (*Vesp.*=*Vespasian*)

Tac.   Tacitus (*Hist.=Histories*)
Wis.   Wisdom of Solomon

3 Secondary Sources, etc.

AB   Anchor Bible
COQG   Christian Origins and the Question of God
JSNTSup   Journal for the Study of the New Testament Supplements
JTS   *Journal of Theological Studies*
KJV   King James Version
LNTS   Library of New Testament Studies
NEB   New English Bible
NRSV   New Revised Standard Version
SBL   Society of Biblical Literature
TDNT   *Theological Dictionary of the New Testament*, ed. G. Kittel and
           . G. Friedrich. 10 vols. Grand Rapids, MI: Eerdmans, 1964–1976.
WBC   Word Biblical Commentary
WUNT   Wissenschaftliche Untersuchungen zum Neuen Testament
ZNW   *Zeitschrift für die neutestamentliche Wissenschaft und die Kunde*
           der älteren Kirche

I
Introduction to *The Language and Imagery of the Bible* by G. B. Caird

George Caird was the last man in the world to think of establishing a 'school'. Precise historical scholarship and thoughtful theological reflection were his stock-in-trade, and were what he strove to inculcate in his pupils, rather than specific 'right' answers to key questions. Nor was he a campaigner, pushing a particular line in season and out. It is only in long retrospect that his major impact can appear, and it is still in my view sorely needed: his understanding of Jewish eschatology and its relevance to Jesus and the New Testament. The book to which the present piece was a second-edition introduction is perhaps the place where his thesis is most obviously displayed. I was honoured to be invited to write this piece – though it went through some severe rewriting after I had sent an early draft to Caird's widow, Mollie, who was not one to hold back criticism. I think in the end she was pleased with it, and I have been glad to maintain occasional links with their remarkable children as the years have gone by.

[xi] I

I was conducting a seminar in San Francisco when a participant asked me for some guidance on interpreting the different levels of language in the Bible. By way of reply, I pulled out of my bag the book the reader is now holding [*The Language and Imagery of the Bible*; see fuller details in the acknowledgments section]. At that, a different participant (a Presbyterian minister) exclaimed, 'That book saved my life!' I understood what he meant.

I happened to be in Oxford, visiting George Caird, the day that *Language and Imagery* was reviewed in *The Times*. He was like a dog with two tails. Not only was the review excellent (no surprises there). What gave him far greater pleasure was that in the same issue of *The Times* there were mentions of a play directed by his son, John, and of the Wigmore Hall debut of his oboist son, George. Such a simultaneous triple score must be some kind of record.

It is also an appropriate scene-setting for the reissue of the book in question. Caird was writing about, if one can put it like this, the drama and music of the Bible, and was writing as one to whom such things were not incidentals, peripheral enjoyments on the fringe of serious work, but were woven into his whole approach to life, teaching and scholarship. His was a rich and rounded personality, to which anything that was worthy of interest was also worthy of enthusiasm. He would conclude a lecture with an appropriate rhetorical flourish, gather up books, notes and the folds of his gown in a single movement, and leave the room with the last well-turned phrase still echoing. One might see him, a few minutes later, striding up Mansfield Road to watch the last half-hour of the morning play in a cricket match between Oxford University and one of the English counties. I recall him coming out of the inaugural lecture of one of his fellow professors to be greeted with the news that his beloved Mansfield College [xii] had, in his absence, scored a great success on the river. His reaction made it quite clear where he would rather have been that summer afternoon.

George was the kind of classical scholar for whom all of life came together in an intricate and exciting whole. Not for him the learned monograph that says more and more about less and less and ends by swallowing its own tail. He was a big-picture person, whose grasp of God, life, music, theology, family, sport, ornithology, biblical exegesis, carpentry, ecumenism and much else besides held these diverse interests together in a unique and compelling unity. The detail mattered vitally, as anyone who has read his articles on the Septuagint, his commentaries or, indeed, the present book, will bear witness. But the care he would lavish on an individual tree never made him, or his readers, forget where they were in the forest. Reader as well as author could sense different worlds attaining a fresh integration. (As I wrote this paragraph, I pulled down from my shelf the 1968 and 1969 issues of the *Journal of Theological Studies* (*JTS*), containing his articles on Septuagint lexicography. I inherited these issues from George himself, but had never before consulted them. Inside one of them, on a piece of blue card, was a note in his hand about the meaning of the rare word *apartia* in the Septuagint of Numbers 31.17, 18. Curious, I turned the card over. It was an advertisement for an Oxford concert of music by Bach, Bartok and Haydn, conducted by George Caird, junior. I rest my case.)

George Bradford Caird was born on 19 July 1917. His parents (as George never forgot) were Dundee Scots, but he himself was born in London, where the family was living because of war service. They then settled in Birmingham, at the heart of the English Midlands, where George's father was an engineer. The family attended Carr's Lane Congregational chapel, where the preaching was first-rate, and where in all probability George learned the pacifism that he was to hold throughout his life. Like many schools in those days, King Edward's in Birmingham offered an excellent classical education, and George took full advantage of it. He acquired a loving and exact knowledge of the Greek and Latin classics, which saw him to a scholarship, and then a Classical 'double first', at Peterhouse, Cambridge, and to a lifetime of fascinated continuing study. His move to [**xiii**] Mansfield College, Oxford, for his ministerial training was natural, given the college's high academic reputation, with former faculty members of the calibre of A. S. Peake, C. H. Dodd and T. W. Manson.

He combined his training with doctoral studies (under the auspices of Merton College, since Mansfield did not at that time have full university status). His thesis was, characteristically, both a word-study and a wide-ranging theological exploration. It was on the meaning of *doxa* ('glory') in the New Testament. Though it was never published as such, parts of it kept finding their way into his other writings, not least the present volume.

He added other languages to his repertoire. When, after a wartime pastorate in north London, he was invited to the chair of Old Testament at St Stephen's College, Edmonton, Alberta, the college administrators discovered after the invitation had been issued that George's doctorate was in New Testament, not Old. As Henry Chadwick told the story in his memorial address, they sent a telegram to Dr Micklem, the principal of Mansfield: 'Can Caird teach Hebrew?' The reply puts most New Testament scholars to shame: 'Yes – and if you give him an hour or two's notice, he can also teach Aramaic, Syriac, Coptic, Akkadian, Sogdian and Sumerian.' Hearing this anecdote put me in mind of the time when I commented to Caird on the fact that he had reviewed a book written in Italian. He explained that, as editor of *JTS*, he had hunted for someone who could read Italian and was interested in the subject. Failing to find anyone appropriate, he had decided to write a 'short note' (a review of only a few lines) himself. Having, however, equipped himself with an Italian dictionary, he discovered that he could read the book with increasing ease; having finished it and understood it, he wrote a characteristically lucid review.

The move to Edmonton came in the year following his marriage to Mollie (née Viola Mary Newport). In all that follows, one will not understand George unless one thinks of him as Mollie's husband. Where he could sometimes be austere, with minimal small-talk (at a party: 'Hello. I'm George Caird. I teach New Testament' – then silence), she was bubbling over with books read, plays seen, music enjoyed, birds spied and catalogued, children and grandchildren, people coming and going. George enjoyed [xiv] all these as keenly, and felt them all as deeply, as she; their way of expressing it was different, and naturally complementary. Mollie is a published poet. One can understand that when George wrote, in the preface to the present volume, that she had been to him 'at all times both Muse and critic', this meant just what it said. Her own delight in words matched his, and she and the children, as he also said, opened doors for him into worlds hitherto unknown.

From Edmonton he moved in 1950 to be Professor of New Testament at McGill University in Montreal, a position he occupied for nine years. (He was still warmly remembered when I arrived to take up the same chair thirty-one years later.) In Montreal he became Principal of the United Church College (the United Church of Canada had brought together Methodists, Congregationalists and some of the Presbyterians), and found himself acquiring a new string to his bow: a commitment to ecumenical work, which took him to the Second Vatican Council as an observer, and made him a frequent participant in, and commentator on, ecumenical endeavours of all sorts. In an article published in the year of his death he described himself as a 'lifelong ecumenist'.

During his time at McGill he published his first three books, and various articles, including his substantial piece on 1 and 2 Samuel in *The Interpreter's Bible*. The broad sweep of *The Truth of the Gospel* (1950), and the detailed learning of *Principalities and Powers* (1956), illustrate again the principle of the forest and the trees. His inaugural lecture at McGill had already announced that the time had come, after decades of dissection of the New Testament, to put things back together again. The very title – 'The New Testament view of life' – speaks both of the boldness of the scholar who dares to sum up so vast a topic, and of the proclivity to see the big picture, within which the details would find themselves not only included but enhanced.

There were those at Mansfield College who hoped that one day, when the then Senior Tutor retired, George would return to Oxford to take his place. Nobody knew, however, quite when this would happen, until the invitation arrived in 1959. Few academics so well launched on a North American career would have been prepared to accept the substantial drop in salary that such [xv] a move involved, but back the Cairds came, spending eleven years in the post before George, as again was only to be expected, succeeded to the Principalship in 1970. He had returned to North America to give the Birks Lectures at McGill, the Shaffer Lectures at Yale and the Fall Lectures at Union Seminary (Richmond, Virginia) in 1969. During his time as Senior Tutor he had given the Grinfield Lectures on the Septuagint and had published several articles, his masterly commentaries on Luke and Revelation, his book on the Second Vatican Council, and his slim but ground-breaking lecture *Jesus and the Jewish Nation*. The university elected him to a Readership, an honour as rare then as it is common now: since there was then only one 'Professor' in each subject area, the status of Reader was as far as anyone else could advance.

His literary ability was outstanding. George Caird, unlike a good many New Testament scholars, knew how to write good English. He was always polishing his prose, and a work would go through many revisions (and, one suspects, discussions with Mollie) before he was satisfied. His clear, crisp sentences say more in a few words than some scholars manage in several pages. A slim volume from Caird, easily mistaken for a slight or negligible work, is likely to be an explosive charge, packed with pithy wisdom.

This virtue is displayed to great effect in the commentaries, where the reader needs to see both what the paragraph under discussion is all about, and where its peculiar problems, and the possible ways of solving them, may lie. George, the master of the broad summary and the sharp analysis, blended both in section after section, painting the picture, explaining the allusions, sorting out the mare's nests, and then standing back and letting the reader appreciate the text for itself.

George's years as Principal of Mansfield were extremely busy. The mixture was as before, only more so: training ordinands, running a college which was playing an increasingly large part in the wider university, translating parts of the New English Bible (NEB) (once, in a lecture, he read, or rather declaimed, a splendid passage from Ben-Sirach, after which he paused, looked up and said 'I wrote that'), writing hymns, giving lectures, teaching graduates and enjoying his family. I first heard Britten's 'Metamorphoses' [xvi] while in the study with George Senior, having one of my early essays on Paul skilfully and devastatingly dismantled, with George Junior practising his oboe somewhere within earshot in the Principal's Lodgings.

On top of all this, he took a leading role in bringing together the 'Permanent Private Halls', as they were called (the theological training colleges, including the Roman Catholic and Nonconformist colleges), and setting up, for the benefit of all the ordinands in Oxford, the University Diploma in Theology. In addition, he was for two years Chairman of Oxford University's Theology Faculty Board (a demanding, not to say exhausting, post). As if all this were not enough, he became in the following year Moderator of the General Assembly of the United Reformed Church. The latter post, held by each occupant for a year, carried a kind of honorary archiepiscopal status. George decided that, rather than giving lectures or addresses, he would spend his year visiting as many congregations as he could and answering people's questions about the Bible. For him, it meant living on adrenalin; for his hearers, it was a wonderful chance to hear a world-class mind address problems that not all local clergy were equipped to handle. It is perhaps not surprising that in the eight years he was Principal he wrote only one major book, his commentary on Paul's 'Letters from Prison'.

He continued, however, to lecture and teach, as brilliantly as ever. One of those lecture-courses formed the basis for the present book, about which I shall say more presently. Two other courses he gave regularly were on New Testament Theology and New Testament Ethics. The latter, so far as I know, perished with him. The former was half way through being turned into a book at the time of his death, and has now been triumphantly finished by my one-time fellow research student, L. D. Hurst, and published by Oxford University Press. That is the book, above all, which draws together the major themes and emphases of Caird's thought.

His election to the Dean Ireland Chair meant that he had to move out of Mansfield after nearly twenty years, and become a Fellow of The Queen's College. George had initially hoped to retain the Principalship while holding the chair; an Oxford professor, unlike a Cambridge one, is not allowed by statute to be [xvii] the head of a college at the same time, but since Mansfield was still not (as it now is) a 'proper' Oxford college he hoped the regulation would not apply to him. When the authorities insisted that it would, he got his own back: he applied for permission to live in the country cottage that had been his holiday retreat, on the edge of the Downs, in excellent walking and birdwatching country. It was, by car, further away from Oxford than the regulations would allow. But, as he said in his official request, it was just inside the limit as the crow flies; 'and for this purpose professors should be deemed to be crows'. He won.

As far as his scholarship and teaching were concerned, he made a seamless transition to the Dean Ireland Chair, where, no longer having a college to run, he was able to devote himself to a new responsibility for which he was admirably equipped, that of co-editing the *Journal of Theological Studies*. Those unfamiliar with such matters may not appreciate the significance of the way he went about this task. Editors often content themselves with a short note either accepting or rejecting a proffered article. Frequently they delegate the task of reading and selecting manuscripts to other colleagues. George threw himself into editorship with characteristic thoroughness, employing much the same method he used when reading an essay or draft chapter from one of his graduate students. The form was always the same. In his own neat longhand (often on the back of something else, such as a list of forthcoming religious broadcasts, sent to him in one of his many consultative roles; ever the parsimonious Scot), he would go straight to the point:

- 'P. 2, para. 3, line 15: You have made an important point here, but you seem to have overlooked the following . . .
- P. 3, para. 1, line 10: But surely in that case Paul would have written *archē*, not *telos*?
- P. 4, para. 2, line 6: But see now the article in *ZNW* 1974, which demonstrates the opposite.
- P. 5, para. 3, line 14: [etc. etc.]'

Often the greatest compliment of which one would be aware at the time was when two pages passed without comment. On reflection, though, the compliment was that he would give such **[xviii]** attention to the detail of one's work. For the graduate student, the process could be devastating: that paper, one reflected ruefully, took eight weeks to write, and back it comes (always within a few days of submission) with all these criticisms. It made one determined not to let him do it again, though he always did. For writers submitting articles to the *Journal*, one suspects that in many cases it was the first time they had ever received such treatment. Articles revised accordingly and re-submitted could not but be greatly improved. Like Caird's translation work, the long hours of unglamorous labour had as their reward the knowledge that the world of scholarship and Bible reading were being well served. Clarity and discipline of thought; easy intimacy with the relevant literature; forceful, brief, lucid expression. An unstoppable combination.

As a teacher he could be formidable, sometimes devastating. He had thought the matter through and reached a decision, and there was no point wasting time discussing it further. (I remember him saying, of Philippians 2.5–11, 'Neither here nor anywhere else in all his writings does Paul make any use of the [Isaianic figure of the] servant of the Lord' – an opinion that many, myself included, have challenged.) One could imagine some pupils buckling under the strain. But if one accepted the challenge, there was great reward. Sometimes, late on in my own doctoral studies, I would arrive at his room in Queen's to be greeted with 'Ah, come in, come in; I'm not at all sure I agree with the line you took in your piece, but here's a cup of tea; sit down and we'll go at it.' There would follow a couple of hours or more of intense hand-to-hand fighting, ranging to and fro over texts, Hebrew roots, rabbinic allusions, greco-roman contexts, theology, occasionally a bit of church politics thrown in on the side, all with the sense that, whichever British Academy committee he was to chair the next day, this was the thing that really mattered in life. (Of course, he was like that with everything else as well.)

The Language and Imagery of the Bible came out in early 1980. None of us thought at the time that it would be the crown of his publishing career; that was to be the forthcoming *New Testament Theology*. But in retrospect, that was what it was. The following year he won the much-valued British Academy Burkitt Medal for Biblical Studies, and the book went [xix] on to win the Collins Religious Book Award. A few articles followed. He had a sabbatical and visited New Zealand, stopping off in Canada on the way back to visit old friends, the present writer included (and giving me a quick rundown on Canadian ornithology). He and Mollie were looking forward to retirement, which would have taken place in autumn 1984. Unknown to him, two of his former research students were plotting a volume of essays to commemorate his seventieth birthday in 1987. He intended to settle down and finish off the *New Testament Theology*, as well as the 'Past Master' volume on Paul (which was eventually written by his successor in the Dean Ireland Chair, Ed Sanders).

He spent some time turning the garage of their cottage into a study, where his practical skills were well employed fitting bookshelves. But on Easter Eve, 21 April 1984, at the cottage, he suffered a massive heart attack.

The news was telephoned round the world to friends and former students. Easter Day passed in a fog of sadness and memories. The funeral was held in Mansfield College Chapel the following Saturday (28 April); Dr Donald Sykes, his successor as Principal of Mansfield, gave the address. A memorial service was held in the Church of St Mary the Virgin, Oxford, on 13 October 1984, at which Professor Henry Chadwick gave the eulogy. Fittingly, the Allegri String Quartet came to the service and played the 'Cavatina' from Beethoven's Quartet, Opus 130; the musicians had become close friends of the family, and their presence reminded the large congregation of the many sides of George's life.

Donald Sykes's funeral address was published in the *Mansfield College Magazine*, no. 186, pp. 48–9. Henry Chadwick's was printed in the same publication, pp. 50–4, and reprinted on pp. xvii–xxii of the memorial volume (*The Glory of Christ in the New Testament*, ed. L. D. Hurst and N. T. Wright, Oxford University Press, 1987), which took the place of the planned Festschrift. A fuller memoir, discussing George's scholarly writings in some detail, was written by his friend and colleague of many years, Professor

James Barr, and published in the *Proceedings of the British Academy*, vol. 71 (1985), pp. 493–521. (This was, of course, before the posthumous publication of the *New Testament Theology*.) George's full curriculum vitae can be found in *The Glory of Christ in the New Testament*, pp. xv–xvi, and a bibliography of his published works [xx] is printed in the same volume, pp. xxiii–xxvii, and in the Caird–Hurst *New Testament Theology*, pp. 427–30. The published memoirs have, of course, been of invaluable assistance in the course of preparing the present biographical note.

II

The Language and Imagery of the Bible stands out as the final major literary achievement of Caird's lifetime. In it, as he says, he has tried 'to set out systematically for the ordinary reader the questions he needs to ask if he is to enhance his understanding of the Bible and his delight in its inexhaustible treasures'. It is unlike other books by biblical scholars, not least in that it combines all the conventional resources of the biblical specialist with the interests, discussions and insights of the grammarian, the literary critic, the psychologist and many others besides. Caird describes himself in the preface as being like an amateur gardener who 'accepts cuttings from everyone, hoping that they will take in his own soil'. They do.

On the day I described earlier, when his book was reviewed in *The Times*, I had myself just finished reading it. (I hadn't heard the original lectures; a quirk in the timetable had prevented me from attending them.) He asked me what I thought of it. I said I thought that he had basically wanted to say what he says in the three last chapters, and that he had found out he needed to write the previous eleven to prepare the ground for them – and that he had obviously thoroughly enjoyed the whole process. He was delighted (and I was relieved) that I had described exactly what his aim had been.

To get the full flavour of the book, therefore, one should read it as one might watch a great cathedral being built. The foundations and walls are crafted superbly, but they gain their real meaning from the arches, towers and spires which they support. And since the final pinnacle – the last chapter, on 'the language of eschatology' – is perhaps the most important thing in the book, it is there that we should start, to see where the whole project was going all along. We can then appreciate why the rest of the book is what it is. [xxi]

The problem of eschatology, and the language that expressed it, was one that Caird returned to again and again. He addressed it piecemeal in the Luke commentary; he dealt with it wholesale when commenting on Revelation (the key question is in the preface: 'What *on earth* is all this about?'). He published an article in French on 'Les eschatologies du Nouveau Testament'. The key essay, *Jesus and the Jewish Nation*, depends heavily on Caird's understanding of first-century Jewish eschatological language for its reconstruction of the historical ministry of Jesus.

The basic argument of the chapter is as follows. The word 'eschatology' has become such a slippery term in scholarly discourse that it is almost useless:

> during the last eighty-five years [that is, since Weiss and Schweitzer] it has been subjected to a series of tactical definitions which have rendered it more useful to those who want to win an argument than to those who aim at exact knowledge.

We must, then, distinguish between several different senses of the word. Eschatology^H (historical) speaks of the world having a literal end. Eschatology^I (individual) reflects on the eventual fate of the individual; when the biblical writers talk about this, they do not expect their language 'to be taken with flat-footed literalness' (a regular Cairdian protest). Eschatology^K (as in the German *konsequente Eschatologie*) is the sense proposed by Weiss and Schweitzer a century ago, and accepted with remarkable readiness on all sides: first-century Jews expected the literal end of the world to occur at any moment, and Jesus and the early Christians shared this belief. The problems this generated – in particular, the sense throughout early Christianity that the kingdom of God was in some sense already present – were addressed by C. H. Dodd in his proposal of 'realized eschatology' (Eschatology^R). Rudolf Bultmann then proposed a different variation on the theme: when Jesus used 'eschatological' language, he was using it to denote, not the literal end of the world, but the challenge to each individual to an encounter with God. This existentialist interpretation (Eschatology^E) could have pointed Bultmann in what Caird believed was the right direction, had it not been so ruthlessly individualistic. Other definitions come in around the edge as well; clearly the word 'eschatology' needs taking by the scruff of the neck and defining more tightly if it is to serve any useful purpose. **[xxii]**

Caird's own definition focuses on the central point: the biblical writers 'regularly used end-of-the-world language *metaphorically* [my emphasis] to refer to that which they well knew was not the end of the world'. It is because this is so important that he found himself forced to write five earlier chapters on metaphor. In the chapter we are considering, he illustrates his thesis copiously from the Old Testament and other Jewish writings. He then applies it, with typical brevity and clarity, to John the Baptist, to Luke's portrait of Jesus, to Mark 13 and its parallels (making the point he frequently stressed, that warnings about fleeing to the hills, or not stopping to get your belongings, make far more sense to someone threatened by imminent military invasion than they do to someone facing the Last Trump), and to Paul. 1 Corinthians 7, so much beloved by the advocates of Eschatology[K], does not after all declare that world history is coming to an end, but that, 'in a period when the old regime is cracking up, Christians must expect to live under harsh social pressure'.

So Weiss and Schweitzer were right to stress eschatology, but wrong to take the language literally. Bultmann was right to see it as concerning self-understanding, but wrong to make that self-understanding non-historical and individualistic. Dodd was right to stress realized eschatology, wrong to flatten out the continuing story-line. Here are three hammer blows at the most influential New Testament scholars of Caird's lifetime. And, the final touch, with the preacher's voice audible under the scholarly peroration:

> Wherever in the course of time men and women come face to face, whether for judgment or for salvation, with him who is the beginning and the end, that event can be adequately viewed only through the lenses of myth and eschatology.

The penultimate chapter, on myth, follows a similar pattern. The biblical writers use the language of mythology, not because they believe the myths concerned were literally true, but because this is the only available and appropriate lens through which to see the full significance of certain events. As with eschatology, the word 'myth' is used with a confusing range of meanings. The mythological language used in the Bible is a complex metaphor-system in which the writers add colour to their address to [xxiii] their own times by using a well-known tale told in a well-known way: the creation, for instance, seen in terms of the defeat of the chaos-monster, and retold again and again in relation to God's defeat of empires and tyrants. One of the most influential developments of the story is found in Daniel 7, after which no Jewish or Christian writer 'could use the lens of this myth except as it had been reground by Daniel'. This point, of course, underlies Caird's own influential and important understanding of Daniel 7 in the gospels.

The mythological language most often associated with Caird, though, has to do with the 'Principalities and Powers', and the chapter closes with a fresh treatment of this topic, to which he so often returned through four decades of scholarship. The 'powers' are not abstractions, but personal beings. They are not simply the human authorities referred to in (for example) Romans 13. They are not God's attendant angels. They are not the 'denizens of a fantasy world of demons'. They are, rather, 'heavenly beings who represent the power structures of the old world order which Paul believed to be tottering to its end'. Paul, like other biblical writers, is using mythological language to interpret actual historical events. But he is also using language about history to reinterpret the myths. As a result (again, we hear the preacher's voice rounding off the chapter):

> henceforth the victories of God over all the forces in the universe which are resistant to his will are to be won, not by the thunderbolts of coercive might, but by the persuasive constraints of self-sacrificing love.

Continuing to work backwards, we reach the chapter on language and history. Once again, there are distinctions to be made, this time between 'history', 'historical', 'historic' and the like. History is to be distinguished from saga, legend, novel and pseudepigraph. Most events are not described, perhaps are not describable, in 'neutral' terms: when Exodus says that the sea piled up at the blast of YHWH's nostrils, and when Paul says that on the cross the principalities and powers were disarmed and put to shame, they are referring to historical events, and 'we cannot say that where there is more interpretation there is [xxiv] less history'. Just because the gospel-writers are preaching theologians, that does not mean they are making their stories up. When they spoke of the resurrection of Jesus, the fact that they wrote out of Christian faith cannot disguise the fact that they intended to speak, not of their own inner experience, but of something that had actually happened. Here as elsewhere, history involves recognizing the consequences of a particular action or event, which is why 'we cannot write a history of our own times'. The historian was – and, Caird implies, still is – in a position analogous to that of the prophet in the Old Testament: making moral judgments, giving the true interpretation of what might otherwise remain random events, and being judged accordingly.

The final three chapters, which sum up so much of the method and content of Caird's other major writings, rest on the foundation of the middle section of the book (chs. 7 to 11). This deals with metaphor. Caird grasps at once the problem that, in contemporary usage, linguistic statements are often confused with metaphysical ones. Saying (as one must) that the phrase 'the body of Christ' is a metaphor is not to deny the existence of a reality to which that metaphor refers. (This problem persists. Some scholars have disputed Caird's metaphorical reading of apocalyptic language by suggesting that he made it into 'mere metaphor' – a phrase that would have guaranteed a snort of defiance from G. B. C.) The discussion is wide-ranging. Different types of non-literal speech are carefully distinguished, with fascinating and well-chosen examples. We are treated to further discussions of parable, allegory, the hidden poetry of Paul, anthropomorphism and Bultmann's programme of 'demythologization'. We are also introduced to metaphors about metaphors: 'All words are liable to fatigue and exhaustion through overuse, and metaphors are particularly susceptible.' It is vital to understand the particular point of a particular comparison:

> when the psalmist tells us that a united family is like oil dripping down Aaron's beard on to the skirts of his robe, he is not trying to persuade us that family unity is messy, greasy or volatile; he is thinking of the all-pervasive fragrance . . .

Metaphor, rightly understood, is a lens through which we see things we would otherwise miss. This, then, is the basis for the particular examples of metaphor dealt with in the final three [xxv] chapters. To understand history, myth and eschatology you must understand how metaphor works, particularly how it is used in the Bible.

To understand metaphor, however, you must understand language and imagery in general. This is the wide-ranging subject of the first part (roughly the first half) of the book. There is not much point attempting to summarize this coherent, step-by-step, yet copiously illustrated and diverse discussion, which ranges far and wide through linguistics, semantics, etymology (pausing to note that the word 'etymology' encapsulates a mistake, since according to its own etymology it suggests that true meanings are contained in a word's derivation, whereas in fact true meaning is a function of usage) and much besides. The same section which points out the ambiguity of the sentence 'I'm mad about my flat' (is the speaker an Englishman enthusiastic about his living quarters, or an American furious about her puncture?) also highlights the momentous fact that, according to the writers of the New Testament, 'with the coming of Jesus the whole situation of mankind has so altered as to change the semantic content of the word "God".' There are brief but powerful vignettes of topics close to Caird's heart throughout his career: the argument and theology of the letter to the Hebrews, the authorship of Ephesians, the problem of the 'son of man'. And much more.

We are warned about the pitfalls that open up before us if we fail to recognize the linguistic usage we are faced with. We are advised not to try to discover meanings beyond, or behind, those the original writers intended (had Caird lived to see the full flowering of postmodernism, we can predict what his reaction might have been). He points out that when the biblical writers used a word, we should not assume they meant what we today would mean by it – advice that, if heeded, would enable a good many theologians, both scholarly and popular, to stop wasting time and to concentrate on the real issues. He remarks that those who apply surgery to a biblical text are, as often as not, tacitly admitting their failure to understand it. Here, again, we meet the principles that guided Caird throughout his own work as a biblical scholar, a preacher and also, interestingly, as a practising biblical translator. One feels that, when he discusses the Septuagint, he does so as a fellow professional, recognizing the trans-[**xxvi**]-lator's efforts to grapple with problems he himself knew at first hand.

III

Yes, I am an enthusiast. I would not have undertaken this task unless I believed that this book, whose influence is already considerable, has the potential to teach a new generation of readers, preachers, translators and scholars how to read the Bible for all it's worth. But I am not, I hope, an uncritical enthusiast. There are certain points which, were he still alive, I would wish to question or challenge.

Caird was uncompromisingly loyal to the New English Bible, on which he had, of course, himself laboured. I do not know which sections he drafted himself, though I believe (since he had returned to the UK some time after the project's inception) that he was mostly assigned portions of the Apocrypha. But I do not share his enthusiasm. I have used the NEB in daily public reading, and it does not wear well. Its occasional triumphs are more than offset by its frequently ponderous style. Try reading 2 Corinthians 3 out loud, and ask yourself whether the repeated 'splendour' would not have been rendered better as 'glory'. The Revised English Bible has made several important improvements – including replacing 'glory'; but it has not, to my mind, alleviated the underlying problem.

A particular question of interpretation arises at a point where one might have supposed that Caird's varied interests would have come together in a way other than they did. In discussing the parables, he remarks that an explained parable is about as effective as an explained joke, and suggests that, though the interpretations of (for example) the parable of the sower may well have captured something of what Jesus actually intended, they are none the less probably secondary. Caird was rightly critical of the line of interpretation begun by Jülicher and brought down by Boucher and others, in which 'allegorical' interpretation was ruled out as being necessarily late, and the parables were reduced to moral lessons; but at this point he did not, I think, go far enough. What he did not see – surprisingly, given his careful and nuanced reading [xxvii] of apocalyptic literature – is that the *form* of Mark 4.1–20 is precisely that of the apocalyptic vision. First the somewhat strange story, step by step; then the question of meaning, and the comment about the special privilege of knowing the secrets of the kingdom of God; then the point-by-point interpretation. Of course, since this is a parable told by a prophet, not a vision reported by a seer, we may be forgiven for not seeing the parallel at once. But, once seen, I submit that it is irresistible. Recognizing this point would, I think, have enhanced rather than undermined certain other aspects both of this book and of Caird's thought in general.

Another controversial matter, in which I think the last word has yet to be spoken, is Caird's continued insistence that the New Testament writers spoke of Jesus being *appointed* to his divine 'sonship'. This has sometimes given readers the quite erroneous impression that Caird himself held an 'adoptionist' Christology, a suggestion that his work on (for example) Philippians 2.5–11 or Colossians 1.15–20 should dispel (see, too, his essay on 'The development of the doctrine of Christ in the New Testament' in *Christ for Us Today*, ed. N. Pittenger, SCM Press, 1968, pp. 66–80). But I am not sure that, granted that some of the New Testament does indeed speak of Jesus' 'appointment' to divine sonship, this is, even in the relevant contexts, the central or the most appropriate way of getting to the heart of what was being said.

These are small queries. Looking again through the book, what strikes me is its sheer richness. Page after page sparkles both with fascinating examples and with Caird's own sharp prose and dry wit. If one is going to write a book about language and imagery, it is as well to show oneself a master of it. If one is going to write a book about the Bible, it is as well to show oneself able to handle it from beginning to end, from creation to apocalypse, from the similes of the Song of Songs to the puzzles of Pauline theology. Caird does all this and more. On page after page he shows himself both a master exegete and, equally important, a deep and thoughtful lover of scripture. He obviously relished it, pondering its nuances, surveying its broad sweep, delighting in its poetry, puzzling out its obscurities. Some things are better caught than taught. Readers who come to Caird through this book will put themselves in the way of catching the sheer excitement of reading the Bible, as well as learning [**xxviii**] the major lessons it has to offer. Had he lived, he would have written several more books, each important in its own way. But even George Caird would have found it hard to write a better book than this one.

2

The Lord's Prayer as a Paradigm of Christian Prayer

It was a delight to get to know Richard L. Longenecker when he was in Toronto and I was in Montreal (where I was professor from 1981 to 1986). We kept in touch, and when he organized a series of symposia on various topics, and the subject of 'prayer' came round, I was honoured to be invited to give a paper on the Lord's Prayer. As one might expect, I have written about this prayer in various places, including *The Lord and His Prayer* (Wright 1996b). That gave me a platform for further reflections at the symposium itself.

[132] 'As our saviour Christ hath commanded and taught us, we are bold to say: "Our Father . . ."' So runs the old liturgical formula, stressing the Pater Noster as a command and its use as a daring, trembling, holy boldness. At one level, this is entirely appropriate. At another level, however, it fails to catch the most remarkable thing about the Lord's Prayer – and so fails to grasp the truly distinctive feature in Christian prayer that this prayer points us to. For the Lord's Prayer is not so much a command as an invitation: an invitation to share in the prayer-life of Jesus himself.

Seen with Christian hindsight – more specifically, with Trinitarian perspective – the Lord's Prayer becomes an invitation to share in the *divine* life itself. It becomes one of the high roads into the central mystery of Christian salvation and Christian existence: that the baptized and believing Christian is (1) incorporated into the inner life of the triune God *and* (2) intended not just to believe that this is the case, but actually to experience it.

The Lord's Prayer, along with the eucharist, forms the liturgical equivalent to what Eastern Orthodox church architecture portrays and western Gothic architecture depicts – both developing, each in its own way, the central Temple-theology of Judaism. The God worshipped here, says this architecture, is neither a remote dictator nor simply the sum total of human god-awareness. This God is both intimately present within the [133] world *and* utterly beyond, other, and different from it. He is present to celebrate with his people and to grieve with them, to give them his rich blessings and to rescue them from all ills, because he is also sovereign over heaven and earth, sea and dry land, all the powers of this world, and even over the urgings of the human heart. The Lord's Prayer is an invitation to know this God and to share his innermost life.

All this is so, more particularly, because the Lord's Prayer is the 'true exodus' prayer of God's people. Set originally in a thoroughgoing eschatological context, its every clause resonates with Jesus' announcement that God's kingdom is breaking into the story of Israel and the world, opening up God's long-promised new world and summoning people to share it. If this context is marginalized – or regarded as of historical interest only (because, for instance, as some would suggest, the *parousia* did not arrive on schedule) – the prayer loses its peculiar force and falls back into a generalized petition for things to improve, albeit still admittedly to God's glory. In order for it to be prayed with anything approaching full authenticity, therefore, it is necessary to be grasped afresh by the eschatological vision and message of Jesus himself, who announced the true exodus, the real return from exile, and all that is implied by these wide-ranging shorthand expressions.[1]

I begin this article, therefore, with some reflections on the rootedness of the Lord's Prayer within the ministry and kingdom-announcement of Jesus. This will lead to a fuller exposition of the way in which the Lord's Prayer opens up the heart of Jesus' 'new exodus' project and invites those who so pray to become part of it. And this will then lead to some reflections on the shape and content of Christian liturgical praying and private praying, and, finally, to some concluding remarks moving on from the 'Our father' of Jesus' ministry to the 'Abba' cry of which Paul speaks in Galatians 4 and Romans 8.

I The Lord's Prayer and Jesus' Own Prayer-Life

References to Jesus' own practice of private prayer are scattered throughout the gospels and clearly reflect an awareness on the part of his first followers that this kind of private prayer – not simply formulaic petitions, but wrestling with God over real issues and questions – formed the undercurrent of his life and public work. The prayer that Jesus gave his fol-[134]-lowers embodies his own prayer-life and his wider kingdom-ministry in every clause.

---

1   On these topics, see Wright 1996a.

Father/Our Father

Jesus' own address to God, it appears, regularly included 'father'. Though the Aramaic word *Abba* is only found in the gospels in the Gethsemane narrative at Mark 14.36, there is a broad consensus (1) that Jesus indeed used this word in prayer, and (2) that the notion of God's fatherhood – though, of course, known also in Judaism – took central place in his own attitude to God in a distinctive way. So when the prayer given to his followers begins with 'Father' (Luke 11.2) or 'Our father' (Matthew 6.9; *Didache* 8.2–3, which also begins 'Our father'), we must understand that Jesus wants them to see themselves as sharing his own characteristic spirituality – that is, his own intimate, familial approach to the creator. The idea of God's fatherhood, and of building this concept into the life of prayer, was not, as must again be stressed, a novelty within Judaism. But the centrality and particular emphasis that Jesus gave it represents a new departure.

Hallowed Be Your Name

The sanctifying of God's name, as in the clause 'hallowed be your name' (Luke 11.2//Matthew 6.9), is not a major theme in the gospels. Where it does occur – as, for example, in Mary's exclamation, 'Holy is his name!' (Luke 1.49); or Jesus' prayer, 'Father, glorify your name'; and the father's response, 'I have glorified it, and will glorify it again' (John 12.28) – it appears as a natural, and typically Jewish, affirmation of God's holiness and majesty. But the hallowing or sanctifying of God's name is thoroughly consistent with the sort of work that Jesus conceived himself to be undertaking.

Your Kingdom Come

The coming of God's kingdom, however, as expressed by the petition 'your kingdom come' (Matthew 6.10//Luke 11.2), is a major theme throughout the entire gospel tradition. And though its interpretation has some-[135]-times been controversial, there is no doubt (1) that Jesus made this the central theme of his proclamation, and (2) that he meant by it that the long-awaited kingdom or rule of God, which involved the salvation of Israel, the defeat of evil, and the return of YHWH himself to Zion, was now at last happening.[2]

Inaugurated eschatology, or the presence *and* the future of God's kingdom, was a hallmark of Jesus' public career – as it was, probably, of the Teacher of Righteousness a century or more earlier and of Simeon ben-Kosiba a

---

2 See Wright 1996a, chs. 6–10.

hundred years later.[3] Where the leader, God's chosen one, was present, the kingdom was already present. But there was, of course, still work to be done, redemption to be won. The present and the future did not cancel one another out, as in some unthinking scholarly constructions. Nor did 'present' mean 'a private religious experience', and 'future' mean 'a *Star Wars*-type apocalyptic scenario'.

The presence of the kingdom meant that God's anointed Messiah was here and was at work – that he was, in fact, accomplishing, as events soon to take place would show, the sovereign and saving rule of God. The future of the kingdom was the time when justice and peace would embrace one another and the whole world – the time from which perspective one could look back and see that the work had, indeed, begun with the presence and work of the anointed leader.[4]

To pray 'your kingdom come' at Jesus' bidding, therefore, meant to align oneself with his kingdom-movement and to seek God's power in furthering its ultimate fulfilment. It meant adding one's own prayer to the total performance of Jesus' agenda. It meant celebrating in the presence of God the fact that the kingdom was already breaking in, and looking eagerly for its consummation. From the centrality of the kingdom in his public proclamation and the centrality of prayer in his private practice, we must conclude that this kingdom-prayer grew directly out of and echoed Jesus' own regular praying.

Your Will Be Done

The performance of God's will, as voiced in the entreaty 'your will be done on earth as it is in heaven' (Matthew 6.10) – whether one sees that clause as [136] subordinate to the clause 'your kingdom come' (Matthew 6.10//Luke 11.2) or as distinct – chimes in with the emphasis of Jesus at several points in his recorded work. This is particularly noticeable in John's gospel. But it finds many echoes in the synoptic gospels, not least in Luke's repetition of how God's will *must* be fulfilled.

Give Us Today Our Daily Bread

The prayer for bread, as in 'give us today [or, 'day by day'] our daily bread' (Matthew 6.11//Luke 11.3), awakens echoes that resound throughout Jesus' public ministry. The two evangelists who give us the Lord's Prayer also give

---

3 See Wise 1999, which is a stimulating and suggestive book, even if the argument is possibly pressed too far.
4 Wright 1996a, ch. 10.

us the temptation stories, where Jesus' hunger and his refusal to create bread for himself feature prominently (compare Matthew 4.2–4; Luke 4.2–3). The wilderness feeding stories suggest both a literal feeding and a symbolic act that demonstrated God's power, operative through Jesus, to provide for the needs of the people (compare Mark 6.32–44 par.; 8.1–10 par.). Jesus' own prayers of thanks on these occasions (compare Mark 6.41 par.; 8.6 par.; see also Luke 24.30) are translated by the Lord's Prayer into a trustful prayer for God's regular provision.

One of the most securely established features of Jesus' public ministry in recent discussion, with only an occasional dissenter,[5] is his frequent participation in the festive meals of his day, where he celebrated the kingdom with all comers. One does not have to go all the way with the members of the Jesus Seminar, who have described Jesus as 'the proverbial party animal', in order to appreciate that the sharing of food, both actually and symbolically, was a central feature of his life.

The sequence of meals in the story of Jesus reaches its climax, of course, in the Last Supper. The bread there was – again in the context of prayer – given a special meaning, which echoes back throughout Jesus' lifetime and on to the cross and his resurrection. To pray for bread (whether for 'today', as in Matthew, or for 'day by day', as in Luke), therefore, is once again to align oneself with one of the most central and practical symbols of Jesus' kingdom-work. Bread follows from and symbolizes the kingdom, both in the Lord's Prayer and in Jesus' own career. [137]

Forgive Us Our Debts/Sins

The prayer for forgiveness – 'forgive us our debts, as we also have forgiven our debtors' (Matthew 6.12); 'forgive us our sins, for we also forgive everyone who sins against us' (Luke 11.4) – is the one instance of a prayer Jesus taught his followers to pray that they did not suppose he needed to pray himself. The well-known scene of John the Baptist's initial objection to baptizing Jesus (Matthew 3.14–15) and the very early tradition of Jesus' personal sinlessness (compare John 7.18; 8.46; 2 Corinthians 5.21; Hebrews 4.15; 1 Peter 2.22) bear witness to the great divide at this point between Jesus and his followers. They needed to repent and seek God's forgiveness, but he did not.

This exception, however, clearly proves the rule that the Lord's Prayer was intended by Jesus to bind his followers closely to the agenda of his whole ministry. Forgiveness, which is offered freely and without recourse to the Temple-system,

---

5 E.g. Allison Jr 1998.

was another hallmark of Jesus' work – indeed, so much so that it was the cause of scandal (as, for example, in Mark 2.5–12). Furthermore, there is good reason to think that Jesus regarded this free offer of forgiveness as a central part of his inauguration of the new covenant, and that he saw the corresponding obligation to mutual forgiveness as a necessary badge of membership.[6] This prayer for forgiveness, therefore, though not aligning itself with anything in Jesus' own spirituality, belongs very closely with the total picture of Jesus' public ministry, as his ministry is set out in the gospel narratives.

Lead Us Not into Temptation, but Deliver Us from the Evil One

With the prayer about deliverance from temptation (*peirasmos*) and the evil one (*ho ponēros*) of Matthew 6.13, we are back again with Jesus. Again, the temptation narratives of Matthew 4.1–11 and Luke 4.1–13 are close at hand as part of the context; and again, the Gethsemane scene and the complex of 'trials' before Caiaphas and Pilate offer themselves as the wider setting.

Jesus' whole public career was marked by 'trials' of one sort or another – by what he, and the evangelists, saw as a running battle with the powers of evil, whether in the form of possessed souls shrieking in the syn-[138]-agogues or angry souls challenging in the market-place. The fact that Jesus was not spared these trials, but had to face them at their fiercest, suggests a clue as to the meaning of this controversial clause, which we will pursue later.

Here in the prayer of deliverance is, once again, one of the clearest overtones in the Lord's Prayer: 'Let me be as my master.' 'You are those', says Jesus in Luke 22.28, 'who have continued with me in my trials (*en tois peirasmois mou*)'. So in giving this prayer, Jesus is inviting his followers to share his own struggles and to experience the same spirituality that sustained him.

This brief survey is enough to demonstrate that the Lord's Prayer is by no means simply a collage of vaguely suitable material culled from the liturgical culture of second-Temple Judaism. Its shape and content remind us of the public career of Jesus at every point. And since Jesus' public career was solidly rooted and reflected in his own life of prayer, we must conclude that the Lord's Prayer is an invitation to share Jesus' own prayer-life – and with it his agenda, his work, his pattern of life and his spirituality. The Lord's Prayer marks out Jesus' followers as a distinct group not simply because Jesus gave it to them, but because it encapsulates his own mission and vocation. And it

---

6   See Wright 1996a, 268–74.

does this in a form appropriate for his followers, which turns them into his co-workers and fellow labourers in prayer for the kingdom.

Of course, if one thinks of Jesus simply as a great human teacher, then summoning his followers to share his own pattern and style of prayer is a reasonable commonplace. But if we accept the early Christian assessment of Jesus – with its dramatically high, though still Jewish, Christology – what has been said so far strongly implies that here within the Lord's Prayer we are meeting the beginnings of Trinitarian soteriology: the son is inviting his followers to share the intimacy of his own life with the father.

2 People of the New Exodus

All of what we have set out above, however, leads us to the present, main section of this article. In this section the theses will be proposed (1) that Jesus saw his kingdom-work in terms of the much-hoped-for 'new exodus', and (2) that the Lord's Prayer encapsulates this vision. [139]

The Lord's Prayer as Encapsulating and Celebrating a New-Exodus Vision

The events of Israel's exodus from Egypt, the people's wilderness wanderings and their entry into the promised land were of enormous importance in the self-understanding and symbolism of all subsequent generations of Israelites, including Jews of the second-Temple period. The geographical 'return' of the nation from exile, however, had not been matched by the fulfilment of the promises that the people of Israel would be free from pagan domination and free to serve YHWH in their own land. When that happened, it was expected that the exodus would form the backdrop for that much-longed-for real return from exile.[7]

When YHWH restored the fortunes of Israel, it would be like a new exodus – a new and greater liberation from an enslavement greater than that in Egypt. There are signs of this theme scattered liberally throughout the gospels. The reported conversation of Moses and Elijah with Jesus on the Mount of Transfiguration in Luke 9.31, where the focus of their discussion is on Jesus' 'exodus' that he was about to accomplish at Jerusalem, is one prominent example of this theme. And the Lord's Prayer can best be seen in this light as well – that is, as the prayer of the new wilderness-wandering people.

---

7 See Wright 1996a, xvii–xviii; 1999b.

Typological correspondences between the exodus of Israel's memory and the new exodus of Christian proclamation are complex, and should not be pressed for exact one-to-one correspondences. That is not how this sort of thing works. None the less, it may be reasonably claimed that for the evangelists – and arguably for Jesus himself – the equivalent of the crossing of the Red Sea is the death and resurrection of Jesus. The Last Supper is the Passover meal that anticipates, and gives meaning to, the great act of liberation. From that point of view, the wilderness wandering, led by the pillar of cloud and fire, does not occur until the post-Easter period – where exactly this theme is picked up, as we will see, by Paul in Romans 8.

There are some signs, indeed, that Jesus saw the period of his ministry as, at least in certain respects, parallel to that of Moses at the court of Pharaoh. Luke 11.20, for example, alluding to Exodus 8.19, portrays Jesus as saying: 'If I by the finger of God cast out demons, then the kingdom of God has come upon you.' The parallel in Matthew 12.28 has 'spirit' for 'finger', so it is, of course, possible that Luke deliberately created an exodus al-[140]-lusion in a Jesus-saying where it was not originally present. But even if an accumulation of such points were held to prove that Jesus regarded his followers prior to Calvary and Easter as still 'in Egypt', I would still argue that the Lord's Prayer was designed to constitute them as 'exodus people', 'freedom people' – in fact, as 'new-covenant people'.

The Lord's Prayer, in fact, was designed to encapsulate and celebrate, in the presence of God, the liberation that had already begun to take place and that had yet to be completed. It was designed to enable Jesus' followers to beseech the father that they would be enabled to remain loyal to his freedom purposes through all the tribulations that lay ahead. This can be seen more particularly as we look again at each of the clauses of the Lord's Prayer from a new-exodus perspective.

Father/Our Father

In highlighting echoes from the exodus tradition in the Lord's Prayer, we must begin, of course, with 'father': 'Israel is my son, my firstborn; let my son go, that he may serve me' (Exodus 4.22–23); 'When Israel was a child, I loved him, and out of Egypt I called my son' (Hosea 11.1). Calling God 'father' not only evokes all kinds of associations of family life and intimacy; more importantly, it speaks to all subsequent generations of God as the God of the exodus, the God who rescues Israel precisely because Israel is God's firstborn son. The title 'father' says as much about Israel, and about the events through which God will liberate Israel, as it does about God.

Jesus' own sense of vocation, that of accomplishing the new exodus, was marked principally by his awareness of God as father.[8] Now in the Lord's Prayer he invites his followers to consider themselves exodus-people. Their cry for redemption will be heard and answered.

Hallowed Be Your Name

God revealed himself to Moses in the burning bush, speaking his name and giving it as the main reason why he could be trusted to bring the children of Israel out of captivity (compare Exodus 3.13–16). And it was the honour and [141] reputation of YHWH's name that Moses would subsequently use as the fulcrum in his great prayer for Israel's forgiveness after the episode of the golden calf – a theme that was also picked up by Joshua after the debacle at Ai (compare Exodus 32.11–14; Joshua 7—9). The sanctifying of God's name, in other words, has to do once more not merely with God's own reputation in, as it were, a private capacity, but with the fact that he is committed to and in covenant with the people of Israel. To pray that God's name be hallowed, therefore, is to pray that the exodus may not only happen but be followed through to its proper conclusion – that is, that Israel be redeemed not only from the original slavery of Egypt, but also from the sin and rebellion that keeps the nation from arriving and safely settling in the promised land.

Your Kingdom Come

The sovereign rule of the one true God is, of course, the main subtext of the battle between Moses and Pharaoh. As with Elijah and the prophets of Baal, the story of the exodus is a story about which God is the stronger. It is in deliberate evocation of the exodus theme that Isaiah 52.7–10 writes of the great return:

> How beautiful upon the mountains
> are the feet of the messenger who announces peace;
> who brings good news, who announces salvation,
> who says to Zion, 'Your God reigns.'
> Listen! Your sentinels lift up their voices,
> together they sing for joy;
> for in plain sight they see YHWH returning to Zion . . .
> YHWH has made bare his holy arm before all the nations;
> all the ends of the earth shall see the salvation of our God.

---

8   Cf. Wright 1996a, ch. 13.

The exodus is the background; the great return the foreground; the kingdom of YHWH the main theme. This is the context of Jesus' own kingdom-announcement, the setting that gives meaning to the kingdom-clause in the Lord's Prayer. [142]

Your Will Be Done

The doing of YHWH's will on earth as in heaven is, of course, part of the whole apocalyptic theme in which heavenly truths and events become embodied in their earthly counterparts. Part of the point of the whole Sinai theophany – the central part, in fact, of the exodus-story – was the meeting of heaven and earth, with Moses as the intermediary who went to and fro between the two spheres, so that laws and instructions made in heaven could be carried out on earth. This anticipates (or, depending on one's view of Pentateuchal origins, reflects) the Temple-theology in which the sanctuary was considered to be quite literally the place where heaven and earth met. If Torah was the means by which, within Israel, God's will was to be done on earth as in heaven, and if the Temple was the place where this was embodied in cultic celebration and sacrifice, to pray that this might happen anew – within the context of the new-exodus motifs already so strongly present – was to pray not merely that certain things might occur within the earthly realm that would coincide with plans that God had made in the heavenly realm, but that a fresh integration of heaven and earth would take place in which all that Temple and Torah had stood for would be realized afresh. It was to pray both that God's saving purpose for Israel and the world would come about through God's personal action, and that God's people would find themselves not merely shaped by a law, however divine, or focused on a building, however God-given, but embraced by a saving personal love.

'Thy will be done on earth as in heaven' can, of course, carry all sorts of further overtones, such as prayers for wise political solutions to world-shaking crises, prayers for bread for the hungry and prayers for justice for the oppressed. But at its heart lies a prayer for the appropriate integration of heaven and earth that the early Christians came to see already accomplished in Jesus himself – who was like Moses, but so much more so – and came to long for in God's eventual future (compare Revelation 21; see also Romans 8.17–30, which we will discuss later).

Give Us Today Our Daily Bread

The prayer for bread has its historical background in the provision of manna in the wilderness. God's daily gift, following the people's grum-[143]-bling, became the stuff of legend. Jesus' actions in the feeding miracles alluded to the wilderness stories, as the evangelists (especially John) suggest. In the context of the Lord's Prayer, this clause aligns the followers of Jesus with the people of the wilderness generation and their need to know God's daily supply of not only literal bread but also of all that it symbolized.

Manna was not needed in Egypt. Nor would it be needed in the promised land. It is the food of inaugurated eschatology, the food that is needed because the kingdom has already broken in and because it is not yet consummated. The daily provision of manna signals that the exodus has begun, but also that we are not yet living in the land.

Forgive Us Our Debts/Sins

The story of the manna, however, was also the story of Israel's sin and lack of faith. The prayer for forgiveness, therefore, is quite appropriate in this context, and not merely another item in a shopping-list of spiritual needs and wants. In the light of Jeremiah 31 and Jesus' offer of forgiveness as the central blessing of the new covenant – that is, the great return that was happening through his work – forgiveness is raised to a new height. If the Egypt from which the new exodus is freeing God's people is the Egypt of sin and all that it produces, then the prayer 'Forgive us our sins' becomes precisely the prayer of those still in Egypt: 'Deliver us from Pharaoh!'

Matthew and the *Didache*, of course, present Jesus as speaking of the forgiveness of debts (as in Matthew) or debt (as in the *Didache*). I have elsewhere agreed with those who see in this a sign of the Jubilee, and of Jesus' intention being that his followers should celebrate it among themselves.[9] The Jubilee provisions, of course, look back to the fact that Israel had been enslaved in Egypt and that God had rescued and delivered it (see Leviticus 25.38, 42, 55). They were part of the exodus-theology. In the same way, Jesus' demand that his followers should forgive one another belongs precisely within the same logic. Redeemed slaves must themselves live as redemption people. The inner connection between forgiving others and being forgiven oneself, which is so strongly emphasized in Matthew 6.14–15 and 18.21–35 (compare Sirach 28.1–7), grows directly out of this exodus-motif. **[144]**

Lead Us Not into Temptation, but Deliver Us from the Evil One

In this wider context the difficulties about the clause 'Do not lead us to "the testing"', which are reflected in current debates about the wording for

---

9   See Wright 1996a, 294–5.

liturgical use, may be addressed with some hope of success. Who is testing whom, with what intent and with what result?

The normal assumption is that the prayer is asking to be spared having one's faith tested by God. But the tradition throughout early Christianity that sees the testing of one's faith as a necessary part of discipleship – indeed, as a following of Jesus – speaks strongly against such an understanding. Is it, then, as Albert Schweitzer thought, the eschatological *peirasmos* – the Great Tribulation, the worst moment in history – that the prayer is asking to be spared from? A strong case for this reading can be made out, and I have myself taken this line in the past.[10]

On this view, Jesus believed that 'messianic woes' were coming on Israel, and that it was his particular task and vocation to go out ahead and take the full weight of them on himself, so that the people would not need to undergo them. This would explain the repetition in Gethsemane of his command to his disciples: 'Watch and pray, that you may not enter the *peirasmos*' (Matthew 26.41; Mark 14.38; Luke 22.46) – meaning by that command: 'Pray that you may be spared this great moment of anguish; it is my task to enter it alone.' (We may note, however, that when Jesus himself prayed a somewhat similar prayer the answer was 'No'.) And such an interpretation fits well with what I have elsewhere argued to be Jesus' perception of the moment of crisis in which he saw himself as having a central role.

But it remains somewhat strange to see this as the complete explanation of 'lead us not into temptation'. For if the early Christians came to believe that in some sense the great *peirasmos* had, indeed, happened to Jesus on the cross, why would they have continued to pray this clause in the Lord's Prayer thereafter? Granted, the fall of Jerusalem, which was still in the future for those who handed on the early traditions, had been spoken of by Jesus in similarly dramatic terms, as witness Mark 13 and its parallels. But what about after that, in the period when we must assume the *Didache*, at least, to have been written – and most likely the gospels of Matthew and Luke as well?

One possible answer, of course, is that in the days following AD 70 [145] the church looked beyond the fall of Jerusalem to the final moment when God would redeem the whole of creation – and that such a futuristic vision included a final, yet-to-occur tribulation. But this possibility, which we can see reflected perhaps in the book of Revelation, only sharpens the question. For then we must ask: did the church expect to be in some sense spared the sufferings of this final tribulation? Did not salvation consist, rather, in

---

10 Cf. Wright 1996a, 577–9.

remaining faithful within it? This, then, leads us to reconsider the exodus tradition and to search for other possible meanings.

The most probable explanation, I propose, is that the 'testing' is not God's testing of his people but the people's testing of God.[11] One of the central charges against the members of the wilderness generation was that they, in their unbelief, 'put YHWH to the test' by challenging him to produce demonstrations of his presence with them (compare Exodus 17.7). The particular issue, of course, was YHWH's provision of water from the rock, which followed directly on the people's grumbling about food and YHWH's provision of manna. The Deuteronomic memory of the wilderness 'testings' echoes on in the prophetic traditions, with Ahaz using the old warning as an excuse not to look for the sign that Isaiah was offering (compare Isaiah 7.12; see also Psalms 78.18, 41, 56; 95.9; 106.14). In one of Paul's alignments of the church with the wilderness generation, he cites this specifically as a central failing that the church must not emulate (1 Corinthians 10.9). This was, more specifically, one of the key failings of the wilderness generation that Jesus specifically avoided during his initial temptations (compare Matthew 4.7//Luke 4.12, quoting Deuteronomy 6.16).

The passage in Paul's letters in which this theme finds expression – that is, 1 Corinthians 10.9: 'We must not test the Lord [or, 'the Christ'] as some of them did' – also suggests that the early church had become used to taking 'the *peirasmos*' in a wider sense than simply the sharply focused eschatological one. For in 1 Corinthians 10 Paul draws a close parallel between the church and the wilderness generation, speaking of the people of that earlier generation as having been 'baptized' into Moses (v. 2) and as having all eaten 'spiritual food' and drunk 'spiritual drink' (vv. 3–4). Their testing of the Lord – or, as the preferred reading has it, of 'the Christ' – was one aspect of their many-sided failure.

None the less, when Paul speaks of *peirasmos* a few verses later, it is clear that he means not the Israelites' testing of God but the 'temptations' that come on God's people, not least from the pagan environment in which they live. In 1 Corinthians 10.13 he gives us the clearest statement of what *peirasmos* [146] had come to mean in the early church and of how, with its exodus overtones, it was being reapplied:

No *peirasmos* has overtaken you but that which is normal to the human race. God is faithful: he will not allow you to be tested beyond your

---

11   Gibson 1998.

strength. He will make, with the *peirasmos*, also the way out, so that you are able to bear it.

This can only refer to the much more general 'temptation' within which the temptation to put God to the test is one, but only one.

What we see here in this reapplication of the exodus tradition is not so much the downgrading of eschatology into moralism, but the taking up of moral instruction into typological eschatology. Paul will not rest content with simply telling the Corinthians how to behave and chiding them if they go wrong. He will teach them to think of themselves as the people of the true exodus, and within that framework show them how the moral struggles they face – including the temptation to devise tests to see how strong their lord is – are the equivalent of the temptations which brought the wilderness generation to ruin. They must now succeed where their typological predecessors failed.

Who, then, is the author of this 'temptation' of 1 Corinthians 10.13? Paul does not say directly, but the context strongly implies that it is the evil one. Despite the apostle's firm conviction regarding the sovereignty of God, such 'testings' come from 'the satan' (compare 1 Corinthians 7.5; the word *peirasmos* occurs in the Pauline corpus only in 1 Corinthians 10.13; Galatians 4.14; and 1 Timothy 6.9). 1 Corinthians 10, therefore, might be seen as a practical commentary on the Lord's Prayer, particularly on its concluding clauses. What Paul, in effect, is saying is: you are the exodus generation; therefore trust God to lead you out of your moment of testing without succumbing to it – that is, to deliver you from the evil one.

If this is accepted, then we may understand the last part of the Lord's Prayer (that is, the last two clauses in Matthew's version and the *Didache*) as follows: Jesus' followers are instructed to pray that they may be spared the great *peirasmos* that is coming on Jesus himself *and* the cognate tribulation that is coming on Jerusalem and the whole world. To this extent, the petition is similar to what Jesus urges in Matthew 24.20//Mark 13.18: 'Pray that your flight may not be in winter'.

But the petition also broadens out to include all of what Paul speaks [147] about – namely the variegated temptations which, coming from 'the satan', include the temptation to put God to the test but also include such other sins as idolatry and grumbling. Thus 'Lead us not into temptation' would then mean, in that broader context, 'Do not let us be led into temptation [from which we cannot escape]'. The fact that God has promised to be faithful and to provide the way of escape does not mean, in the logic of New Testament prayer, that one should not pray for it, but rather the reverse. Those who pray the Lord's Prayer are designed by Jesus to be those who remain faithful to the God who intends to remain faithful to them – and who thereby constitute the true eschatological Israel, the people of the new exodus.

The Lord's Prayer as the Heart of the New-Covenant Charter

We may now stand back briefly from this exodus-based exposition of the Lord's Prayer and examine the results. Certain features from our investigation can be highlighted. The prayer is given by Jesus to constitute his followers as the true exodus-people. They are to succeed, not least by prayer, where the original wilderness generation failed. The prayer moves from the disciples' relation to God, through the honouring of God's name and the doing of his will, to provisions for bodily needs and dealing with evil. Furthermore, the prayer has something of the same shape – and, within the new eschatological moment, something of the same role – as the Decalogue within the exodus-narrative. Thus the Lord's Prayer may be seen as being to the church as the Ten Commandments were to Israel: not just something to do, a comparatively arbitrary rule of life, but the heart of the new-covenant charter.

Of course, it is not quite as easy as that. Matthew, who one might have expected to make this point, may be thought to have hinted at it by his placing of the Lord's Prayer within the Sermon on the Mount, redolent as it is of exodus typology. And it would be sheer folly to think that the Decalogue has no abiding significance within the church, albeit reinterpreted in various ways – just as it would be folly to suppose that Israel BC was not also commanded and invited to pray the intimate covenantal prayer, the *Shema*, that Jesus himself reaffirmed (though, interestingly, as ethic rather than prayer, as in Judaism; compare Matthew 22.34–40; Mark 12.28–31; Luke 10.25–28). Nevertheless, there is an important point here, which is at [148] the very heart of our investigation: if we are looking for characteristic marks of the church, the Lord's Prayer offers itself more readily than the Ten Commandments, despite the parallel use of them in some systems of Christian education, as though they were, respectively, simply a timeless prayer and a timeless moral code.

The Lord's Prayer takes its place, rather, alongside baptism and the eucharist. Both are thought of in exodus terms in the New Testament, not least in 1 Corinthians 10. It is, therefore, appropriate that praying the Lord's Prayer should take place corporately and publicly within the liturgies for both baptism and the eucharist. But it is also the case that the Lord's Prayer will be most fully understood and most fully 'meant' within those exodus-based narratives, which are symbolically and dramatically acted out in their new Christ-centred form. These sacraments are precisely among those moments when – within the inaugurated eschatology through which alone Christianity makes sense – both past and future, heaven and earth, are brought together in one dramatic action.

The Lord's Prayer is the means by which the church celebrates what has been accomplished already in Christ and strains forward for what lies ahead. And in the course of living between the present and the future, the church prays in the Lord's Prayer for grace and strength to remain faithful to its lord and not to fall away from the bracing agenda of his kingdom-announcement.

3 Prayers and Paradigms

The church that prays the Lord's Prayer claims, thereby, the status of the eschatological people of God. In so praying, it locates itself between Calvary, Easter and Pentecost, on the one hand, and the great consummation (sometimes, by metonymy, called 'the *parousia*'), on the other hand. The Lord's Prayer is thus a marker, a reminder to the church of who and what it is and why.

To locate oneself on this historical scale is, of course, to look with dismay at the many times when the church, like the wilderness generation, has betrayed its lord, put its God to the test, and committed various idolatries and immoralities. But it is, at the same time, also to claim that, with the cross and resurrection of Jesus behind it, forgiveness and restoration are ever-present realities as well. [149]

A Paradigm for the Church's Liturgy

The shape of the church's regular worship, therefore, ought to be ordered, I suggest, in ways that highlight this identity. All sorts of Christian traditions have been tempted in various ways to de-eschatologize themselves, and so to settle down into being simply a religion, with or without an accompanying moralism. It is this, perhaps, that has allowed so much contemporary thought to assume, without more ado, that Christianity is simply one 'religion' among many – a view that the New Testament's characteristic eschatology would never permit.

One obvious way of keeping the church's eschatological focus would be to allow the shape as well as the content of the Lord's Prayer to inform its liturgy more strongly, not just in that part of the worship service labelled 'prayer' but also in the structure of the whole. Invocation of God as father; worship and prayer that sanctifies God's name; prayer for Jesus' kingdom-work to find its complete fulfilment on earth as in heaven – all of these might come first. Intercession for particular blessings, of which bread is among the most basic and hence symbolic of the rest, would occur within this larger context.

Furthermore, we should note that, against the grain of some post-Augustinian liturgies, the church is not instructed by its lord to approach its father with 'Sorry' as its first word. Even the prodigal son began his speech with 'Father'. There is, to be sure, an appropriate place for penitence, both for communities and individuals. But the normal Christian approach to the creator God is the unfettered and delighted 'Father'. There is a time for penitence, but its location within the Lord's Prayer suggests that it should not take pride of place in regular liturgical worship.

There are, of course, some theologies still current in which all penitence is pushed to one side as gloomy or doleful. That this is a gross caricature should not need to be said. The Lord's Prayer indicates both that penitence is a regular necessity and that it is not the most important element. Pride and paranoia are alike to be avoided.

If the Lord's Prayer is correctly understood in its new-exodus eschatological context, a liturgy that grows up on this basis is likely to choose scripture readings in such a way as both to celebrate God's deliverance of his people and to remind members of the congregation that they belong within this overarching story. This does not mean the avoidance of the non-narrative parts of scripture, such as the book of Proverbs. But it does mean that the [150] sequence from the Old Testament to the New has some importance, and that at some point that sequence, which gave birth to the church, should be brought into explicit focus, whether by prayer or song.

The church's task in using the Lord's Prayer as a paradigm for liturgy, therefore, is (1) to thank God for its identity as the people of the new exodus, (2) to pray that God's achievement in Jesus Christ may reach its complete fruition for both the church and the entire creation, and (3) to pray for grace and strength to remain faithful to God's calling in the present. In so doing, the church is explicitly identifying with Jesus himself in his own prayer and work (as we have highlighted in the first section of this article) – a stance that can only be taken without gross arrogance when it is remembered that the prayer, as given by Jesus, is not simply a command but an invitation. Like a good deal in the gospel accounts, it requires a belief in the holy spirit to make full sense of this picture (which is what John and Paul, in particular, supply, as we will note later in this article).

A Paradigm for Christian Living

The Christian is also called to make the Lord's Prayer paradigmatic in his or her own personal life. The context in Matthew 6 includes Jesus' command to go into one's own room, shut the door and pray to the father who sees in secret (6.6). (We might want to ask: how many of Jesus' original hearers had private rooms into which they could retreat, with doors by which they could shut out all others?) The life of the individual Christian is lived out between baptism and bodily death and resurrection on the same principle as the life of the corporate church. It is true, of course, that the story of Israel's wilderness wanderings has been more regularly applied to the Christian life than to church history, and the symbolism is well enough known: the crossing of the Jordan symbolizing death, and so forth – or, as in some 'second blessing' traditions, altered so that the crossing of the Jordan signals an entry into a 'higher life' of full sanctification. None the less, the exodus-story is still a fruitful source of imagery for reconstructing a genuinely Christian spirituality.

The Lord's Prayer, as used by a Christian who is conscious of his or her pilgrimage to the eventual promised land, celebrates the great beginning of that pilgrimage when, in baptism, that individual is united with Christ in his death and resurrection. Calling God 'father' says and cele-[151]-brates all of that. The early petitions of the prayer, with their focus on God's name, God's kingdom and God's will, can all be used in this context as the framework for focusing in one's private prayer on God himself, and for claiming already in the present – as, indeed, is done in the sacraments – the blessings of the future that are already secured in Christ. And within private prayer, as with public prayer, all of the other elements take their place: intercession, the prayer for forgiveness, and the clear-eyed plea against *peirasmos* and against the *ponēros*. These all find their appropriate, though still subordinate, home. The individual Christian is called to be a man, woman or child of prayer as a new-exodus person.

But that cannot be the whole story. For, as I said in the first section of this article, at its heart the Lord's Prayer is an invitation to each Christian to share in the praying life of Jesus himself. The early Christians were very conscious of Jesus' exalted presence before God's throne, where his constant task is to intercede on behalf of his people (compare Romans 8.34; Hebrews 7.25; 9.24). The Lord's Prayer, therefore, by uniting Jesus' people with their lord in the prayer that formed the inner core of his own life, brings about the situation where those who pray it are even now, whether they realize it or not, 'seated in the heavenly places in Christ Jesus' (Ephesians 2.6; compare Colossians 3.1, 3).

There are different ways of appropriately embodying this reality. Precisely because we are to pray God's kingdom into existence 'on earth as it is in heaven', it is always worthwhile exploring and reflecting on those ways – including matters of place, posture, timing, musical accompaniment and so on. These are not mere incidentals. They will, of course, vary quite widely with culture, personality and opportunity. Such variations, however, do not suggest that there are not some more and some less appropriate outward forms and fashions. Rather, the reverse is true. Each individual Christian and every church community is responsible, under God, not just for maintaining a human tradition – or, for that matter, demolishing one – but for discovering the forms that the Lord's Prayer itself prompts and suggests within a particular culture and for the particular people who are going to be using it.

4 *Abba*, Father: Conformed to the Pattern of Christ

It is striking that at the two places where Paul quotes Jesus' use of *Abba*, the Aramaic word for 'father', he also speaks in dramatic language of the [152] two things that have formed the underlying structure of this article: (1) the new exodus in Christ, and (2) the incorporation of the worshipping Christian into the inner Trinitarian life of God. I conclude this article, therefore, with a brief look at these two passages and some suggestions as to what they mean for our regarding the Lord's Prayer as a paradigm of Christian praying.

In Galatians 4.1–11, as is fairly obvious though not always fully drawn out, Paul tells the story of the exodus again. Only it is not now the exodus from Egypt, when God sent Moses and gave the law, but the exodus of God's people in Christ, both Jews and gentiles, in long-term and complete fulfilment of the promise to Abraham. Thus in verses 4–7 he says:

> When the time had fully come, God sent forth his son . . . to redeem . . . and because you are children, God has sent the spirit of his son into our hearts, crying 'Abba, father'. So you are no longer a slave, but a son; and, if a son, then an heir, through God.

As a result, as he emphasizes in verses 8–11, there can be no 'going back to Egypt'. God has now been revealed, not in a burning bush but in the son and the spirit – or, rather, as the one who sent the son and now sends the spirit of the son.

The God of the new exodus is the God revealed as father, son and spirit. The only alternative is some kind of paganism, even if, paradoxically, it is hiding underneath the Jewish Torah. And the revelation of God as Trinity is completed in the experience of Christian prayer – that is, in the *Abba*, which certainly refers to Jesus' own usage and may well refer to the practice of saying the Lord's Prayer in the early Aramaic-speaking church.

Two reflections on the use of this *Abba*-prayer by Christians may be of note. First, just as the Lord's Prayer is still known as the 'Pater Noster' by many Roman Catholics who actually now say it in English, so perhaps – though it can only ever be a guess – the same prayer may have continued to be known as the 'Abba' by those who said it in Greek. Second, it may be asked: is it simply a coincidence that the key prayer-word of the early Christians, like some of the key prayer-words of their pagan counterparts, was a palindrome (that is, a word or number that reads the same backwards or forwards) – indeed, one of the simplest possible palindromes?

The point, anyway, is that the Lord's Prayer – by (1) reflecting the prayer of Jesus and inviting his followers to share it, and (2) embodying [153] the new-exodus stance that summed up so much of Jesus' whole agenda – is now the appropriate vehicle of a specific type of prayer. This prayer is not shouting across a void to a distant and perhaps unknown God. Nor is it simply getting in touch with one's own deepest feelings and self-awareness. Nor is it getting in tune with the wider spirit of the whole cosmos. It is prayer that grows directly out of the Jewish experience and knowledge of the one creator God, but that finds, without leaving that Jewish base behind, that the knowledge of this one God has three intertwined aspects – not least of all because Jesus himself, as a human being, remains at the heart of it.

Romans 8.12–30 completes the circle.[12] Here we find the fully inaugurated, but not yet consummated, eschatology that so perfectly reflects Jesus' own kingdom-announcement, albeit seen now from the post-Easter perspective. We are saved in hope; but hope that is seen is not hope. And this salvation is precisely the new exodus. Led by the spirit, who here takes on the role of the pillar of cloud by day and of fire by night, we are called the children of God. We are no longer slaves, and must not dream of going back to Egypt. Rather, because we are those who cry 'Abba, father!' we are not only children but heirs, heirs of the true promised land.

---

12   See Wright 1999d.

The true promised land is not a strip of territory in the Middle East or elsewhere, nor yet 'heaven' as a far-off and basically disembodied final resting-place. Rather, it is the renewed creation itself. It is God's world restored, healed and flooded with the spirit, sharing in the freedom that goes with the glorification of God's children. Creation itself, in other words, will have its own exodus. Our exodus experience in the death and resurrection of Jesus Christ is both the key starting-point of that long project and the guarantee that God will complete what he has started.

In the midst of all of this, the characteristic Christian prayer is that which, inspired by the spirit, catches the Christian up in the mysterious, and even painful, dialogue of the father and the spirit (compare 8.26–27). It is this that forms the Christian according to the pattern of the crucified and risen son (8.17, 29). And it is this that constitutes Christians as 'those who love God' (8.28) – in other words, those who fulfil, at last, the great exodus prayer-command of Deuteronomy 6.4–5: 'Hear, O Israel, YHWH our God, YHWH is one; and you shall love YHWH your God with all your heart, and with all your soul, and with all your might.'

The Lord's Prayer, then, though not explicitly referred to by Paul, [154] points on to what in many ways must be seen as the crown of early Christian theology and practice. For the *Abba*-prayer, inspired by the spirit of Jesus, is the characteristic Christian prayer. It encompasses within itself that celebration of God's goodness and kingdom, that intercession for and grief over the world in pain and need, and that anguish over trials and temptations that still beset and besiege what is the normal state of Christian existence. More than all that, however, as an invitation to share in Jesus' own prayer-life and as the new-exodus prayer, it enables the baptized and believing Christian to share – humbly, wonderingly, painfully, joyfully – in the life of God himself, father, son and spirit.

3

God and Caesar, Then and Now*

I served as Canon Theologian of Westminster Abbey from January 2000 to July 2003, working under the leadership of the remarkable Dean, the late Very Reverend Wesley Carr. Wesley held a doctorate in biblical studies and was always most supportive of my work. At his behest, I gave various public lectures in the abbey, including some that turned into books in their own right. (That was the origin, for instance, of *Surprised by Hope* (Wright 2008) and also of *Evil and the Justice of God* (Wright 2006a).) Westminster Abbey is, of course, at the heart of the 'Establishment', being a 'royal peculiar', that is, an Anglican church responsible not to any bishop or archbishop but directly to Her Majesty the Queen. As such, it raises all sorts of questions for those – particularly in the USA! – who are conditioned by various cultural narratives to regard all such linkage between church and state with grave suspicion. The reality is quite different, in my experience, from what most people imagine. Westminster Abbey has a unique opportunity to raise questions of import- ance and does not usually attempt to dictate the answers. So it was that when Queen Elizabeth was approaching her Golden Jubilee (she became Queen in 1952 on the death of her father, George VI, though the coronation did not take place until June 1953) we hosted a series of lectures which related, one way and another, to the monarchy and its role in the national life. This was mine. When, some while later, I was asked to contribute to the Festschrift for Wesley Carr, this piece seemed obviously suitable.

[157] 'Render unto Caesar', declared Jesus, 'the things that are Caesar's; and unto God the things that are God's.'[1] That famously cryptic comment serves not only as a title for this article but as a reminder of the question-mark that hangs over life in an established church, not least in that most established of churches, Westminster Abbey. Having served under Wesley Carr and

---

* 'God and Caesar, Then and Now.' Pages 157–71 in *The Character of Wisdom: Essays in Honour of Wesley Carr*. London: Ashgate Publishing, 2004. Copyright © Martyn Percy and Stephen Lowe 2004. Reproduced with permission of the Licensor through PLSclear.
1   Mk. 12.17 KJV (adapted) and parallels.

experienced the joys and puzzles, the stresses and opportunities which the intermingling of church and state produce, I am delighted to offer these reflections in gratitude for his brave leadership and wise collegiality.

How, today, should we approach the question of God and Caesar – of Christ, church, crown and state? To answer, I shall first outline some current assumptions, and suggest that they are currently challenged from within contemporary culture itself. Then I shall suggest that the biblical basis for the topic is more solid and multifaceted than normally imagined. Finally, I shall argue for a way of understanding church, state and crown in our own day.

The Legacy of the Enlightenment

I begin by drawing attention to three influential features of Enlightenment thought that are taken for granted today. The first is the assumption of a split-level world in which 'religion' and 'faith' belong upstairs, and 'society' and 'politics' belong downstairs. This assumption has effectively privatized religion and faith on the one hand, and on the other has emancipated politics from divine control or influence. God lives upstairs (many of the Enlightenment philosophers were deists) and doesn't bother about what goes on downstairs. Our modern word 'state' is itself an Enlightenment invention, designating a self-operating system, free from religious influence. Thus even to phrase the question in terms of 'church and state' may run the risk of deciding things in advance. [158]

Many today assume this split-level world as the norm. Indeed, when people hear Jesus' 'God-and-Caesar' line from Mark 12, they assume that it affirms and legitimates this divide. That is why many assume, further, that any link between church and state must be ill-conceived. Surely, they think, we are now a *secular* society? Surely a church–state link belongs with witchcraft and superstition, with crusades and prince-bishops? Surely – one of the favourite lines in Enlightenment rhetoric – it's *mediaeval*?[2]

Well, it is and it isn't. This brings us to the second Enlightenment assumption often taken for granted today: that political beliefs and attitudes come in two packages, and that everyone has to choose one or the other. There is the package of the Right: rigid social structures, hierarchy, law and order, a tough-minded work ethic and a strong view of national identity. Then there is the package of the Left: freedom and revolution, overthrowing hierarchies, blurring old lines, doing things in new ways. It is assumed that, with local

---

2   See Bradley 2002, 143.

variations, you are basically in one camp or the other, and that many other decisions are determined by it. In the USA many assume that if you believe in God and the Bible you are also opposed to gun control and in favour of the death penalty – or that if you believe in abolishing the death penalty and introducing gun control you probably doubt the Incarnation and the bodily resurrection of Jesus. The packages vary from one country to another, but it is assumed that political beliefs line up on one side or the other and that a recognizable package will be held in common on either side. It is also often assumed (this, too, was part of Enlightenment rhetoric) that the church, and belief in God, are part of the right-wing package. The more democratic, let alone revolutionary, you become, the less you will have to do with God.

Things are not that easy, but old assumptions stick hard. The very idea of Left and Right dates only to the French Revolution. Those who have discovered in our own day that Jesus announced the kingdom of God, and that Paul spoke of Jesus as the world's true lord, often assume that this implies some variation on today's left-wing package, just as for generations people who have discovered that Paul insists on obeying 'the powers that be' have assumed that this implies some kind of right-wing package. This too is anachronistic; but it explains why many today look at the combination of God, church, crown and state and declare that it's all part of a right-wing conspiracy and must be got rid of; or, if they understand the New Testament as supporting a left-wing package, that God and the church are hopelessly compromised [159] by having anything at all to do with crown and state and must be set free at once.[3]

The third influential Enlightenment assumption, which affects how people see the other two as well, is the belief in progress. History (it is believed) reached a climax in Europe in the eighteenth century; humanity's calling ever since has been to implement this achievement. If recalcitrant elements in earlier worldviews have proved harder to shift than the early revolutionaries had imagined, they must be mocked or shamed into giving themselves up. Surely, we are told, 'in this day and age' certain things are inappropriate? Surely 'now that we live in the twenty-first century' it's time to get rid of some types of social organization or constitution? The assumption here is that everyone 'really' knows that the undoubted advances in science and technology have made older religious and political beliefs redundant, banishing God upstairs on the one hand and redefining politics into Left and

---

3   See e.g. Horsley 1997; 2000.

Right, with a strong inclination towards some kind of egalitarian, one-level social democracy.

The Enlightenment agenda is, of course, far more complicated than this, but I hope these three aspects are recognizable. The achievement of the Enlightenment was to shape the way people think and feel so thoroughly that many today unquestioningly assume these radical innovations. This is simply part of 'living in the modern world'.

But just when the Enlightenment empire sits back and surveys its achievement, the Goths and Vandals are at the gates. Postmodernity, growing up within the western world over the last generation, has challenged every aspect of the Enlightenment package. Things are again more complex than we can explore here; I simply sketch, in reverse order, some of the effects of the current revolution against the modernist assumptions.[4]

Belief in progress has been under attack, not least politically. 'Progress' has often been associated with the Left, but in the more radical post-war Left, especially in France, 'progress' itself has been accused of being a covert excuse for imperial domination. The word *developed*, and its little sister, *underdeveloped*, encapsulate the position now under threat from post-colonialism. Belief in 'progress' has enabled western modernists to trample over much of the world in [160] search of wealth and power, just as belief in 'Roman justice' excused Caesar's first-century imperialism.

Likewise, belief in our own political right-and-left alternatives as a one-size-fits-all map is hard to sustain. Western parliamentary-style democracy is only one of several options that different societies find appropriate. 'Democracy' means something different in the UK from what it means in the USA and the different European countries. We whose histories include rotten boroughs and beer-for-votes rallies should not be surprised at how difficult it is to stage one-person-one-vote elections in many parts of the world today. Fewer people voted in the last UK general election than in the *Big Brother* TV series. We are not in a wonderful position from which to offer the rest of the world a permanent political solution. Anyway, the Enlightenment didn't only produce democracies. It also produced Napoleon, Bismarck, Mussolini, Hitler and Stalin.

In particular, the western world has become disillusioned with secular modernism, the child of Enlightenment deism. We may have banished the older image of God upstairs, leaving him there to mumble in his beard while we run the world by ourselves, but theology like nature abhors a vacuum,

---

4   On the postmodern turn, see Wright 1999c and e.g. Walsh and Middleton 1998.

and new gods have been bubbling up from below to replace the absentee landlord. New Age movements, Druids, shamans, crystals and horoscopes: the 'religion' section in any bookshop will reveal that 'spirituality' is big business. The spiritual starvation diet offered by secularism made people so hungry that they now eat anything. People are rediscovering their awareness of something or someone they call God, or 'the divine', not least in and through symbols, rituals and stories. People speak eagerly of 'mystery', 'magic' or 'other dimensions' – all things which the Enlightenment tried to ban as mumbo-jumbo and superstition. Some still try to enforce that ban, but mystery has come back to our lives, and we like it and won't be put off. The question now facing us is: how should we put God and the world back together again after an artificial divorce of two centuries? That we must do so is increasingly apparent. And all this means that the cultural assumptions within which the God–church–crown–state debates have traditionally been conducted have been eroded.

The Kingdoms of the World and the Kingdom of God

This brings us to the foundational question: what does the New Testament say on the whole subject? Above the High Altar in Westminster Abbey are inscribed words from Revelation 11.15: 'The kingdom of this world is become the kingdom of our God and of his [161] Christ.'[5] This is typical of what the New Testament declares: God is king, and the kingdoms of the world are thereby demoted. The crucified and risen Jesus of Nazareth is God's Messiah, lord of the world; he is already reigning at God's right hand; he will reappear to complete this rule by abolishing all enemies, including sin and death themselves.[6]

This early Christian belief goes back, through Jesus himself, to the ancient Jewish world. Throughout that world, both Jewish and Christian, the assumptions of the Enlightenment simply do not hold. God and the world are not separated by an ugly ditch; the political options are not polarized along the lines of authority versus revolution; and, though history does indeed move towards a great climax and then out to implement this in the world, this has

---

5 Actually, the inscribed text has made the 'kingdoms' plural; in the Greek the word is singular, and only occurs once in the sentence (literally, 'the kingdom of this world is become of our lord and of his Messiah').

6 The classic statement is in 1 Cor. 15.20–28.

nothing to do with automatic progress and everything to do with sacrifice, vocation and the strange purposes of the living God.

The story of how this works out is far too long to tell here. In many periods of Christian history the Israelite monarchy was invoked as the model for Christian kings and queens; but in the Old Testament itself kingship is ambiguous, and hardly supports a triumphalist use. In any case, the really formative period for Jewish political thinking, the period that set the tone for the New Testament, was during and after the Babylonian exile. Jeremiah urged the exiles to seek the welfare of Babylon, and to pray to God for it.[7] God, he declared, had raised up his servant Nebuchadnezzar, king of Babylon, and given him authority over all the nations.[8] Second Isaiah spoke of the pagan Persian Cyrus as God's anointed, who would rescue the exiles and send them home.[9] The exiles rebuilt Jerusalem and the Temple under the ambivalent auspices of pagan rulers. Despite some prophetic hopes, no Davidic king emerged to create a new, independent kingdom. Instead, Jewish writers from the exile to Jesus and beyond wrestle with the ambiguities of living as God's people under non-Jewish rule. Two books stand out.

Daniel tells stories of Jews who refuse to compromise with paganism. When they are vindicated by God, however, they (like Joseph under Pharaoh) are promoted to positions of service within the pagan kingdom. Jews may face martyrdom (not least because they refuse to privatize their faith), but they are committed to being good [162] citizens even under a regime at best penultimate and at worst blasphemous. Of course, there comes a time when the true God will judge the pagans, and then God's people must get out and run.[10] There will come a time when all regimes, including the one within which Daniel is a loyal civil servant, will give way to the kingdom that God will set up, which can never be shaken.[11] Combining apocalyptic visions of God's coming kingdom, and public service within the present one, appears shocking to the Enlightenment mindset. But something like this is what we find in the New Testament and the early church.

The Wisdom of Solomon offers a stern warning to pagan kings and rulers. They have been appointed to their high office by the living God, but he will judge them for what they do and fail to do. They therefore need Wisdom,

---

7 Jer. 29.7.

8 Jer. 27.4–8.

9 Isa. 45.1–7; cf. 2 Chr. 36.22f.; Ez. 1.1–4.

10 Isa. 52.11–12; cf. 48.20; Jer. 50.8; 51.6, 45; Zech. 2.6, 7.

11 Dan. 2; 7; 9.

who has been active throughout Israel's traditions, and who (we gradually discover) is more or less an alter ego for God himself.[12] This is not the *absent* God of Enlightenment deism; it is the wise, guiding, judging, rescuing God of the biblical tradition. This God does not divide the world between Right and Left, authority and revolution. Both of those are too brightly lit, too unambiguous, to be ultimately useful in guiding our steps in the right paths. Wisdom herself proposes a different way.

Some Jews, of course, took more extreme positions. Some sought to ape the pagan kings; the Hasmonean dynasty went that route, as did Herod and his sons. Equally, there was a long tradition of revolt, from the Maccabees to Bar-Kochba, sometimes using the slogan 'No king but God'.[13] But when Jesus of Nazareth announced that God's kingdom was breaking in, he seems not to have meant it in that sense. What was he talking about? How did Jesus' vision of God's kingdom stand in relation to the kingdoms of the world?

From the start, Jesus' proclamation of God's kingdom was fighting talk.[14] Everybody knew that God's kingdom didn't refer to a place, perhaps a place called 'heaven', where God ruled and to which God's people would be gathered, well away from the wicked world, at the end of their lives. Only a deist could think like that. God's kingdom, said Jesus, was coming, and people should pray for it to come, *on earth as in heaven*; and here he was, on earth, making it happen before people's very eyes. When Herod heard, he was angry; he was King of [163] the Jews, and rival claimants tended not to live long. When the chief priests heard, they knew that it meant a challenge to their power base, the Temple. If Caesar had heard, he would have reacted similarly. What none of them could figure out, and what even Jesus' closest associates had difficulty understanding, was what *kind* of a challenge Jesus intended to pose: what sort of a kingdom he was advancing, and what kind of a king he considered himself to be.

The answers begin to emerge when Jesus arrives in Jerusalem and symbolically purges the Temple, pointing ahead to its imminent destruction. This precipitates a string of debates, in which Jesus is virtually on trial, like someone being interviewed by a hostile media knowing that any verbal slip might prove fatal. Mark 11 and 12 offer a sequence of these debates, all of them politically and theologically freighted. This is where we find the trick question, and the opaque answer, about the tribute penny, about Caesar and

---

12   Wis. 6.1–11.

13   On these Jewish movements, see Wright 1992, Part III.

14   On Jesus and the kingdom, see Wright 1996a; 2000b.

God. It is not an isolated 'political' comment in an otherwise non-political sequence of thought. It fits exactly where it is.[15]

Tax revolts against Rome were nothing new. A large-scale one had taken place during Jesus' boyhood, and had been crushed with typical Roman brutality. Saying 'Yes, pay the tax' would be to say 'I'm not serious about God's kingdom'. But to incite people not to pay would at once incur trouble.[16]

Jesus gets his interlocutors to produce a coin, tacitly admitting that they kept the hated coinage, with its blasphemous inscription and its (to a Jew) illegal image, a portrait of Caesar himself. Whose is it? he asks. Caesar's, they answer. Well then, says Jesus, *you'd better pay back Caesar in his own coin* – and pay God back in *his* own coin!

The closest echoes to this double command are found in 1 Maccabees 2.68. Mattathias is telling his sons, especially Judas, to get ready for revolution. 'Pay back to the gentiles what is due to them,' he says, 'and keep the law's commands.' Paying back the gentiles was not meant to refer to money. I am sure that some of Jesus' hearers would have picked up that revolutionary hint. Because he was standing there looking at a coin, his surface meaning was, of course, that the tax had to be paid; but underneath was the strong hint that Caesar's regime was a blasphemous nonsense and that one day God would overthrow it.

The setting and the saying show decisively, against what is so frequently asserted by both Right and Left within the Enlightenment tradition, that Jesus did not mean it as indicating a separation between the spheres of Caesar and God, with each taking responsibility for a [164] distinct part of the world. Even at the surface level, the saying must have meant that God claimed the whole of life, including questions about taxes. Of course, Jesus acknowledges, you may have to pay taxes to the pagans, just as Jews in exile had to pray to God for the welfare of Babylon; but that doesn't mean that God is only concerned with a different, 'spiritual' world. God is present in the ambiguity, summoning people to an allegiance which transcended but certainly included the position they found themselves in vis-à-vis the occupying power.

Jesus' death can itself be seen as Jesus' own offering, simultaneously, of what was due to Caesar (crucifixion was what Caesar did to rebel kings) and what was due to God. Mark at least may have that in mind; certainly the primary meaning of his crucifixion narrative is what we would call

---

15   On the passage, see Wright 1996a, 502–7.

16   Indeed, Luke (23.2) indicates that this charge was levelled at Jesus before Pilate.

'political', though it is also theological and personal as well. Once again, the Enlightenment categories are simply unable to cope with the meanings the writers intend us to discover in their narratives, let alone the meanings that the central character, it seems, intended his followers to discern in his death. The death of Jesus brings to a head the ambiguous character of the Israelite monarchy from Saul and David right on through history. Calvary and Easter become the focal points of the apocalyptic and wisdom traditions, and hence of second-Temple Judaism's political theology: God's new world is born, claiming the kingdoms of the world as its own, because their central and most powerful weapon, death itself, has now been broken.[17]

Most of the fixed points in our knowledge of the early Christians are stories of persecution and martyrdom, as God's gospel and Caesar's gospel came into conflict.[18] Think of the aged Polycarp, on trial for his life. The Roman government applies two tests: first, you must blaspheme or curse Jesus Christ; second, you must swear 'by the genius of the emperor'. No loyal Christian could do either. Polycarp's answer is a specific rebuttal: 'I've served him for eighty-six years, and he's never done me any wrong; how can I blaspheme my king who saved me?' Caesar claimed to be king and saviour; Polycarp is giving Jesus titles claimed by Caesar. But then, against our expectations, Polycarp proposes to explain to the governor what Christianity actually is. He respects his office, since 'we have been taught to render honour to the rulers and authorities who are appointed by God'. Even when Polycarp is on trial for his life, he is content to say, like Jesus before Pilate in John 19.11, that God has appointed the pagan governor who is about to [165] pass sentence. This is puzzling to us, but it would have made sense to the authors of Daniel, Wisdom, Mark or John.[19] Or, for that matter, to Paul or Peter.

Polycarp's double point (Jesus, not Caesar, is lord, king and saviour, but God has also appointed people, however unfit, as authorities in the world) is echoed in the epistles. 1 Peter 2.9 declares that Christians form a royal priesthood. Well, then, we conclude, they owe no loyalty to any other royalty or priesthood. On the contrary, says Peter (2.13–17): you must respect the rulers; fear God, honour the emperor. So, we conclude, he's saying that earthly rulers are always right. Not so; the next paragraph (2.18–25) discusses what to do, not when justice is done, but when injustice is done, resulting

---

17 On the political significance of the defeat of death, see Wright 2003, chs. 12 and 19.

18 For details, see Wright 1992, ch. 11.

19 Polycarp adds, interestingly, the phrase 'as long as it isn't to our harm': we render honour, as long as that honour is not damaging to us. Where this modification to Rom. 13 came from, and what precisely is meant by it, are matters of debate.

in suffering. Most of the letter is about suffering and possible martyrdom. Daniel would have understood, though the ambiguity would confuse the superficial and over-bright lights of Enlightenment political analysis.

The centre of early Christian reflection remains Paul. It is often supposed that Paul's only political comment is Romans 13.1–7, where he states that God has ordained 'the powers that be'; but this just shows how far our traditions have taken us away from reality. There is no space to explore this in detail, but in almost every letter Paul demonstrates that Jesus is lord, and that Caesar isn't; that the 'gospel' of Jesus upstages the 'gospel' of Caesar; that the true salvation is achieved through Jesus, not Caesar; that the world needs God's justice, not Roman justice; and, with great irony, that the cross, a hated symbol of Roman rule, had been transformed into the life-giving symbol of God's self-giving love. Paul's central arguments constitute a massive outflanking movement against the imperial rhetoric of his day (emperor-worship was the fastest-growing religion of the time).[20]

So why did Paul write Romans 13?[21] Because of the whole tradition of Jewish monotheism and political thought to which he was heir. God does not want anarchy. Nor, of course, do we. It's fine to point out the wickedness of earthly rulers, but when someone [166] steals my car I want justice. It's all very well to say that people in power are self-seeking, but if nobody is in power the bullies and the burglars have it all their own way, and the weak and helpless suffer most. God doesn't want that. God has therefore instituted rulers and authorities (even at the obvious risk that most of them don't acknowledge him and only have a shaky idea of what justice actually is), so as to bring to his world such order as is possible until the day when the rule of Jesus himself is complete on earth as in heaven. This is the Christian version of the political viewpoint we find in Daniel, Wisdom and other Jewish texts. Romans 13 is not, then, a carte blanche for rulers to do what they like. Paul is not setting rulers on a high pedestal, above criticism. Instead, he is reminding them that they have been instituted by God and remain responsible to him for the authority they bear.

The final book of the New Testament, of course, has its own point of view. Just as Ephesians 6 indicates that there is still a battle to be fought against the wicked powers, so Revelation 13 paints an apocalyptic picture of an empire that has gone so bad that the only word to be spoken is one of judgment. God will judge blasphemous wickedness, especially when it uses violence against

---

20   See esp. Wright 2002a. This is a lightly revised version of Wright 2001. See too Wright 2000b.
21   On this, see esp. Wright 2002b, 715–23.

the helpless. That is part of the means by which the kingdom of this world is becoming the kingdom of our lord and his Messiah. But nothing in the Jewish tradition within which the book must be interpreted suggests that this would indicate a blanket condemnation of all rulers and authorities, or a refusal to give them the honour of being God's agents, however misguided and dangerous on occasion they may be. Rather, what the early Christians offer is inaugurated eschatology: like the Israelites under their monarchy, chafing at its imperfections and looking for the fulfilment still to come, the followers of Jesus are to live under the rulers of the world, believing them to be appointed by God but not believing that that makes them perfect or that they do not need to be held accountable. On the contrary. Because they are God's servants they may well need to be reminded of their duty, however dangerous and uncomfortable a task that may be. The stories of Paul in Acts suggest that he sometimes did just that.[22]

There is no space here to speak of the time between the suffering church in the third century and the church of Enlightenment modernism. One of the major achievements of Enlightenment rhetoric was to pour scorn on this long period, from the settlement of Constantine right through to the eighteenth century, as a hopeless compromise, maybe even 'the fall of the church'. The very word [167] 'Christendom' has become a sneer. But, though there is a vital point to be made about the dangers of assuming too ready an identification between the cause of the gospel and the cause of any particular country, nation or state (a danger which the Enlightenment has not helped us to avoid), this criticism is trivial and superficial, and fails to take into account the long, complex and by no means compromised tradition of serious Christian political thought throughout the millennium and a half from AD 300 to AD 1800.[23] It is false to suggest that from Constantine onwards the church was muzzled, forced to do what its political masters told it. Of course, that happened sometimes – just as it does today, even in countries where, as in the United States, non-establishment is much vaunted. There were also many times when the church was able to confront and challenge the state and crown directly. Establishment and martyrdom are closer than we might suppose. Think of Becket. But for our present purposes we skip over all this and more, and arrive at our present British institution of monarchy and its supposedly Christian meaning. How can the biblical theology of rulers and authorities be reinterpreted appropriately in this setting?

---

22   E.g. Ac. 16.35–39; 23.3–5.

23   See particularly O'Donovan 1996; O'Donovan and O'Donovan 1999.

The Angled Mirror

The New Testament offers a theology of rulers and authorities as appointed by God. This places a huge weight of responsibility on the authorities which many modern democratic rulers cheerfully ignore. What is striking about the British monarchy, and some others that still remain, is that they openly acknowledge and, indeed, celebrate this responsibility.[24]

Earthly rule is a kind of sacrament. Dangerous to say; more dangerous to ignore. Sacraments can be abused and turned into sympathetic magic, an attempt to tap in to God's power and life without paying the price of obedient loyalty. That is what Protestants and rationalists have always objected to. But abuse does not destroy the proper use. Proper sacraments – action, drama, symbol and ritual on the one hand, words and prayers that tell God's story and invoke [168] his presence and power on the other – are neither magical nor empty. Monarchy, like all sacraments, needs to be held within a strong theology of the ascended Jesus, lord and king of the whole world, the one who has all authority.

All human power-systems are subject to Christian critique. All power can become idolatrous. Every knee shall bow at Jesus' name, and we must never tire of saying so. But there is another side to the story. Today's cheap-and-chattering republicanism owes nothing to the Christian critique of human power, and everything to the sneer of the cynic, noting the price of every-thing but ignoring its value. Monarchy at its best is a symbolic reminder that the power games of this world do not stand alone, but in a curious and many-sided relation to a transfiguring love and power which exists in a different dimension. In a constitution like that of the UK, monarchy is meant to be an angled mirror in which we see around the dark corner to that other dimension of reality, and realize the provisionality of all earthly power. Woe betide a monarchy that merely mirrors a society back to itself, or that becomes an idol instead of a mirror. The monarchy we have had for the last fifty years, however, has done its best to avoid those dangers, and to reflect and embody the self-giving love that calls mere power to account. Let us not be naive. But let us be appropriately cynical about cynicism itself.

What about the constitutional questions we face today? We are in danger of doing to our national institutions what developers in the 1960s did with our ancient buildings. They tore down wonderful structures that had

---

24 In what follows, I am indebted (not without some disagreements) to Ian Bradley's striking new book, Bradley 2002.

survived centuries of fire, flood and bombs, and they put up concrete and glass monstrosities, reflecting the soul-less secularism that created them. We now have agencies to stop that kind of thing; but our human institutions have no protection against the same unwelcome attention. Of course, traditions and institutions must develop. But to tear them down because 'we live in the modern world' or because they are deemed inappropriate 'in this day and age' is to capitulate to an outworn ideology. There is nothing inevitable about a 'progress' towards flat secularist republics. Do we really want a French-style, or American-style, presidency? Why do so many of our friends and neighbours envy us?

A Swiss doctor once said, 'British doctors don't know what tonsils are for, so they take them out; I don't know what tonsils are for, so I leave them in.' I think we *do* know, or are perhaps starting to rediscover, what monarchy is for. Monarchy is a reminder that the justice and mercy which rulers must practise are not their possession, but come from elsewhere; they are part of the God-given created order. Nations and states that have shed symbols which speak of responsibility to God have often become totalitarian. Of course, [169] republics too can have such symbols. The United States maintains several, despite its official separation of church and state.

I am not suggesting that the present form of the British monarchy is necessarily ideal for the next century and beyond. That is an open question. But it is hard to deny, on Christian premises, that it is vital for the health of a nation and society to have such symbols, and the accompanying rituals with, yes, all their sacramental overtones. Since we have such a symbol, let us not be so foolish as to throw it away, especially when we have nothing else in mind to replace it. Before you cut down an oak tree without knowing what to plant in its place, ask yourself what you are about to lose, and whether you could ever get it back. Before you throw away real royalty, and turn the living representatives of our heritage into a theme park of themselves, ask yourself if you would choose the obvious alternatives. Grey politicians standing for one last election; glitzy media stars improvising their own soap operas – neither can compete with what we already have. The stability and morale of the UK and many parts of the world (we should not underestimate the importance of the Commonwealth, or the extent to which it is held together by personal allegiance to the Crown) may be at stake.

What then about the interlinking of church, state and crown? The word 'establishment', granted, is a millstone around our necks. It has heavy and negative overtones. But the reality is very different. Away from the sneering world of the journalists, out in the country where it counts, the Church of

England is still looked to by all kinds of people, from Lords Lieutenant to town councillors to groups of gypsies, not only to preach the gospel and minister the sacraments, but to be an honest broker, to hold the ring, to provide stability, focus and hope. Some sneer at 'implicit religion' and the inarticulate faith that, for instance, turns up at an Advent carol service but can't say why. I don't sneer at it; I want to work with it and nurture it, to take every spark of faith and help it, in its own time, to become a flame. Establishment means, among other things, that the church is there for everybody. Of course, that sometimes means nobody bothers, but it also means that much of the society regards the church as its own. To cut the link, to insist that the church is only there for the fully paid-up members, would be to send a signal to the rest of our world that we were pulling up the drawbridge, that we were no longer there for them.

Arguments for disestablishment regularly make points that cancel one another out. Establishment, say some, means a powerful church; the gospel is about weakness, not power; therefore establishment must go. Establishment, say others, means the church is ruled by the state; the gospel is about the powerful rule of Jesus Christ; therefore we should not abandon establishment. You can't have it both ways. Either [170] we are dangerously powerful or we are dangerously weak. The truth, as usual, is more complex.

The main motive for disestablishment, in the press and elsewhere, is the old secularist agenda. Many are offended that the Enlightenment has not had its way with every area of society. When people argue that we live in a religiously plural society, they usually don't want to take those religions seriously; they are just repeating another bit of Enlightenment rhetoric, that there are so many religions that they are all equally irrelevant. In fact, though of course non-Christian faiths must be taken seriously, they still represent only a tiny minority of people in the UK.[25] The evidence suggests that many Jewish and Muslim communities are happier to have Christianity as the established religion than to live in a secularized state. The Jews in particular know what that might mean.[26]

---

25 After I wrote the first draft of this chapter, the census figures for 2001 were published, showing that a remarkable 71.7 per cent of the UK consider themselves in some sense Christian. The next figure down is 2.7 per cent (Muslims).

26 It is often said that a future coronation might be a 'multi-faith' event. But it is by no means clear whether what the Christian church has understood to be the meaning of coronation (including, for example, anointing) over the last thousand and more years would be something that any of the 'other faiths' would want to endorse. If it means that the religious and spiritual significance of the coronation would be reduced to having various religious bodies all saying prayers in their own way and to their own deities, this would simply be a late victory for the Enlightenment's downgrading of

There are, of course, different models of establishment. The Scottish one is not the same as the English; we might profitably explore the differences.[27] I assume, as well, that establishment ought to find ways of including, at whatever level, the other Christian churches – though I regard as disingenuous the anti-establishment polemic from some Roman Catholic journalists, who conveniently forget the 'concordat' arrangements that still obtain, officially or unofficially, in many Roman Catholic countries.[28] As we move towards increased mutual understanding, cooperation and sharing of a common life, I would hope that more flexibility might emerge on the axis between ecumenism and establishment. [171]

The Establishment may well develop, then, but I see no reason to dismantle it. The negative signals sent by disestablishment would be profound, and unhelpful to both church and world. Do we really want the major turning-points in our national life to be conducted without prayer, and solemn seeking of God's blessing? Do we want leaders and rulers who will pledge themselves, not to ideals of justice and mercy which come ultimately from God, but simply to whatever the people may want? It is obviously not of the essence of the church that it should be established. The early church wasn't, and most churches are not today. But I believe it is of the *bene esse* of the church in England that it should continue to be established, while allowing for flexibility and development. Let us not capitulate to the tired, flatland world of secularism and modernism. Let us go on, learning from past mistakes but also building on existing strengths, confident that our God has not led us up a blind alley these last thousand and more years, but that the gospel of his kingdom can and will guide and transform our national life as well as our personal lives for generations to come.

all religions to 'what people do with their solitude', and would not honour either the other religions themselves or Christianity. On the spiritual significance of coronation, see Bradley 2002, ch. 4.

27 In Scotland, the monarch is not 'supreme head of the church'.

28 The classic ones being in France under Napoleon (1801) and in Italy (the 'Lateran Treaty' of 1929). Both were, of course, subsequently modified, but de facto arrangements still obtain. The question of the Act of Succession, which is endlessly raised at this point in the discussion, is more complex than it seems. Would the Roman Catholic church be prepared to give up its insistence that children of mixed marriages be brought up as Roman Catholics?

4

Christian Origins and the Question of God

The Rutherford House symposia (held in Edinburgh) provided a welcome forum in which I was able from time to time to explain, sometimes to a puzzled audience, ideas that I had been expounding at more length elsewhere. I have tried, in particular, to live at or near the interface between historical exegesis and systematic theology, and I have often run into a measure of incomprehension, and sometimes even hostility, from colleagues who are more obviously rooted in one camp or the other. Whether or not the present paper convinced, or even mollified, the theologians at the seminar in 2007 I could not say. But the piece may still have its usefulness in explaining how I see the urgent tasks facing Christian thinkers today, not only to clarify and explain what we mean when we say the highly contested word 'God', but also to commend this meaning, and this belief, to others.

[21] Introduction

The question of God is raised constantly throughout early Christianity and is routinely given the same answer: if you want to know the meaning of the word 'God', look hard at Jesus of Nazareth. Indeed, much of the New Testament is written precisely to enable people of all sorts and conditions to do precisely that, and in case the point gets lost, the writers re-emphasize it now this way, now that: no-one has ever seen God, but the only-begotten God who is in the bosom of the father has made him known; he is the image of the invisible God; he bears the very stamp of God's nature; or in Thomas's unforgettable confession when faced with the risen Jesus, 'My lord and my God'. Not only in John (as people sometimes misguidedly suppose) but throughout the early church it is affirmed that those who have seen Jesus have seen the father.

What this means within its historical context is an enormous topic, and to do justice to it, I really ought to discuss in detail the magnificent recent

53

book by Larry Hurtado.[1] That, however, would give me a particular focus which is not my intention, and I leave such a review as a worthwhile [22] road not taken on this occasion. Instead I want to look at two questions which interlock in various ways and which have come into focus and, I hope, will continue to come into focus in my own multi-volume project. I do not just want to look at what the early Christians thought about the meaning of the word 'God', as redefined around Jesus and (in a measure) around and, indeed, by the holy spirit. I want to dig beneath that and ask: where did the early Christians stand on what we might call 'the question of God' as it presented itself in their day, both in Judaism and in the wider pagan world into which Christianity made its way with astonishing speed? And, second, I want to ask: what does the *story of Christian origins* itself contribute to our own reappropriation of this early Christian vision of God?

Two words by way of general introduction. First, the title of my overall project, which is the title I was originally given for this essay, was a way of not settling in advance the question of whether there is something called 'New Testament theology' and whether I wanted to contribute to it. The two questions of (1) what we can say as historians about the origin or origins of Christianity and (2) what we can say about God are both, in my view, perfectly valid in their own right. But whereas, from within some worldviews, these two questions might appear to exist in watertight compartments, this option is denied to the Christian at least, who is faced with the wonderfully complex and entertaining further question of how these two things overlap and interlock. The sub-discipline that has called itself 'New Testament theology' (with well-known examples of the genre from Bultmann, Kümmel and others) has come at things rather with the assumption that our task is to collect and compare the statements about central theological topics that we find in the different New Testament writers.

This is important, but I sense a further set of questions underneath, which have to do with something the New Testament writers were all keenly interested in but which many in the then dominant German Lutheran world – and, to my dismay, some in today's evangelical world – are not only not interested in but downright hostile towards, namely, the events themselves through which Christianity began long before even Paul started dictating his letters. As I have said in other places, the risen Jesus does not say to the disciples that all authority in heaven and on earth is given to the

---

1 Hurtado 2003.

books they are to go off and write. The question of God precisely as it is posed to us by the New Testament writers is one that cannot be addressed, let alone answered, by exegesis of their key passages alone, but only by this exegesis in combination with the serious and sustained historical task of enquiring what it was that actually happened in the reign of Tiberius and under the governorship of Pontius Pilate. Neither the Christian apologetic to the wider world nor the Christian instruction of those within the fold [23] can confine itself to the New Testament text alone; to do so is to falsify the text itself. This is the puzzle, the metapuzzle if you like, of the interplay between the historical study of Christian origins and the theological enquiry about the meaning and/or reference of the word 'God'. I decided in 1989, when roughing out my own project, that the only thing I could decently do was to set the questions out side by side as best I could and see what sparks they began to knock off one another. This work, clearly, is still in progress.

A second word of general introduction: I am very much aware that all talk about God is necessarily self-involving and that the mode of this involvement will vary according to what is being said, or at least what is being meant, about God himself. You can discuss the distant gods of Epicureanism and/or deism with a shrug of the shoulders and with your hands in your pockets. But if you mention the God of Abraham, Isaac and Jacob and intend to take this God seriously, you are bound to adopt an attitude which some first-century Jews formalized in the way we see already in Paul: to mention this God, remind yourself that he is the one who is blessed for ever, amen. And the Christian who knows what he or she is about will constantly reflect that the most natural modes of God-talk are adoration, thanksgiving, confession, supplication and proclamation, not theorization. This is not an attempt to marginalize systematic theology – far from it. It is simply a reminder of what the greatest systematic theologians have always known and recognized – that theology is a matter of loving God with our minds and that loving does not mean merely admiring or 'being intellectually interested in'. This is why (to link my second introductory point to my first) it is difficult to mount a historical argument about Christian origins, because the question of God swirls around the whole project, and different implicit answers to it will result in different implicit attitudes to everything else – history, of course, very much included.

Anyway, so much for introduction. I want to address my topic in three sections, which bounce off one another cheerfully all the way through: the kingdom of God, the righteousness of God and the love of God.

The Kingdom of God

As a matter of history, it was central to the early Christian claim, belief, witness and corporate life that the one true God had established his kingdom in and through certain events, the events to do with Jesus of Nazareth, who had been demonstrated to be Israel's Messiah and the world's true lord. When the early Christians spoke about God's kingdom (as, by the way, they went on doing, despite the drop in references in [24] the Pauline letters as compared with the gospels), they were demonstrably conscious that Jesus' constant reference to this as the major theme of his proclamation and purpose was both in line with the Old Testament celebration of YHWH's kingship, and its promise that this kingship would come to fresh expression, and in dialogue with the kingdom-expectation and kingdom-movements of the time. If we are to study Christian origins with proper historical sensitivity, we must remind ourselves constantly that neither Jesus nor his first followers had a monopoly on Jewish kingdom-of-God discourse in the first century and that the so-called revolutionary usage we associate with Judas the Galilean and other rebel groups at the beginning of that century did not suddenly disappear just because the Christians, following Jesus himself, had picked up this dangerous language and seemed to be reshaping and remoulding it. The question of God as posed in Palestine in, let us say, AD 45, certainly included the question of different visions of the kingdom of God: what would it mean, what would it look like, that God would become king? What changes would come about as a result? When would it happen – or in the case of the Christians, how was one to express one's belief that it had already happened and in another sense was still to happen? And not least important as part of that God-question, who would be vindicated when the kingdom arrived in all its fullness? How could you tell in the present time who God's true kingdom-people might be?

Already, by dipping our toe into the turbulent water of first-century Judaism, we discover the key questions that the word 'God' raised at the time. They were not so much theoretical questions about attributes as practical questions about actions. What was God up to? Who spoke for God, who was acting for God, how did you know and what should we be doing about it? We ought not therefore to be surprised that the major writings which emerged over the first generation of Christian faith, the writings which the very early church, quite correctly in my view, put at the head of that extraordinarily bold and visionary thing, the emerging canon of the New Testament, were writings which dealt head-on with the question of God but did so in an utterly first-century Jewish way, *by telling a story of actual events as the story of how God at last became king.* The gospels as wholes in their forms and intentions – and their constituent parts, large and small, in their traceable history such as it is (begging several large questions at this point) – show us a community determined to express its identity in terms of things that had actually happened, events (as we say) within history, in and through which the being they called God had become king. It is not simply, then, that the gospels contain within themselves some remarkable pictures of God – the prodigal father, for instance, or the king who gives a wedding feast for his son; it [25] is, rather, that by their very nature, and by what they tell us about the earliest Christianity as a storytelling and storyliving community, they point us to the God of creation and providence, the God of Israel, the God of justice, the God who, having made a good and beautiful world, has remained committed to it despite its rebellion.

The gospels have been emasculated in much of the church by being split up into small portions and never seen as a whole, rather as if a great symphony were only ever heard in twelve-bar snatches; and it is this, incidentally but importantly, that has left the door open to those who want, for quite other reasons, to suggest that works such as the so-called *Gospel of Thomas* belong in the same category as Matthew, Mark, Luke and John. *Thomas* does not; it consists of detached aphorisms, and even if they all or mostly turned out to be authentic sayings of Jesus himself, the work as a whole, and the others like it, would represent a falsification of what Jesus was saying and doing as well as a falsification of what the early church believed. Ultimately, the so-called 'gnostic gospels' would be a denial of what Jesus and the church believed *about God himself* and what the canonical gospels are inviting the rest of the world, ourselves included, to believe about God. The canonical gospels are saying, in form and overall substance, that the word 'God' properly belongs to the creator God, the God of Israel, the God who has kept his promises to creation and to Israel *and has done so in this way.* And they are the stories told by and within the early Christian community that in its worship and witness was living by and out of the belief that these things were so.

Ironically, therefore, the evangelical imperative to believe that everything in the gospels really happened is pushing in the right direction for, all too often, the wrong reason. The reason it matters that the events really happened is not 'so that the Bible can be true after all', as though that were the bottom line, but 'so that God really has become king on earth as in heaven' – a truth to which all evangelicals give lip-service but not all, I fear, actually reflect on or work at in practice. More of this, perhaps, anon. My underlying point is that one of the most secure things we know about Christian origins is that the earliest Christians told these stories about Jesus not simply to reinforce (à la Bultmann) small points of doctrine or practice, but to sustain the whole early Christian worldview, which necessarily expressed itself in narrative because the worldview was precisely about things that happened, about events unfolding and reaching a climax. This is why the question of the form and genre of the gospels has proved so difficult: because the evangelists, and I assume but cannot argue here their major sources, took it for granted at point after point that the story they were telling was (at least) four different stories rolled into one.

First, it was the story of the creator God launching his project of new creation from within [26] the womb of the old. Second, it was the story of Israel's God bringing the long story of the covenant to its appointed goal. Third, it was the story of how the life that the early Christians experienced had begun. Fourth, of course, joining all these together, it was the story of Jesus himself. No wonder the gospels are complex documents. None of these elements can be omitted in a full account of what the gospels actually are; and they all interact, not least in the strong implicit belief that the story of the covenant always was the story of how the creator God had purposed to deal with the problem of evil within his creation and so to put creation itself to rights once more. All of this is implied in the very structure, layout and narrative design of the four gospels, different though they are. And together they all add up to a fifth story, which remains the projected title for the putative fifth volume in my own project, after the fourth volume on Paul: *The Gospels and the Story of God*. The reason the gospels are what they are is that they are doing on a large scale what Jesus in so many parables is doing close up: they are telling these narratives in such a way as to say, 'Look closely, ponder and pray your way through this story, and discover thereby who the one true and living God actually is.'

And this does not mean, simply and univocally, that we should leap to the high Christology to which all the gospels, not only John, subscribe. It does not, that is, lead simply to a one-for-one replacement, so that where before we might have said 'God', now we simply say 'Jesus'. Things are more subtle: the gospel-writers, like Paul, are implicit pretheoretical Trinitarians. 'Who then is this?' ask the disciples, and Jesus does indeed act and speak as one who believes that he has been called to do what in Israel's scriptures only YHWH, Israel's sovereign and saving God, can and must do. But this same Jesus prays to the one he calls 'Abba, father', and sometimes that prayer is anguished and answered in the negative. And at the last the godforsaken cry on the cross, as Moltmann and others have seen so clearly, compels us to formulations of Trinitarian theology with paradox at their heart and renunciation of triumphalism as their mode.

The gospels thus offer us the narrative mode of discourse, not presumably as the only appropriate mode of God-talk but as at least a primary mode, not to be translated out into non-narrative modes without loss. In doing so, they are reaffirming one of the central underlying themes of the Old Testament; indeed, one might say *the* central underlying theme, as highlighted by John Goldingay in the first volume of his remarkable *Old Testament Theology*: Israel's story (which is itself the focal point and encapsulation of creation's story) as the story of what the one true God is up to, the story which in the Old Testament, as in the intertestamental literature, remains always a story in urgent search of an appropriate [27] ending.[2] In reaffirming this and in offering the story of Jesus as the appropriate ending (and the appropriate beginning of another story or, if you prefer, the translation of the single-language story into the many-language story of the early church), the gospels are standing over against the wide world of ancient paganism, which had various things to say about the creation of the world and about the interplay between divine beings and the world, not much to say about the future of the world, and several overlapping stories about divine power at work in the world through human empire. When Jesus tells his disciples that the rulers of this earth behave in one way but his disciples must behave in a different way, he is saying in a nutshell what the gospel-writers are then saying in their choice of form and mode: live within this story, and you will discover who the true God really is, what God is like, and what you must be like as a result. The theological challenge thus constitutes for the evangelists the political challenge to live in the pagan world as the people who know Israel's God, who believe that this God has brought his covenant plan to its long fruition, and who are now living under the rule of the one who has claimed all authority in heaven and on earth. This is what the kingdom of God is all about, and the gospel-writers insist that it has been redefined around Jesus and brought to birth through his death and resurrection.

My argument so far is that the gospels, by their very form as well as their detailed content, are stating in the strongest possible terms that the being who can properly be called God is the creator God, the God of Israel, that he has revealed himself in decisive and climactic action in Jesus of Nazareth, Israel's Messiah, and that God has thereby called into being a people, a rejuvenated

---

2   Goldingay 2003.

or regenerated Israel if you like, through whom his purposes for the world are now to be taken forward. What we theorize as the doctrine of creation lies at the heart of the whole thing; history matters because creation matters. When the writers we think of as constituting the wisdom tradition invite their readers to embrace wisdom and live by it, this is not a wisdom that takes you away from creation. Wisdom is the one through whom God made the world in the first place. The deep anti-historical impulse in a fair amount of western Protestantism to this day is ultimately an anti-Judaic impulse, ultimately a step towards the gnostic rejection of creation. And along with creation goes what might be called God's justice, by which I mean loosely the utter determination of the creator God to put his world to rights and thereby to re-establish his kingship, his sovereignty, over it. It is because of this impulse to put things to rights that God called Abraham; and [28] this is why God's faithfulness to his covenant is also his faithfulness to creation, something which much theology and exegesis, over the last couple of generations at least, have found hard to hold together. It is this justice, this faithfulness to creation and covenant, to which the next main section now turns.

The Righteousness of God

It is with Paul, and particularly in Romans, that we meet the full-dress exposition of God's faithful covenant justice – my preferred longer translation for that impossible phrase *dikaiosynē theou*. When I talk in what follows about God's faithfulness or God's justice, it is this phrase, with its many overlapping connotations, that I shall have in mind. I have written about this at length in various places and can only here summarize what I have said elsewhere.

It is important from the outset to stress that in moving from the gospels to Paul, we are not moving from a narrative world to a non-narrative one. The form of Paul's writings is epistolary, not straightforward narrative, but as I and others have shown at length, understanding the underlying narratives in Paul is not simply a matter of teasing out a bit of peripheral embroidery but a way of getting to the very heart of things. Paul draws on and redeploys an almost bewildering variety of interlocking stories: the story of creation, of humankind, of Israel; of Abraham, Isaac and Jacob; of Moses and the exodus and the giving of the law; of David and the prophets and the whole history of Israel; of Jesus himself, summarized in a dozen different ways but always so as to highlight the cross and resurrection as the events through which, as Paul says, one world is crucified and another is reborn and we with it;

and, almost equally important, the stories of himself and the early church in various places and the story of what it means to be a Christian, to start as a sinner, to be grasped by God's call through gospel and spirit, to believe, to be baptized, to live the life in Christ, to work for the gospel, to die in the hope of being with Christ immediately and of being raised to new life at the last. At this point, too, the story of creation itself comes round to meet us once more, with Paul's glorious prediction that creation itself will be set free from its slavery to corruption and will share the freedom of the glory of God's children. And for Paul, as for the gospels, whether we look at his larger arguments or his smaller summaries, it comes down again and again to the story of God: the God who made the world, the God who will judge the world and put it back to rights, the God who called Abraham, who gave Torah, who sent Jesus and condemned sin in his flesh, who raised Jesus from the dead and seated him at his right [29] hand, who now sends the spirit to enable the church to be the sign to the powers that their time is up. All this and much more can be said about the stories that inform and undergird the specific things which Paul says to one church after another.

All this means that Paul, like the gospels, must be seen not least in terms of his view of God as the God of Israel – with all the problems and puzzles which this entails in terms of his insistence that God did indeed give the law and did indeed call ethnic Israel, and his equal insistence that God had now acted apart from the law and that God had called a people not from Jews only but from gentiles also. The reason Paul faces these problems is clearly that he has not thought of abandoning the Jewish view of God, rooted in the Old Testament, as though the gospel of Jesus Christ revealed some other God. And this puts him on a direct collision course, more obviously than the gospels because of his particular situation and the reason for his writings, with the pagan world of his day. It is in Paul that we see as clearly as anywhere else the confrontation between the God of Israel, now seen as the God revealed in Jesus and by the spirit, and the pagan gods of the surrounding nations. For Paul, the origin of Christianity posed in a fresh way the question of God that had always been at stake between Jews and non-Jews. And when he wrote about the righteousness of God, God's saving faithful covenant justice, he was aware that it was this large theme in Jewish literature, most notably in Isaiah 40—55, which formed the basic challenge from the God of Israel to the pagan gods. The creator will be faithful to the covenant through the work of the 'servant', and the mighty gods of Babylon will find themselves tottering and crashing to the ground while God's people are rescued and the whole creation is renewed. When Paul went about his work as the apostle to the gentiles, this image was of great importance to him. He wrote of pulling down strongholds and destroying proud systems that opposed the truth. He wrote not least of the way in which the living God had called people to know and serve him instead of their lifeless idols. And he spoke especially of the defeat of the principalities and powers through the cross of Jesus and of the folly of doing anything that would approximate to going back to serving them once more – an echo of the exodus-narrative which haunts a considerable portion of his thinking and writing.

It is this exodus context which provides the two strongest and clearest examples in Paul of the redefinition of the meaning of 'God' around Jesus and the spirit. The first is Galatians 4, where he tells the story of people moving from slavery through redemption to freedom – in other words, the exodus-story. The exodus was the time when the meaning of the name YHWH was first revealed; this was when the Israelites discovered who it really was that their ancestors had worshipped when he rescued [30] them from slavery. Paul, drawing on the same Abrahamic background, describes God as the one who sends the son and then sends the spirit of the son and declares that 'now that you have come to know God, or rather to be known by God, how can you turn back to the *stoicheia*, the elements of the world?' (Galatians 4.9). The gospel events, in other words, have unveiled the full character of the true God; the God who made promises to Abraham is the God who now claims the whole world as his own and who does so by showing himself as the son-sender and the spirit-sender. Either you have the Trinity, or something remarkably like it, or you have a return to slavery. God's saving covenant faithfulness, his putting of things to rights, has been unveiled before the whole world.

The second passage is Romans 8, a more sustained exposition of the same theme and one which brings to its first great climax Paul's explicit treatment of the *dikaiosynē theou*. God's promise to Abraham, Paul had said in Romans 4, was that he would inherit the world – not just one piece of territory but the entire planet. Romans 8 describes how it is that God will be faithful to this covenant promise and thereby to the whole of his creation: God will do for the whole world, at the end, what he did for Jesus at Easter. Indeed, Easter is hereby revealed as the secret of both the future of the world and the character of God, as Paul had already said in Romans 4, describing God as 'the one who gives life to the dead' (Romans 4.17) and then as 'the one who raised Jesus from the dead' (4.24). This is part of the central point of Easter, that it is the decisive work of the creator God, who is utterly determined to put his creation to rights. (One of the many interesting things I noticed when working on my book on the resurrection was that, for the early Fathers and the rabbis alike, resurrection is what you get when you insist on a strong doctrine of creation and a strong doctrine of God's justice. Conversely, for Paul, having got resurrection – the resurrection of Jesus – as his starting-point, he is able to announce to the whole world that God will redeem it and to invite those who have worshipped the world rather than God to forsake their idols and meet their maker.)

In all of this Paul is not merely stressing the greatness of the salvation promised to those who are in Christ and indwelt by the spirit, though, of course, he is doing this as well. Nor is he simply standing over against the kind of Judaism he had formerly taught and lived, though he is doing this too. He is deliberately outflanking the pagan worldviews, not least the views of divinity, which he knew only too well from the streets of Ephesus and Corinth. He does not need (as people used to imagine) to translate the Jewish ideas and beliefs of earliest Christianity into quasi-pagan thought-forms to make them attractive or accessible. What the world needs, Paul believed, is the God of Abraham, Isaac and Jacob and the Messiah of Israel, who is the world's rightful lord and coming judge. [31] And though this message was sheer folly to the pagan world – a crucified Jew as the lord of the world! – Paul discovered that when he announced Jesus as lord, the message itself, what he called the powerful word of the gospel, did its own work and brought people to 'the obedience of faith'. That which paganism could not provide, a genuine humanity reflecting the image of the creator God, was generated by the gospel. And in this generation the question of God, the central question underneath all worldviews, was given a fresh set of answers that enabled Paul to engage in debate with all comers.

This ongoing debate is brilliantly encapsulated in the Areopagus address in Acts 17. It is, of course, hugely abbreviated (there is no way that Paul would have let them off with a couple of minutes), but it demonstrates – and by its multiple links to his letters this demonstration could be considerably elaborated – that the view of God to which Paul had come by rethinking his basically Pharisaic theology afresh in the light of Jesus and the spirit was able to trump the major answers which ancient paganism gave to the question of God.

To begin with, the classic polytheism that had left temples and images scattered all around the ancient world simply would not do. Worthless idols, Paul calls them – dismissing with a wave of the hand some of the finest ancient works of art as simply unnecessary category mistakes. Serious pagan philosophers of the time would have agreed with him. But what about the major options as catalogued a century earlier by Cicero? The Stoics believed that the world was itself divine; Stoicism is a form of monotheism, since, if everything (*to pan*) is divine, then there is only one divinity. The great strength of pantheism is that it takes seriously the signals of transcendence, of strange innate power and glory, within creation itself, but Judaism trumps this by speaking of the world as the wise handiwork of a good creator and also offers what Stoicism cannot find, an analysis of the problem of evil with the promise that something is to be done about it.

Conversely, if the strength of Stoicism is its recognition of the signs of divine life within the world, the strength of Epicureanism is its recognition that the world, as it stands, also shows signs of being, to put it mildly, other than God. But Epicurus and his great disciple Lucretius then go off into full-blown deism with a god or gods who are absent and uncaring, leaving the world to manage by itself as best it can. Judaism once more trumps Epicurus by speaking of the world as still known and loved by its creator and of the creator's desire that all people, instead of merely acknowledging him at a distance, feel after him and find him.

The third option, that of the Academy, declared that there was not enough evidence to decide the question, but one should keep traditional religion going just in case – a position not unknown in today's western world and church. But at this point Paul moves beyond [32] what Judaism would have said. The devout Jew would have said that the one true and living God would, in the end, put the world to rights; some devout Jews would have said that God would do this through the coming Messiah. Paul goes one further. He knows the name of the Messiah, and the whole picture has come sharply into focus through God's raising him from the dead.

The resurrection of Jesus the Messiah thus provides, for Paul, the epistemological as well as the theological fulcrum for his mission to the pagan world, for his announcement that there is a God, a creator God, who loves the world and has remained in sustained and searching contact with it and that God will one day put it to rights. The resurrection informs the Academy that a new knowledge has arrived which will settle the question after all; it informs the Epicurean that the living God has acted and is continuing to act within our world and not a great distance away; it insists to the Stoic that, though the world is full of signs of God's presence, the living God is not limited by the entropic possibilities visible within the cosmos as it is but has acted and will continue to act as its sovereign, to judge it and to save it. The Areopagus address thus offers a concise account of the intellectual question of God as seen by the author of Romans 1 and Romans 8.

This brings us back to the larger question of God's saving, faithful covenant justice and especially to the question of Israel. Though we divide traditional Jewish belief into monotheism, election and eschatology, the latter two are really ways of speaking about the first: there is one God, and Israel is his people; there is one God, and through the covenant he will put the world to rights. Just as the Jew further demarcates the meaning of 'God' by the second clause ('and Israel is his people') and, for that matter, the Muslim substitutes an equally defining clause ('and Muhammad is his prophet'), so Paul the Christian, and with him the whole church ancient and modern when it knows its business, declares that there is one God and that Jesus is his son. The sonship of Jesus – remembering that 'son of God' was a title for Israel as well as for the Messiah – is the climax of election as well as the fullest self-revelation-in-action of the sovereign God. Paul is thus precipitated in Romans 9—11 into a long discussion of Israel precisely because the Messiah is from Israel according to the flesh but is also God overall, blessed for ever (9.5). And only when he has worked through the underlying christological logic of Israel's election can he conclude his great discussion of God's justice by speaking, doxologically, of the unsearchable depth of God's wisdom and ways. The question of election and the concomitant question of eschatology are part of the question of God because they concern God's ultimate saving faithful justice.

This in turn – though we have no time to speak of this here – flows directly into the life of the community within the larger pagan environment. Romans 12—16 is part of the logical whole, the exposition of [33] God's *dikaiosynē*, precisely in its appeal that the Christian community live within the present world under the rule of God's new creation, not least in its struggle for united worship across traditional boundaries. And this in turn contextualizes the appeal for obedience to authorities in Romans 13; part of the question of God in every culture is, implicitly or explicitly, the question of what obedience is owed to earthly authorities, and Paul gives the question the classic Jewish answer, that the existing powers are called into being by God (who, as the creator, certainly does not want anarchy), even though they are constantly disobedient to their call to be agents of God's just and wise rule and must themselves be summoned back again and again to that obedience. I have written extensively elsewhere of Paul's reworking of this Jewish political theology and his quite explicit lining up of Jesus as lord over against Caesar. I just note it here as one element, a very important one, within the overall early Christian question of God. Suffice it to say here that Paul offered the pagan world an answer to the question of whether a god, or the gods, could ever actually put the world to rights. Caesar had claimed to do so, awarding himself the titles 'saviour' and 'lord' and claiming that Roman justice and peace would solve the world's problems. Paul called Jesus 'saviour' and 'lord' and declared that it was through his gospel alone that genuine justice and peace could be found. Paul's exposition of the justice of God, the ancient Jewish doctrine reformulated around Jesus, offered a standing challenge to the powers of the world and their claims to justice, as indeed to divinity.

The Love of God

No serious reader of Paul could make the mistake one still sometimes encounters, that of supposing that his stress on God's justice was somehow antithetical to an emphasis on God's love. Once you put the terms back into Hebrew, things become far less polarized, precisely because God's 'righteousness', God's justice, is his ṣĕdāqâ, whose covenantal and relational spread of meanings encloses a good deal of what our English translations are representing by the word 'love'. And though agapē has a wider meaning elsewhere in ancient Greek, including the Septuagint, than it does in the New Testament, behind it again and again stand words such as ḥesed and 'ahăbâ, Hebrew terms which speak of the constant, utterly reliable, generous and warm-hearted love of the creator God for Israel, yes, but also for the whole of creation, not least for human beings.

The other mistake is to suppose that an emphasis on the love of God is going to lead, before too long, into a kind of mushy relativism [34] where no lines are drawn very clearly, judgment disappears like a bad dream, and God simply becomes an indulgent grandparent. Again, no-one who knows the Old Testament, not least the passages where God's ḥesed and ṣĕdāqâ are emphasized, could make this mistake. And no-one who knows John's gospel and his epistles, the documents that stake a claim to be the New Testament's central expositions of God's love, could imagine such a thing there either. The love of God, which Paul and John together insist is revealed centrally in the saving death of Jesus the Messiah, has nothing to do with an idea that evil does not really matter after all. It has everything to do with the fact that evil does matter and that it matters so seriously that nothing short of the cross will deal with it. Justice, in fact – the insistence that God will at the end put the world to rights – is itself for the early Christians a form of love, the form that God's love takes when confronted by evil. God loves the world so much that he will not allow it forever to wallow in the corruption and decay into which the rebellious human race has plunged it. Calling a halt to evil – condemning it on the cross and bringing it to a final end still in the future – is the great act of love itself.

This answer to the question of God – that the one true God is the God of love – is itself generated (from the Old Testament, it is true, but generated afresh) from within the very origins of Christianity. I return to the point at which I began. The earliest Christians were aware of the generous, healing love of God at work in Jesus. Even if he only did a quarter of the things ascribed to him in the gospels, we would have to say that he must have been one of the most remarkable human beings of that or any age and that one of the truly remarkable things about him was his embodiment and living out of a wonderfully generous, self-giving love. When we add the other three-quarters back in and construe the gospel stories, as I believe we must, in terms of Jesus' constant implicit reference to his acting out of the vocation to do and be what YHWH himself had promised to do and be, and when we see the narrative lines all leading up to the cross, we find our conclusion strikingly stated and confirmed over and over: 'Having loved his own who were in the world, he loved them *eis telos*, to the uttermost' (John 13.1); 'God commends his love for us in that while we were yet sinners the Messiah died for us' (Romans 5.8).

Those who knew themselves to be traitors, yet found themselves welcomed and commissioned, would have found it hard to separate their understanding of how the movement began from their knowledge of a love that had found them, forgiven them and now equipped them. In then retelling the story of the exodus in a new way as their own story, they naturally found themselves speaking, like Moses in Deuteronomy, of a love which reached out to them and thereby to the whole world, not because of any qualities which that love found to approve but simply because it was love [35] indeed. And with this Jewish root of the doctrine of God's love re-formed, like everything else, around the person and the death of Jesus and the power of the spirit, they found once again that they had an answer to the question the pagan world had long asked. A glance through ancient pagan literature, or for that matter inscriptions and letters, will reveal that one of the primary attitudes of ancient pagans towards the gods was a sense of their unreliability. You could never be quite sure if this or that god was going to be pleased with you, would do something to help you, or if you were going to be let down, on the one hand, or tripped up, on the other. Over against this sense of helplessness, of not really knowing, of being tossed to and fro on a sea of theological and cosmic uncertainty, place Paul's finest paragraph on God's love, itself the central climax of a letter which has expounded God the creator and God the faithful judge. Who shall separate us from God's love? Neither death nor life nor angels nor rulers nor the present nor the future nor powers nor height nor depth nor anything else in all creation shall have the power to separate us from the love of God in the Messiah, Jesus our lord. This great peroration, one of the most spectacular in all literature ancient or modern, is also the ultimate answer to the question of God as it is raised and answered afresh from within the very origins of Christianity.

Conclusion

I have written elsewhere about the detailed ways in which the early Christians drew on Jewish language about God's involvement with Israel and the world to talk of Jesus and the spirit. Early Trinitarian theology drew heavily on Jewish roots, concerned from the outset to maintain Jewish-style monotheism rather than collapse in any way into any kind of paganism, merely adding Jesus to a pantheon. Instead, the early Christians drew on the Jewish language of God's word, God's wisdom, God's tabernacling presence, God's law and God's spirit to make it clear that what they were saying about Jesus was not destroying Jewish monotheism but fulfilling it. That is a whole other area.

The only thing I have to add here, by way of conclusion, is that by doing so they were giving Jewish monotheism the stability that it might otherwise appear to have lacked. The Jewish narrative was always open-ended, a line petering out and a hand pointing forward, a claim awaiting validation. The Christian story, while offering a new kind of open-endedness in the fresh framework of the gospel and its worldwide mission, insists that at the centre of history, the history in which God's sovereign and saving purposes have been at work, the incarnate son of God died and rose again as the condemnation of evil and the launching of the project [36] of new creation. In these events the world can see, as never before or since, that when the powers of the world do their worst, the creator of the world does his uttermost; that when lies and treachery and idolatry and power games and demonic forces get together and make the world dark even at noon, then the living God comes to the heart of the darkness and takes its full force on himself.

Thus the four great questions that collectively form the question of God received fresh answers from within the womb of Christian origins. To the question of the relationship between God and the world we know and live in, Judaism always said, against paganism, that the God of Abraham was the creator of the whole world. Paganism, even supposing it took any notice of this absurd claim, shrugged its shoulders and wrote it off. The early Christians *were* early Christians because the event that brought them into being was the event that showed the creator dynamically at work within his world, renewing both it and his own intimate relationship with it in incarnation and resurrection. To the question of the fact of evil, Judaism always said that evil was serious and that God's choice of Israel was designed to reverse its effects. Paganism, again if it took any notice, shrugged its shoulders and continued on its cynical way. The early Christians *were* early Christians because the event that brought them into being was the condemnation of sin on the cross and the launching of God's new, sinless creation. To the question of God and the present running of the world, Judaism always said that God wanted good earthly rulers but they would have to answer to him. Paganism sneered, persecuted the Jews and divinized its own rulers. The early Christians *were* early Christians because in his resurrection and ascension Jesus had been enthroned as the lord before whom all would have to bow. Finally, to the question of God and the future, Judaism always said God would put things to rights, and paganism always scoffed at such a notion. The early Christians *were* early Christians because in Jesus the Messiah Israel's God *had* put the world to rights and would complete the work on his return. The question of God emerges naturally with fresh answers from the very events that generated Christianity in the first place.

Christianity takes its origin, after all, not from fresh speculation about God or the gods, not from what the modern western world calls 'religious' experience, but from events through which, in their occurrence and in their continuing power when announced to the world, the question of God has been given a decisive and fathomless answer. This answer, now as then, calls forth the worship of the creature for the creator, the work of justice to implement that of the God of justice, and the love for God and one another which is both the reflection and the re-embodiment of the love of God himself, enacted in Jesus and shed abroad in our hearts by the spirit.

5
Faith, Virtue, Justification, and the Journey to Freedom

The choice of 'faith' as a topic for the Festschrift for Richard Hays was natural. Ever since his famous PhD, Hays has been seen as the pioneer of new ways of understanding what Paul said on this central topic. But what aspect should one then choose? The decision was made for me by an unexpected invitation to lecture in London on 'Faith as a virtue in tomorrow's world'. I had misheard the original verbal invitation, remembering it simply as the general theme of 'Faith in tomorrow's world', and only in the last week before the lecture did I discover that the whole series, of which my lecture was I think the start, was on the theme of 'virtue'. It was an exciting moment: suddenly my distantly remembered work on Aristotle's 'virtue' theory from undergraduate days came into creative partnership with my more recent reflections on Paul. All sorts of things clicked into place, and I was delighted to rework the lecture into this article. The other, larger, result of this thought-experiment was my book *Virtue Reborn* (Wright 2010), renamed by the US publisher *After You Believe* on the grounds that Americans don't buy books with the word 'virtue' in the title. I still think the whole theme is an idea whose time needs to come again, perhaps especially in the study of early Christian thought and, more importantly, life.

[472] Introduction

The first time I met Richard Hays was at the Annual Meeting of the Society of Biblical Literature (SBL) in Dallas, Texas, in December 1983. Dallas was having an ice storm at the time, but we were warm and safe in a huge hotel, along with thousands of other scholars, reading papers to one another and, equally important, making friends in the margins of the meetings. Richard read his (now well-known) paper on Romans 4.1, which I instantly recognized as solving the notorious translation problem in that verse and raising important questions about the reading of the whole chapter, questions that he and I have continued to explore in dialogue.[1] I introduced myself, and within minutes we were sitting in a cafe with a couple of expensive gin and tonics and, again equally important, open Greek Testaments. We were talking, particularly, about faith. Thus it began; thus it has continued. And thus, nearly a quarter of a century later, I come to be writing about faith as a small tribute, expressive of heartfelt thanks, to a great friend and a great scholar.[2]

We did not, however, talk in those days about faith as a virtue. 'Virtue' was not a topic that Pauline scholars even considered back then, except per-[473]-haps in a sidelong allusion to 'virtue lists' at certain points in the letters.[3] It is fair to say that the very idea of 'virtue' would have at once aroused suspicions. This might be, after all, a way of smuggling in 'works' by the back door, into Paul's soteriology (something we Paulinists are trained to watch out for, like sniffer dogs at an airport ready to detect the slightest whiff of hard drugs). And since one of the many things that Richard Hays and I had had in common from our early theological formation was an anxiety about some readings of Paul in which, it seemed to us both independently, 'faith' might actually become a 'work' in the sense of something a person does to earn God's favour, the idea of faith itself as a 'virtue' would have seemed highly suspicious to us both.[4] (There is an irony in this. We were both conscious of thereby taking a more 'Reformed' line, over against a prevailing 'Lutheran' reading of faith, and insisting on the importance of grace. Yet it is from the 'Reformed' camp that a good deal of criticism has come against the lines of thought that we have both subsequently pursued.)

Since then a good deal has changed, not so much at this point within the world of Pauline scholarship but rather in the world of current ethical discourse. Virtue has been making a come-back, not least among Richard Hays's colleagues at Duke Divinity School. Within an overall understanding of Christian life as generated and sustained by God's grace (in other words, ruling out from the start any suggestion that the 'virtue' we are going to talk about is something that 'we do' through self-effort, still less self-justification), thinkers like Stanley Hauerwas, Gregory Jones and Samuel Wells have explored

---

1   Hays 1985; Wright 2002b, 489.

2   An earlier version of this paper was given as a lecture at the Priory of the Assumption, Bethnal Green, London, on 8 February 2007. I am grateful to my hosts on that occasion for warm hospitality and fascinating discussion.

3   E.g. Col. 3.12–15.

4   See esp., of course, Hays 2002 [1983].

Christian behaviour in ways that, though ancient enough in themselves, have until recently been dormant.[5] Christian behaviour, they have insisted, is more than merely the 'automatic' way in which spirit-filled people find themselves acting, more than merely a spirit-driven obedience to *this* moral precept in *this* situation, but instead more like what Paul him-[474]-self calls *dokimē*, 'character' in the sense of 'a well-formed character, a tried and tested personality': a life formed by a long succession of choices that have become habit forming, choices that are often difficult to make, and often involve pain and suffering, but choices that have enabled people eventually to exhibit a deep Christlikeness, structural and not merely on the surface.[6] This, broadly, is the discourse of 'virtue', and in my judgment, as an interested onlooker of contemporary ethical discussions, it is potentially enormously fruitful.

But why *faith* as a 'virtue'? To return to the anxious Paulinist: is this not just what we suspected? Might this not imply after all that faith itself, the faith by which we are justified, is something that we have to 'work at', to generate from within? But at this point the theological tradition insists: in addition to the 'cardinal virtues' of temperance, courage, justice and prudence, some of the greatest ever Christian thinkers have added the 'theological virtues' listed by Paul himself, not only in 1 Corinthians 13 but in other passages as well, indicating that he already thought of them as, in some sense, a set.[7] And my intention in this paper is to offer some creative reflections on how a Pauline scholar might reinhabit this tradition of 'virtue' discourse, and perhaps even refresh it from its putative scriptural origins.[8] In doing so I am hoping, as it were, to throw a bridge across into the area of ethics and moral theology that Richard Hays has made his own but in which I have published almost nothing. One of the (to me) interesting and unresolved questions within our long friendship has been why Richard has moved on from Paul to ethics while I have moved on (back?) from Paul to Jesus. Perhaps this venture of mine into his field will tempt Richard to try his hand, in return, in the study of Jesus . . .

---

5   See e.g., among many others, Hauerwas and Pinches 1997; Wells 2004; Jones 1995. A useful summary of recent work on virtue in the context of its classical background is Porter 2001. A good deal of this work looks back with appreciation to MacIntyre 1985 [1981].

6   On *dokimē* in Paul, cf. e.g. Rom. 5.4; 14.18; 2 Cor. 2.9; 10.18; Phil. 2.22.

7   1 Cor. 13.13; Col. 1.4–5; 1 Thess. 1.3; 5.8.

8   I find, in rereading the paper at editorial stage, that I have subconsciously echoed various themes from Hays's seminal paper on 1 Corinthians in Hays 2005.

I Virtue and Eschatology

Many discussions of virtue, and many discussions of faith, begin from where we presently are, as muddled, sinful, half-believing human beings, and explore the ways in which virtue (including 'faith' in some sense) can help us move forward to become the people God wants and intends us to [475] become. In this, as in many areas of theological exploration, I find it helpful to start instead from the far end, from the ultimate goal. I propose that we begin with the picture of what God intends us to be, and has promised that we shall be, and to work back from there to where we are. This is, I suppose, rather like the procedure adopted by some management consultants: to ask where the company ought to be twenty years from now, to imagine that we are already at that moment of presumed or anticipated success, and then to ask the question: how did we get here? What steps did we take on the way?

If that is the shape of my account, much of the raw material for reflection will be drawn from the scriptures. Obviously, in the discussion of virtue both in general and in particular there is an enormous tradition stretching from Augustine through Aquinas to many interesting discussions in the modern period. But, though I am aware of the broad outline of this tradition, it has not been my specialty, and I hope that what I have to offer as scripturally based reflection will bring a fresh contribution to that tradition rather than a re-evaluation of some part of it from within. And, as is perhaps predictable given the subject, my own specializations and my desire to engage Richard Hays yet one more time, I will draw particularly on St Paul.

To work back from the future that God intends for us is actually suggested already by the classic accounts of virtue. Aristotle spoke of the goal or end, the *telos*, of human moral behaviour. We are on a journey towards that point, which he called *eudaimonia*. That has normally been translated as 'happiness'; but the meaning Aristotle had in mind was not the one that word often suggests in today's western world (the feeling of contentment or pleasurable excitement) but the more organic one of becoming our full and true selves, discovering in practice the best and highest activity of which humans are capable. The virtues are the particular 'strengths' (that is the meaning of the Latin word *virtus*) that enable us to grow into that full being, to advance towards that eventual goal. Taking the word 'goal' in its obvious current sporting usage, the virtues are like the different skills that different soccer players possess (passing, tackling, dribbling, shooting and so on), which are all aimed, eventually, at getting the ball into the net.

But Aristotle's description of that goal, not least in terms of 'reason' as the highest human faculty (so that the highest goal is the clearest and best use of reason), is, of course, challenged by the early Christian writings. There, again and again, we find the New Testament writers emphasizing instead love, *agapē*, as the highest activity, the one that binds everything else to-[476]-gether.[9] They speak of this 'love' as the fruit, not of unaided human effort, but of two things: the work of grace of the creator God, and the individual human response to that grace, which consists of faith. And one of the key questions we thus have to consider in thinking of Christian faith as in some sense a 'virtue' is the extent to which, once you add the 'theological' Christian virtues of faith, hope and love to the 'cardinal' virtues of temperance, courage, justice and prudence, the notion of 'virtue' itself has subtly but deeply changed. But since within the ancient hebraic worldview, and particularly within its Christian offshoot, the notion of a journey towards a goal remains central and vital, giving us a picture of an unfinished story whose intended conclusion can nevertheless be glimpsed, we can take Aristotle's idea of *telos*, and of the virtues as the steps by which we advance towards that goal, and reflect on the Christian version of this, starting from the *telos* itself and working back towards where we are, faced with the question of faith in our contemporary world.

But are Aristotle's goal and the Christian goal the same thing? Yes and no. Yes: it is the goal of discovering that for which humans were made, that in which they will find their deepest fulfilment. No: the hebraic and early Christian sense of the ultimate goal is quite different from that of Greek philosophy. The New Testament is clear about the goal towards which we are journeying. It is not, as in Platonism, an ultimate disembodied immortality in a non-spatio-temporal world. It is, rather, the new heavens and the new earth promised by Isaiah, Revelation and other biblical books; the redeemed, renewed cosmos spoken of by Paul in Romans 8; the 'summing up of all things in heaven and on earth in Christ' spoken of in Ephesians 1.10. Despite the widespread and misleading impression today that being a Christian has as its ultimate goal simply 'going to heaven', the early Christians, like many of their Jewish contemporaries, looked back to Isaiah and similar prophecies and spoke, with them, not of God's abandonment of the good creation, but of God's rescue of that good creation from corruption and decay, both physical and moral, and of God's creation of a new world out of the old one, a world

---

9   Col. 3.14: love is 'the bond of completeness', *syndesmos teleiotētos*. This already includes the eschatological note, the sense of an envisaged ending or goal, a *telos*.

in which the wolf would dwell with the lamb, in which peace and justice would flourish, and in which, above all, human beings would find their true fulfilment. This big picture is the soil in which the ancient Jewish belief in the resurrection of the dead flourished and grew, until the time when, to everyone's surprise, resurrection actually happened in the [477] case of Jesus of Nazareth, causing his followers to declare that in him God's new creation had already begun, confirming the ancient Jewish expectation and indicating that it had already started to come true.[10]

This already gives to the Christian understanding of the journey a sense, as Eliot said, that 'the end is where we start from'.[11] The end, the *telos*, the goal, has already happened in Jesus. We are not merely journeying towards a distant, and largely unknown, destination; we have glimpsed it already in microcosm. A small but highly significant part of the future has come forward to meet us, and is now firmly embedded in what is the fixed and unalterable past of this world. Having already been grasped by that *telos*, we now advance towards it in quite a different mood, quite a different mode, from those who travel without having already arrived.

This eschatological reshaping is closely cognate with the Christian redefinition of classical virtue in terms of a life lived through the calling of God's grace and in the power of his spirit. We do not simply make ourselves good by learning about virtues and then trying hard to practise them, ending up producing a self-made human being that could, in the end, be presented before God for inspection and approval. Rather, we find ourselves caught up by the story of Jesus, by the events of his life, his kingdom-announcement, his death and his resurrection, and we find both that he is himself the goal, the fullness of humanity as well as the fullness of divinity, and that he himself is the way, the journey by which we may ourselves come to that goal.

2 Virtues, Pagan and Christian

All of this does not mean, as Augustine seems to have thought, that virtue seen from a Christian point of view is completely discontinuous with virtue seen from a pagan point of view (whether Aristotelian, Stoic or any other). On the contrary. The early Christian view, built foursquare on the ancient Jewish theology, was that the one God known to the Jews as the God of Abraham, Isaac and Jacob, the God of the exodus, of Moses, of David and

---

10 On all of this, see Wright 2003; and now also Wright 2008.
11 From 'Little Gidding', in Eliot 2001 [1979], 42.

the prophets, was the creator of the whole world, heaven and earth alike, and had made all humans in his own image. The ancient Jews thus assumed [478] (and the early Christians carried on this assumption) that in all kinds of ways the vision of genuine humanity that they glimpsed in God, in Torah and in Wisdom constituted the overarching goal that included within itself, even though it also transcended, the goal glimpsed by pagan philosophers.

Some Jewish writers, such as Philo or the author of 4 Maccabees, explored this explicitly. Often it is assumed, taken in en route. The result is that temperance, courage, justice and prudence are seen, not as irrelevant or dispensable for the Christian, but rather as intermediate goals, steps on the road to the higher and in some ways quite different goal marked out by faith, hope and love. What is more, they are seen as intermediate goals that are themselves to be reached, not by sheer unaided moral effort, but by the grace of the creator God, and the renewal, by that grace and through faith, of the image-bearing capacity of all human beings. More in line with Aquinas than with Augustine, this means that the classical virtues, like every other aspect of God's created world, can themselves, as it were, be redeemed – but only if they submit, as all creation must submit, to the process of baptism, being put to death with Christ and being raised again. This, I think, is more or less what Paul means when he speaks of 'taking every thought captive to obey Christ' (2 Corinthians 10.5).

But whenever that putting-to-death and raising-to-life takes place, there are some things that are left firmly behind, and other things that emerge in quite a new light. One of the obvious results of putting to death in Christ the classical notions of virtue, and of the individual virtues themselves, is immediately apparent: pride is stood on its head. Pride was a virtue in the classical world. It was the sense of self-worth that came from knowing one's own value and position, particularly from contemplating one's own social, cultural, military, personal, moral or other achievements. And pride is the great casualty of the Christian journey; that is one of the main thrusts of Paul's two letters to Corinth. If the goal has already been given in Jesus Christ, our journey is not one of achievement but of implementation, not of unaided goodness but of unmerited grace. And this leads us back to faith, hope and love, the theological virtues, which Paul lists in that way precisely in the first letter to the Corinthians at the point where he confronts the pride of the community and shows them 'a more excellent way' (1 Corinthians 12.31). Indeed, Aquinas takes the daring step, as well as dethroning pride, of reinhabiting passion: over against the Stoics, with their desire for *apatheia*, he declares that the ultimate goal is the passionate love of God. Nothing that

76

is put to death cannot be raised, but nothing that is not put to death can or will be.

This is the point where we glimpse one of Paul's many visions of the ulti-[479]-mate end, the *telos*. Now, he says, these three things abide: faith, hope and love; but the greatest of these is love (1 Corinthians 13.13). The point he is making, in that fascinating and powerful poem on *agapē*, is precisely not that love is a virtue to which you should aspire in the old sense of a hard, unaided moral struggle. Half of the chapter consists in his attempt to explain to the Corinthians, who were used to thinking in that static pagan way, that for a fully Christian virtue you need a fully Christian eschatology. He contrasts the 'now' with the 'not yet': now we see through a glass darkly, but then face to face; now I know in part, but then I shall know as I am known. Paul is drawing on the picture of the ultimate future, the resurrection life, which he will expound in detail two chapters later, in order to insist to the Corinthians both that the highest form of virtue is love and that the way to this virtue is to recognize it *as an eschatological reality*, that is, something whose *telos* lies in the ultimate future but something that is already given in Jesus Christ and given to others in Christ and by the spirit. Thus, the eschatological nature of Christian virtue provides the key to understanding both the convergence and the divergence between pagan and Christian.

That sense of a reality given in Christ and through the spirit is, by the way, the biblical reality that lies behind the rather fuzzy talk in some Christian circles about Christian behaviour being a matter of allowing the spirit to work in one's life. This can sometimes degenerate into the Romantic or existentialist idea, a kind of parody of the theology of grace, that sees the only good deeds as those that 'come naturally', those in which one is being 'true to oneself', living 'authentically' in the sense of there being a close fit between deep intention and practical action. The trouble with that, of course, is that it would be all right if we were already at the goal in the sense of already being completely filled with the spirit, already raised from the dead; but at the moment we are still on the way, *in via*. The resurrection has not already occurred, except in the case of Jesus, and for that reason moral effort (always with the Pauline proviso, 'not I, but God's grace'; compare 1 Corinthians 15.10) is still essential.

This, I think, is the reason why there has been in our day a renewed emphasis on the virtues, as we noted at the start. It stems from a recognition that Christian Romanticism is not enough. You can have as strongly inaugurated an eschatology as you want *as long as you realize that it is not yet complete*, as Paul himself insists throughout 2 Corinthians and in

Philippians.[12] Every time you say 'already', you must always insist 'not yet' (and vice [480] versa, but that is not my present point). Not that Christian experience is simply an undifferentiated muddle, though it may sometimes feel like that; but that we can understand clearly what it means to live between the resurrection of Jesus Christ (and the power of the spirit that flows from that) and the final renewal and resurrection that has clearly not yet taken place. And those who live in that intermediate time need a framework of thought-out and understood moral shaping: not just individual commands for individual situations, to be obeyed (or perhaps disobeyed) in a kind of ad hoc fashion, but a sense that, in order to obey those commands, we are not simply miscellaneous Christians who happen to obey or disobey, but that we can actually *become the kind of people* who are more likely to obey than not, and that this will come as we cultivate the habits of mind, heart, body and life – in short, the virtues – that will dispose us to obey. We can become, in other words, people for whom the Romantic or existentialist dream might eventually begin to come at least partially true. But this is not, or not for the most part, something straightforwardly and completely given in baptism and in initial Christian faith.

The Christian teaching and practice of virtue, then, can be understood in terms of the life that is lived within the story whose goal, whose *telos*, is that complete, redeemed, renewed and perfected human life, within God's new and redeemed heaven and earth and among God's ultimately restored people. For the Christian, virtue is the practised art of being the sort of person who is already anticipating, in the present, the life of the coming age. The point of 1 Corinthians 13 is that love is not our duty; it is our *destiny*. It is the song that is sung in God's new world, and we are to become the sort of people who practise it in the present (even against the other jangling tunes the world is singing) so that we are all the more ready to sing it in the future, and so that we can be a sign of that future coming already into the present.

When we grasp this shaping of the Christian moral life, we may perhaps suggest that the relationship between the cardinal virtues and the theological virtues (and, behind them both, the pagan and Christian ideals of moral habit-forming) is not simply that the latter, by supplementing the former, gives them a new context, changing the abstract idea of virtue itself. It may also be that some of the thrust of the former is transformed, by that putting-to-death and bringing-to-life we noted earlier, into the thrust of the latter.

---

12   Cf. e.g. Phil. 3.12–16.

Thus, most obviously, the cardinal virtue of justice, giving to each person what is his or her due, is transformed into *agapē*, giving to each not simply what is due but more besides, including 'justice' itself (since *agapē* will **[481]** never wrong anyone, as Paul says elsewhere[13]), but going beyond it into generosity, giving to each in the way God gives to each, that is, lavishly and without thought for cost. That transference, that taking up of the lesser (justice) into the greater (love), works more or less in that particular case. It is not so obviously the case, or not to me at any rate, when we consider the relationship between faith and hope, the other two 'theological' virtues, on the one hand, and temperance, courage and prudence, the other three 'cardinal' virtues, on the other. Maybe this is a sign that we should not be overly restricted by the fourfold and threefold pattern of classical pagan and Christian virtue discourse. Indeed, if we ask where 'prudence' comes within early Christian ethical thinking, the straightforward answer is 'wisdom', which itself, as has been argued, is a matter of recalibrating pagan prudence in the light of the command to love: that is, that knowing the love command to be the highest there is, we drastically reorder our sense of priorities.[14] And one could easily argue that what Aristotle meant by 'courage' is included en route within Paul's exhortations to live by faith, patience and hope; also, that 'temperance' corresponds quite closely to what Paul meant by 'self-control', which is a fruit of the spirit (Galatians 5.23).[15] But to pursue any of this would take us too far afield.

3 Faith among the Virtues

With this framework of eschatological virtue, and of the convergence and divergence between pagan and Christian virtues both in themselves and in the way they 'work', I return more specifically to the question of faith as a virtue. It is fascinating to see in 1 Corinthians 13.13 that faith and hope, like love, are among the things that 'abide', that last into the future, that are (in other words) among the things that form bridges from the present age into the age to come. Putting this the other way round, it seems that for Paul, faith is a quality that we shall possess in God's new age, and that we anticipate in the present. Paul, indeed, gives both faith and hope as qualities of love: love

---

13   Rom. 13.10.

14   See Pinches 2000, 742.

15   So, of course, for that matter, is 'love' itself, and also 'patience' (*makrothumia*) (Gal. 5.22).

bears all things, *believes all things, hopes all things*, endures all things (13.7).[16]
[482]

Most people do not, I think, see 'faith' in this Pauline way. A well-known hymn specifically differentiates between faith and hope on the one hand and love on the other:

> Faith will vanish into sight,
> Hope be emptied in delight;
> Love in heaven will shine more bright,
> Therefore give us love.[17]

There is some justification within Paul himself for saying something like this in relation to hope: 'Who hopes', he asks, 'for what he sees?' (Romans 8.24). But if we explore what that means, we discover that hope is not so much emptied as fulfilled. If 'hope' is the longing to possess what God promises in the future, when we possess it *we do not abandon our hope; we fulfill it.* 'I've got what I hoped for,' we say, and hope is thereby affirmed. (There is a potential semantic catch here: when we speak of 'gaining our hope', what we really mean is 'gaining the thing we had hoped for', leaving it open in what sense the activity of hoping still continues.) It is, of course, possible too, perhaps even likely, that in God's new creation there will be new projects and aspirations, tasks to work on, plans to fulfil.[18] In that case, 'hope', which at present is always darkened by the shadow of uncertainty, will be a glad looking-forward from which that shadow has been removed, since we shall then want and intend what God wants and intends. Perhaps there is, in that sense as well, a future for hope, a future in which hope itself will be transformed, not abandoned.

What then about faith? Is faith part of our present journey, which will be unnecessary when we arrive, in the way that a boat becomes unnecessary when we reach the opposite shore? Or is it like love, something we know in part at the moment, which will be given more fully and richly in the future, in the way that the giant cluster of grapes offered the weary Israelites a foretaste of the promised land? I think it is both. For this we need some kind of

---

16 Again, note the presence of patience in this catalogue of what 'love' will do.
17 'Gracious Spirit, Holy Ghost' (1862), by Christopher Wordsworth (1807–1885), Bishop of Lincoln (and a nephew of Wordsworth the poet).
18 That seems to me at least to be implied by passages like Rev. 21 and 22. In 22.2 the leaves of the tree of life, growing by the water of life that flows from the new Jerusalem, are to be 'for the healing of the nations'. Who will administer that healing?

typology of the New Testament idea of 'faith', which is more polymorphous than many readers, I think, give it credit for. We need to set this out before we can understand what exactly faith is from the Christian point of view, in [483] what sense it may be classified as a virtue, and (presuming a positive answer to the latter question) what the effects of practising this virtue may be in personal and public life.[19]

The word *pistis* and its cognates cover, in fact, quite a wide semantic range, with four main and broad areas that merge into one another, and that thereby provide a large open field across which one can move in various directions, while each retains something of its individual flavour. All four senses are important if we are to understand the full early Christian picture of faith; not that we can parcel each occurrence of the relevant words confidently into one or another of the categories, but that all these meanings are readily available as part of the immediate field.

First, there is faith as *trust*: relying on someone or something, a person or a promise. Here 'faith' denotes both a single action, an act of trust, and also a wider attitude, a trusting approach to God, to a particular person (not least, in the gospels, to Jesus himself), and hence more or less an attribute of the person doing the trusting. In this sense, 'faith' becomes as it were a *property* of the person concerned. Such a person becomes a 'trusting' person, a 'faithful' person in that sense.[20]

Second, there is *belief*, in the sense of believing a particular statement to be true (which will often, but not always, involve believing, or trusting, the person making the statement). This is, if you like, a more focused aspect of the more general 'trust': believing *that* as opposed to simply believing *in*.[21] (In case anyone should try to play these two senses off against one another, we should note that both belong together in central New Testament formulations: in Romans 4.24–25 Paul speaks of 'believing *in* the God who raised Jesus from the dead', and in Romans 10.9 he speaks of 'believing in your heart *that* God raised him from the dead'.) The famous *fides qua creditur*, the faith 'by which' one believes, is in the New Testament a combination of these first two senses.

---

19 There are, of course, many typologies of 'faith' on offer, not least Bultmann's classic (though in my view flawed) account in Bultmann 1964. This is not the place for detailed engagement with different ways of organizing the material.

20 Several of the occurrences in Rom. 4 clearly belong here, while shading also into the second sense by the end of the chapter at least. Cf. too, e.g., 1 Cor. 2.5; 2 Cor. 5.7; Col. 1.4. For a 'faithful' person, cf. e.g. Gal. 3.9 ('those of faith').

21 Cf. e.g. Rom. 4.3, 18; 6.8; 10.9; also in a related sense 14.2; 1 Cor. 15.11; 1 Thess. 4.14.

Third, there is *fides quae creditur*, the faith itself *that is believed*. Here 'the faith' has become the proposition or the set of propositions or, indeed, the entire potential and later actual multi-volume corpus of systematic theology [484], that is thought to form the substance of that which Christians believe. Paul uses this, too: 'the one who formerly persecuted us', say the Jerusalem Christians according to Galatians 1.23, 'is now *preaching the faith he once tried to destroy*'.[22] Here 'the faith' is more or less 'the Christian message' or 'the gospel'. At this point, obviously, 'faith' in this sense cannot be a 'virtue', since it has shifted from describing the act or attitude of the believer to describing its correlate, the thing believed. It might be possible to argue that 'the faith' in this sense includes or presupposes the virtue of 'faith' in the other senses, but 'the faith' itself in this sense cannot be a virtue.

This is emphatically not so in the fourth sense. Here 'faith' and its cognates mean, more or less, faithfulness, loyalty, reliability, trustworthiness and even, in consequence, something like our word 'integrity': the quality of being so fully in tune, all through one's thinking and acting, that others know they are with someone on whom they can lean all their weight. (This is perhaps part of what Revelation means in calling Jesus the 'faithful' witness.[23]) More particularly, to put it anthropomorphically, someone of utter faithfulness is someone on whom *God* knows that he can lean all his weight.[24] In this sense, of course, none of us (except Jesus himself) is fully trustworthy in the present life. But part of the point of the eschatological perspective is that when we shall know as we are known, we shall have become people of utter faithfulness, utter reliability. Just as there is a striking contrast between Peter on the night Jesus was betrayed and the same Peter standing boldly before the crowds and the high priests in Acts, so there will be a contrast between our present fickleness and our utter integrity and reliability in God's new creation.

And, once more, Paul uses the *pistis* root in this sense, both of God and of Israel. In Galatians 2, he speaks of having been 'entrusted' with the gospel to the gentiles. In Romans 3.2–4, he speaks of Israel being 'entrusted' with God's oracles, and of some proving unfaithful to that trust – not, in other words, of them simply not believing in God's oracles themselves, but in

---

22 Emphasis added. Cf. too, e.g., Ac. 6.7; Rom. 10.8?; 1 Tim. 5.8. And 1 Cor. 15.14, 17 appear to belong here, though with strong overtones of senses 1 and 2; also 2 Cor. 13.5; Gal. 6.10 (though again, in the context of the whole letter, we must assume that echoes of senses 1 and 2 are also present); Eph. 4.5, 13; Phil. 1.27.

23 Rev. 1.5; 3.14; 19.11.

24 For 'faithful' in this sense, cf. e.g. 1 Cor. 4.2, 17; 7.25; Eph. 6.21; Col. 1.7.

being unreliable, untrustworthy, 'unfaithful' in the sense of 'unfaithful to their commission': they should have passed on 'the oracles' to the world, but they did not. This 'infidelity' in the sense of unreliability does not, Paul declares, call into question the 'faithfulness' of God himself, because God [485] will be true even if all humans are false. (At this point, we note, the concepts of faith and faithfulness need to be calibrated against the concepts of truth and truthfulness, but that too would take us too far afield, except to note the use of the older word 'troth', where 'I give you my troth' means, more or less, 'I put my truthfulness on the line by making a promise to which I will be faithful'.) A further example may be in 2 Corinthians 4.13, where Paul quotes Psalm 116.10, which may be best translated here, not 'I believed, and so I spoke' (NRSV), but '*I kept faith*, and so I spoke'. The point of the passage, and of the psalm being quoted, is not so much a statement of 'faith' in the second sense, as is often assumed, but in the fourth: 'I remained loyal', even under all the pressures and suffering that might have blown me off course.

How then does 'faith', in any of these senses, constitute a proper anticipation of an aspect of the ultimate future life, the resurrection life in God's new heavens and new earth? How, in other words, can 'faith' be seen to be the practice of something that will last, something that is a necessary part of that growing of a human being towards the full *telos* for which God has made us? Is faith, after all, also among the virtues?

We must face, to begin with, the problem that Paul and others sometimes speak of 'faith', in parallel with 'hope' in Romans 8.25, as something that will not be needed in the age to come: 'We walk by faith, not by sight' (2 Corinthians 5.7 NRSV). But the apparent conflict between this passage and 1 Corinthians 13.13 is only superficial. If 'faith' means trust (more specifically, for the Christian, trust in the God who raised Jesus), this trust will obviously continue and be perfected in the age to come. If it means 'belief that Jesus is lord and that God raised him from the dead', that too will not be abandoned but rather celebrated in the age to come. If it means 'loyalty to this God', and utter trustworthiness of character as a result, then this too will be consummated and perfected in the coming age. (And the one remaining sense, 'the faith', *fides quae*, will, of course, remain just as true in the coming age as in the present one.) In every sense, then, 'faith' is something that will last into God's new world and, indeed, be enhanced there.

Of course, part of the thrust of 'faith' at the present time, as in 2 Corinthians 5.7, is precisely that it is trust, belief and trustworthiness under conditions that threaten to destroy trust, to deny belief and to undermine trustworthiness. And perhaps, to jump to our conclusion, this is what gives 'faith' its peculiar character precisely as a virtue, but a virtue leading towards a *telos* in which, when perfected, the activity to which the virtue leads will 'come naturally', while in the present it does not. At the moment, to put it bluntly, 'faith' in any specifically Christian sense appears difficult or [**486**] impossible. The observed fact of universal death – observed and commented on, of course, not just since the Enlightenment, but as early as Homer and Aeschylus! – makes it difficult if not impossible to believe in the resurrection, either of Jesus or of his people. At the moment, the fact of evil in the world makes it difficult for many, and impossible for some, to believe in a good creator. At the moment, the changes and chances, the problems and pressures of life make it difficult for any of us to be utterly trustworthy, utterly loyal, utterly faithful in any sense or context. It is true that being trustworthy in general terms might be thought an aspect of the cardinal virtue of justice, part of giving to each individual his or her due (we owe to other people a duty of being true to what we have said, to what they may properly expect from the sort of person we have presented ourselves to them as being), and for that matter part of the virtue of temperance (controlling one's desire to behave in an untrustworthy manner) and, indeed, prudence (reckoning that trustworthy behaviour is more likely to have desirable consequences). It could thus be argued that there might be some aspects of 'faith' that could be seen as virtuous even outside a Christian context. But the demands of the Christian meanings of 'faith', in the senses explored above – faith as trust, belief, and loyalty to the God revealed in Jesus – are such as to transcend this completely. The gospel, as Paul knew, is folly to pagans. Trusting it would appear, not as a virtue, but as a vice. 'Faith' of this Pauline sort can therefore come about only *in response to the grace and revelation of the God of Abraham, the God who raised Jesus from the dead.*

This mention of Abraham and resurrection leads us to one of the most central Pauline statements of faith. In Romans 1 Paul declares that all humans have an innate knowledge of God but that they suppress this knowledge: they refuse to acknowledge God or give glory or thanks to him, even though they can see his eternal power and deity in the created order. As a result, he says, their humanness deconstructs and they become futile (Romans 1.18–23), worshipping lifeless idols and so courting death. By contrast – and recent studies have made it clear that Paul fully intends this contrast at the end of the epistolary section of which Romans 1.18 is the opening – Abraham believed God's promise, since despite the counter-evidence he trusted God as creator, gave glory to him and was 'fully convinced that God could do what he had promised' (Romans 4.16–22).[25] That was why he became fruitful despite his and Sarah's old age. [487]

Paul designed this rather careful analysis of Abraham's faith, of course, in order to demonstrate that Christians share essentially the same faith, because they are trusting the same God to be the creator and life-giver (4.23–25). This is the point at which one of the most important features of Christian faith comes into view: *Christian faith means responding in trust to the trustworthy God*, who is trustworthy precisely as creator and redeemer, as maker and judge, as the one who calls all things into being and promises to set all things right at the end. Here the first, second and fourth senses of 'faith' all come together. Christian faith is not a thing in itself, an independent decision to pin one's flag on God's map, but is always and necessarily the answer to an invitation, the gratitude for grace, the response to a call. This is part of the very grammar of 'faith' in the Christian sense. And the third sense of 'faith', *fides quae*, is not left out of this picture, since Paul's formulation insists on it: Christian faith is not a general trust in a divine presence or possibility, but belief in *this* God, the God who raised Jesus, that is, belief in 'the faith' that Jesus is lord, that God raised him from the dead and that God's new age, his new creation in which all is judged and all is set right, has already begun in him.

From this perspective, we should not be surprised to see Paul describing faith itself as a gift, as one of the results of the sovereign 'word of God' preached in the gospel, one of the consequences of the spirit's working. 'By grace you are saved, through faith; and this is not of yourselves, it is God's gift' (Ephesians 2.8). This raises, of course, but does not answer, the puzzling question of predestination: 'the word of God, which is at work in you believers' (1 Thessalonians 2.13; compare 1.4–5); 'no-one can say "Jesus is lord"' except by the holy spirit' (1 Corinthians 12.3). This has been a bone of contention in much protestant dogmatic theology. Reformed thought has strongly emphasized faith as the gift of God, ruling out any sense that 'faith' is something that 'I do' to become pleasing to God – in other words, preventing 'faith' from becoming 'a work'. Lutheran and Arminian thought has sometimes apparently insisted on faith as free, uncaused human belief – not least in supposed reaction to a perceived mediaeval Roman view of faith as an infused virtue.[26]

---

25 On the links between Rom. 1 and 4, cf. Wright 2002b, 500–1; and e.g. Adams 1997.

26 The idea of 'infused virtue' in mediaeval thought seems to be the result of Aquinas's drastic modifi-cation of Aristotle by the inclusion of Rom. 5.5, read in an Augustinian sense (i.e. taking 'the love of

But if faith is in any sense a gift, we are back with Augustine's paradoxical and (to some people) disturbing formulation: give what you command, [488] and command what you will! While some might hear this as a shoulder-shrugging excusing of moral incapacity ('God simply hasn't given me the grace to keep this particular commandment, so clearly he can't want me to do so'), Augustine's saying can, and in this case certainly should, be read in the much more bracing sense: the sign that God is indeed commanding this virtue, and also giving it, is that we now clearly perceive our inalienable obligation to be working at it in the power of the spirit. Simply to pray for a particular virtue (or for the disappearance of a particular vice) and then to expect it all to be done for us without our having to think about it, or to undertake particular and no doubt very difficult acts of will and moral self-discipline, is to capitulate once more to a Romantic dream of what the moral life ought to be like. Such a dream would be the moral or even emotional equivalent of a poor person suddenly winning the lottery: without effort, suddenly all your problems are over! Just pray about it and there won't be any more moral battles!

But virtue is not like that, and Christian moral living is not like that either. The Romantic dream of an inner transformation that will make moral effort unnecessary is untrue both to the New Testament and to worldwide and millennia-long Christian experience. Romantics may suppose that they have been installed in a hotel where everything they want is brought by room service at the touch of a button, but in fact they inhabit a house with a well-stocked larder from which they must choose ingredients and do their own cooking. The point of virtue, in other words, is the recognition that there is such a thing as building up a habit of taking regular small decisions to be a certain type of person, so that gradually one becomes that type of person indeed. And the point of virtue within a Christian frame of reference is that recognizing the utter gift-character both of the new age itself (the new age that has broken in with Jesus' resurrection) and of our own participation in that new age (the gift of faith and baptism, of membership in the eschato-logical people of God) does not take away but rather sets in its proper context the life of moral effort, of virtue that really does flow from the new life of Jesus' resurrection and that really does anticipate the *telos* to which it tends, the fully redeemed life of our own resurrection within God's new world. And, once again, this contextualizing of Christian virtue within the redemptive

God has been poured into our hearts through the spirit' to mean that the gift of the spirit has enabled *us* to love *God*).

eschatological framework underscores the great revolution in virtue ethics that took place from Paul onwards, or as Paul would say, from the cross of Jesus Christ onwards: the dethroning of pride and the enthroning of humility and gratitude. Not for nothing are Paul's two chapters on fundraising, on giving money as a sign of gratitude to God, framed within the letter [489] where above all Paul stands ancient pagan virtue-culture on its head: when I am weak, then I am strong![27]

Faith, then, is indeed a virtue. It demands hard work, not because it isn't a gift, but because it is; not because it isn't authentically flowing from within us, but because it is. The gift is the gift of the path to a richer, more responsible humanness; authenticity includes the choice to make an act of will despite desire, not simply bringing desire and will into line. To choose to believe, to choose to continue to believe, to choose to be faithful, loyal and trustworthy, despite all the pressures to unbelief and disloyalty, is typical of the choices that constitute, or contribute towards, the life of Christian virtue.

4 Faith, Virtue and Justification

It is in this light that we can, I believe, make some fresh sense of 'justification by faith' itself. At first sight, as we said earlier, the traditional reading of, and language about, justification by faith would seem to exclude all talk of 'virtue' as being dangerously prone to human pride and self-glorification. That, it seems, is why Augustine wanted to deny that there could be such things as 'natural virtues' apart from faith, hope and love; and why Karl Barth, the greatest Augustinian of modern times, avoided the language of virtue altogether (though the substance of virtue discourse is still to be found in his work). Let it be said again, as clearly as possible, that in attempting to put justification by faith and our discussion of faith-as-virtue into some kind of mutual correlation, I have no intention of 'smuggling in "works" by the back door'.[28] But justification by faith, as Paul makes extremely clear in a way that has sadly remained opaque to many of his ardent followers, must itself be understood quite strictly within its eschatological context. How does this work, and what will it say to our pursuit of faith as a virtue, a virtue that moreover will help us take large steps towards that freedom that God desires for his children? [490]

---

27 2 Cor. 8; 9; cf. 12.10.

28 I have discussed this and cognate topics frequently, not least in Wright 2002b; 2005a, ch. 6. See in addition, e.g., Wright 2004; 2006b.

Paul's fullest statement of justification is, of course, in Romans and, despite what many think, the first statement of justification is actually about justification by works. In Romans 2.1–16, he sets out a classic Jewish framework of the final judgment, revised at every point around the gospel of Jesus Christ. There will come a day when God will judge the secrets of all through Jesus Christ, and in this judgment Jew and gentile will stand on level ground. On that day, Paul declares – to the horror of those who would much rather he hadn't uttered such unReformed nonsense – that those who *do* what is right will be justified, will (that is) be declared by God to be in the right (2.13). (We later discover, in chapter 8, that the *form* of this future justification is precisely resurrection to immortal and eternal bodily life, the event through which God will declare who are his true children, just as, in 1.4, the resurrection of Jesus declared that he had all along been God's unique son.) Paul does not, in Romans 2, explain how it is that, with all humans being roundly declared to be sinful (3.9–20), any at all can in fact be discovered 'to have persevered in well-doing' (2.7). This causes problems for those who suppose, ahead of the evidence, that the sequence of thought in Romans corresponds to the sequence of ideas in a classic protestant *ordo salutis*. Such readers normally suggest that Paul is here merely offering a hypothetical position, which he will then undermine in chapter 3. The mirror image of this is the suggestion that Paul is in fact cheerfully acknowledging that there are indeed some good pagans who, without the grace of the gospel, do what is right and will thereby be justified on their own merits on the last day.[29]

But Paul is far more subtle, and his writing is far more symphonic, than that. He has drawn attention, as a good theologian of inaugurated eschatology might well do, to the eventual picture, the future day when God will set all things right. Only in the light of that future day, now disclosed by its anticipation and inauguration in Jesus Christ, can we understand what God is up to in the present time. And it is precisely *in the present time* that the doctrine of 'justification by faith', set out in 3.21–31, means what it means. The point is this: though all have indeed sinned and fallen short of the glory of God (3.23), God's gift of grace in the redemptive death of Jesus Christ (3.24–26) means that all who believe the gospel are declared to be in the right *in the present time*, in other words, as an anticipation of the future day when the secrets of all hearts will be disclosed. Paul's double emphasis that this is the *present* [491] reality[30] is meant to answer to the *future* reality set

---

29 Perhaps the best-known example of the latter is Dodd 1959 [1932], 62.

30 Rom. 3.21: *nyni de*; 3.26: *en tō nyn kairō*.

out in 2.1–16. Justification by faith is God's declaration, in advance of the final judgment, that all who believe in the gospel of Jesus Christ are already marked out as his people, being assured of forgiveness of sins.

Part of the point of this declaration, in advance of the final judgment, is that by giving the believing Christian full assurance of this forgiveness, and of sharing in the sonship of Jesus Christ (8.29), the context is set for that life of moral effort that is spoken of so vividly in chapters 6 and 8: not, in other words, that being a Christian commits you after all to the unrelenting and anxiety-driven pagan search for perfection, which would only result in pride, nor that being a Christian means that you will now 'automatically' behave in a manner that conforms to the gospel, but that being a Christian, believing in Jesus Christ and coming to understand justification by faith, creates a context of grace and gratitude in which the holiness of life commanded in Romans 6—8 is set, in which (in other words) virtues can be pursued without any shred of danger of lapsing back into Pelagianism or anything like it. And, in case there were any doubt about how all of this happens, Romans 12.1–2 makes it very clear: transformation through renewal of the *mind*. You will need to think differently in order that, through sustained moral effort, you may live differently. God, after all, wants redeemed humans, not puppets. Christian living demands that we become more fully human not only in what we do but why we do it.

Equally, part of the point of justification by faith, here in Romans 3 as elsewhere, is the point I have laboured in other places,[31] that because faith, rather than possession of Torah or the attempt to keep it, is the badge of membership in the eschatological people of God, this means that gentiles as well as Jews are full and equal members within that people. This, indeed, sets the ecclesial context for Christian faith, which is important for Paul in a multiplicity of ways for which there is no space here. I want, rather, to probe further into the question, vital for our central topic of faith as a virtue: why should *faith* be the badge that marks out Christians in the present as those who belong to God's eschatological people, those who are already assured of final vindication?

Two obvious initial answers, one negative and one positive, come to mind.

Negatively: the badge cannot be Torah or other signs of Jewish covenant membership, because if it were, as Paul says, only Jews could be members [492] (3.27–30). Even then, this would remain a theoretical possibility only, since they too are in fact sinful (3.19–20). The universal badge must therefore

---

31 Notably, Wright 2005a, ch. 6.

be faith, because faith is open to all. This gets us so far but no further, since several other things are also open to all, such as (obviously) hope and love. Why not justification by hope, or by love?

Positively: faith in the God who raised Jesus has an obvious character, of responding to *this* gospel, the message about *this* God, and thus marks out Christians as persons who are placing their trust *here* rather than anywhere else, leaning all their weight on the events through which God actually accomplished the defeat of sin and death and the launching of his new creation. This too is important but insufficient.

I suggest that both answers point beyond themselves. Where they point, I suggest, is to the important and Pauline idea that actually defines faith itself – and launches it on its new career of being a (Christian) virtue! – namely that Christian faith is the answering, faithful response to the faithful acts and word (both acts-as-word and word-as-acts) of the utterly trustworthy God. *Christian faith is thus the first sign that a particular human being is reflecting God's image*, so that when God speaks the faithful word of the gospel, the word that tells of his personal faithfulness to creation and covenant, in Jesus Christ and his death and resurrection, the human being who believes is answering God's faithfulness with faithfulness. (Some have read Paul's 'from faith to faith' in Romans 1.17 as expressing exactly this point.[32])

What is more, the believing person is thereby re-embodying *the faithfulness to death of Jesus Christ himself.* A long contemporary debate, in which Richard Hays has played the major role, has wrangled over whether by *pistis Iēsou Christou* and similar phrases Paul might actually mean 'the faithfulness of Jesus Christ' rather than 'faith in Jesus Christ'.[33] Though there is no doubt more to be said, I regard this debate as in principle settled in favour of the former interpretation, which appears fresh to us only because of the heavy weight of the long protestant tradition that has stressed the latter. Jesus, says Paul in Philippians 2.8, was *obedient* unto death, the death of the cross. The notions of *faithfulness* to God's plan and *obedience* to God's purpose are here very close. When, in Romans 5.12–21, Paul refers in summary form to what he has said in 3.24–26 and 4.24–25, 'obedience' is the category he chooses, because of the desired contrast with Adam. But the point of [493] Romans 3.1–5 was that God always required a faithful Israelite to carry forward his purposes; and this is what he has now put forward in the person of his son,

---

32   E.g. Dunn 1988, 43–4; and Wright 2002b, 425.

33   See Hays 2002 [1983], esp. the appendices in the 2nd edn.

the Messiah who represents Israel in himself.[34] *Christian faith is thus also the first sign of the Christ-life appearing within a person*, that faithfulness to God, his purpose and his promise that is not just a miscellaneous religious awakening or awareness but a very specifically Christ-shaped refashioning of the person from the heart and mind outwards.

This account of justification by faith will not, of course, satisfy those who are always on the lookout for semi-Pelagianism, ready to warn against the idea that God accepts us because of 'something in us'. But this reaction is a mistake. There is an irony here, not unlike the irony of traditional polemic over the eucharistic sacrifice: Protestants have always suspected Catholics of supposing that they were re-sacrificing Christ, because Catholics always insisted that the mass was not something other than Christ's own sacrifice, while Catholics have suspected Protestants of adding merit of their own to the Lord's Supper, because they said that what they were doing was indeed something different from Christ's death. In the same way, many Protestants have suspected Catholics of semi-Pelagianism, because they say (as I have done) that the faith because of which God declares us to be in the right is itself a gift of God that we now have within us. Catholics, in turn, have suspected Protestants of adding to or even anticipating the gift of God, by insisting that faith is something in some way outside ourselves. I strongly believe that a properly eschatologically oriented account will bypass this difficulty (and for that matter the problem about eucharistic sacrifice, though that again is a topic for another time).

Part of the problem has been, I think, that for many in the protestant tradition there has been a large-scale muddling up of several things, including conversion, justification, receiving the holy spirit, coming into a 'personal relationship with God', sensing and practising the presence of God, and even 'salvation' itself. Within this general muddle, 'justification by faith' has often come to mean simply believing and trusting in God and coming to know him through Jesus Christ, and discovering that this personal relationship, not the attempt to perform moral good deeds or religious or liturgical actions, is the centre of everything, and the guarantee and foretaste of final salvation itself. Theologians have often talked of 'saving faith', or even of 'salvation by faith', though Paul only once appears to use the latter formulation (Ephesians 2.8). But Paul does not mean that one is 'justified', that is, 'declared to be in the right', [494] by 'coming to know God personally'. Of course, 'coming to know God in a personal way' is part of the complex event that includes

---

34 See Wright 2005a, ch. 3.

'conversion', 'regeneration', 'being saved' and so on. But the slipperiness of popular language about this complex event should not allow us to blur the very precise and specific thing Paul is referring to when he speaks of justification. To be justified means to be declared 'in the right' by God (that is, (1) that one's sins are forgiven through the death of Jesus Christ, and (2) that one is a fully accredited member of God's single, worldwide covenant family). This declaration takes place in the present time (Romans 3.21-31) in anticipation of the declaration that will take place on the last day (Romans 2.1-16). And this 'justification', which is, of course, possible only because of the sheer grace and mercy of God acted out in the death and resurrection of his son, is made not on the basis of a new 'personal relationship with God' or some other religious experience but rather on the basis of the belief that Jesus is lord and that God raised him from the dead. Such belief acknowledges that because of God's grace, the believer *finds him- or herself within the eschato-logical purposes, the eschatological people and the eschatological narrative of the one true God, known in and through Jesus Christ.* And when God makes exactly that declaration about believers – in the future, by raising them from the dead, and in the present, by declaring them in advance to be thus 'in the right' – that declaration is what is called 'justification'.

5 Faith, Virtue and Freedom

This at last opens the way for important final points. First, the faith I have described, which includes trust, belief and faithfulness, does indeed become a virtue in the Christian sense. Second, this faith leads to a freedom, both personal and social, that is vital to be grasped if Christian life is to be renewed and Christian freedom to be celebrated in the public square today.

First, this faith really does become a virtue, in the Christian sense. The initial reaching out in grateful response, itself precipitated by the work of the spirit and the preaching of the word, is the start of a lifelong reaching out, a faithfulness that, like the initial faith, is the answer to God's faithfulness in Jesus Christ and in the word of the gospel. But this lifelong faithfulness, sharing as it does the nature and character of the initial faith by which one is justified, is not (again, as in some Romantic or existentialist dreamings) a matter of giving expression to how one happens to be feeling at the time. (One of the evils of our age is first to say 'I feel' when we mean 'I think'; [495] then to pass, subtly, to the point where *actual* feelings have taken the place of *actual* thought; then to pass beyond that again, to the point where 'feeling' *automatically trumps* 'thinking'; then to reach the point where thought has disappeared altogether, leaving us merely with Eliot's 'undisciplined squads of emotion'.[35] At that point, one of the nadirs of postmodernity, we have left behind both the classical and the Christian traditions, though tragically you can see exactly this sequence worked out in various would-be Christian contexts, not least synods.)

This lifelong faithfulness is a matter of practice. It means acquiring a *habit*: making a thousand small decisions to trust God *now*, in *this* matter, to believe in Jesus and his death and resurrection *today*, to be faithful and trustworthy to him *here and now*, in *this* situation . . . and so coming, by slow steps and small degrees, to the point where faith, trust, belief and faithfulness become, as we properly say in relation to virtue, 'second nature'. Not 'first nature', doing what comes naturally. No: *second* nature, doing from the heart that which the heart has learned by practice and hard work. Christian faith thus reaches out, by spirit-inspired and eschatologically framed moral effort, towards the *telos* for which we were made, that we should be image-bearers of the faithful God. This means, in the terms I have posed in this paper, that faith is indeed one of the things we learn to do in the present time that truly anticipates the full life of the coming age. This is the sense, I think, in which lifelong Christian faith, though not different in kind or content from the faith by which one is justified (but only in temporal location, that is, ongoing rather than initial), is indeed to be reckoned among the virtues.

Second, and perhaps still more urgently, Christian faith – belief and trust in the creator God who raised Jesus from the dead, and trustworthy loyalty to this God – sets us free in our personal lives from the need to worship or trust idols, and in our public lives from the pressure to serve the needs of an idolatrous state. In our personal lives, as Paul sees in Romans 1, what matters above all is worship, the worship which acknowledges that God is God, the creator and life-giver, the all-powerful one. All sin proceeds from a diminution in this trusting faithfulness, and the replacement of some or all of it by the worship of idols of one sort or another. And idols, when worshipped, first enslave, then dehumanize and then kill. I am not by training a spiritual director, but I know enough from pastoral work – not to mention the evidence of my own heart and life! – to know how idols work and how faith in the God who raised Jesus displaces and dethrones [496] them, and thereby sets the Christian free to be, at last, the person God is calling him or her to be.

---

35   From 'East Coker', in Eliot 2001 [1979], 19.

Likewise, in our public lives, as in the first century, to believe that Jesus is the Lord and that God has raised him from the dead is to believe that Caesar, in whatever form, is not lord, and that Caesar's proper sphere of work is not to usher in the new world in which justice and joy dwell for ever (as Caesar-figures often claim).[36] Only the one true God will do that, in a fresh and further act of grace, the final outworking of the achievement of Jesus Christ. Rather, Caesar's proper and limited task is to bring a measure of order to present society, to anticipate in specific acts of judgment (putting-to-rights) such elements of God's final putting-to-rights as can be done within the present age.[37] Part of our difficulty in today's world is that we are completely unclear about what it is that governments can do, and should try to do, and how they should go about finding a moral basis for doing it. We live in a confused time, with democracy in apparent decline and with the church and Christian consciences increasingly at risk from governments, in various parts of the globe, that, having made a mess of almost everything else, decide to distract attention by stirring up anti-Christian sentiment and passing laws designed to make life difficult for those who want to be faithful followers of Jesus Christ.

This is where faithfulness, loyalty and trustworthiness will stand out, where that fourth meaning of *pistis* is needed over against the shrinkage of 'faith' to merely 'my personal belief'. The rhetoric of the Enlightenment has been extremely keen to squash 'faith' into 'private, personal belief' so that it can then insist that such 'faith' should stay as a private matter and not leak out to infect the wider world. But since the Christian's personal belief is in the creator God who raised Jesus from the dead, this personal belief can never remain *only* a personal belief but, rooted in the trust that is the first meaning of *pistis*, must grow at once into the loyalty, the public trustworthiness, that is the fourth meaning. This too is part of the virtue of 'faith': to take the thousand small decisions to be loyal, even in public, even when it is dangerous or difficult, and so to acquire the *habit* of confessing this faith (sense 3) both when it is safe and when it is dangerous. Just as Mother Teresa spoke of recognizing Jesus in the eucharist and then going out to recognize him in the poor and needy, so we need to learn the virtue of affirming our faith in our liturgical and prayer life so that we [497] can then go out and affirm it on the street, in public debate, in pursuit of that freedom for which the second-century apologists argued.

---

36   See Wright 2005a, ch. 4.
37   On this point, and the whole paragraph, see esp. O'Donovan 2005.

Christian faith, then, does indeed belong among the virtues. But we can only understand that in the light of the full biblical and eschatological narrative, in which God's eventual new creation, launched in Jesus' resurrection, will make all things new. Christian faith looks back to Jesus, and on to that eventual new day. It tastes in advance, in personal and public life, the freedom that we already have through Jesus and that one day we shall have in all its fullness. The *practice* of this 'faith' is, on the one hand, the steady, grace-given entering into the habit by which our character is formed, a habit correlated with those resulting from the similar practice of hope and love. On the other hand, the practice of this faith is the genuine anticipation in the present of that trust, belief and faithfulness that are part of the *telos*, the goal. That goal, already given in Jesus Christ, is the destination towards which we are now journeying in the power of the spirit. Virtue is one of the things that happen in between, and because of, that gift and that goal.

6

Neither Anarchy nor Tyranny: Government and the New Testament[1]

In the first decade of the twenty-first century, I found myself becoming more and more involved in questions about the political process, particularly in the UK, in Europe and in the USA. This was partly because of working in Westminster Abbey; partly because subsequently, as Bishop of Durham, I had a seat in the House of Lords (though like all other bishops, the pressure of normal diocesan work is such that one is seldom able to be in the Lords more than three or four days in a month); and partly because my own work on Paul and the gospels was increasingly making me reflect that when Paul said 'Jesus is lord' he meant, among other things, that Caesar was not – in some sense or other. Teasing out what that might have involved took me in various directions. In terms of Paul, I have pulled it together in *Paul and the Faithfulness of God* (Wright 2013b), chapter 12. In terms of wider cultural and political reflections, I have published various small books such as *Creation, Power and Truth* (the Noble Lectures in Harvard University, 2006, eventually published in 2013) and *God in Public* (Wright 2016b). The middle lecture of the Noble series was then recycled in various forms and for various occasions. One version, overlapping with the second chapter of *Creation, Power and Truth* but sharpening up some themes, is presented here.

[61] The New Imperialisms

There is a current debate as to whether what we see in today's world is really a form of empire. The hegemony wielded by the western world, particularly by the United States as the current sole superpower, has some close affinities

---

1   This chapter is adapted from the second Noble Lecture given at Harvard University on 24 October 2006.

with earlier empires. But there are also considerable differences: the United States does not exercise direct governmental control over far-flung states in the way that, say, Queen Victoria ruled over a worldwide empire through viceroys, governors general and other imperial officials. Such differences are significant, but I would nevertheless side with those who use the word 'empire' to describe today's reality.[2]

Empires have a certain logic to them. If we have attained a new level of civilization, people think, we have a duty to share it with the world. This was exactly how the ancient Roman imperial rhetoric worked, as a glance at Cicero and similar thinkers reveals. We Romans are naturally free, we naturally possess 'justice', we believe in and maintain 'peace', and this gives us an obligation to share our unique gifts with everybody else. Of course, they come with a price tag, but [62] that is only to be expected granted the great benefits that are being conferred. As with the Roman empire, so with more modern ones, be they the British of the nineteenth century or the American of the twentieth and twenty-first. The political systems that evolved in the wake of the Enlightenment combined the ancient logic of imperial rule with modern ideas of progress and made a potent story. Once the divine right of kings had been rejected as an obvious power-play, 'vox populi, vox Dei' provided an inexorable alternative, and with atheism on the increase the 'vox Dei' bit was set aside, leaving 'vox populi' as a law unto itself. If only the people's voice could be heard and harnessed, then the world would attain its long-denied utopia.

Many of today's political puzzlements arise, at least in part, from the failure of this expectation to materialize. We have all been voting for a long time now and utopia has failed to arrive on schedule. Modernist rhetoric kept up the pretence for a while, suggesting that a little more reform, better housing and healthcare, more appropriate foreign aid, the export of democratic freedoms to other countries, and so on, would enable us to turn the corner and bring about utopia at last. Yet this hasn't happened and isn't going to happen, a fact highlighted dramatically and tragically for us by events of recent years. The problem of evil – not the philosopher's puzzle about explanation, but the global puzzle about what to do – is the guilty secret that the rhetoric of empire seeks to hide.

This is not a uniquely modern problem. Paul had scathing words for the imperial delusion in 1 Thessalonians 5: 'When they say, "Peace and Security" [as the Romans did say to their subject peoples], then sudden destruction

---

2   Such as Ferguson 2004; 2005.

will overtake them, and there will be no escape.' Imperial protection rackets can only last so long. Sooner or later there will be a day of reckoning, as the system topples under its own [63] lazy, top-heavy weight. Today's global empire is essentially an economic one, kept in place by electronic transactions rather than viceroys on the ground, but the same analysis remains true, as evidenced by today's global economic crisis.

And so long as we maintain the historic split of religion and politics, of faith and public life, we will be powerless to do more than lament before the errors of misplaced imperial ambition. The good news is that the great scriptural narrative, which we have for so long hushed up, tells a different story, one which calls all human empires – ancient or modern, military or economic – to account. This is the biblical story of the strange lordship of Jesus Christ. It has compelling implications for the conduct of the UK government today.

Jesus as Lord

One of the extraordinary reversals in scholarship over the course of the last thirty years has been the rediscovery of the political dimension to the New Testament. In the 1970s hardly anyone was writing about the Roman empire in relation to early Christianity. It was assumed, partly because of the Lutheran 'two kingdoms' doctrine, that the early Christians were concerned with worshipping Jesus, living in the spirit, being justified by faith, and explaining to one another how precisely to go to heaven, rather than with earthly politics. Paul's political views were dismissed with a wave at Romans 13, and Jesus' attitude to the state was summed up in the saying about rendering to Caesar, which was taken as marking a rigid separation of powers. The book of Revelation was thought of as a strange farrago of apocalyptic nightmares, which eager fundamentalists would systematize into end-times datelines and shocked liberals would dismiss as [64] bloodthirsty fantasies. It was taken for granted that the early Christians were uninterested in serious political theology.

All that has changed in the last thirty years. In the Society of Biblical Literature[3] several groups have looked excitedly for critiques of empire in early Christianity. Matthew, Mark, Paul, John and especially Revelation are all deemed thoroughly counter-imperial. Indeed, the pendulum has swung so far so fast that it is in danger of flying off altogether into politically driven

---

3   An influential gathering of mostly American biblical scholars.

speculations with as little historical basis as the dualism they replace. Some assume, ridiculously, that since the New Testament now seems to be about politics it cannot after all be about theology. Somewhere in the middle of all this there is fresh wisdom to be found, and it comes both in the repeated assertion that Jesus is lord – meaning, among other things, that Caesar is not – and in the emphasis that it is *Jesus*, the crucified one, who is lord, thereby redefining the very notion of 'lordship' itself.

John's Gospel

It has often been remarked that, whatever we think of the historical value of the rest of the gospel, the Johannine narrative of the trial before Pilate (John 18—19) offers a remarkably authentic picture of how a suspected rebel leader might be tried before a provincial governor.[4] But it is, of course, much more. It is the climax, within John's astonishingly skilful narrative, of the gospel-long dialogue between Jesus and 'the world' (as introduced by the prologue's statement that 'he was in the world, and the world was made by him, but the world knew him not') and also between Jesus and his fellow Jews (of whom the prologue at once goes on to say that 'he came to his own, and his own received him not'). Pilate stands for the world, the world made by God but run by Caesar. Jesus stands for the [65] kingdom of God, as announced by psalms and prophets, by Isaiah and Daniel in particular.

The scene displays not just two kings but two types of kingdom. Here is Caesar's kingdom: a kingdom in which truth is relative to power. Jesus has come, he says, to bear witness to the truth, and Pilate's famous response, 'What is truth?' [John 18.38], indicates the gulf between the two empires. Caesar's empire only knows the truth of Roman rule, the truth that comes out of the scabbard of a sword (or, as we would say, the barrel of a gun): the 'truth' of taxes and whips, of nails and crosses. But the kingdom Jesus comes to bring is not 'from this world'. If it were, he observes, his servants would have been fighting to stop him being handed over: that's what kingdoms originating in the present world always do.

This, we must insist, does not mean that Jesus' kingdom is a 'purely spiritual' one, a gnostic dream of escape that has nothing to do with the present world and hence has no challenge to offer to Caesar. No: Jesus' kingdom does not *derive from* this world, but it is *designed for* this world. But precisely because it is the kingdom of the wise creator God who longs to heal his world, whose justice is aimed at restoration rather than punitive destruction, it can

---

4   Sherwin-White 1963, 24–47.

be neither advanced nor attained by the domineering, bullying, fighting kingdom-methods employed in merely earthly kingdoms. Jesus thus redefines what it means to be 'lord of the world' at the same time as he redefines, with heavy Johannine irony, what it means to be 'king of the Jews'. And the Jewish leaders, meanwhile, now with crowning irony, declare that Jesus cannot be their king, since they have 'no king but Caesar' [John 19.15].

In the middle of this extraordinary dialogue, Jesus says something yet more striking. Pilate has warned that he has the power to crucify or release him. Jesus comments that Pilate couldn't have this authority if it were not given him [66] from above, so that the greater sin is ascribed to the one who handed him over – in other words, Caiaphas. It is truly remarkable, in the midst of the contrast between the two types of kingdom, to find this note, alerting us to the deeply Jewish perception, itself rooted in the doctrine of creation, that even in the present rebellious state of the world, God does not want anarchy or chaos. There must be rulers, even if they are bound to be themselves drawn from the ranks of the wicked. To have no rulers is even worse. The resulting paradox, that God-given rulers send the son of God to his undeserved death, lies close to the heart both of the New Testament's doctrine of the principalities and powers, and of its multiple interpretations of the meaning of the cross.

Thus, when we read John's gospel as a whole, and allow the confrontation with Pilate to shape the meaning John intends us to find in the story of the crucifixion and resurrection, we discover a deeper meaning to those climactic events than we get if we treat the political build-up as mere scene-setting for an essentially apolitical doctrine of redemption. Jesus has come not to destroy the world but to rescue it from evil, and if the structures of human authority are part of the good creation, the abuse of those structures constitutes a double evil. Jesus' task, driven not by the love of power but by the power of love, is to take the full force of that double evil on himself, and thereby to complete the work of redemption just as the father completed the work of creation at the end of the sixth day. The final cry from the cross in John ('It is accomplished!') resonates all the way back to God's *finishing* of creation on the sixth day.[5] The darkness of evening brings in the seventh day, the day of rest, before the arrival of the eighth day, 'the first day of the week', the day in which – if we are to allow John's massive build-up of imperial and counter-imperial [67] themes to resonate as far as chapter 20 – the new creation is launched, and Jesus prepares to ascend, like the 'son of man' in

---

5   Gen. 2.2.

Daniel 7, to rule the world with a new kind of power, the transformative and healing power of suffering love.

The Synoptic Gospels

This spectacular Johannine political theology, routinely ignored by preachers and theologians alike, conforms closely to what we find in the synoptics. Matthew's risen Jesus insists that all authority in heaven *and on earth* has been given to him, which deserves further exploration in terms of Matthew's plot and major themes. Luke contrasts the posturing of Augustus Caesar in Rome with the humble but decisive birth of Jesus. Then, in Acts, he describes what it means that the kingdom is indeed 'restored' to Jesus as Israel's king and to his followers acting as ambassadors. In Acts 17 we find Paul accused of heralding 'another king, namely Jesus'. The book ends with Paul in Rome itself, announcing God's kingdom and preaching Jesus Christ as lord 'openly and unhindered'. No first-century reader would have missed the point, which was in any case implicit in the initial ascension narrative. Within modernism the ascension is merely a supernatural embarrassment, but within first-century worldviews (whether derived from Daniel 7, or based on Roman emperor-cults, or, like those of the early Christians, rooted in one and confronting the other) it clearly meant that Jesus was now constituted as the true, and divine, lord of the world.

Mark's political theology has been variously explored,[6] and I simply focus on his redefinition of power in 10.35–45. James and John ask to sit at Jesus' right and left. Jesus responds that they don't know what they are talking about (though the reader will soon know, as two others end [68] up in those positions when Jesus is at last labelled publicly as 'king of the Jews'). But then comes the great redefinition: the rulers of the earth lord it over their subjects, but with you, the greatest must be the servant, and the leader must be the slave of all – *because* 'the son of man came not to be served but to serve and to give his life a ransom for many'. That famous verse (10.45), drawing together Isaiah 53 and Daniel 7, is not, as so often imagined, a detached statement of atonement-theology, but rather the clinching point in this devastatingly counter-imperial statement about power. That does not mean that it is *not* about (what we have come to call) 'atonement'. Rather, it is an invitation to understand atonement itself – God's dealing on the cross with the sin of the world – as involving God's victory not so much over the world and its powers (as though God were simply another cheerful 1960s anarchist) but over the

---

6 See e.g. Myers 1990.

worldly *ways of* power, the ways in which the powers that were created in, through and for Jesus Christ have rebelled and now themselves need to be led, beaten and bedraggled, in his triumphal procession, in order eventually to be reconciled.

Paul

That last sentence is a deliberate echo of Colossians 1 and 2, and points us to Paul. It used to be thought that Paul was a quietist, accepting magistrates and emperors with a shrug of the shoulders. I have argued elsewhere that this is a serious misreading of Romans 13, and that Romans as a whole, and for that matter Philippians too, offer a sustained if sometimes coded challenge to the absolute rule of Caesar.[7] Think of the opening of Romans (1.1–17): Jesus, for Paul, is the king, the *kyrios*, the son of God, whose 'gospel' calls the whole world to loyal obedience, and generates a world of justice, freedom and peace. Paul was able, while deriving his gospel from a Christ-shaped rereading of psalms and [69] prophets, to phrase it in such a way as to challenge, point by point, the normal rhetoric of Caesar's empire.

When Romans 8 offers a Christian variation on the Jewish eschatological hope for the renewal of creation, it upstages the boast of Rome that, under the emperor, the world was entering a new age of fruitfulness. Philippians 2 and 3 make the same point in different though related ways. 1 Thessalonians, as we saw, mocks the normal imperial boast of 'peace and security', and in chapter 4 provides a picture of the *parousia* of Jesus which seems designed to upstage the regular imperial panoply of the *parousia* of Caesar, 'arriving' at a city, or back in Rome after some great exploit, with the grateful citizens going out to meet him and escort him into the city. Of course, 1 Thessalonians 4 has become notorious as the proof-text for a 'rapture' in which God's people will be snatched away from earth to heaven, thereby leaving them without the promised new heavens and new earth, leaving Paul without one of his more powerful pieces of anti-Caesar rhetoric, and leaving us less able to mount any critique of empire.

Central to Paul, of course, as to John and Mark, is the theology of the cross, which is again to be seen not only in terms of traditional 'atonement'-theology but also in terms of counter-imperial polemic. As any student of Roman history knows only too well, crucifixion was not just a very nasty mode of execution but also a clear statement of power. It warned subject peoples, slaves and insurgents that Rome ruled the world, that Caesar was

---

7   See Wright 2009, esp. ch. 4.

lord, and that resistance was both futile and very, very foolish. It made the theological point that the goddess Roma ran the world, and required her subjects – especially in the Middle East, which supplied the grain essential to the well-being of the overcrowded city of Rome itself – to do what they were told, when they were told. It took not only genius but considerable [70] chutzpah to see, and to say, that the symbol which spoke of the horrible 'justice' of Caesar's empire could now speak of the restorative justice of the true God.

All this is based, of course, on the resurrection. If death is the ultimate weapon of the tyrant, then resurrection is the reassertion that the creator God rules over the world which the tyrants claim as their own. To speak only of 'atonement' in the dehistoricized and depoliticized sense of 'Christ dying for my sins' as a kind of private transaction, while in itself highlighting one of the majestic truths at the heart of the Christian faith ('the son of God loved *me* and gave himself for me'[8]), is to run the risk of colluding with empire, implying that the redemption that I enjoy will enable me to escape the world where imperial powers continue to behave as they always do. Equally, of course, to imagine that we can reduce Matthew, Mark, Luke, John or Paul to terms simply of 'politics', as though their political stance is not non-negotiably rooted in their theology of creation, atonement and new creation, is to reduce them to echoes of our own largely impotent political posturing.

It is the underlying theology, in fact, which enables the New Testament writers to avoid that kind of shallowness and lay the foundations for a mature political theology. We trace their thinking, through books such as the Wisdom of Solomon, all the way back to the biblical story of God's people under pagan rule. The line from Genesis 3 to the Tower of Babel in Genesis 11 then gives way to the call of Abraham; Abraham and his family end up in Egypt, rescued when God judges their pagan overlords; the decidedly ambiguous conquest of Canaan results in the still ambiguous kingdom of David and Solomon; and eventually we find ourselves back in Babel, in the Babylonian exile, which creates the context for those two most deeply political prophecies, Isaiah and Daniel. The Psalms, meanwhile, celebrate the kingship of [71] YHWH over the nations, and YHWH's placing of his Messiah as the one who will bring the kings of the earth to order. It is this story that formed the matrix within which the early Christians fashioned their own political stance.

---

8   Gal. 2.20.

At the heart of this stance we find the affirmation, the good news: Jesus is lord. *Jesus*, the crucified one, is lord; not another Caesar to bully and threaten, but the one whose life and death redefined power for ever. The book of Revelation is now widely and correctly seen as one of the great documents of early Christian political theology, offering a further account of the victory of the creator God over the rebel powers of the world, a victory rooted in God's determination to restore and fulfil the creational intent and accomplished through the self-giving death of the 'lamb'. Revelation joins the rest of early Christianity in announcing that Jesus is lord of earth as well as heaven, and that at his name every knee shall bow.

The lordship of Jesus is thus to be understood in harmony with the larger theological themes of creation and judgment, themes that together constitute the good news of the creator God over against the darkness of a world gone astray. Jesus' lordship is not outside, or over against, the restorative purposes of the creator God. Rather, he is exalted through his resurrection and ascension to the place where the God who made the world through him now rules the world through him. As Paul says, quoting Isaiah 11 at the final climax of his greatest letter, Jesus is the one 'who rises to rule the nations; and in him the nations shall hope'.[9] Only those who have lived with the hopelessness of human empire will fully appreciate that promise, just as only those who have lived with the violence of empire will fully appreciate the meaning of the victory over violence itself won on the cross.

The New Testament's theology of creation, resurrection and new creation thus forms the solid platform for the [72] central gospel assertion that Jesus Christ is lord, the good news for those in a newly imperial world. The good news is that this lordship is not a mere heavenly lordship, distracting attention (and critique) from the tyrannies of the world, but a lordship designed for earth as well as heaven, not only in the ultimate future when heaven and earth are one, but also in the penultimate future, in which Jesus' followers work to bring signs of his healing and hopeful rule to birth in the present time. It is to this task, difficult and complicated though it may seem, that we now turn.

Living in God's Alternative Empire

The last decade has forcibly reopened the question many in our world had considered closed for ever, that of the interrelation of faith and public life. It

---

9 Rom. 15.12.

has never really gone away, of course, but for much of the last two centuries, particularly in the North Atlantic world, it has been regarded as effectively off limits. I have noticed that in the USA the idea that church and state might have anything to do with one another is often attacked with real venom, perhaps because of long memories of George III sending bishops to the colonies. Now, with the proliferation of multi-faith communities in many formerly monochrome parts of the world, and particularly with the rise of a militant Islam, we face old questions in new ways.[10]

Politicians and columnists to left, right and centre have chipped in with comments which indicate that we are totally unused to addressing questions of religion, culture and public life, and unaware that there might be some old maps which would help us find our way through countryside which is virgin territory to us but which was well known to many of our forebears in all the great world-faiths. Two years running, the editors of *New Statesman* magazine have highlighted [73] big features on 'God' which have shown, basically, that they know there is a question out there which needs addressing but don't know what it is – and that they are afraid of letting God get too close to public life. How can the early Christian political theology I have been exploring help us to think afresh about all of this, and navigate our way through this complex and dangerous territory?

The biblical theology that runs from Genesis and Exodus, through the ambiguous narratives of conquest and monarchy, through Isaiah and Daniel, through, indeed, the Maccabaean literature and the Wisdom of Solomon, and out with a new focus into John, the synoptics, Paul and Revelation – and for that matter Ignatius of Antioch, Polycarp of Smyrna and Irenaeus of Lyons – approaches questions of earthly power and the kingdom of God through the doctrines of the good creation, the promised new creation, and the lordship of the crucified, risen and ascended Jesus. This invites us today to a massive task of retrieval, in implicit dialogue with political theologians of all sorts, but for which there is here only time for a short summary.

As I said above, it is part of the doctrine of creation that the creator intends the world to be ordered and structured, with a harmony of its parts that enables flourishing, fruitfulness and the eventual fulfilment of the creator's intention. From the beginning, according to the ancient poetic story, the creator God gave to humans the task of reflecting the divine image into the world, being the bridge between the creator and the creation, representing the presence of God within the creation and the presence of creation before

---

10   The question is now of urgent interest. See e.g. Wallis 2006.

God, and doing so with a rich awareness of both elements. The risk that the humans would rebel, and set up on their own, is a point in Genesis 1 which resonates deeply with several subsequent layers of the story: because, when evil [74] enters the world, the creator does not abandon it to chaos, does not unmake creation itself, but works from within to produce an eventual restoration.

It gradually emerges, throughout the Hebrew and Aramaic scriptures, that part of this divine purpose is to call and equip rulers, not only within Israel itself but also within the pagan nations of the wider world, to bring a measure of order to the world – and even sometimes, as in Isaiah 10, judgment on God's people! – even though they themselves remain part of the problem, abusing their vocation to further their own ambitions of violence, greed and hollow glory. The ambiguity of human power – the necessity of it on the one hand, and the inevitable temptations of it on the other – thus fleshes out the precarious position of the humans at the beginning and of Israel throughout the story, as the Israelites, like Adam and Eve (and that may be part of the point), rebel against the creator and are eventually ejected from the garden, the promised land.

The promises to which Israel clung over the following centuries combined the two elements that give shape to early Christian political thought as well: first, God's use of non-Jewish powers to restore and give order and security to the post-exilic community; second, God's challenge to those very powers (and God's promise to the chosen people) that the coming Messiah, and/or the messianic community, would eventually put the whole world to rights, which would involve the demotion of all powers from the proud, arrogated position they routinely occupy.

Let me put it like this, in a threefold typology, based on the doctrines of creation and redemption: (1) God intends the world to be ordered, and will put it in proper order at the last; but (2) he doesn't want chaos between now and then, and uses human authorities, even when they don't acknowledge him, to bring a measure of his order in advance [75] of the end; and (3) since that puts awful temptations in the way of the authorities, God's people have the vital calling to speak the truth to them and call them to account in anticipation of that same final day.

I hope it is clear that this gives to second-Temple Jewish thought, and thereby to early Christian thought, a complexity and density which does not correspond to the (over)simple political alternatives familiar in today's western world. Perhaps it is also clear that this complexity corresponds much more closely to the way in which much of the rest of the world sees public life, and that if we are to engage with the world we live in, instead of assuming that our post-Enlightenment political mindsets are automatically superior, we would do well to think the matter through more fully.

The early Christian political theology includes the application to power of the achievement of Jesus Christ in his death and resurrection.[11] The problem of evil within the world cannot be reduced to the sum total of individual sin, hugely important though sin and forgiveness are. It includes, and the evangelists and apostles knew it included, the victory by the creator God over all the powers that have rebelled within the world, and hence the announcement to the principalities and powers that their time is up, that Jesus is lord and that they are not. (That, of course, is the message of Ephesians 3.10: the revelation of God's many-coloured wisdom to the rulers and authorities.) The rulers are therefore to be summoned to obedience to the 'prince of peace'. The church was from the beginning entrusted with this dangerous message, and necessarily and inevitably suffered for it, but went on claiming, as in Acts, the moral and political high ground of reminding the authorities what their job really was, and holding them to it. The apostles found far less difficulty than we do in holding this package together. We, who have inherited the post-Enlightenment [76] antithesis of anarchy and tyranny and have turned it into two-party systems of left and right, are called to relearn the more subtle, and more useful, biblical analysis of how the rule of Jesus Christ makes its impact on the kingdoms of the world.

The church is therefore called to reject both tyranny – all rulers must bow before Jesus! – and also the anarchist dream of no powers, no 'order', no structure to God's world. In the promised new heavens and new earth there will be order. How much more, then, within the present world where evil still infects the human race, is it necessary that there be rulers and authorities who can hold it in check?

Equally, the church must also reject the Marxist dream of a simple inversion of power, of the rule of the previous underclass but by the same means as before. Rather, the church must affirm that the creator God intends the world to be ruled by properly constituted authorities, but insists that they be held to account, and that it is part of the task of the church to do this, to speak the truth to power, to affirm power in its proper use and to critique it in its regular abuse.

Here, I think, we in the western world have been too in love with our own modernist democratic processes, and have imagined that the only really

---

11   Wright 2006a.

important thing about power is how people attain it, since 'vox populi' will give them the absolute right to do what they want after being elected. Part of our difficulty today is precisely that this implicit belief is held so strongly that the idea of a democratic 'mandate' is, for many, part of an unchallengeable worldview, and far too much weight then attaches to all the expensive fuss and bother about elections.

The early Christians, like the Jews of the same period, were not particularly interested in how someone, or some system, [77] came to power. They were much more interested in what people did with that power once they had it, and in holding up a mirror to power, like Daniel with Nebuchadnezzar or Darius, so that those in power might be reminded that they are responsible to the creator God and that, ultimately, they are called to bow the knee to Jesus as lord.

If the church could recapture this vision, there might emerge a more mature political theology that would avoid the sterile left–right polarization or the more recent but equally sterile centre–centre polarization (if that isn't too paradoxical) that has characterized so much western politics. Our political discourses have become shallow and naive, not only in descending to spin and smear, but also, more worryingly, in appealing to social and cultural feeling rather than to genuine issues of justice, power and freedom.

The church is called to bear witness to the promise of new heavens and new earth in which justice will dwell, to refuse to be conned by the rhetoric of either the new Right or the new Left, and to insist on bringing signs of that future to birth both in its own life and in the world around, based on the resurrection of Jesus and the power of the spirit.

The church must, in short, learn from Jesus before Pilate how to speak the truth *to* power rather than *for* power or merely *against* power. This needs working out, of course, in economics both local and global; in ecology and stewardship of the whole creation; and, not least, in structures of global governance. Thus, for example, the suspicion or downright rejection of the United Nations on the part of some on the American Right must be rejected if we are genuinely to work for justice and peace across the globe. Neither the USA nor the UK, nor some combination of the two, can ever again be as they stand a credible global police-force, especially in the Middle East. Yet some kind of transnational policing is [78] necessary in some parts of the world, and if the UN cannot currently provide it we must find ways of enabling it to do so.

To take another example, I am disappointed at the shallow level of engagement on many fronts over the question of establishment. From where

I sit (namely in the House of Lords), it is clear that two regular objections to the present position are simply ill-informed. First, establishment does not mean that the church tells the state what to do; bishops have a voice, and often use that voice to speak up for the voiceless in their regions and, indeed, for other denominations and other faiths, but we are not in any sense 'in charge'. Sometimes it is the representatives of other faiths who are the strongest supporters of establishment. Many Jews, for instance, have often said they would rather have someone speaking for God in public life than have a secular republic which could do what other secular republics have done in the past.

Equally, establishment does not mean that the state tells the church what to do. The cartoon on the cover of Theo Hobson's little book *Against Establishment*, with Her Majesty The Queen walking a dog on a lead, the dog's face being that of the Archbishop of Canterbury, is not only straight-forwardly wrong (that simply isn't how establishment works), but ironically so: Hobson's own position is that the Church of England should reflect the mood and whim of the society in which it is set, going with the flow of contemporary moral positioning. In other words, for the Queen, substitute your favourite political columnist.

In fact, the present position does give the church (and those wider communities for whom it has a chance to speak up) a voice at the table; not the only voice, and not an easy voice to maintain in good order, but a voice none the less. There might well be other ways of achieving the same end, but [79] there is an end there to be achieved, and the present system is at least a way of maintaining something of what ought to be done while the swirling currents of confused political rhetoric go round and round in circles.

The church now has a chance, granted the general decaying feel of western democracy (think of the billions spent on elections in the USA; think of the refusal of the accountants to sign off on the European Union's accounts; think of the House of Commons' 2009 expense-claims scandal and the British public's near-ubiquitous anger and cynicism towards all politicians . . .), to speak up about the big issues of justice, freedom, the very nature of government and democracy, the responsibility of all rulers not just to their own political backers or financiers but to those they rule.

God wants there to be good government, and the church – and Christian politicians – must bear public witness to that fact in every way possible. That, after all, is what Christians are doing when they pray, as Jesus himself taught us, for God's kingdom to come on earth as in heaven.

7

The Bishop and Living under Scripture

This essay was originally a lecture, given at the request of the Archbishop of Canterbury, during the Lambeth Conference 2008. It was one of many 'extra' sessions designed to feed in to the main programme, rather than being on the main agenda itself; but a good number of my fellow bishops turned up to it, and we had some lively discussion – though I was recovering from a heavy cold and my main memory is of relief that my voice just about lasted through the session. The piece was then republished in a collection of related essays. As I say at the start, there was a discussion group (known at Lambeth as an 'indaba' group) on the use of the Bible, and this was intended as a contribution to it. How much effect these reflections have had on global Anglicanism in the last ten years it is impossible to say; but I remain convinced that, without serious attention both to what scripture says and to the question of how we use it responsibly and wisely, the chances of renewal within this or any Christian church remain slim.

[144] Introduction

My theme in this chapter has obviously been designed to go with the indaba group-work on our use of the Bible. This is an opportune time, as our conference quickens its pace, to reflect on how we use scripture, not least how we bishops use scripture as part of our vocation, as in the main theme of this conference, to be 'bishops in mission'.

Let me draw your attention to a book of mine which is foundational for what I'm going to say. *Scripture and the Authority of God* grew directly out of my work on both the Lambeth Commission and the International Anglican Theological and Doctrinal Commission.[1] It was published in the USA under

---

1   Wright 2005b.

the strange title *The Last Word*[2] – strange, because it certainly wasn't the last word on the subject, and also because if I were going to write a book called *The Last Word* I think it ought to be about Jesus Christ, not about the Bible. But such are the ways of publishers.

The puzzle about the book's title, though, points forward to the first thing I want to say, which is about the nature of biblical authority and the place of the Bible within the larger edifice of Christian theology and particularly missiology. I turn to my first main section. [145]

Scripture and the Authority of God

I Scripture as the Vehicle of God's Authority

Debates about the authority of scripture have tended to get off on the wrong foot and to turn into an unproductive shouting-match. This is partly because here, as in matters of political theology, in the words of Jim Wallis 'the Right gets it wrong and the Left doesn't get it'.[3] And sometimes the other way round as well. We have allowed our debates to be polarized within the false either/ or of post-Enlightenment categories, so that we either see the Bible as a holy book, almost a magic book, in which we can simply look up detached answers to troubling questions, or see it within its historical context and therefore claim the right to relativize anything and everything we don't immediately like about it. These categories are themselves mistaken; the Bible itself helps us to challenge them; and when we probe deeper into the question 'What does it mean to say that the Bible is authoritative?' we discover a new and richer framework which simultaneously enables us to be deeply faithful to scripture, and energizes and shapes us, corporately and individually, for our urgent mission into tomorrow's world.

Consider: how does what we call 'the authority of the Bible' relate to the authority of God himself – and the authority of Jesus himself? When the risen Jesus commissions his followers for their worldwide mission, he does not say, 'All authority in heaven and earth is given to . . . the books you people are going to go and write.' He says that all authority is given to him. When we say the closing words of the Lord's Prayer, we don't say that the kingdom, the power and the glory belong to the Bible, but to God himself. And when Jesus commissions the disciples for mission in John 20, he doesn't say 'Receive this

---

2   Wright 2005b.
3   Wallis 2006.

book' but 'Receive the holy spirit'. Authority, then, has a Trinitarian shape and content. If we want to say, as I certainly want to say in line with our entire Anglican tradition, that the Bible is in some sense our authority, the Bible itself insists that that sentence must be read as a shorthand way of saying something a bit more complicated, [146] something that will enable us to get some critical distance from the traditional shouting-match.

From very early on in the church, it became clear that those entrusted with God's mission included some who were called to write – to write letters on the one hand, and to collect, edit and write up the stories about Jesus, and the story of Jesus, on the other hand. The composition-criticism of the last few decades has moved us on a long way from the old half-truth that the biblical authors 'didn't think they were writing scripture'. Paul certainly believed that God had entrusted him with an authoritative mission, and that his letter-writing formed part of that spirit-given, Christ-shaped, kingdom-bringing activity. And the gospel-writers, in their different ways, write in such a manner as to say, with quite a rich artistry: here is the continuation and culmination of the great story you know from Israel's scriptures, and this is how, through its central character, it is now transformed into the narrative of God's dealings not just with Israel but with the whole world. Any first-century Jew who has the nerve to begin a book with 'In the beginning', weaving the themes of Genesis and Exodus, of Isaiah and the Psalms, into the story of Israel's Messiah, and doing so in such a way as to provide a framework around and energy for the mission and life of the followers of this Messiah – anyone who does something like this is either astonishingly un-self-aware or is making the definite claim to be writing something that corresponds, in a new mode, to the scriptural narrative of ancient Israel.

From very early on, the first Christians discovered that the church was to be shaped, and its mission and life taken forward, by the work of people who were called to write about Jesus, and about what it meant to follow him in his kingdom-mission. The new dispensation, the messianic age, did not mean the abandonment of the notion of being shaped by a God-given book, but rather its transformation into something new, new genres and themes developing out of the old. But this already indicates that the Bible was not something detached, an entity apart from the church, simply standing over against it. The Bible as we know it, Old and New Testaments, was, from the first, part of the life [147] of God's people, and remained so as it was read in worship, studied in controversy and made the basis for mission. But this did not mean then, and does not mean now, that the Bible can be twisted into whichever shape the church wants at a particular time. You can't say, as some have tried to say, 'The church wrote the Bible, so the church can rewrite the Bible.' Paul would have had sharp words to say about that, as would the author of Revelation. From very early on, all the more powerful for being implicit and not yet much thought through, we find the first Christians living under scripture, that is, believing that this book is its peculiar gift from its lord, through the work of his spirit, designed to enable the church to be the church, which is, of course, as we have been thinking throughout this conference, not a static thing, but to be the church in mission, to be sent into the world with the good news of God's kingdom through the death and resurrection of his son and in the power of that same spirit.

2 God's Authority and God's Kingdom

When we say 'the authority of scripture', then, we mean – if we know our business – God's authority, Christ's authority, somehow exercised through the Bible. But what is 'God's authority' all about? To look again at scripture itself, it is clear that one of the most common models assumed by many in today's world simply won't do. We have lived for too long in the shadow of an older deism in which God is imagined as a celestial CEO, sitting upstairs and handing down instructions from a great height. The Bible is then made to fit in to the ontological and epistemological gap between God and ourselves; and, if it is the deist God you are thinking of, that gap has a particular shape and implication. The Bible is then bound to become merely a sourcebook for true doctrines and right ethics. That is better than nothing, but it is always vulnerable to the charge, made frequently these days, that it is after all only an old book and that we've learned a lot since then. The Left doesn't get it, and often all the Right can do is to respond with an ever more shrill repetition of 'the [148] Bible, the Bible, the Bible'. As the late great Phil Ochs sang during the Vietnam War:

> And they argue through the night,
> Black is black and white is white,
> And walk away both knowing they are right;
> And nobody's buying flowers from the flower lady.

I know that quoting a Vietnam protest song dates me, but I guess that I'm not the only one in this room radically shaped by the events of the late 1960s . . .

The real problem with the deism that infected so much of the western world in the eighteenth century and dominates it still – thank God for our brothers and sisters from elsewhere who didn't have that problem! – is that it lives by serious reaction against the whole notion of God's kingdom coming 'on earth as in heaven'. (Actually, much protestant theology couldn't really cope with this idea either, perhaps in reaction against the perceived worldly kingdom of mediaeval Catholicism, which is why it privileged a particular reading of St Paul over against the gospels, a problem still with us in the guise of the Bultmannian legacy.) But when we reread the gospels and the kingdom-announcement we find there into the centre of our own life and thought, we discover that God is not a distant faceless bureaucrat handing down 'to do' lists, our 'commands for the day'. The God of scripture is with us in the world, his world, the world in which he lived and died and rose again in the person of his son, in which he breathes new life through the person of his spirit. Scripture is the vehicle of the kingdom-bringing 'authority', in that sense, of this God. That is why the Left, which prefers a detached deism so it can get on and do its own thing, disregarding instructions that seem to come from a distant God or a distant past, gets it wrong, and why the Right, which wants an authoritarian command from on high, doesn't get it.

There is a particular problem here, because our Anglican formularies speak of scripture and its authority in terms of 'things which are to be believed for eternal salvation'. Living as they did [149] within the early modern western view, our Anglican forebears rightly saw scripture as the norm that guided you towards God's promised salvation through faith in Jesus Christ; but, like everyone else at the time, they saw that salvation less in terms of God's kingdom coming on earth as in heaven and more in terms of being rescued from this earth for a 'salvation' somewhere else. We can't go into this in any detail, but I just want to note that part of the exciting work today of reintegrating gospels and epistles and rethinking the whole notion of the kingdom and particularly new creation and resurrection is not without its effect on the place and role of scripture in the whole process. Basically, I believe that scripture is the book through which the church is enabled to be the church, to be the people of God anticipating his sovereign rule on earth as in heaven, and that this fleshes out what our formularies say in a three-dimensional and energetic fashion.

3 Scripture and the Story of God's Mission

So how does the Bible function in the way I have described? Answer: by being itself; and 'being itself' means, primarily, being itself as story. I do not mean by this what some have seen as 'mere story', that is, a cheerfully fictive account to be relegated to the world of 'myth'. The Christian Bible we know is a quite astonishingly complete story, from chaos to order, from first creation to new creation, from the garden to the city, from covenant to renewed covenant, and all fitting together in a way which none of the authors can have seen but which we, standing back from the finished product, can only marvel at. Speaking as a student of ancient literature, I am continually astonished by the shape of scripture, which can't simply be explained away as the product of some clever decisions by a third- or fourth-century council. Of course, scripture contains many sub-plots, and many parts that are not in themselves 'narrative' at all – poems, meditations, wisdom sayings and so on. But the narrative shape continues to stand out and, indeed, to stand over against all attempts to flatten scripture out either into a puzzle-book of secret gnostic wisdom, which deconstructs the stories, or into a book of true [150] answers to dogmatic and ethical questions, which also deconstructs the stories but from a different angle.

And this raises the question: how can a narrative be authoritative? This is the right question to ask, and it raises some exciting possibilities. As I have set out at length elsewhere, scripture offers precisely the unfinished narrative of God's heaven-and-earth project, God's great design, as Paul puts it, echoing the Law and the Prophets, to join everything in heaven and earth into one in Christ. And the unfinished narrative functions like an unfinished play, in which those who belong to Jesus Christ are now called to be the actors, taking forward the drama towards its intended conclusion. This is actually a far stronger, and more robust, version of 'authority' than the one which simply imagines the Bible as a sourcebook for true dogmatic and ethical propositions. Of course, such propositions are to be found in it, and they matter; but they matter as the tips of a much, much larger iceberg, which is the entire drama. And it is by soaking ourselves in that whole drama that we, God's people in Christ Jesus, are to live with and under scripture's authority, not simply by knowing which bits to look up on which topics, but by becoming people of this story, people formed and shaped in our imaginations and intuitions by the overall narrative, so that we come to know by second nature not only what scripture says on particular topics but why it says those things. And living under scriptural authority, contrary to what has been said by liberalism ever since the eighteenth century, does not then mean being kept in an infantile state, shut up parroting an ancient text, but rather coming alive, growing up, taking responsibility for seeing how the narrative has gone forward and where it must go next. We are, in short, to be improvisers, which as any musician knows doesn't mean playing out of tune or out of time but rather discerning what is appropriate in terms of the story so far and the story's intended conclusion.

This, I submit, has a strong claim to be an intrinsically Anglican way of thinking about scripture, insofar as there can be said to be such a thing. I am always intrinsically suspicious of claims to discover a specifically or intrinsically Anglican approach to [151] anything, not just because of the myriad of local variations but also because of the characteristic Anglican claim that Anglicans have no specific doctrine of their own – it's just that if something is true, Anglicans believe it. The truth behind that old joke is that we have tried over the years, when it comes to scripture at least, to nourish a tradition of careful scholarship, rooted in philology, history and the early Fathers, hand in hand with a readiness to let the Bible resonate in new ways in new situations. As an example of this, I cherish Brooke Foss Westcott, Bishop of Durham a hundred and ten years ago, who is buried close to J. B. Lightfoot in the great chapel at Auckland Castle. Westcott is known, of course, for his meticulous textual criticism, and his magisterial commentaries on John and Hebrews. But in Durham he is also remembered for being the bishop who, before the days of trade unions, settled a long and damaging miners' strike by negotiating so hard with the mine owners that eventually they met the workers' demands. For Westcott, careful biblical scholarship and hard street-level work for God's kingdom were two parts of the same whole, and we should be proud when Anglicanism reflects similar combinations.

All this is, of course, nurtured by the straightforward but deeply powerful tradition of the daily offices, with the great narratives of scripture read through day by day, preferably on a *lectio continua* basis, so that 'living prayerfully within the story' is the most formative thing, next to the eucharist itself, which Anglicans do. Classic matins and evensong, in fact, are basically showcases for scripture, and the point of reading Old and New Testaments like that is not so much to 'remind ourselves of that bit of the Bible', as to use that small selection as a window through which we can see, with the eyes of mind and heart, the entire sweep of the whole Bible, so that our 'telling of the story' is not actually aimed primarily at informing or reminding one another but rather at praising God for his mighty acts, and acquiring the habit of living within the story of them as we do so. That, I suggest, is the heart of Anglican Bible study.

Seeing the Bible in terms of its great story enables us, in particular, to develop a layered and nuanced hermeneutic which retains [152] the full authority of the whole Bible while enabling us to understand why it is, for instance, that some parts of the Old Testament are still directly relevant to us while others are not, and how this is not arbitrary but rooted in serious theological and exegetical principle. In the book, I have developed the model of the five-act play, with Creation and Fall as the first two acts, then Israel, then Jesus himself, and then the act in which we ourselves are still living, whose final scene we know from passages like Romans 8, 1 Corinthians 15, and Revelation 21 and 22. The point of this model is partly to explain the notion of 'improvising' I mentioned earlier – when living within the fifth act, we are required to improvise our way to the necessary conclusion while remaining completely faithful to the narrative, and the characterizations, of the earlier acts and, indeed, to the opening scenes of our own present act, namely Easter and Pentecost. But it is also partly to provide a way of understanding how it is that though, for instance, the book of Leviticus is part of our story, a non-negotiable part of that story, it is not the part where we presently live. When you live in Act 5, you cannot repeat, except for very special effect, a speech which was made in Act 3. Thus we do not offer animal sacrifice; the letter to the Hebrews makes that abundantly clear. A similar argument is mounted by Paul in Galatians about God's gift of the Mosaic law: it was good and God-given, but those of its prescriptions which separate out Jews from gentiles are no longer appropriate, since we are not any longer in Act 3 but in Act 5, and with that eschatological moment the old distinctions are done away.

This argument could be pursued at much greater length, but let me just make one particular and important point. There are, of course, a good many features of the Pentateuch which are not only retained but also enhanced in the New Testament; one cannot assume because some features of Mosaic law are abolished that all are equally redundant, just as it would be a bad mistake to suppose that the reason some parts have become redundant is simply because they're old or because we now 'know better'. Things are not that shallow. In fact, it gradually becomes clear that the Old Testament is continually calling Israel to a way of life which is about discovering a genuinely human existence, [153] and that, granted the achievement of Jesus the Messiah in Act 4, a good many features of the Mosaic law are not only retained but enhanced. This holds true for the Decalogue itself, with the sole exception of the sabbath law, and it certainly holds for the codes of sexual conduct, as a great wealth of scholarship has shown again and again. In the whole Bible, what men and women do sexually resonates with larger cosmic issues, and particular commands and prohibitions are not arbitrary, detached rules, but tip-of-the-iceberg features revealing a deep and structured worldview underneath. I commend the five-act model to you as a creative and fresh way of understanding and using the Bible for all it's worth.

But it is, of course, particularly designed to explain how the great story of the Bible points us to our mission and to equip us precisely for that mission. The story begins with the creation of heaven and earth, and it ends with their eventual marriage, their coming together in fulfilling, God-ordained union. The biblical story reaches its climax, of course, in Jesus Christ, where this union of heaven and earth was inaugurated, modelled and accomplished – against all the powers that would keep them apart – through his death and resurrection. And the mission of the church in the power of the spirit is to implement the achievement of Jesus and so to anticipate the eventual goal. Mission, in other words, takes place within the overall narrative of scripture, and is reinforced and kept in place by the reading and studying of the text that speaks this way, drawing together all features of wider culture that point in this direction and standing over against all features of wider culture that point elsewhere. It is only by living within this overall narrative that we, as bishops committed to leading the church in mission, can keep our bearings when so many elements of our own culture and our various traditions would threaten to sidetrack us this way or that. As I have written elsewhere, the larger biblical narrative offers us a framework for developing and taking forward a holistic mission which refuses to split apart full-on evangelism, telling people about Jesus with a view to bringing them to faith, and full-on kingdom-of-God work, labouring alongside anyone and everyone with a heart for [154] the common good so that God's sovereign and saving rule may be glimpsed on earth as in heaven.

Anglicanism has tended to oscillate between these two, between a primary reading of the epistles as being about private and personal salvation and a primary reading of the gospels as being about 'social justice'. The two need one another, and in the best Anglican traditions they join up, like all the other complementarities in God's world. So my point at this stage is this: a serious Anglican reading of scripture can and should generate a five-act hermeneutic in which our goals in mission are greatly clarified and our energy and sense of direction for that mission reinforced, as the spirit uses our telling and retelling of the story to shape the habits of our hearts, minds and wills. And to say that is, of course, to say that, at the very heart of it all, the point of scripture is to root, form and shape our spirituality as a people and as individuals. We are to be a scripture-shaped praying people, which must then mean a Jesus-shaped praying people, which naturally includes being a scripture-shaped and Jesus-shaped eucharistic people. It is out of

that scripturally formed well of personal and corporate spirituality, continually confronting, transforming and directing us, that we draw water to be
refreshed as we find our way forward in the service of God, his gospel and his
kingdom. But all this points us on to our present culture and the challenges it
presents. How can scripture form us for mission in tomorrow's world?

Scripture and the Task of the Church

I Foundation: Bible and Culture

The confrontation between Christian faith and contemporary culture,
between (if you like) Jerusalem and Athens, is as old as the gospel itself. It
is rooted in turn in the confrontation between the Old Testament people
of God and the surrounding cultures of Egypt, Canaan, Assyria, Babylon
and then, later, Persia, Greece, Syria and eventually Rome. Indeed, cultural
confrontation and [155] the complex negotiations it generated are woven into
the very fabric of scripture itself. Jonathan Sacks, whom we so revelled in
listening to last night, wrote an article the other day[4] about the way in which
languages without vowels, such as Hebrew, tend to go from right to left, driven
by right-brain intuition, whereas languages with vowels, such as Greek, tend
to go from left to right, as the left-brain passion for getting things worked out
accurately drives from that side. I asked him at dinner whether he'd had any
feedback on the article, and he said rather disappointedly that he hadn't; but
he drew the moral, which I now develop, that part of the power of the early
Christian faith was to take a right-brain religion such as Judaism and express
it within a left-brain language like Greek. (Of course, you could argue that
the rabbis made up for lost left-brain time with the Mishnah and Talmud,
but that would be another story.) From the very beginning, Christianity was
engaged with its many surrounding cultures, and no one model – Niebuhr,
you recall, explored five in his classic book *Christ and Culture*[5] – will catch
all the nuances we might wish.

Even in a short address such as Paul's on the Areopagus (Acts 17.22–31) we
can see all kinds of different things going on. Paul is in head-on collision with
the great temples all around him, and the endless stream of sacrifices being
offered at them, yet he can begin from the 'altar to the unknown God' and
work up from there, quoting Greek poets on the way. And, reading between

---

4 Sacks 2008.
5 Niebuhr 1952.

the lines, we can see how the message he brought could say both 'Yes' and 'No' to the Stoic, the Epicurean and the Academic. The Stoic supposes that all is predetermined, that divinity is simply suffused within the world and working its purpose out. Well, says Paul, you are right that God is not far from any of us, but wrong to suppose that God and the world are the same thing. The Epicurean supposes that God, or the gods, are a long way away, and that the best thing to do is make such shift as we can in this world. Well, says Paul, you are right that God and the world are not the same thing, but you are wrong to suppose that God is not interested in the world, and us human creatures. The Academic sits on the fence: there isn't really enough evidence to [156] be sure about the gods, so it's best to keep the old state-religion going just in case (a position not unfamiliar, alas, to some Anglicans). Well, says Paul, you are right that there hasn't really been quite enough evidence to be sure of anything; but now all that has changed, because there is a man called Jesus whom God raised from the dead, and he is going to sort everything out from top to bottom.

Now, of course, the point of all that is not simply an interesting set of skirmishes about different ideas. The point is that these ideas had legs, and went about in the ancient world making things happen. They altered the way you saw things, the way you did things, the goals you set yourself, and the ways you ordered your world and society. From the beginning no serious Christian has been able to say 'This is my culture, so I must adapt the gospel to fit within it', just as no serious Christian has been able to say 'This is my surrounding culture, so I must oppose it tooth and nail'. Christians are neither chameleons, changing colour to suit their surroundings, nor rhinoceroses, ready to charge at anything in sight. There is no straightforward transference between any item of ordinary culture and the gospel, since all has been distorted by evil; but likewise there is nothing so twisted that it cannot be redeemed, and nothing evil in itself. The Christian is thus committed, precisely as a careful reader of scripture, to a nuanced reading of culture and a nuanced understanding of the response of the gospel to different elements of culture. You can see this in Philippians, where Paul is clear that as a Christian you must live your public life in a manner worthy of the gospel, and that whatever is pure, lovely and of good report must be celebrated – but also that Jesus is lord while Caesar isn't, and that we are commanded to shine like lights in a dark world. There are no shortcuts here, no easy answers. Prayer, scripture and complex negotiation are the order of the day.

There is, of course a very particular Anglican spin to some of this. Many parts of the more traditional Anglican world, not least here in England itself, have become very used to going with the flow of the culture, on the older assumption that basically England was a Christian country so that the church would not be compromised [157] if it reflected the local social and cultural mores. That strand of Anglicanism has always been in danger of simply acting as chaplain to whatever happened to be going on at the time, whether it was blessing bombs and bullets in the First World War or going to tea at Buckingham Palace. Within that world, the Bible has often been quietly truncated. We don't like the bits about judgment, so we miss them out. We are embarrassed by the bits about sex, so we miss them out too – and then we wonder why, in a world full of hell and sex, people imagine the Bible is irrelevant! The Bible is a kind of spiritual Rorschach test: if you find you're cutting bits out, or adding bits in, it may be a sign that you're capitulating to cultural pressure. Equally, of course, there are many parts of the Anglican world where nothing but confrontation has been possible for a long time, and there people may have to learn the difficult lesson that actually the world is still charged with the grandeur of God, and that the biblical Christian must learn to rejoice with those who rejoice and weep with those who weep, no matter who they are, what they believe or how they behave. It is crucial to our vocation, and to our particular vocation granted our particular histories, that we rediscover the art, which itself is rooted in scripture, of discriminating (as Paul says) between things that differ, and of affirming what can and must be affirmed and opposing what can and must be opposed. Those of us who are involved in the business of politics and government know that this is a difficult and often thankless task, but it must be undertaken.

2 The Bible and Gnosticism

All this brings us to three particular features of tomorrow's world which stand out particularly and call for a biblical engagement as we take forward our God-given mission. I am here summarizing the Noble Lectures I was privileged to give at Harvard University two years ago, which are yet to be published. The three features are Gnosticism, empire and postmodernity, which fit together in fascinating ways and which provide a grid of cultural and personal worldviews within which a great many of our contemporaries [158] live today. I speak particularly of the western world, and I regret that I am not qualified to do more of a 'world tour'. But I remind all of us that, whether we like it or not, when the west sneezes everyone else catches a cold, so that cultural trends in Europe and North America will affect the whole world. (I notice that, though the current US election will affect everybody on the face of the earth for good or ill, only Americans get to vote. This strikes me as odd, though, of course, we British were in the same position for long enough and didn't seem to mind at the time.)

Addressing these three issues could sound like an abstract intellectual exercise, but believe me it isn't. This is the real world where people struggle and sin and suffer, and it is fatally easy for the church to be pulled down into the cultural assumptions of the day and so have no gospel, nothing to offer, no basis for mission or content to it either.

The first of the three makes this point graphically. When I was in college, we studied Gnosticism as a strange ancient phenomenon, little imagining that it was already alive and well in western culture and that it would sweep through our world dramatically, not only in obvious things like *The Da Vinci Code* but also in the subtext of half the Hollywood movies and, more sadly, half the would-be theological thinking in our church. Two features stand out. First a radical dualism, in which the created order is irrelevant because we, the enlightened ones, are just passing through it and can use or ignore it as we please. At this point the Gnosticism of the Right says: we can do what we like with our planet, because it's all going to be destroyed soon and we'll be snatched away to a distant heaven. And the Gnosticism of the Left says: we can do what we like with our bodies, because they are irrelevant to the reality within us. And both are held in place by the larger Gnosticism of the western Enlightenment itself which has said, for the last two hundred years: we westerners are the enlightened ones, with our modern science and technology; we can make up the rules, we can saunter around the world exploiting its resources and its people, we can drop bombs on people to make whole countries do what we want, and it doesn't matter much [159] because we, the enlightened ones, are the natural possessors of justice, freedom and peace so those other people don't matter as much as we do.

Along with the radical dualism goes Gnosticism as a religion, not of redemption, but of self-discovery. This is the real 'false gospel' at the heart of a good many contemporary debates. Gnostics do not want to be rescued; they want to discover 'who they really are', the inner spark of divine life. There is even a danger that we Anglicans spend time discussing 'who we really are', as though there were some inner thing, the Anglican spark, and if only we could identify that then we'd be all right. And in some of our most crucial ethical debates people have assumed for a long time that 'being true to myself' was all that really mattered (at this point the existentialism and Romanticism of the last two hundred years reinforce the underlying Gnosticism). This is a religion of pride rather than of faith, of self-assertion rather than of hope, of a self-love which is a parody of the genuinely biblical self-love that is regard for oneself, body and all, as reflecting the image of the creator.

And this false religion, though it often uses the language of Christianity, makes it impossible for people to have real Christian faith, or for that matter real Jewish faith; because in the Bible you discover 'who you really are' only when the living God, the creator, is rescuing you and giving you a new identity, a new status, a new name. The Bible is itself the story of, and the energy to bring about, the redemption of creation, ourselves included, not the discovery within ourselves of a spark which just needs to express itself. Gnosticism hates resurrection, because resurrection speaks of God doing a new thing within and for the material world, putting it right at last, rather than God throwing the material world away and allowing the divine spark to float off free. And it is resurrection – the resurrection of Jesus in the past, and of ourselves in the future – which is the ground of all Christian ethical life in the present. Christian ethics is not a matter of 'discovering who you truly are' and then being true to that. It is a matter, as Jesus and Paul insist, of dying to self and coming alive to God, of taking up the cross, of inaugurated eschatology, [160] of becoming in oneself not 'what one really is' already but 'what one is in Christ', a new creation, a small, walking, breathing anticipation of the promised time when the earth shall be filled with God's glory as the waters cover the sea. A biblically based mission must learn from the great narrative of scripture to set its face against all Gnosticism, because it cuts the nerve of the mission both to the world of politics and society and to the life of every man, woman and child.

3 The Bible and Empire

Second, empire. We British had an empire on which the sun never set, and we have spent the last hundred years puzzling over what went wrong, and counting the cost. As I have said often enough, I hope and pray my beloved American friends don't have to do the same. Let's be clear: there is nothing absolutely wrong with empire in itself; empires come and go – they always have done – and the point is not 'Wouldn't it be a better world without empires at all?' but 'How can empires be called to account, be reminded that God is God and that they are not?' All empires declare that they possess justice, freedom and peace; Greece did it, Rome did it, the British did it a century ago, the Americans do it now. Who will be next, and are we ready for that with a biblical narrative of empire that will say, with Colossians 1, that all the powers in heaven and on earth were created in and through and for Jesus Christ and were redeemed by the blood of his cross? Are we ready, in our biblically shaped mission, to transcend the futile rhetoric of left and right – a very recent invention, in fact itself an invention of the Enlightenment – and to understand power the way the Bible understands it, as given by God to bring order to his creation on the one hand and, on the other, to anticipate in the present that final putting-to-rights of all things which we are promised?

If we are thinking biblically, we have a narrative which encodes a mission, the mission of God both to the rulers of this age and to those whose lives are either enhanced by them or crushed by them, or quite often simply confused by them in the middle. We [161] in the west need to learn from our brothers and sisters who live under regimes which are deeply hostile to the church and would prefer that it disappeared altogether. And, dare I say, we need to learn these lessons quite quickly, because people are already talking about the next great superpower, and whether it is India or China we can be sure that, unless something truly extraordinary happens, the world will be dominated for the first time since ancient Rome by a superpower that does not stand within the Judaeo-Christian tradition, and which will see that tradition as a threat. If we don't prepare ourselves now for the future reality, and if we don't learn the biblical lessons here and now of what Christian mission looks like under empire, we will fail not only the world of our own day but also the world of our children's and grandchildren's day.

Notice how empire and Gnosticism go together. Gnosticism arises under empire, because when you are powerless to change anything about your world you are tempted to turn inwards and suppose that a spiritual, inner reality is all that matters. Carl Jung put it nicely, if chillingly: who looks outside, dreams; who looks inside, awakens. Welcome to the world of navel-gazing. That's why second-century Gnosticism arose when it did, following the collapse of the final Jewish revolt in AD 135. And the empires of the world are delighted when people embrace Gnosticism. Again, in the second century the people who were reading the *Gospel of Thomas* and other books of the same sort were not burnt at the stake or thrown to the lions. That was reserved for the people who were reading Matthew, Mark, Luke, John and the rest. There is a massive lie out there at the moment, which is that the canon of scripture colludes with imperial power while the gnostic literature subverts it. That is the exact opposite of the truth. Caesar couldn't care less if someone wants to pursue a private spirituality. But if a person goes around saying that all authority in heaven and on earth is given to the crucified and risen Jesus, Caesar shivers in his shoes. And going around saying that is at the heart of Christian mission, which is sustained and energized by scripture itself, the book that will keep not only individual Christians but whole churches steadfast and cheerful [162] in that mission when everything seems bent on blowing them off course.

4 Postmodernity

Whenever I mention postmodernity my wife either groans or yawns, but before you have those same reactions let me say what I mean. We live in a world – the western world, but increasingly the global community – where truth is at a discount. Relativism is everywhere; there is only 'your truth' and 'my truth'. Facts don't matter; spin is all that counts. Likewise, and deeply worrying for the church, because we easily get sucked into this, argument and reason are set aside, and instead of debate we have the shrill swapping of hurt emotions. 'I am a victim; you are prejudiced; end of conversation.' Or, in one of those worrying irregular verbs, 'I am speaking from the heart; you are prejudiced; he or she is a bigot.' My friends, this entire way of thinking – a world where the only apparent moral argument is the volume of the victim's scream – is an affront to the biblical world, to the Anglican world, to the world of scripture, tradition and reason. Reason is not the same as emotion or, indeed, experience. Genuine screams of genuine victims matter enormously; they are all taken up into the cry of dereliction from the cross. But they are to be addressed, not with more screams, still less competing ones, but with healing, biblical wisdom. The reaction against scripture within postmodern Christianity is no worse than the reaction against reason itself. And 'experience', which for John Wesley when he elevated it alongside scripture, tradition and reason meant 'the experience of God the spirit at work transforming my life', has come to mean 'whatever I feel' – which is no more a safe guide to anything than a glance at the English sky in the morning is a safe guide to the weather later in the day.

Of course, postmodernity doesn't stop with the deconstruction of truth. It deconstructs the self as well. At this point the Gnostic would do well to hide, because in postmodernity there is no such thing as the inner spark, the true inward reality. That's why, for instance, in today's debates among the gay community, [163] the essentialist position ('This is who I am') is increasingly discounted by the constructivists ('This is what I choose to be today') – though you wouldn't know that from the way the church still talks about the matter. But the greatest deconstruction of all is, in fact, that of the overarching narrative, the great stories. Big stories, like truth-claims, declares the postmodernist, are claims to power. Live within the modernist story and the modernists will end up running the show. That's how the world has worked for long enough.

And, of course, that presents quite a challenge to the Christian; because the Bible, as I have stressed, is precisely a great narrative, the huge, sprawling story of creation and new creation, of covenant and new covenant, with Jesus in the middle of it. That is why many Christians today shrink their mission to the mere attempt to give some people, here and there, a spiritual life and a hope out beyond, rather than taking the mission where it needs to go, into every corner of God's world and its systems and structures. But please note: the deconstruction of power-stories is itself a claim to power. Pontius Pilate asked Jesus 'What is truth?' because for him the only truth was what came out of the scabbard of a sword. Indeed, the conversation between Jesus and Pilate in John 18 and 19 stands near the heart of a biblical theology of mission, though sadly I'm not sure if that will come out in our Bible studies in the next few days. In other words, though postmodernism sneers at empire and its grandiose dreams, in the final analysis it colludes with it. It can scoff, but it cannot subvert. All those years of Jacques Derrida, and we still got George Bush. And Tony Blair.

So what does the Bible itself have to say on the matter? How can the great story I've been speaking of respond to the postmodern challenge – because make no mistake, if it doesn't, our mission will shrink into a sad little parody of its true self. The answer is that the story of scripture is not a story of power, but a story of love – genuine love, overflowing love for the world God made. Note carefully what happens at this point.

I said postmodernity had one moral value only, the scream of the victim. That isn't quite true. It has one other: the duty to, as is [164] often said, 'embrace the Other'. This has come from various sources and it's sometimes joined up, though I have to say with minimal justification, with some elements of the work of Jesus. This is at the heart of the appeal that we 'live with difference' and so on. I have spoken about that elsewhere; it all depends on a decision as to which differences you can and should live with and which you shouldn't and can't. There is an enormous amount of begging the question currently on this matter. But when we consider the biblical narrative we discover that here again postmodernity has produced a parody of the reality. In scripture, God makes a world that is other than himself, and that is full of complementarities: heaven and earth, night and day, sea and land, vegetation and animals, and ultimately humans, with the complementarity of male and female growing more evident within that world until it is finally affirmed, producing a picture of a world of radical differences with the differences made for one another. Within the biblical narrative, of course, this reaches its great conclusion when heaven and earth finally come together, with the new Jerusalem as the bride of Christ. This is the biblical story of love: the love of God for his world, the love within that world for that which is radically different from me, from us, the love which really does 'embrace the Other', not in a casual and floppy sense of 'anyone who's a bit different from me', but in the deep ontological sense of a love which goes out into a different country altogether to affirm the goodness of God's creation there and to discover, in that affirmation, the greatest delight which mirrors the delight of God the creator, the delight of Christ the lover.

What we desperately need, if we are to pursue a biblical, Christian and, indeed, Anglican mission in the postmodern world, is the 'spirit of truth'. There is no time to develop this further, but it is vital to say this one thing. We have got so used to the postmodern sneer that any truth-claim is instantly suspect. And at that point many Christians have lurched back to the apparent safety of a modernist claim: conservative modernists claim that they can simply look up truth in the Bible, without realizing what sort of book it is, while radical modernists claim they find truth in today's science, without realizing what sort of a thing that is [165] either. But we cannot go back; we have to go on; and the spirit of truth, often invoked in favour of any and every innovation in the church, is actually at work when we live within the great story, the love story, God's love story, and become in turn agents, missional agents, of that story in the world. Truth is not something we possess and put in our pockets, because truth is grounded in the goodness of creation, the promise of redemption for that creation, and the vocation of human beings to speak God's word both of naming the original creation and of working for new creation – the word, in other words, of mission. The spirit of truth is given so that, living within the great biblical story, we can engage in those tasks.

Conclusion

There is much more to say, as Jesus himself said in the farewell discourses, but you cannot bear it now. I hope I have said enough to spark off some discussion and open up some topics of more than a little relevance to who we are as bishops in the Anglican Communion and what we should be about in our mission in tomorrow's world. I have tried to offer a robust account of the way in which the Bible is designed to be the vehicle of God's authority, not in an abstract sense but in the dynamic sense of the story through which God's mission in the world goes forward in the power of the spirit. And within that larger picture, the small details slot into place, not as isolated fragments of disjointed moral or theological musings, but, as I said before, as tips of the iceberg which show what is there all along just under the surface. There are other questions I haven't addressed, not least the way in which the Bible demands to be read both individually and corporately in each generation, so that each generation can grow up intellectually, morally, culturally and Christianly. We will never get to the point where scholarship has said all that needs to be said and subsequent generations will just have to look up the right answers. Thank God it isn't like that. But, as we in turn give ourselves to the tasks of being bishops-in-mission, of being [166] biblical-bishops-in-mission, we must always remind ourselves that the Bible is most truly itself when it is being, through the work of God's praying people and not least their wise shepherds, the vehicle of God's saving, new-creational love going out, not to tell the world it is more or less all right as it is, but to do for the whole creation, and every man, woman and child within it, what God did for the children of Israel in Egypt, and what God did for the world in the death and resurrection of Jesus: to say, 'I have heard your crying, and I have come to the rescue.'

8

Imagining the Kingdom: Mission and Theology in Early Christianity

Among the many reasons why I was delighted to accept the invitation to teach New Testament at the University of St Andrews was the chance to work on historical biblical scholarship alongside an 'Institute for Theology, Imagination and the Arts'. Though the pressure of time makes it difficult to sustain detailed cross-disciplinary engagement, I have always had the sense that, at St Andrews, one is encouraged to look beyond the immediate borders of the discipline as it has been developed. That is what I wanted to do in this inaugural lecture, delivered in October 2011 after I had been in post for just over a year.

Three interests converged at this point. First, there was my ongoing sense that the four canonical gospels are to be read as telling the story of 'how God became king' – which then itself became the title of a popular paperback in 2012. Not enough study, in my view, has been given to the ways in which the story told – in very different ways – by the four gospels made sense within the story-laden Jewish world of the day and also, by implication, in confronting the narratives of imperial Rome. Second, there was my interest in the analysis of post-Enlightenment western culture in terms of the modern retrieval of types of Epicureanism, a seam of thought which was opened by my reading of Stephen Greenblatt's *The Swerve* and which I have now developed a good deal further in my 2018 Gifford Lectures (Wright 2019a). Third, a different kind of cultural analysis was opened up by Iain McGilchrist's remarkable book *The Master and His Emissary*. Though he was speaking of much wider concerns, his analysis of the increasingly left-brain-driven western world struck me so forcibly as an account of how my own discipline has developed that an inaugural lecture seemed a good moment to bring this out. Putting all this together was exciting and, though as I write this I am approaching official retirement from St Andrews, I still hope to work it all out more fully in due course.

[380] The four gospels stand magisterially at the centre of early Christianity, as they stand at the head of the canon. Despite the occasional efforts to push them out of their central position and substitute other documents, whether actually existing (such as the wrongly named *Gospel of Thomas*) or reconstructed (such as the hypothetical document 'Q'), the majority of scholars still believe, rightly in my view, that Matthew, Mark, Luke and John deserve their place. We might put it this way: if they had been lost for centuries, and then dug up last year in the sands of Egypt or Syria, they would be hailed as among the most extraordinary ancient documents we possess. The fact that they are well known should not blind us to their remarkable blend of page-turning narrative, vivid portraiture (especially of their central figure), historical verisimilitude and sophisticated theology.

And yet. Reversing what St Paul says about himself in 2 Corinthians 6.9, it remains the case that the gospels, though well known at one level, are unknown at another. An oversimplification, of course; but I refer to the overall drift of gospel studies and, indeed, to the general perception of the four gospels in the wider church community to which the biblical studies academy remains tangentially, and sometimes uncomfortably, related. Huge strides have been made in helpful directions, not least by my predecessor but one, Professor Richard Bauckham, both in his work on the wide intended readership of the gospels and in his award-winning book on the gospels and the eyewitnesses.[1] If his thesis is even half right – and I think it is at least that – then all kinds of assumptions, including some of those blessed things they used to call 'the assured results of criticism', will need to be torn up and worked again from scratch. But I believe we need to go still further. Despite generations of care and attention being lavished on the gospels as wholes rather than as assemblages of parts, I am not convinced that the main message of all four gospels has been grasped – and then, having been grasped, has been reflected in the methods employed for further study. And since I shall contend here that the four gospels stand at the centre of the *missionary* and [381] hence *theological* life of the early church, a failure to understand their central thrust is most likely an index of a failure to grasp several other things as well about the life and work of the first Christians.

I don't want to be thought alarmist. Fine work in many directions has been done on the gospels, a generation ago by another predecessor, Matthew Black

---

1 See Bauckham 1998; 2006. The present article is an edited version of the inaugural lecture I delivered on 26 October 2011 as Research Professor of New Testament and Early Christianity at the University of St Andrews. References to 'my predecessors' are to former holders of the title of chair.

of blessed memory. And, of course, Robin Wilson, of more recent memory, contributed much to our appreciation of the hinterland of early Christianity within which the gospels and their early reception must be understood. But there comes a time in every discipline when one has to take a deep breath, stand back a bit and say, 'Well and good; but perhaps we're still missing something.' I think this is one of those moments. And, at such times, what is required is not simply more attention to detail, vital and central though that remains. What is required is precisely *imagination*: a willingness to think beyond the fence, to ask questions that have hitherto been screened out. And, to complete the list of predecessors over the last fifty years, Markus Bockmuehl published a remarkable book, *Seeing the Word*, in which he offered an eloquent and wide-ranging plea for just such an imaginative leap, a reassessment of the tasks and methods of the whole discipline.[2] That is the kind of exercise to which I now want to give attention.

I have three basic things to say. First, I shall propose a fresh thesis about the gospels, stressing the invitation they offered to their first readers to imagine a new state of affairs being launched into the world, a state of affairs for which the natural shorthand was 'the kingdom of God'. This might seem rather obvious, but in fact the history of gospel scholarship for at least the last century has included many avoidance mechanisms, drawing attention away from the uncomfortable claim which the gospels are actually making. This will lead to the second section, in which I want to pull back and survey the wider intellectual and cultural climate in which the discipline of 'New Testament studies' was born and nurtured, and suggest that the failure to grasp the central message of the gospels flows directly from the post-Enlightenment agendas which have dominated the discipline. It is important, though, to stress both that my proposal is neither for a return to a pre-Enlightenment or anti-historical method, nor for a too-enthusiastic embrace of postmodern modes of operation, and that I regard a good deal of what has passed for 'conservative' or 'orthodox' responses to the mainstream Enlightenment agenda as sharing in, rather than solving, the underlying problems. This will send us back, third, to the gospels and the other New Testament writings with some fresh possibilities before us. I want to stress what seem to me the central grounding [382] features of early Christian mission, and the way in which what came to be called 'Christian theology' grew out of that, not as a detached intellectual exercise but as the necessary anchoring of the central Christian symbol.

2 Bockmuehl 2006.

How God Became King: The Story of the Gospels

My proposal about the gospels is that they all, in their rather different ways, tell the story of Jesus of Nazareth as the story of *how God became king*. They all, in other words, announce the launch of what can only be called a 'theocracy'. And my contention here is that, by and large, research into the gospels has for the last hundred or more years managed not to notice this, to screen out the claim which would have been obvious in the first century and which sustained the early church in its life and mission.[3]

The word 'theocracy', of course, sends shivers down many spines today. In our current climate, with the uneasy stand-off between secularism and fundamentalism, the idea of a 'theocracy' sounds uncomfortably like a return to what people vaguely imagine as the situation of the Middle Ages, with popes, bishops and priests ordering everyone about – or, indeed, to the forms of theocracy envisaged and sometimes even implemented in other religions today. (When I was lecturing in Ireland recently, someone asked me to comment on the fact that only two countries in the world have clergy sitting as of right in the upper chamber of Parliament: the UK on the one hand and Iran on the other.) And most modern westerners, not least in our great universities, react very strongly against any type of larger oversight, rightly valuing their freedom both of action and of thought. Theocracy is what we thought we'd got rid of, not something we wanted to discover in some of the western tradition's most central texts.

But 'theocracy', in a sense yet to be defined, is, of course, what is meant by 'the kingdom of God', which the synoptic gospels highlight as the central motif of Jesus' public announcements and which the fourth gospel presupposes as his central theme.[4] We know from Josephus that the revolutionaries, in the last century before the disastrous Roman–Jewish war, took as their battle-cry the slogan 'No king but God!'[5] Presumably they thought they knew how God would exercise that kingly rule; presumably they imagined that they themselves might act in some way as divine agents. But **[383]** that 'God's kingdom' denoted the long-awaited rule of Israel's God on earth as in heaven there should be no doubt. The widespread assumption today that 'the

---

3 Wright 2012.
4 The first time we meet the expression in John (3.3), it seems to be assumed that this is what Jesus is all about.
5 Jos. *Ant.* 18.23; see the discussion in Wright 1992, 302–7.

kingdom of God' denotes another realm altogether, for instance that of the 'heaven' to which God's people might hope to go after their death, was not on the first-century agenda. When Jesus spoke about God's kingdom, and taught his followers to pray that it would arrive 'on earth as in heaven', he was right in the middle of first-century Jewish theocratic aspirations.

So when the gospels tell the story of Jesus, they do so (to repeat) as the story of 'how God became king'. It wasn't, for them, just an aspiration; it was an accomplishment. We can see this in three narrative strands which work together in all four gospels (though not, interestingly, in any of the non-canonical gnostic materials). As throughout this article, I here summarize material that could be set out in considerably more detail.

The three strands in question come in addition to, not in competition with, the two more normally observed. Gone are the days when people could confidently affirm that the gospels were in no sense 'biographies' of Jesus. Several studies have indicated the reverse: when placed alongside greco-roman *bioi*, the four canonical gospels clearly belong in something like the same genre.[6] Nor is there any problem in continuing to affirm that the gospels tell the story of Jesus as the story of the launching of the movement which, perhaps anachronistically, we refer to as 'the church'. How precisely the gospels reflect early Christian faith and life is another matter, but that they do so is not in question. The gospels are, in a perfectly proper sense, 'biographies'; they are also foundation documents for Jesus' first followers. But the three further interlocking dimensions we must now explore are key elements which have, all too often, been missing from the discussion.

The first of these missing dimensions is that the four canonical gospels tell the story of Jesus as the *continuation* and *climax* of the ancient story of Israel. To say this is more than to say that the gospels portray Jesus as the fulfilment of ancient prophecy. That is obvious. It is the *kind* of fulfilment which matters here. The gospels give every sign – admittedly in four different ways – that they belong to that feature of the Jewish world of the day in which the longer story of Israel was being told in search of an ending, and that they are writing in order to provide such an ending. What matters – and what, I think, goes radically against the grain of western thought for many centuries – is the idea of *narrative continuity*. Not just 'narrative' as such; that might lead simply to a repeated pattern, which we naturally find as well, for instance in the strong sense of a 'new exodus', the fresh and final repetition of ancient [384] Israel's greatest story. That is important, but it points beyond itself to the belief,

---

6 See particularly Burridge 2004.

which we can track in many Jewish texts of the time, that all these repeated patterns were part of a larger sequence that was going somewhere. History might be in some sense cyclic, but in a more important sense the cycles contributed to a forward, linear movement.

Thus, for instance, the book we call Pseudo-Philo tells the ancient story of Israel and breaks off at the point where David is about to become king. Its recounting of the tales of the judges seems to be designed as a model for militant messianic movements in the writer's own day. Similarly, the book of Wisdom recounts the story of the exodus, not simply as a great historic moment in Israel's ancient past, but as the model for the new and decisive act of judgment that Israel's God is about to perform, condemning the wicked and vindicating his wise and righteous sufferers. At that level, despite the radical difference of genre, this is much the same as what we find in *4 Ezra* and *2 Baruch*, whose writers look back to the horrible events of 586 BC as a kind of model for what they have now experienced in AD 70, and retell the ancient story as a way of leading the eye up to the great messianic deliverance which is about to burst upon the world, with (in *4 Ezra*'s vision) the messianic lion triumphing over the pagan eagle.[7]

All of these, in their different ways, look back to the scriptures, and particularly the book of Daniel, with its intriguing combination of the genres of wisdom and apocalyptic. In fact, the storytelling at which we have just glanced belongs within a much larger movement of thought in which Daniel 9 in particular became seminal. In Daniel 9 the prophet asks how long the exile is going to be: will it not, as Jeremiah prophesied, last for seventy years? Back comes the answer: not seventy years, but 'seventy weeks of years'; that is, seventy times seven.[8] There are important echoes here of the Jubilee theme from Leviticus 25, but for our purposes the point is that this 490 years, predicted in Daniel 9, haunted the minds of devout Jews in the centuries immediately before and after the time of Jesus. There is plenty of evidence to indicate that people within various movements were calculating, as best they could, when that time would be up, and when the long-awaited deliverance from pagan domination would therefore occur. Their answers varied wildly. The Essenes, it appears, pinned their hopes on the climax coming around the time when Herod the Great died. Some rabbis, however, did their sums quite differently (it all depends, of course, where you begin the sequence), so that when Akiba hailed Simeon ben-Kosiba as Messiah in AD 132 some of

---

7   *4 Ez.* 11.1—12.39.
8   Dan 9.2 (cf. Jer. 25.11; 29.10; Zech. 1.12; 7.5; 2 Chr. 36.21; 1 Esdr. 1.58); 9.24.

his colleagues opposed him, not so much because Ben-Kosiba was not [385] a suitable candidate but because, according to their calculations, the 'son of David' was not due for at least another century.[9]

All this, interesting though it is, simply points to the widespread phenomenon which is, I suggest, the presupposition for the story the gospels tell in the way they tell it: that Israel's history, under the guidance of a strange and often opaque divine providence, had not come to a standstill, but was moving forward towards its appointed goal. The story has many twists and turns, and many flashbacks and, indeed, flash-forwards, advance hints of what is to come. But it is a single story-line, and it is awaiting its proper and fitting fulfilment. My first point, then, is that all four gospels, in their different ways, are written so as to say that the story of the public career and fate of Jesus of Nazareth provides that proper and fitting, if highly surprising and subversive, fulfilment. Jesus is not, for the evangelists, simply the anti-type of the various types such as Moses, or David, or the Passover lamb. He is the point at which the millennia-long narrative has reached its goal. Matthew makes the point, graphically, with his introductory genealogy. Mark does it with his opening quotations from Malachi and Isaiah; Luke, by telling the story of John the Baptist as a reprise of the story of Samuel. (They do it in many other ways, too, but these stand out.) John goes right back to the beginning, to the opening of Genesis, and structures his gospel so as to say that in Jesus not only the story of Israel but the story of all creation is reaching its decisive goal. And in all four gospels there are clear echoes and references back, in a variety of ways and contexts, to the various prophecies of Daniel, including those of chapter 9.

It is in Daniel, of course, that we find the strongest statement of what the climax will be, when it comes: it will be the arrival of God's own kingdom, his sovereign rule, trumping the rule of all pagan powers. And it is to Daniel that we should look to find the text which, according to Josephus (echoed at this point by Suetonius), most incited Jews to rebel against Rome: the text according to which a world ruler would, *at that time*, arise from Judaea.[10] Josephus and Suetonius, of course, refer this to Vespasian, called back from the campaign against Jerusalem to become emperor in Rome. The four gospels, clearly, have another candidate in mind. And, for that matter, a different sort of kingdom. But to that we shall return. [386]

9   On all this, see esp. Beckwith 1996.
10   Jos. *War* 6.312–15; cf. Suet. *Vesp.* 4, and also Tac. *Hist.* 5.13. See the discussion in Wright 1992, 312f. Compare Jos. *Ant.* 10.267, where Josephus highlights, as the distinctive feature of Daniel, that his prophecies had a specific chronological reference.

Much more could be said about the way in which the four gospels tell the story of Jesus as the climax of the continuous story of Israel, with the kingdom of God arriving at that climax. But I move rapidly to the second point, which is that the gospels tell this story *as the story of Israel's God*. Here we must take a step back once more, because it is not as well known as it ought to be that in the world of second-Temple Judaism there was a strong sense, not just that Israel's fortunes needed to change, but that Israel's God needed to come back to his people, to the Temple. Ezekiel had described the divine glory leaving Jerusalem, and had prophesied that it would return to a rebuilt Temple, but nobody ever said they'd seen it happen. There is no scene anywhere in the literature of the period to correspond to Exodus 40, where the divine glory fills the newly constructed tabernacle, or 1 Kings 8, where the same thing happens to Solomon's Temple. There is no sudden appearance, as was granted to the prophet Isaiah. Plenty of texts say that it will happen (I think, obviously, of Isaiah 40 and 52; of Zechariah and Malachi), but none indicate that it has already done so.[11]

Here the four evangelists are quite explicit. John is perhaps the most obvious: 'the Word became flesh', he says (1.14), 'and tabernacled, pitched his tent, in our midst; and we beheld his glory.' In case we missed the point, John rubs it in again and again by his constant positioning of Jesus in relation to, or in the place of, the Temple (for example in 2.21). Mark, outwardly so different from John, hits exactly the same note with his opening quotations from Isaiah and Malachi. Both passages concern the return of the divine glory, and the messenger who will prepare the way for it. Mark leaves us in no doubt that he thinks this has now happened, in and through Jesus. Matthew and Luke in their own ways get at the same point, Matthew not least with the Emmanuel promise (1.23 and 28.20), and Luke not least through the terrifying scene in chapter 19 where Jesus, arriving in Jerusalem, tells the story about the king who comes back at last only to find a disobedient servant, and then announces Jerusalem's imminent destruction on the grounds (19.44) that 'you did not know the moment when God was visiting you' (*ton kairon tēs episkopēs sou*).

This rather simple observation, clearly, puts the cat among several of the older critical pigeons. I grew up in a scholarly world where it was taken for granted that while John had a high (and most probably Greek) Christology, the synoptics had a low (quite possibly Jewish) one. That only shows the extent to which people were asking the wrong question. Once we think into

---

11 I survey the evidence in Wright 1996a, 615–24.

the world of first-century Jewish narrative, a very different picture emerges. [387] To the old sneer that Jesus talked about God but the early church talked about Jesus, we may reply that Jesus did indeed talk about God and God's kingdom – in order to explain what he himself was doing and would accomplish.

It is this picture, third, which confronts – as Israel's stories normally did confront – the power of pagan empire. The four gospels, again in their very different ways, are all written to tell the story of Jesus as the story of Israel, and the story of Israel's God, reaching their proper climax, *so as thereby to tell the story of how Israel's God becomes king of the whole world.* This is the clue to the mission, and the missionary theology, of the early church, to which I shall return.

Think for a moment of the narrative which had burst upon the world around the time that Jesus of Nazareth was born. The intellectual *coup d'état* which Augustus accomplished through his court poets and historians was every bit as stunning as the political coup he achieved in the double civil war that followed the assassination of his adoptive father, Julius Caesar. Everybody in Rome knew that Augustus's attaining of supreme and unchallengeable power meant the overthrow of a centuries-long tradition of fierce republicanism (Augustus, of course, insisted that he had merely restored the republic, but nobody was fooled). But for Livy to tell the history of Rome through the long years of the republic and climaxing with the rule of Augustus, with whom he had a lasting friendship, was a remarkable achievement. Scholars differ on the extent to which Livy himself believed that the rule of Augustus was an unqualified good thing, and Tacitus records (*Annals* 4.34) that in one of the later, and sadly lost, books of his great work Livy felt able to praise the conspirators Brutus and Cassius. But he knew which side his bread was buttered on, as is evidenced for instance by his distorting of key political details to suit the new regime.[12]

The greatest writer to tell the long story of Rome as a history leading the eye up to Augustus was of course Virgil. His early *Eclogues* refer to the turbulent events of the civil war, and include the mysterious fourth, hailing the birth of a child who will usher in the golden age. Virgil read the *Georgics* to Augustus in person after his victory at Actium in 31 BC; and he was regularly in the company of Augustus during the years in which he composed the *Aeneid*

---

12 E.g. 4.20, where Livy suggests that Cornelius Cossus was consul, not merely a military tribune, when celebrating his single-handed victory over an enemy commander four centuries earlier, thus supporting Augustus's jealous retaining of military glory for himself in his own day.

itself, the greatest poem of the period. Here there is, as is well known, a 'strong narrative teleology',[13] invoking 'Fate' as the force which will lead Aeneas to found Rome and Rome to produce, eventually, the wonderful new empire [388] of Augustus. Already in the first book the scene is set, with Jupiter himself prophesying to the world, back then in the time of Aeneas, that from his noble line there will be born 'a Trojan Caesar, who shall extend his empire to the ocean, his glory to the stars' (1.286–7). His empire will be lavishly prosperous, and will bring peace to the world (1.289–96). Indeed, Aeneas himself is seen as a type of the coming Augustus, an indication that here, too, typology can flourish within an overall grand narrative. I am not aware of anyone before Augustus causing the story of his own accession to power to be told as the climax of a much longer narrative.[14]

It is only when the first of my three points is fully grasped (which, as I've suggested, is not normally the case) that the breathtaking phenomenon emerges. There is no sign that the Romans are borrowing from Jewish tradition the idea of a centuries-old history climaxing in a surprising but victorious, prosperous and peace-bringing reign. Nor is there any suggestion that Matthew, Mark, Luke or John had read Livy or Virgil.[15] But their story of Jesus as bringing the long history of Israel to an unexpected climax was not only a remarkable parallel to the great Roman narrative, which Augustus and his successors were busily reinforcing in statues, coins and other symbolic artefacts. It was bound to be set on a collision course. The Jews, too, had cherished a prophecy about a coming king whose peaceful rule would extend from one sea to the other, from the River to the ends of the earth.[16] And the four evangelists declare that this king has arrived, and that his name is Jesus. It is not surprising – to anticipate a later point – that we find the early church accused, in northern Greece which was such key terrain for the early empire, of behaving contrary to the dogmas of Caesar, and saying that there was 'another king (*basilea heteron*), namely Jesus' (Acts 17.7).

Rome is, of course, scarcely mentioned in the four gospels, yet for those with first-century ears attuned its presence is everywhere presupposed. John's great climactic scene of Jesus and Pilate – the kingdom of God against the kingdom of Caesar, challenging one another's visions of kingdom, truth and

---

13 Fowler and Fowler 2012, 1606.

14 Cf. the full exposition in Wallace 2008, Part 1.

15 Though Wallace makes a case for thinking that Virgil at least was widely known across the empire by the middle of the century.

16 E.g. Pss. 72.8; 89.25; Zech. 9.10.

power – shows where, for him, the story was heading all along.[17] Luke stages the birth of Jesus carefully in relation to the decree of Caesar Augustus, and his second volume ends with Paul in Rome announcing God as king and Jesus as lord, 'with all boldness, and with no one stopping him'.[18] Matthew and Mark draw heavily on Daniel [389] 7, the passage above all where God's kingdom confronts and overthrows the kingdoms of the world, seen as a succession of four increasingly horrible monsters. There is no doubt, in the first century, that the fourth monster would have meant Rome. And it is possible that Mark himself may have deliberately framed his gospel with strong hints that in Jesus an empire was coming to birth of a completely different character from that of Caesar. A recent article contrasts the dove that descended on Jesus at his baptism with the Roman eagle, appearing as an omen to further the cause of Augustus or his successors.[19] Furthermore, an increasingly common interpretation of Jesus' triumphal entry into Jerusalem is to see that event not only as the staged fulfilment of Zechariah 9 but also as a deliberate parody of the regular entry into Jerusalem of Pontius Pilate, on horseback surrounded by soldiers, coming from his quarters in Caesarea.[20] Whether or not that is correct, we should certainly see the muttered remark of the centurion (15.39) at the foot of the cross as vital. Mark hopes that his Roman readers will come to share this astonishing viewpoint. In a world where Caesar, unambiguously, was hailed as 'son of God', the centurion looks at the dead Jesus and transfers the title to him.

The cross, in fact, is for the evangelists the point where all the lines meet: the lines that run forward from Abraham, David and the exile; from 2 Samuel 7, Psalm 2 and Psalm 72; from Exodus 40 to 1 Kings 8 and Ezekiel 43; and, above all, from Isaiah 40—55 all the way into the mindset of Jesus himself and the interpretative work of the writers. The story told by all four gospels is the story of 'how God became king': not by the usual means of military revolution, but by the inauguration of sovereignty during Jesus' public career, and the strange but decisive victory on the cross itself. All four evangelists report that Jesus was executed with the words 'king of the Jews' over his head; and, as they all knew, though many scholars have long forgotten, the ancient

---

17   Jn. 18.28—19.16.
18   Lk. 2.1; Ac. 28.31.
19   Peppard 2010.
20   Though not directly described in ancient sources, this seems to have become a common theme in sermons and popular addresses, and works such as Borg and Crossan 2007, 2–5. An earlier scholarly study of the possibilities is Kinman 1994; his proposal is based on the known behaviour of Roman governors elsewhere rather than on direct evidence about Pilate's own coming to Jerusalem. However, the suggestion is certainly very plausible.

Jewish dream was that the king of the Jews would be king of the world. Of course: if Israel's God was the creator of the world, one would expect nothing less. And what the four evangelists are asking their readers to [390] do, as they ponder this strange multi-layered narrative, is precisely to *imagine*: to imagine that *this*, rather than something else, is what it would look like when God became king. Along with music and the visual arts, narrative is a primary human means of stimulating the imagination. This, I suggest, is precisely what the four gospels are aiming to do.

These are the themes which I see prominently in the gospels but not so prominently in contemporary scholarship. Indeed, one might observe that much of the effort expended on the gospels over the last hundred years and more has been directed not towards grappling with these issues but precisely towards holding them at bay. Narrative and imagination have been at a discount; the mechanical study of dismembered fragments has been the rule. Most of the much-vaunted 'methods' proposed in gospel scholarship have been generated from within a world where all that I have just said was ignored. Such methods are not neutral; they reflect the underlying assumptions of their makers, and I am suggesting that those underlying assumptions were deeply flawed. But why should this have been so? To try to understand that I turn to the second main section of my lecture.

Avoiding the Kingdom: The Story of Biblical Scholarship

Histories of biblical scholarship cover many issues, and it is important that in engaging with our predecessors as historically minded critics of the New Testament, we contextualize them, as we must ourselves, in the climate of thought in which they lived. An obvious example, related directly to what I have just said about dismembered fragments, is the great German Rudolf Bultmann. He was himself keenly aware of his own presuppositions, though many of his followers, not least in the UK and USA, were inclined to treat his work as simply the objective results of neutral scholarship. Anything but: he was writing his major work on the gospels at a time when, after the First World War and the demise of the Kaiser and other 'great men', Germany was trying to become simply a 'community', a *Gemeinde*, in the Weimar Republic. What did Bultmann do? He wrote about the gospels as the collections of stories which members of *die Gemeinde*, the 'community', told among themselves to sustain their present faith, not at all intending reference to a recently departed 'great man', except for the sheer fact of his crucifixion.

No thought of 'kingdom' there in any sense that a first-century Jew might recognize.

But that observation is simply the tip of the iceberg. So, too, is the necessary warning issued a generation ago by Hans Frei, that for much of the last two centuries narrative itself has been 'eclipsed' in biblical scholarship, which had regarded stories as secondary and looked instead for nuggets of doctrinal and [391] ethical teaching.[21] (We might compare the recent anti-Bible put out by the philosopher A. C. Grayling which, despite its attempt to parody the actual Bible, consists of no narrative at all but only wise sayings and advice.[22]) But, again, one has to go further back and ask why. This is a question which demands a multi-volume answer, and all I can do here is to put two or three items on the table for further discussion as we seek to understand how and why the discipline has gone in the directions it has. I shall, of course, greatly oversimplify many complex issues. My aim is to stimulate the disciplined imagination, not here to nail down exact arguments.

First, ever since the Renaissance the implicit narrative of western culture has been tripartite. There is the good early period; then there is the bad or boring middle period; then there is the sudden reawakening, the shining of a great light, and we can retrieve the good early period – or some of it, anyway – in a newly formed culture or worldview. Thus the Renaissance itself, fed up with what was seen as the stodgy and unimaginative categories of the late Middle Ages, saw itself as a break with the immediate past and a retrieval of an earlier golden age. The Reformation, in its turn, went exactly the same route, returning not to the Renaissance's pagan sources but to the Bible and the early Fathers, largely agreeing about the dark middle period from which one needed a clean break. The Enlightenment, some of the seeds of which were sown in both the Renaissance and the Reformation, has constantly tended to portray everything before it as ignorant superstition, hailing modern science and technology as the signs of the brave new world which enable us to draw an even thicker line between ourselves and our predecessors, retrieving only those bits and pieces of earlier wisdom which may commend themselves from time to time. One way or another, though, all these great movements have contained an implicit (and often explicit) narrative in which precisely what one does not want is continuity. Within Protestantism in particular – and until fairly recently most of the running in biblical scholarship was made by Protestants of one stripe or another – the

21   See Frei 1974.
22   Grayling 2011. See the telling review by Martin 2011.

sense of a major break in the narrative is deeply important. Anything else might signal, at least by implication, that the Catholics had been right all along, even though ostensibly the story being told would have been about the first century rather than the sixteenth. There has, then, been deep visceral resistance to any idea of a continuous narrative, and this itself has greatly impeded a recognition of what the gospels were actually doing. **[392]**

Second, however, the movement of thought from the Renaissance to the Enlightenment can be characterized especially by the major revival of Epicureanism. Ever since Poggio Bracciolini rediscovered Lucretius's great poem *De Rerum Natura* in an obscure European monastery in 1417 – exactly a century before Luther's supposed rediscovery of Paul's theology led him to nail his thesis to the Wittenberg door – the great alternative philosophy of the first century (alternative, that is, to the otherwise dominant Stoicism) had been making its way in European circles.[23] It came to its full flowering with the thinkers of the Enlightenment, taking in such seminal figures as Giordano Bruno, Montaigne, Galileo, Bacon, Hobbes, Newton, Hume and, not least, Thomas Jefferson, who famously proclaimed 'I am an Epicurean'. (That claim has to be taken seriously, despite Jefferson's attempts to have his cake and eat it by also noting his admiration for Epictetus, a first-century Stoic, and, of course, for Jesus himself; the latter two being subject to Jefferson's own rather heavy-handed attempts to decontextualize them and present the cleaned-up results in a way which sustained his other agendas rather than undermining them, as left to themselves they might have done.)

The point, of course, is that in Epicurean philosophy, over against the confused and often frightening paganism of the ancient world and then the confused and often frightening religion of the Middle Ages, the gods are removed far away, off to a distant heaven from which they don't even bother to look down, let alone to get involved in the affairs of the present world. The world itself, according to the first-century Darwinism of Lucretius, consists of atoms, and the objects made up of them, moving under their own steam, without divine intervention, developing and transforming themselves according to their own energy, their innate 'swerve' (*clinamen*, a crucial Epicurean term), and the survival of the fittest. Human society, likewise, should be able to order itself from within, needing no divine intervention whether through kings or priests or anybody else. The modern movement of liberal democracy is thus the twin sister of modern atheistic science, both sharing Lucretius as the primary ancestor and the Enlightenment

---

23   See now esp. Greenblatt 2011.

philosophers as the immediate parents. Biblical scholarship as we know it today was born in a world where the gods had been banished far away, a world in which humans and their societies moved under their own steam.[24]

It is important to stress this matrix, because the majority of westerners today simply do not realize either that they are Epicureans by default or [393] that Epicureanism always was only one philosophy among others. As a young theologian, I was taught, quite fiercely, that the Enlightenment had opened up a new *saeculum* (as, indeed, the American dollar bill declares to this day), and that we could not think of challenging it. Everything earlier was therefore relativized; just as George Washington had suggested that the world prior to the eighteenth century had been full of superstition, so modernist theologians insisted that we simply could not, today, share 'ancient worldviews'. That, of course, was the grand narrative against which postmodernity has protested so strongly, shaking the old Enlightenment certainties to the core. But people usually do not realize that the Epicurean stance of separating God or the gods from the world was always simply one option among others, philosophically speaking; that it was always an unstable option (since the gods always tended to sneak back in by other means, as in the Romantic movement's pantheistic answer to Enlightenment rationalism); that it was always a costly option, easier to embrace if you were rich enough to enjoy the Epicurean lifestyle.[25] But the most important point is that this unstable and costly option was always going to be a very bad framework for understanding the Jewish traditions, especially the New Testament itself.

Now, of course, as a historian, I believe that people with all kinds of different worldviews can and should study the evidence of the past and offer what interpretations they can of it, and particularly – the heart of good history – what made people tick. As the great contemporary historian, Asa Briggs, has written in his recent account of his time at Bletchley Park, what made young historians such good code-breakers is that they were 'well read, drawn to lateral thinking, and taught to get inside the mind of people totally different from themselves'.[26]

But there's the point. To use the anthropologist's jargon, historians of whatever background and context ought to have a stab at offering an *etic*

---

24 On Epicureanism as a key element in modern western thought, cf. esp. Wilson 2008.
25 Not, except in some debased forms (cf. e.g. Gay 1966, 306–8), in the sense of 'hedonism', but in the classical sense of retirement to a quiet and peaceful life.
26 Briggs 2011, 78.

account of the societies they are studying, that is, an outsider's fair analysis of the phenomena before them. But, as with anthropology, so with history, the pressure is there to provide what purports to be an *emic* account – an account of how the people themselves actually thought – but which turns out to be the *etic* one in disguise. And when, in the case of Enlightenment historiography, the *etic* account was offered from within Epicurean principles, the chance of **[394]** getting anywhere near the *emic* account that first-century Jews (including the early Christians) might have offered was severely reduced. In fact, within the Epicurean worldview Judaism was reduced, first, to being a 'religion' (the word 'religion' having been already severely redefined to reflect Epicurean principles, meaning now 'that which humans do with their solitude'), and then to being *the wrong sort* of religion (since the Jews persisted, perversely from the Epicurean point of view, in believing that the real world of creation, and human actions within it, actually mattered as part of the whole).

Those who embraced the Enlightenment but sought still to be good Christians thus portrayed themselves in a different light. Martin Luther's Protestantism, in which Paul rose and smote the wicked Judaizers, came to birth in a new form, as Christianity had to become unJewish in order to hold up its head in European culture. I'm talking here about the 1830s, not yet the 1930s (and leaving the 1530s to fend for themselves), but the point should still be clear. Religion and ordinary life had to be kept as far apart as possible. That was part, it seemed, of the point of justification by faith. The French went all the way with the Enlightenment agenda, and tried to wipe out religion entirely – an attempt which is still in progress today with the banning of Muslim headscarves. The Americans compromised, and insisted simply on a rigid separation of church and state. The English, as usual, looked this way and that and muddled along. As a newcomer to Scotland, I had better not try to describe what happened north of Berwick-upon-Tweed, though the simultaneous influence of John Knox and David Hume has no doubt left an interesting legacy. As for Ireland, I am reminded of the remark of my good friend the Irish American biblical scholar Dominic Crossan, who has said more than once in my hearing that the Irish never really got the Enlightenment, but they got the British instead, which they found most enlightening in other ways. But my point is this: Epicureanism, and its social and political outworkings, may or may not be the best way for us today to organize our world. I would argue not, though that's not the point. But it is certainly not a good way for us to understand the world of the early Christians.

The discipline of New Testament studies has reflected this, on both sides of various great debates. The fateful Enlightenment split between the gods and the world has generated a new meaning for words like 'natural' and 'supernatural'. It is now widely believed by would-be Christian apologists that part of the task is to defend something called 'the supernatural', in which a normally distant divinity invades the 'natural' world to perform 'miracles' or even, in the Christian story, to become human. But this merely reinscribes and perpetuates the Epicureanism that still serves as the framework for the discussion. Thus, in the study of the gospels, so-called 'liberals' have done their best to offer would-be historical accounts in which Jesus was [395] 'really' a Jewish revolutionary or teacher or apocalyptic prophet (the notion of 'apocalyptic' itself, by the way, has suffered radically through this process, but that's another story), while the so-called 'conservatives' have done their best to offer a historical account in which Jesus really was a 'supernatural' being who really did do miracles and rise from the dead.

Since in my own work I have done my best to counter some of the revisionist proposals, it might be easy to suppose I was simply taking the latter path. Rather, I want to insist that to understand the first Christians we must understand the radical difference between the ancient Jewish worldview and the ancient Epicurean worldview (remembering not least that one of the sharpest insults a rabbi could offer to heretics was to call them *apikorsim*, Epicureans). In the ancient Jewish worldview, the one God was not removed from the world, but was mysteriously present and active within it, at least in theory, so that if he remained absent, as in the second-Temple period, there was precisely a sense of that absence. And the modes of his presence and activity were concentrated on the major Jewish symbols: Temple, Torah, land, family, and not least the great narrative that was continuing and would be fulfilled even though it might have seemed for the moment, like a submerged stream, to be running underground. This was the air Jesus and his first followers breathed. And the task of describing, from an *emic* viewpoint, the mindset and motivation of the earliest Christians is thus one for which the Epicurean worldview is singularly badly suited. And to the extent that the movement of nineteenth-century biblical scholarship was done from within that Enlightenment framework, in its various forms owing much to Kant, Hegel and later Feuerbach, it was bound to misunderstand and misrepresent what those earliest Christians were about. And since some of the nineteenth-century proposals are still alive and well, as the sheer inertia of a complex discipline keeps them alive long after their sell-by date, we still find ourselves facing categories like 'Jewish Christian' and 'gentile Christian', like 'early

Catholicism' and 'enthusiasm', which actually demand such radical overhaul that it might be better to draw a line, in our turn, across the false would-be *Heilsgeschichte* of triumphalist scholarship, and try to start again.

There is another element to all this which I just mention before turning to my final point about the cultural context of modern biblical scholarship. Much of the work I have described has been done within the Lutheran tradition. But, for all its strengths, the Lutheran world has long embraced a 'two kingdoms' theology in which God and Caesar simply won't mix. And that, when coupled with the Enlightenment's Epicureanism, has produced several generations of scholarship in which, for instance, it is simply off limits to imagine that Paul might have regarded Jesus as Israel's Messiah, with all the overtones of world sovereignty which that word carried. The [396] general view of scholarship has colluded with the general view of popular western Christianity, that the purpose of the whole thing is 'to go to heaven when you die', rather than discerning, 'imagining' shall we say, the kingdom of God on earth as in heaven and working for that end. Of course, liberation theology and its various exegetical offshoots have tried to present a rival view. But, as with the so-called 'conservative' reaction, this has often simply maintained the split world of the Enlightenment, proposing (for instance) that Paul was 'really' a politician *and therefore not really a theologian after all.*[27] Similar things might be said about some of the work, important in its own way, that has gone under the umbrella of 'sociology' or 'anthropology'. From the post-Enlightenment standpoint, this appears to be on the 'worldly' side of the divide while God, or the gods, remain elsewhere. From the Jewish and early Christian perspective, such a division already gives in to one version of the paganism which both were determined to resist.

One final element of our modern world which has militated against imagining the kingdom in our reading of the gospels, and much else besides, is the triumph of left-brain thinking over right-brain thinking that has been massively and memorably set out by Iain McGilchrist in his breathtaking book *The Master and His Emissary.*[28] McGilchrist has been attacked from within his own field (he is both a brain scientist and a literary critic, and as such has a unique perspective on the history of ideas). His careful and detailed exposition of the way in which the left and right hemispheres of the human

---

27 This position is implicit, and sometimes explicit, in some of the work of Horsley, e.g. his introductions in Horsley 1997; 2000.

28 McGilchrist 2009.

brain function will, no doubt, be modified as research progresses.[29] But as I read his account of the way in which, in the last three centuries, the left-brain activities of analysing, calculating and organizing have steadily taken charge of our world, squeezing out the right-brain activities of imagination, story-telling and intuitive thinking, I find it uncannily accurate as a description of our world in general and of biblical scholarship in particular. And McGilchrist argues strongly on the basis of brain science itself that our human brains are designed to work in a two-way movement: from the right brain with its initial [397] intuitions, to the left brain which works on the detail, and back to the right brain to implement. The right brain is thus the 'master', and the left brain the 'emissary', working at its best within the framework given by the right and intending to pass the results back across. But, as with some observable pathologies (not least schizophrenia), the left brain has taken over, and we have (says McGilchrist) a world in which the master has been betrayed.

McGilchrist is not trying to talk about the world of biblical scholarship, but the following paragraph jumped out at me as a pretty accurate summary of how the discipline has often gone:

We could expect that there would be a loss of the broader picture, and a substitution of a more narrowly focussed, restricted, but detailed, view of the world, making it perhaps difficult to maintain a coherent overview . . . This in turn would promote the substitution of information, and information gathering, for knowledge, which comes through experience . . . One would expect the left hemisphere to keep doing refining experiments on detail, at which it is exceedingly proficient, but to be correspondingly blind to what is not clear or certain, or cannot be brought into focus right in the middle of the visual field. In fact one would expect a sort of dismissive attitude to anything outside of its limited focus, because the right hemisphere's take on the whole picture would simply not be available to it.[30]

I recognize this picture. Having worked for the Church of England for nearly twenty years, I recognize it as an account of what has happened, damagingly, to our institutions. Whether it has happened in the universities too, in the years I have been absent, I couldn't possibly say. My point is that this has

---

29 Cf. e.g. Borst, Thompson and Kosslyn 2011. I am grateful to Professor Malcolm Jeeves for this and other references and for important discussion on this subject.

30 McGilchrist 2009, 428f.

manifestly happened in biblical studies, and especially in New Testament studies, and not least in the study of the gospels. All too often the microscopic analysis of details, vital though it is in its place, has been made to seem an end in itself. 'Objective facts' are all the rage, and whether you're a left-wing hunter of objectivity, determined to disprove the gospels, or a right-wing hunter, determined to show that they are after all 'factual', you may still be missing the point and losing the plot. Facts are left-brain business; vital in their place, but only part of the whole.

Thus, on the one hand, those who presently trumpet the need for a purely and exclusively 'secular' study of the Bible are simply following through the anti-metaphorical agenda of the French Revolution.[31] Meanwhile, those who respond with an attempted rationalistic proof of, say, Jesus' divinity are often [398] themselves remaining within the same sterile antithesis. Like Marxism and capitalism, secularism and fundamentalism are simply the left and right boots of Enlightenment Epicureanism. Only when the detailed left-brain analysis can be relocated as the emissary to the right-wing intuition, with its rich world of metaphor, narrative and above all imagination, can the discipline become healthy again.

The good news is that the gospels themselves resist the destructive, atomizing, Epicurean left-brain analysis on its own. They go on telling the story of 'how God became king', and demanding that serious readers learn to imagine a world in which that might be the case, a world reshaped around their account of Jesus. Perhaps, after all, biblical studies might be one place where the return of the master, a theme indeed made famous by some of Jesus' own stories, might begin to take place. This is a challenge, particularly, for those engaged in doctoral studies. It is much easier to do a purely left-brain doctorate, and there is still plenty of room for that. But we also need, and quite urgently, a new generation of scholars who won't be afraid to see the bigger picture and, without in the least going slack on the necessary left-brain analytic and philological exactitude, come back and articulate a new, freshly imagined vision of the kingdom of God.

Early Christian Mission and Theology

All this leads to my concluding remarks on early Christian mission and theology. For over a century now it has been commonplace within the discipline called 'New Testament studies' to assume that the early church had to

---

31 So McGilchrist 2009, 347.

jettison its Jewishness in order to be relevant to the gentile world into which it quickly went. Thus, as we saw earlier, it has been assumed that Paul had to downplay the idea of Jesus as Israel's Messiah and to switch, instead, to the more readily available category of the *kyrios*, the 'lord'. But this proposal, hugely influential though it has been, simply fails to imagine what 'the kingdom of God' meant to the early Christians, Paul included.[32] Paul, in fact, held firmly to the ancient Jewish belief, rooted in the Psalms, in Isaiah and in Daniel, that a world ruler would indeed arise from Judaea, that Israel's God would thereby return to dwell among and within his people, and that through this the long-awaited new creation of peace and justice would be inaugurated for the whole world. All of that standard Jewish expectation came to fresh flowering in his thought and writing. Of course, the communities that Paul founded were determinedly non-ethnic in their basis. But this **[399]** was not because Paul had as it were gone soft on the essential Jewishness of his mission, or because there was something wrong (as Epicureans imagine) with Judaism, but because he believed that it was precisely part of the age-old divine plan that when God did for Israel what he was going to do for Israel, then the nations would be brought under the healing, saving rule of this one God.[33] Paul's 'gospel', his *euangelion*, was thus much closer in meaning to the various *euangelia* of Caesar than most of modern scholarship has imagined. It was, as Acts 17 (already quoted) indicates, the royal announcement, right under Caesar's nose, that there was 'another king, namely Jesus'. And Paul believed that this royal announcement, like that of Caesar, was not a take-it-or-leave-it affair. It was a powerful summons through which the living God worked by his spirit in hearts and minds, to transform human character and motivation, producing the tell-tale signs of faith, hope and love which Paul regarded as the biblically prophesied marks of God's true people.

The communities that sprang into surprised existence as Paul went around making this royal announcement were remarkably devoid of an obvious symbolic world. They were precisely not defined by the worldview-symbols of Judaism – Temple, Torah observance and so on. They certainly didn't adopt the symbols of the surrounding pagan culture. How could this new community, this new *sort* of community, retain what for Paul was its vital centre, namely its strong unity across traditional social divisions, and its strong holiness in matters of those perennial categories of human life,

---

32 Paul does not, of course, use the phrase often; but when he does it is clear that it remains at the centre of his worldview. Cf. e.g. Rom. 14.17; 1 Cor. 4.20; 6.9. (Full list in Wright 1996a, 668.)

33 This is why, in my view, Barclay's picture of Paul as presenting a puzzle gets off on the wrong foot: see Barclay 1996, ch. 13.

money, sex and power? For Paul the answer was simple. The members of the community needed to understand what it was that had happened in Jesus the Messiah, and in particular who the God was into whose new world they had been brought. What we see in Paul is thus properly characterized as the birth of the discipline that later came to be called 'Christian theology', by which I mean the prayerful and scripture-based reflection, from within the common life of the otherwise disparate body called the church, on who exactly the one God was and what his action in Jesus and by the spirit was to mean. Early Christian theology was not an exercise undertaken for the sake of speculative system-building. It was load-bearing. If the unity and holiness of the early church were the central symbols of the movement, they could only be held in place if a vigorous theology was there to stabilize them in the winds and storms of the first century. Theology, in this sense, serves ecclesiology and thus the kingdom-based mission. Actually, I have come to worry about a post-Enlightenment theology that doesn't do this, that thinks the point is [400] simply to 'prove' the divinity of Jesus, or his resurrection, or the saving nature of his death in themselves, thereby demonstrating fidelity to the Creeds or some other *regula fidei*. In the gospels themselves it isn't like this. All these things matter, but they matter because this is how God is becoming king. To prove the great creeds true, and to affirm them as such, can sadly be a diversionary exercise, designed to avoid the real challenge of the first-century gospel, the challenge of God's becoming king in and through Jesus.

This challenge, of course, required imagination: not the undisciplined fantasy of which left-brain thinking often accuses right-brain thinking, but the imaginative leap into a new worldview, significantly different from the worldviews of paganism, with their many gods who might either be far removed, as in Epicureanism, or rolled into one and close at hand, as in Stoicism – and, indeed, from the worldviews of ancient Judaism, with their fierce concentration on the symbols of land, nation, Temple and Torah. But the leap was not made into the unknown. The imaginative leap required was made on the basis of Jesus, Jesus the crucified and risen Jewish Messiah, Jesus the one in and through whom Israel's God had at last returned in person to rescue his people and the world. And to sustain precisely that leap, the early Christians told and retold, and eventually wrote down, the story of Jesus, not, of course, as 'neutral' reportage (there is no such thing) but as the story of what the one God had done and how he had done it.

The four gospels, then, to return to our starting-point, are thus appropriately named 'gospel', in line both with Isaiah 40 and 52 and with the contemporary pagan usage.[34] They themselves, in telling the story of how God became king in and through Jesus, invite their readers to the imaginative leap of saying, 'Suppose this is how God has done it? Suppose the world's way of empire is all wrong? Suppose there's a different way, and suppose that Jesus, in his life, death and resurrection, has brought it about?' And the gospels themselves, of course, contain stories at a second level, stories purportedly told by Jesus himself, which were themselves, in their day, designed to break open the worldview of their hearers and to initiate a massive imaginative leap to which Jesus gave the name 'faith'. The gospels invite their readers, in other words, to a multiple exercise, both of imagining what it might have been like to make that leap in the first century and, as a second stage, of imagining what it might be like to do so in one's own day. For too long gospel study has been dominated by the attempt to make the gospels reflect, simply, the faith-world of the early church; [401] why, after all, would the early Christians have been particularly interested in miscellaneous stories of what Jesus actually said or did, when all that really mattered was his saving death, making the gospels, as people used to say, 'Passion narratives with extended introductions'? The conservative response has been that early converts would naturally want to know more about this Jesus in whom they had come to place their faith. But this stand-off, on both sides, has usually failed to reflect the larger question: that the gospels tell the story of Jesus not out of mere historical anecdotage or faith-projection, but because this is how Jesus launched the kingdom of God, which he then accomplished in his death and resurrection. Even to hold this possibility in one's head requires, in today's western church, whether radical or conservative, no less than in the non-Christian world, a huge effort of the imagination.

This imagination, like all good right-brain activity, must then be firmly and thoroughly worked through the left brain, disciplined by the rigorous historical and textual analysis for which the discipline of biblical studies has rightly become famous. But by itself the left brain will produce, and has often produced, a discipline full of facts but without meaning, high on analysis and low on reconstruction, good at categories and weak on the kingdom. The task before us – challenging, to be sure, but also richly rewarding – is that of imagining the kingdom in such a way that will simultaneously advance the academic understanding of our extraordinary primary texts and enrich the mission and theology of tomorrow's church. It is, after all, just as difficult today as it was in the first century to imagine

---

34   Isa. 40.9; 52.7. The contemporary pagan usage is now widely discussed; see e.g. Stanton 2004, ch. 2.

what the kingdom of God might look like. Rigorous historical study of the gospels and the other early Christian writings has a proper role to play in fuelling, sustaining and directing that imagination, and in helping to translate it into reality.

9
Revelation and Christian Hope: Political Implications of the Revelation to John

Like many New Testament scholars whose central focus has been on Paul and the gospels, I have not written much on Revelation. But my lifelong amateur interest (Revelation was the first book of the Bible – other than Philemon! – which I ever read at a single sitting) was stirred into something more by the preliminary work for *Revelation for Everyone* (Wright 2011b), and when I was invited to a conference on the book at Duke Divinity School in the autumn of 2010 I was delighted to do what I could. Revelation, of course, has been a magnet for strange interpretative theories of all sorts; but in determining to avoid exegetical folly one must not sink back into the overcautious mood that afflicts some. In particular, as most now recognize, Revelation addresses what we would call 'political' issues, but does so through the vivid 'cartoons' of 'apocalyptic' imagery. In doing so, it opens up the perennial question of how 'apocalyptic' language actually works, a question whose relevance goes much wider than this one book.

Introduction

[105] My primary title, 'Revelation and Christian Hope', would have appeared to many in earlier generations quite straightforward. Revelation is, after all, about heaven. Though it does indeed say some complicated and unexpected things about heaven, we gain an initial glimpse of heaven in chapters 4 and 5, and we then work our way through to the celestial city itself, the new Jerusalem, in the final two chapters. So, in this deceptively straightforward view, the hope is 'heaven', and Revelation offers something of a tourist guide to that destination and perhaps the route towards it.

So ingrained is this perspective that more than one commentator recycles an old joke about someone who has written a commentary on the book of

Revelation finally breathing his last and being carried by angels to the pearly gates. There he is met by several other learned scholars who themselves, in their day, had written commentaries on the book. 'So,' they say, 'you did one too. You will find things very different up here.'

As for political implications within that view: well, that can go two ways. Either we say that, because we're bound for heaven, the rantings and ragings of bestial powers on earth are interesting but largely irrelevant to us. Or we treat those bits as code, rather than symbol, and decode them so that they refer to particular movements within our own day, leading up to Armageddon and the end of the world (which will, of course, happen next week).

When I say that this way of reading the book misses the point in more ways than one, I mean that it subverts the book theologically, politically and, not least, intertextually – the three main focal points of the [106] conference for which this chapter was written. I suspect, in fact, that one of the reasons for the comparative neglect of Revelation in many Christian circles has been a direct result of the embracing of that pseudo-theology about 'going to heaven' that has been the staple diet of much western Christianity, both catholic and protestant.[1] Since I have sometimes been misunderstood on this point, let me say that I have no problem speaking of Christians dying and 'going to heaven', only with the notion that that is the final destination. As I have often said, heaven is important but it is not the end of the world. A glance at the last two chapters of Revelation itself makes the point graphically. Unlike many hymns and prayers, much iconography and enormous unquestioned popular assumption, the final scene of the Christian Bible is not about humans leaving this earth and going up to a place called 'heaven'. It is about the heavenly city coming down to earth. And part of the reason for Revelation's sharp political content is that – again in contrast to the dualist escapism of much modern western Christianity – the coming of God's kingdom on earth as in heaven is not, for John the Seer, something for which we have to wait to the very end. It has already been inaugurated through the victory of the sacrificed 'lamb' who is also the 'lion'. The reason there is any question of political theology in this book is that Jesus is already lord of lords and king of kings, and those who hail him as such need to learn what it means to bear witness to him in the face of the claims and threats of other lords and other kings. That is the burden of my song.

I shall approach this conclusion in four steps. First, I shall set the scene with some reflections on the notion of 'apocalyptic'. Second, I shall look in more

---

1   See Wright 2008.

detail at the hope which Revelation offers, and how it relates to the present vocation of the church as seen in the central chapters of the book. Third, I shall look at the unholy trinity of villains that emerge at the centre of the book, and enquire what sort of political profile they present and what sort of political theology they might engender – in other words, what it means for the church, then and now, to recognize their deceitfulness and escape their clutches. Fourth, I shall offer some reflections on the place of Revelation within the Christian canon of scripture. That will probably be enough for one chapter.

I should add a disclaimer. In writing about Revelation I am venturing to march right in and pluck one or two rather obvious flowers from a garden where others have planted, watered and tended for generations. I hope that more experienced gardeners will forgive my blunderings, and help me gently towards further and deeper insight. [107]

Apocalyptic and the Book of Revelation

The word 'apocalyptic' has been pressed into service in relation to at least three quite different sorts of thing: an experience, a literary genre and a worldview. These sometimes overlap, but should not be confused. (Nor should they be confused with the currently popular meaning of the word, which indicates terrible, cataclysmic upheavals. When journalists have sought to describe the events of 9/11, or subsequent occurrences such as earthquakes and tsunamis, they have often called them 'apocalyptic events'. But this phrase, in this context, neither denotes nor connotes the experience, the genre or the worldview of which we are now speaking.)

First, and I believe foremost, the word can denote a phenomenon in which someone experiences a revelation of things not normally perceptible – sometimes seeing, sometimes hearing, sometimes both. We know about this because the person writes down what happened, but this first meaning has to do not with the writing down but with the event itself, a 'revelation' or 'unveiling', and to the spirituality or tradition that cultivates or hopes for such events. Some might call this a 'religious' phenomenon, though our word 'religion' is at least as misleading as 'apocalyptic' itself. At its heart – this is very important for what follows – this kind of experience, and the cultivation of such events, presupposes that reality is more complex and multi-dimensional than it normally appears, and that, in particular, the sphere of normal human experience (call it 'earth' for the sake of argument) is not separated from the sphere of the angels and their creator by a great gulf, but rather that 'heaven' and 'earth' in fact overlap and interlock in a variety of ways.

The belief that heaven and earth could and sometimes did overlap and interlock is built into the very structure of ancient Israelite life, thought and particularly worship. Israel's central symbol was the Temple, at the heart of the land. The Temple was the place where the two spheres of heaven and earth intersected, where God had chosen to dwell on earth. And the Temple is central for John the Seer, right up to the point where it disappears because its function is swallowed up in the new, complete, heaven–earth reality.

The prophetic tradition thrived on this overlap. Elisha calms his worried assistant through a vision of horses and chariots of fire. Micaiah ben-Imlach stands humbly in the heavenly council so that he can then stand boldly before King Ahab. Isaiah happens to be in the Temple when what is always true suddenly becomes visibly true. Jeremiah finds the overlap crushingly painful but unavoidable. Ezekiel reports strange visions in which symbol and reality flow in and out of one another. And Daniel, the [108] canonical climax of ancient Jewish apocalyptic, combines the wisdom by which he himself can perceive hidden secrets with a sequence of dreams for which he himself needs an angelic interpreter. The book thus moves from accounts of ancient wisdom confronting the principalities and powers to visions that enable the later reader to do the same. In each case, we might note, the meaning and result of these visions is not about the religious experience for its own sake but about (what we would call) the political and social implications.

Nothing in this whole matrix of ancient Israelite and Jewish apocalyptic implies what we properly call 'dualism'.[2] Heaven and earth are distinct, but that duality implies no ontological incompatibility. Earth's inhabitants have gone their own way, and their rulers have abused their power, but heaven's answer to that is not to pull up the drawbridge and provide a back-stair access for those who can escape, but to reassert the claims of the God of heaven and earth on his whole two-sided creation. This always involves conflict with the powers that have usurped his rule on earth, whether pagan or Jewish. The prophets who experience these visions, and speak of them, may be ostracized, threatened and/or punished, but they do not see themselves as part of a tiny little group waiting for the world to go to hell so that they can then be rescued or vindicated. In particular, the prophets are not saying that the world of space, time and matter is coming, or has come, to an end, so that something radically new may happen, generating 'antinomies' and forcing readers to choose between them. Part of the problem of 'the day of the Lord', in Jeremiah and elsewhere, is that it is precisely not, in that crude sense, 'the

---

2 On this point, see the important discussion in Wright 1992, ch. 10.

end of the world'. The morning after the fall of Jerusalem, the created world moves on into a new era of sorrow and shame.

I therefore do not recognize the common antithesis between 'apocalyptic' and 'prophecy', so beloved of an earlier generation. When we come to John's book, he declares up front that his work belongs in both categories, as well as that of 'epistle' (Revelation 1.1–3). The second meaning of 'apocalyptic' is that of the *literary genre* that has come to bear that name. Scholars frequently use it to denote the genre of books which, broadly, stand in the tradition that developed beyond Daniel. Here there is a problem: were these also the result of category 1 events? It is notoriously difficult to tell whether, in books like *1 Enoch*, *4 Ezra* or *2 Baruch*, the writer has actually experienced the visions he records as (what we would call) a 'religious' or spiritual phenomenon. Our suspicions are aroused by the heavy-handed reinterpretation of earlier books; by the exceedingly far-fetched visions that we find in, for instance, *4 Ezra*'s explicit rereading of Daniel; and also by the obvious pseudonymity. Thus, though the literary [109] genre to which these books belong appears to overlap with some parts at least of Daniel, it is I believe a significantly new development. It uses as an expository method what earlier writers had found themselves driven to say through vivid first-hand experience. Please note, I do not say it was any the worse for that. Bunyan's *Pilgrim's Progress* is a literary artefact, using the fiction of an extended dream. We are neither deceived nor disappointed when we realize this.

But in some of these works of 'apocalyptic' genre, made accessible over the last fifty years in a plethora of new editions, we detect signs of what has sometimes been thought of as 'apocalyptic' in the third sense, which is that of a particular *worldview*. Students have routinely been taught that an 'apocalyptic mindset' is dualistic, sectarian, determinist, pessimistic, world-denying, looking to an immediate future not for transformation or healing but for rescue. This may be true of some of the works that use the apocalyptic form as a literary genre. But not only is it not true of those in my first category, it also denies precisely the heaven–earth overlap, that strange open commerce between the twin halves of God's good creation, on which the visionaries rely and which contextualizes and makes sense of their work. I am not hereby committing, I trust, the Romantic fallacy of making original experience good and subsequent formalization bad. I am merely noting that what has been thought of as 'the apocalyptic mindset' does not fit many of the principal writers who stand at the head of the stream of apocalyptic writings.

And – here comes the point – I am convinced of two things. First, John the Divine seems to belong in the first category rather than the second. His is not an 'apocalypse' like, say, *4 Ezra*. He writes in his own name, claiming no ancient alter ego. His fresh use of the ancient prophets is quite unlike that in *4 Ezra*, *2 Baruch* and so on. He does occasionally report conversations between himself and an angelic interpreter, but never do we have that step-by-step interpretation of visions that, beginning with Daniel 7, became the stock-in-trade of later writers. He veers to and fro, as Daniel does, between fairly literal description (as in ch. 18) and reported visions which, uninterpreted, remain dense and impenetrable. He challenges his readers to work things out for themselves, providing clues (albeit sometimes rather obvious ones) rather than explicit one-on-one interpretations. His work has an immediacy that, though not of itself a guarantee of divine inspiration (a sceptic could always blame John's strange diet or, indeed, lack thereof), seems to place him with Jeremiah and Ezekiel, two of his greatest inspirations, rather than with the works of his pseudonymously writing Jewish contemporaries. If, therefore, we come to John's book with the assumption that it exhibits 'the apocalyptic [110] mindset', we are bound to misunderstand and misinterpret it. John is no dualist, no pessimist. In our modern sense, he is no sectarian.

Second, the rather narrow band of thought that has taken up the word 'apocalyptic' in some quarters of New Testament studies – I think of Ernst Käsemann, and his American followers J. Christiaan Beker and J. Louis Martyn – has not made the case for its own fresh meaning of 'apocalyptic'. Since these authors have written about Paul rather than Revelation, I shall not stop on this point, except to say that we are overdue for a reaction based on actual analysis of apocalyptic texts rather than on the assumption of a particular worldview, which looks suspiciously like one variety of mid-twentieth-century systematic theology. A healthy dose of John Collins or Chris Rowland, to look no further, would be a good start. I have no doubt that St Paul was what we could call an 'apocalyptic' thinker and writer. But I do not mean by that what Käsemann and his followers meant. (I note in passing that whereas for Käsemann 'apocalyptic' always referred to the expectation of the imminent end of the world, in his American followers this has been transformed into an understanding of Jesus' death: a sign, I believe, of residual confusion within the putative category.) In exploring John the Seer as an 'apocalyptic' writer, such constructs will not be helpful, primarily because they are generated by contemporary interests that have borrowed the word 'apocalyptic' to give the appearance of historical-critical rootedness, but without exploring what those roots are or what sort of plants they sustain.

The question of the theological interpretation of 'apocalyptic', and of this 'apocalypse' in particular, must therefore remain in abeyance until we have gone further. The tale is told of Karl Barth being asked by a lady whether the serpent in Genesis actually spoke. 'Madam,' he replied, 'it doesn't matter whether or not the serpent spoke. What matters is *what the serpent said*.' In similar fashion, the fact that something is 'apocalyptic' may not be of such theological significance as we have supposed. What matters is *what the apocalypse says*. The exception to this rule is in the presupposition I have spoken of already. The prophetic kind of apocalypse to which John's work belongs presupposes the overlap of, and interplay between, heaven and earth. On that hinges a great deal of theology, and of relevance.

The Hope and the Vision

So what, then, is the Christian hope that John holds out, and how does that hope sustain the calling and identity of the followers of Jesus in the present? The hope is expressed, again and again, in claims such as that of Revelation 11.15: 'The kingdom of this world has become the kingdom [111] of our Lord and of his Messiah, and he will reign for ever and ever.' It is important to note that this is stated at various points throughout the book, even in the midst of trouble and suffering. It is true already. That which is fully realized in chapters 21 and 22 is already anticipated in the sequence that runs from chapter 5, where all creation praises the 'lamb' that was slain because he has won the right to open the scroll of God's eternal purposes, through the various outbursts of praise, to the final conclusion that, in the new Jerusalem which has come down from heaven to earth, 'the dwelling of God is with humans'. In the present time God has a Temple in heaven, which is sometimes glimpsed by the Seer, but when heaven and earth are joined there will be no Temple, because the whole city will be suffused with the presence of God. As Greg Beale has shown powerfully,[3] drawing out its larger significance within biblical theology, the city will be an enormous *cube* – quite unrealistic as an earthly city, even supposing we allow it to be a gravity-free zone with gigantic skyscrapers, but utterly appropriate, symbolically, both in terms of its ultimate perfection and, more particularly, of its being a huge replica of the Holy of Holies. Heaven and earth are one at last.

The dramatic tension which drives most of Revelation is the sharp and horrible realization that this state of affairs has not yet come to pass. But from

3 Beale 2004.

the very beginning we know that something has happened in and through which it has *begun* to be true. Jesus the Messiah, the lion of Judah, has already conquered, is already enthroned. He is worthy to open the seals that otherwise would hold back the divine purpose for the world. Here, as in much of the New Testament, we encounter a christologically based inaugurated eschatology. It is because Jesus has been raised from the dead that his death is seen as salvific, redemptive and above all victorious. And here we discover, too, how mistaken is that reading of the New Testament which supposes that for the early Christians everything depended on a future event still to come. Clearly there was a strong and vital future hope. The eschatology was not realized. But *something had already happened* as a result of which Jesus had already been installed as king of kings and lord of lords. That is what most twentieth-century scholarship failed to realize. The implicit and often explicit denial of the bodily resurrection of Jesus, as I have argued elsewhere, caused generations of liberal scholarship to place all the eschatological weight on the immediate future, whereas for the earliest Christians the main pillar of hope was something that had happened in the immediate past.

The way the hope is articulated, then, and the way it holds in place the vocation and character of the church in the present, is through the tension between the opening vision of heavenly worship in chapters 4 and [112] 5 and the closing vision of the new Jerusalem in chapters 21 and 22. A word about each.

Chapters 4 and 5, we should stress, are not a vision of the ultimate future – despite, for instance, Charles Wesley's magnificent 'till we cast our crowns before thee' (in the closing stanza of 'Love Divine, All Loves Excelling'). They are a vision of the worship which all creation offers to its creator right now, but invisibly within the heavenly throne-room. They are the reality of which the throne-rooms of this world, with their sycophantic worship, are the parody – a theme (reality and parody) which occupies John quite a lot. And the vision of the scroll indicates, remarkably enough, that the world's creator is true to his original plan in Genesis, which was to rule the world, and govern its course, *through obedient humanity*. All others have failed, but the slaughtered lamb steps forward, to do what in scripture the lion of Judah was to do: the messianic task, Israel's task, the human task. The result is that through his redemptive death humans from every nation have become 'a kingdom and priests' (Revelation 5.10) who will reign on the earth – a significant framing theme of the book (Revelation 1.6; 20.6). This vocation derives from the vocation of the redeemed Israel in Exodus 19.6, looking back in turn to the vocation of the human race in Genesis 1 and 2. This is not, then, some specialized, off-beat task peculiar to John's vision. It is the articulation of what it means to be genuinely human, standing between the creator and the creation, summing up creation's praises before God and bringing God's rule to bear on creation. That is the hope which enables this people to praise God in the present despite their immediate circumstances, and to learn that their witness, even unto death if need be, is the means by which the world will be brought under the rule of the 'lamb'. This is the vision, and vocation, which frames in particular the revelation of the mystery of evil at large in the world and the task of God's people to discern it and refuse its seductions. The vision of chapters 4 and 5, in other words, is designed to set the context within which the little communities will take heart and, sharing in the worship already on earth, have courage to hold on, to resist those who speak from other throne-rooms, and so to become victorious and to share at last in the new Jerusalem.

The new Jerusalem, for its part, offers the ultimate hope: the city (the place of human habitation, mutual interchange, and flourishing) that is also a garden, indeed *the* garden. This is not about going back to Eden, but about going on and discovering that the final city is the goal towards which, had they but realized it, Eden's original inhabitants were called to work. In a fresh blending of Genesis 2 and Ezekiel, the river flows through the city, and the tree of life grows on its banks. From Cain's building of the first [113] city (Genesis 4.17) to the original Babel of Genesis 11, we see humans grasping at the ideal from which the primal sin had debarred them, constructing instead murderous and arrogant parodies of that goal. This lies at the heart of the great contrast at the end of Revelation between Babylon and Jerusalem. Babylon represents the ultimate in that Cain-and-Babel story; the new Jerusalem represents the ultimate in the story which begins with the nomad Abraham, but which is anticipated in the city of David. The dualist reaction of Romanticism is to demonize the city and celebrate withdrawn rural life as the only alternative. I recall Stevie Smith's line about those who went to build the new Jerusalem and ended up with New York. But that is not the biblical answer – any more than Richard Neuhaus's opposite position, that when we arrive in the new Jerusalem we will see a sign saying, 'From the people who brought you New York'! No. Now that the lion of Judah has conquered, and according to Psalm 2 will conquer all the kingdoms of the earth, the true city can at last appear. And within that city the redeemed human beings – who appear to be a growing number, not a little withdrawn minority – will share in the rule of the lamb (22.5).

When we understand this relationship between the vision of heavenly worship in chapters 4 and 5, on the one hand, and the final scenes on the other, the long and often puzzling middle section of the book – by which I mean all the way from chapter 6 to chapter 20 – begins to fall into place. The seals are removed from the scroll, one by one, unleashing a sequence of divine judgments, which are necessary in order to overthrow and abolish the ingrained and powerful evil that has taken root in the world through human sin and its sinister empowerment. Among the many highly complex and artistic patterns which have been discerned throughout these chapters we may highlight the rather obvious one: that the judgments, like the plagues in Egypt, are the prelude to the rescue of God's people. The judgments come in three sequences of seven – the seals, the trumpets and the bowls – which are almost certainly to be seen as different symbolic angles on the same events, rather than twenty-one different events. Thus each sequence draws to its climax in terms of terrifying events – thunder, lightning, earthquake and so on (8.5; 11.19; 16.18, echoing 4.5). The judgments themselves are highly stylized, replete with biblical allusions and echoes, evoking the awesome judgments on Sodom, Egypt, Tyre and above all Babylon. But in each case the sequence is interrupted by a vision of the redeemed, celebrating in worship, joining with the heavenly liturgy that had already been witnessed in chapters 4 and 5 and which continues to form the theological as well as liturgical ground-plan for the book: God is the good and wise creator; Jesus is the lamb whose death has ransomed a royal priesthood. [114]

The vision of hope is therefore the vision of a people, a community, a *polis*, which will finally be revealed as the new Jerusalem itself, the bride of the lamb. The fundamental characteristic of this *polis* is worship of the true God for who he is and for what, through the lamb and his death, he has now done. The remarkable sequence of songs of worship, spread liberally throughout the book, indicates the quality and content of that worship (and, incidentally, shows up the lack of quality, and the poverty of content, in much that today passes for 'worship'). And since this worship already takes place in the present, the eschatology is indeed inaugurated. The question thus presses as to what this *polis* looks like in the present time, and how it conducts itself against the other cities, the other communities, that surround it. That is at the heart of the political question, to which we shall shortly turn. But, as quickly becomes clear, all this can only happen because a victory has been won which now opens the way for other victories to be won. What is this victory, over whom is it won, and what are the consequences? Up until chapter 12, it might have seemed as though the church simply faced all kinds of miscellaneous challenges, temptations, dangers and threats. But from chapter 12 onwards it becomes clear that these are neither random nor isolated. They are part of a concerted campaign conducted by an ultimate enemy who will stop at nothing to prevent the purpose of the world's creator from being carried out. Here John's symbolism, culled as usual from many other sources, is on full lurid display as he introduces us to the dragon, the beast from the sea and the beast from the land.

The Challenge of the Beast

With chapters 12, 13 and 14 we are forced to recognize, if we had doubted it, that this book is written from, and to, a very precise context. Detailed studies have shown that, of all the interpretations of the famous 666 in 13.18, 'Nero Caesar' fits the bill extremely well. This is not only because of the numerical value of the name within the familiar gematria. The number possesses other properties that would make it all the more clear what the church was up against. The repeated 'six' is not only a parody of 777, a number of utter perfection, but also more particularly of the hyper-perfect numerical value of the name 'Jesus Christ', which is 888. The beast, supported by the dragon and operating through the 'beast from the land', and thus standing at the centre of the unholy trinity, is a parody of Jesus at several levels, not least the refrain that 'he was, and is not, and is to come'. The reality is that the living creator God wills to rule his world through Jesus the Messiah and his people. The parody is that the dragon rules the world through the beast and his henchmen, notably the 'second beast'. [115]

But if Nero is identified, at least in a preliminary way, with the beast from the sea, where do we go from there? Two questions in particular: first, can we then locate the book's date precisely enough to figure out who all the other characters are? And second, does this mean that the book possessed great meaning for that generation but none, except distant historical reminiscence, for any other generation, our own included? These are major questions and deserve some care.

First, as to the date. A majority of biblical scholars today agrees with Irenaeus in dating the book in the reign of Domitian, towards the end of the first century AD. I have no a priori reason against this, except that there is less evidence than used to be thought for a serious Domitianic persecution. Like a great deal in ancient history, that does not mean that nothing was going on. The reference to Nero would then be explained by the widespread myth of Nero *redivivus* – either that Nero did not actually die but had gone to the east and would return to take vengeance on the Rome that had rejected him, or that he had indeed died but would revive and, once again, take vengeance. There are plenty of signs of this legend in chapters 12—18. But I am not entirely convinced that an earlier date, perhaps in late 68 or early 69, has to be ruled out. I have long thought that if St Paul had lived to see what we call 'the year of the four emperors', that is, 69, with Rome threatening to implode once more into the chaos from which Augustus claimed to have rescued it a century earlier, and then Jerusalem falling at the climax of it all, he might well have reckoned that this was the 'day of the Lord' of which he had warned, the day when the propagandists of 'peace and security' would be overtaken by sudden destruction (1 Thessalonians 5.3). And there is no reason to suppose that John, on Patmos, would have as good information as we do about the quick post-Nero succession of Galba, Otho, Vitellius and Vespasian. The numbered schemes in 17.9–13 may thus be strictly inaccurate yet sufficient to summon up the sense of a quick succession of rulers.

But equally, second, I believe this part of Revelation, though to be sure carrying very specific historical reference, is written in such a way as to open up a window on a much larger issue even than Rome and Nero. The model for Revelation 13 is, of course, Daniel 7, but it is noticeable that whereas Daniel has four beasts emerging from the sea, Revelation only has one – but it resembles three different animals, a leopard, a bear and a lion (13.2). Could it be that the writer is signalling that the real problem is not Nero himself but that which Nero, for the moment, embodies and expresses – something that will emerge in different guises at different times? This has been a popular route in exegesis, and the thing that Nero embodies is often labelled simply 'empire'. This points towards [116] a route, as well, through the fascinating but difficult chapter 17, where the 'great whore' Babylon is, of course, Rome itself, sustained by its sequence of emperors of whom the beast is one. (There is virtually no doubt about this identification. I say 'virtually' because one or two scholars have tried to make out that the great city which is destroyed is Jerusalem in AD 70, making way for the 'new Jerusalem'. This has the considerable apparent merit that it draws Revelation much closer to the so-called 'little apocalypse' in Mark 13 and parallels, which is undoubtedly about the fall of Jerusalem, and uses similar sources, from Jeremiah and elsewhere, to talk about it. If Revelation were written in 69 or 70, the sight of a city in smoking ruin would be spot on. But in Revelation this is more or less insupportable. The great trading city at whose fall merchants from around the world wail for their loss (18.11–19) cannot be other than Rome.)

But if we make this identification, we have three routes then open to us. First, we could say that the writer believed that the fall of Rome and the ushering in of the complete new age was imminent, and he was wrong.

(Unless you say that AD 69 was enough of a 'fall' to be going on with, which seems straining it more than a little.) Or we could say, with the dispensationalists, that though Rome may have been John's model he was in fact writing history in advance – the history, in fact, of our own day. The fact that this has been tried unsuccessfully again and again for a thousand years is, of course, not of itself enough to disprove it. False dawns do not mean that no such thing as a dawn exists. No: the main argument against the dispensationalists is their failure to take seriously the nature of John's symbolism. Or we could say that his prophecies are consistent with the fall of Rome, which happened some four hundred years after his day, in which case he was right – but we would still be left with a large hermeneutical gap, the one between his writing and that event, and then the larger one between the event and everything that has happened subsequently. Or we could say that, though John certainly envisaged Rome's fall, he saw it as encapsulating and embodying the disastrous and self-destructive way of life of all human empires, or all human empires of a certain type. This is the power of using 'Babylon' as *symbol*, rather than merely as *code* – a key hermeneutical point in several parts of the book. The Cain-and-Babel narrative, in which humans grasp at the eschatological city-gift but inevitably corrupt it and use it as an instrument of their own self-aggrandizing power, reaches various climactic moments, of which Rome is the obvious foreground for John. That is the interpretative route to which I am drawn.

This is not to make Rome a mere example of a larger general truth. Just as Jesus and his death and resurrection are not mere examples of the [117] larger truth of God's powerful redemptive love but are actually the midpoint of history, the point at which the ancient door of God's purposes swings open at last to reveal the new world that lies ahead, so Rome – the great power which at that unique moment summed up arrogant human rebellion – will fall. That will be the sign that Jesus has won the decisive victory, however many new Babylons, new Romes, appear between that time and the eventual consummation.

Two main features of the rule of the beast are of particular concern to John. The first is idolatrous worship; the second is aggressive economic exploitation. On the first: it is now well known that the imperial cult was the fastest-growing religion in first-century Asia Minor. Detailed studies, which could really have been undertaken since Deissmann but which had to wait for the failure of the Bultmann school before, like the horsemen of chapter 4, they could be unleashed, have now charged out, showing the way in which the worship of Rome itself, and of the emperor and his family, increasingly dominated city life not only in Ephesus, though that great city remained central, but throughout the province. We remind ourselves, of course, that religion and politics have hardly ever been separable throughout human history, as they still are not for most of the world, and that they were completely intermingled in the first-century Roman world. Ultimately, power was what counted, and power came from the gods. Worship that power and some of it rubs off on you. The dragon who has been thrown down from heaven – chapter 12 is John's reworking of the 'fall from heaven' taunt in Isaiah 14 and Ezekiel 28 – retains the power that is his as a former member of the heavenly court. We should not be surprised that, just as in those chapters an earlier myth of Lucifer's fall is being reworked in terms of oracles against Babylon and Tyre respectively, so here the dragon who has fallen gives his power to a 'beast' who later on supports the woman in whom Rome's seductive power is symbolized. Beast and dragon together appear to present an all-powerful combination. The second beast – now regularly understood to be the local officials who eagerly promoted the imperial cult – acts as a dragon in lamb's clothing (13.11), insisting, on pain of death, that the beast be worshipped.

This power is then worked out, particularly through the second beast in 13.16–17, in economic exploitation. To buy or sell, one must have the mark of the beast. Iron control of economic life, justified by the apparently overwhelming evidence for the beast's supernatural power (13.11–15), is one of the signs of the dragon's power. The kings of the earth have 'committed fornication' with Babylon. This metaphor develops powerfully through chapters 17 and 18, and forms another parody, this time [118] between Babylon as the great whore and the church as the bride of the lamb. In 18.3 we see the unholy combination of money, sex and power, used nakedly and for their own sake instead of for the good of humans and creation, and to God's glory. And, though the last generation of commentators has been quick to insist that 'fornication' is here simply a metaphor for power and money, the regular condemnation of idolatry, and its coupling with fornication in, for example, 2.14, 20, and the final condemnation of it in 21.8 and 22.15, seem to indicate that illicit sexual practices were one of many signs of the same overall bestial and dragon-inspired way of life which John is naming and shaming. The downgrading of responsibility into power for its own sake, of resources into money for its own sake, and of relationships into sex for its own sake, and the multiple combinations of all three, seem to lie at the heart of the critique of 'Babylonian' empire. At this point the 'masters of suspicion' (Nietzsche, Marx and Freud, described thus by Paul Ricoeur) seem to be spot on.

Here, described thus by Paul Ricoeur we must face the problem that the word 'empire', like the word 'apocalyptic', has had a chequered career over recent years. How fashions change. Twenty years ago, one heard almost nothing of 'empire' in New Testament studies; now it is omnipresent. The reasons for this have to do particularly with the shift away from existentialist interpretations to political ones, which itself has to do with the shift away from divinity schools to departments of religion. It also has to do with a rapidly rising awareness that today's world, following the collapse of the earlier European and Russian empires, has entered a new mode characterized by dangerous and unstable post-imperial societies on the one hand and by the rise of a different sort of empire, largely controlled by American interests, on the other. Since my topic here also includes the political 'implications' of Revelation, one can hardly omit this consideration, difficult though it is for a British citizen to tell his American cousins how not to organize their tea party. All this, as you know, came out sharply in the varied reactions after 9/11, with some, including some Americans, placing part of the blame on American imperialism, and others reacting with vitriolic anger to such a suggestion.

Part of our problem, I suggest, is that our mental grid for understanding power, and hence politics, is very different from that of a first-century Jew or Christian – and it is, of course, the latter grid that should control our reading of Revelation. Ever since the two great revolutions (American and French) of the late eighteenth century, European and American politics have increasingly seen themselves on a left–right spectrum (this was an invention of the French Revolutionaries), with the central problem of organizing a society, that of avoiding chaos on the one hand and tyranny [119] on the other, sloping off to the left among those who regard tyranny as the greater evil, and to the right among those who fear chaos most. The tyrannies of the twentieth century have pushed all our spectrums further to the left, with the exaltation of freedom over order, liberty over constraint. This works through contemporary western society in ways, and with multiple and sometimes paradoxical complexities and reactions, far too numerous even to list here.

But the result, especially among liberation theologians and those most aware of the post-colonial imperatives, has been that we have perhaps smiled our approval a bit too easily at the unmasking of the demonic and bestial regimes of Revelation 13 and 17. Again and again one meets the familiar antithesis between Revelation 13 and Romans 13, with the assumption that Revelation 13 is supporting our kind of left-wing politics and that Romans 13 is in favour of our kind of right-wing politics. Quite apart from considerations of canonical readings, and of the old but difficult rule of interpreting scripture by scripture, this simply fails, in both its parts, as a possible reading for first-century Jews or Christians. They simply didn't see things like we do.

Part of the problem, of course, is that various recent regimes and programmes have indeed appealed to these passages in support of nakedly left- or right-wing regimes. I think particularly of the almost obscene misuse of Romans 13 by the apartheid regime in South Africa, but also of the over-eager appropriation of Revelation 13 on the part of those with a rather obvious contemporary left-wing agenda. Another part of the problem is that exegetes have for years simply not been trained in the political thinking of the ancient world, so that just as we have exported sixteenth-century theology back into ancient Galatia and made Paul's letter address our post-Reformation concerns in their own terms, we have exported modern political assumptions back into ancient Asia Minor and made Revelation, and Paul too for that matter, address our political anxieties in their own terms.

The full antidote to this, and the proper ground-plan for a fresh appraisal, would, of course, be a detailed analysis of the larger world of ancient political thought and philosophy. There being no time (or, in my case, expertise) for such a thing, we may simply note the assumption that obtains right through Israel's scriptures, and on into the New Testament and early Christianity: that a proper, wise and effective ordering of society is one aspect of creational monotheism itself. In other words, the creator God wants humans to run his world, to make the wilderness flourish, and to build wise and healthy cities and run them humanely. But, from the Cain-and-Babel story onwards, it was recognized that the humans [120] on whom this responsibility falls will abuse it for their own ends – again, power, money and sex. The people of God, from Abraham onwards, are therefore constantly called to articulate and embody the God-given critique of this abuse of human responsibility; and, where such abuse occurs within God's people themselves, to address it prophetically by critique from within. Even the prophetic critique then needs critique: the distinction between false and true prophecy, so important for ancient Israel as for John the Seer, is the final layer in the multiply structured critique of power. But all this critique happens, not because power is bad in itself, but because it is abused. As with gardens and cities, so with power: the nostalgic or Romantic longing for a world without power is a desire to return to the nursery.

Joseph, the archetypal wise ancient Israelite, becomes second-in-command to Pharaoh – a kind of long-range paradoxical fulfilment of the place of human beings in Genesis 1 and 2. Daniel and his friends, having launched their highly daring critique of Babylonian power and come out smiling, resume their top jobs in the civil service. Paul, on trial in Acts, will respect the office while sharply criticizing the behaviour of its present holder. Polycarp, having declared roundly that he is not going to worship Caesar's image, knowing perfectly well where that will lead, agrees to civilized discussion with the Roman tribune on the grounds that the Christian scriptures teach him to respect those in authority. And Jesus himself, astonishingly, declares to Pilate that he could have no power over him were it not given him from above – meaning that the chief priests, who handed him over, had the greater sin. That Johannine theme is one of the sharpest and starkest: 'the ruler of this world' is cast out, overthrown, defeated – but he still rules by God's appointment. Part of the mystery of the cross itself, in John, lies exactly there. Tyranny is horrible; it is defeated by the cross. But the beasts that tyrannize the world in Daniel, and the great beast of Revelation 13, emerge from the sea. They are actually chaos-bringers. Their enforced and dehumanizing 'order' will in fact result in destruction, devastation and chaos come again.

It will not do, then, to read Revelation 12—19 with the kind of satisfied glow that comes from having all our nice liberal prejudices so easily confirmed. That does not imply, of course, that conservative prejudices are thereby confirmed instead; to imagine that would be simply to return to our normal and highly misleading left–right spectrum. Rather, we are called, I believe, to recognize the way in which bestial regimes rise, gain power, deceive many with their apparent success, attain economic supremacy, and then traffic so readily in all sorts of commodities including, as in 18.13, human beings. We are called to recognize that this happens and will happen, not because we should be aiming at a [121] world without structures of power but because power corrupts and the church must bear witness against that corruption, by critique, by non-collaboration, by witness and if need be by martyrdom. If the world were to listen to the church – and twice in my lifetime it has done so, in South Africa and in eastern Europe – the result should not be, though sadly it has sometimes been, a post-tyrannical chaos, but a fresh order, this time humanizing, this time striving afresh towards the garden city. As we all now know, and should have known long since, it will not do to assume that to overthrow a tyranny will result in the spontaneous growth of a healthy liberal democracy.

Of course, it will not do, either, to assume that what we think of as healthy modern western democracies are themselves the ultimate and eternal answer to the problems of Revelation 12—18. That is part of the eighteenth-century lie. In fact, the very separation of religion from politics which was so vital a part of that essentially deistic settlement on both sides of the Atlantic has resulted in regimes that, claiming their power gave them the right, acted in ways far more like the beasts than like the church. Pushing God out of the equation, politically in the 'vox populi, vox Dei' theory, scientifically with the neo-Epicureanism that created the context for the appropriation and exploitation of Darwin, economically with the 'invisible hand' of the market, and ethically with the post-Freudian assumption that sex will do what it will do – all this has the mark of the beast about it. These questions need to be worked out in other contexts, but it would be unwise to leave the central chapters of Revelation with the impression that bestial regimes are only and always non-democratic tyrannies. They may be closer to home than we like to think. Perhaps this is why the western church, so comfortable now within its present world, is not persecuted.

The vision of hope, then, confronts the regimes of the dragon and the beasts. And the church, caught up within and bearing witness to that hope, must constantly be refreshed in worship of the true God, the real Trinity, and so learn to avoid collusion with the beast in a way that will be much more demanding than any easy-going, one-size-fits-all solution would allow. The church is to live as the alternative *polis*, not by separating itself into sectarian isolation but by bearing witness, like Daniel and his friends, before kings and rulers. The aim is not to damn, but to redeem; the leaves on the tree are for the healing of the nations, and the gates stand open for the kings of the earth to bring their treasures. Only if we keep that goal before us will we avoid the isolation which is the mirror image of collusion. [122]

Revelation in Canon and Tradition

I have said enough, I hope, to give an overall picture of Revelation with particular reference to hope on the one hand and political implications on the other. I conclude with some reflections on the place of this book within the canon of Christian scripture – and on the puzzling relation between canon, itself an early part of tradition, and the larger tradition itself.

We have seen again and again, and could have developed much more, the ways in which Revelation continually draws on and develops many great themes and insights from the Old Testament prophets. This is not, we should stress, because scripture is simply a bran-tub out of which one might scoop enough, now and then, to make into a fresh meal. It is because Revelation, like all the New Testament, sees the Old Testament in terms of a great, complex, multifaceted *narrative* that came to its climax in Jesus the lion of Judah and has now generated a new narrative that is demonstrably the fulfilment of that ancient story but also in a significantly new mode. The fact that one could say just the same thing about Matthew or Paul or John or Hebrews makes the point. Revelation is, in Richard Bauckham's phrase, 'the climax of prophecy'. It seems that the writer is aware of this.

In particular, the story Revelation tells is the same story that all four gospels tell, though the church, which has done its best to hush up this fact about the gospels, has not usually recognized the similarity. The four canonical gospels (unlike the so-called gnostic 'gospels'!) tell the story of *how Jesus of Nazareth, Israel's Messiah, conquered the power of evil through his death and became the lord of the world.* They are not about how Jesus revealed that he was divine and then died so that we could go to heaven. They are about how Jesus acted as the embodiment of Israel's God to overthrow the usurping forces of evil and to establish, through his death, resurrection and ascension, God's kingdom on earth as in heaven. We see this strikingly, for instance, in Mark 10.35–45, where Jesus, faced with the foolish request of James and John, insists on a radical redefinition of power itself, and indicates that his forthcoming saving death will be the means of instantiating that radical redefinition. But the point is perhaps clearest in John, in the passages already referred to: the ruler of this world is cast out, is coming to get Jesus, has been condemned (12.31; 14.30; 16.11). This sequence leads the eye up to the final clash between Jesus and Pilate, where Jesus points out that his kingdom, which is not 'from' this world but is emphatically *for* this world, must be of a different sort from Caesar's, since if it were the normal kind his followers would fight. The attentive reader is left to ponder John's meaning, that somehow the [123] crucifixion that follows is the means by which all this is accomplished. The famous *tetelestai* (John 19.30) means more (though not less) than 'he has dealt with our sins'.

The same is true, though again often ignored, in Paul. By common consent, Romans 8 expresses something like the very heart of Paul, and here we have themes familiar now from a new angle in Revelation: abolition of accusation and condemnation, suffering as the prelude to glory, and particularly the new creation, born from the womb of the old. But then in the glorious coda to that chapter we have, in Pauline language and idiom, the theology of Revelation in a nutshell: God justifies, so no-one can condemn; Jesus died, so all will be well; suffering of every kind will not separate us from his love; and then, particularly, in all these things *we are more than conquerors* through him who loved us. It is not accidental that that Pauline phrase was used as the title for a famous commentary on Revelation: the theme of conquest, the unique victory of Jesus but also the consequent victory of his followers, is foundational for both writers. And, once we understand Revelation and, for that matter, the gospels, we can see that the great poem which Paul has placed at the heart of Philippians 2 is a more exact summary of their combined message than we might have imagined.

What does all this say about the tradition of the church? Sadly, it reveals the extent to which the tradition has got it both right and wrong. Of course, many Christian theologians and exegetes have glimpsed and expressed these themes, often far better than we can. But, equally, many have found them strange and off-putting, and have opted instead to place their emphasis on themes which, though themselves important, do not have the same high profile and urgent insistence in the New Testament itself. In particular, and speaking as one who has lived and worked in an established church, I believe that ever since the fourth century, but particularly in the mediaeval west, the great church has become increasingly alienated from the vision of God and God's kingdom which we find right across the New Testament, and by way of displacement has highlighted themes that, though themselves important, are not the urgent and driving heart of the canon itself. The radical misunderstandings of the dispensationalists are simply one recent outgrowth of this phenomenon. Far more dangerous, I think, are the more deep-rooted misunderstandings which have construed the Christian hope as simply 'going to heaven for ever', which have invoked the divinity of Jesus and his saving death in the service of that vision rather than in the service of the overthrow of the powers and the establishment of God's kingdom, and which have apparently abandoned politics as a dirty, bestial game and then have ended up colluding [124] with the deeper structures of abuse. Revelation shows us, in and through all its puzzling and arcane imagery, a vision of the creator God reclaiming sovereignty over the whole world through the slaughtering of the 'lamb', and entrusting to the present worshipping church the responsibility to bear witness to Jesus as the world's true lord, and to his way of victory as the power that is greater than the power of Babylon. That is the ground of Christian hope. That is the foundation of a Christian vision of the *polis*, in the present as much as in the ultimate future.

10
The Monarchs and the Message: Reflections on Bible Translation from the Sixteenth to the Twenty-First Century

The anniversary in 2011 of the King James ('Authorized') version of the Bible (KJV) was celebrated in various ways, and I was privileged to be part of two of those, one in New York and one in London. This happened to coincide with the publication of my own translation of the New Testament, entitled *The New Testament for Everyone* in the UK edition and *The Kingdom New Testament* in the USA. I was therefore all the more interested to look back to 1611 and to see how the translators had gone about their work and, in particular, how they had used, or modified, the work of the incomparable William Tyndale. I had made Tyndale's acquaintance in the early 1970s when studying the early English Reformation as part of my theology degree, at which point I discovered that though Tyndale himself had been republished many times, his close colleague and fellow martyr John Frith had not. I even managed, by close comparison of Frith's biblical citations with Tyndale's translation, to propose that Frith had done the first draft for Tyndale's 'Ephesians'. Editing Frith's works for a new edition (cited in the following piece) was my first major scholarly project, and Tyndale's vision, of fresh popular Bible translation as a major element in working for God's kingdom, was in my mind the whole time. Those of us who are now surrounded with dozens of new translations should never forget the debt we owe to those whose work cost them their lives.

[309] Introduction: Translation as Part of Biblical Faith

The phrase 'lost in translation' is such a cliché that it even became the title of a movie. There is a famous story about a missionary starting a sermon by quoting Jesus' words, 'I am the good shepherd', only to have the local inter-preter tell the congregation, 'He says he is a good man, and keeps goats.'

But things get lost just as effectively when, instead of translating, we stick with a foreign or ancient language that readers or hearers do not understand. This is so whether we are talking about the Bible or Shakespeare, about Schubert's songs or Wagner's operas. We want to get the force of the original, but we want to understand it as well. To translate is to distort, but not to translate can be a greater distortion still – especially when part of the point of the text is to communicate meaning, not just to produce melodious noise.

Opera-goers often have the luxury of surtitles, so that while the original words are sung on stage the translation can appear on a screen above. Despite the popularity of overhead projectors in church, I have not heard anyone suggesting that we should read the Bible out loud in its original Hebrew and Greek, with a modern English translation above. The reason we do not do that, I think, is not just the lack of competent people to read the original languages out loud. The reason is that *we believe in translation.* Putting the message *of* Jesus, and the message *about* Jesus, into different languages so that people can understand it in their own idiom is one of the things Christians characteristically do. The problems that this poses – the danger of things being 'lost in translation' – have been faced and sur-[310]-mounted again and again. When the church has refused to translate, for instance in the long Middle Ages when the western church had the Bible in an ancient Latin that few could understand, the ordinary people were at the mercy of whichever priest was claiming to interpret it. Now, happily, more or less all churches recognize the glorious duty of getting the Bible to people in their own tongue. One of the delights of being an Observer at the Synod of Bishops in Rome in late 2008, quite apart from the interesting contrast with our own dear Lambeth Conference a few months before, was the appeal from all round the hall for every man, woman and child across the Catholic world to have the Bible in his or her own mother tongue. If only they had said that in 1525, I thought, the entire history of the western world would have been very different.

That imperative to translate is, I take it, one of the powerful meanings that emerges from the story of Pentecost in Acts. When the spirit comes, the followers of Jesus are able to tell people about God's powerful deeds *in their own languages.* Christianity has been a translating faith from the outset.

Jesus' first followers were in any case already almost certainly bilingual. Their mother tongue was Aramaic (a language that developed from the classical Hebrew of the scriptures, a few hundred years earlier). But Greek had been everybody's second language in their part of the world for three hundred years by their day, and it is quite likely that many 'ordinary people' in the Middle East had a smattering of other languages as well. The question of how well Jesus himself could speak Greek – as, for instance, in his reported conversation with Pontius Pilate – remains largely unaddressed, and people can still write books as though Jesus was a monolingual Aramaic speaker.

That is highly unlikely. Bilinguality has historically been the norm in many parts of the world. Those of us who grew up with only one language, and have had to learn others at a later age, are the impoverished exceptions, and I suspect we often project our imagination on to other times and cultures. The little boy selling postcards outside the Church of the Holy Sepulchre in Jerusalem can not only speak Arabic and Hebrew but can also most likely get by in English, French, German and Spanish; why should Jesus not have been able to speak and read Aramaic and Hebrew and also to speak Greek? Only a monolingual world such as ours would need the old tease about the person struggling to learn other European languages: 'The French', says the pupil, 'call it a *cuiller*; the Italians call it a *cucchiaio*; the Germans call it a *Löffel*; the English call it a spoon – which [311] is after all what it is.' There is the easy mistake: the assumption that one's own language 'tells it like it is', that the words we use are the natural names for things, and that other languages are a kind of code for one's own. It is highly unlikely that any of the early Christians would have made that sort of mistake.

The question of translating scripture had already been faced when scribes, after the exile in Babylon, 'interpreted' the ancient Hebrew scriptures into Aramaic so the ordinary people could understand it. It was then faced even more directly by those who, somewhere between one and three hundred years before Jesus' day, translated Israel's scriptures from Hebrew and Aramaic into Greek. Christianity was born into a world where biblical translation was already an established fact. There was little sense, as there is in the stricter forms of Islam, that the sacred language was the 'real thing' and that translation meant desecration.

But if scriptural translation was already a fact of ancient Jewish life, with the Christian gospel there was an extra dimension. It was not just that there were some members of the wider believing community who happened not to read or speak Hebrew or Aramaic. It was, rather, that from the beginning the early Christians believed that Jesus was Israel's Messiah *and therefore the rightful lord of all the world*. This belief is etched across the New Testament, from the magi offering homage to the king of the Jews (Matthew 2.1–12) right through to the grand declaration, in the book of Revelation (11.15), that 'the kingdom of the world has passed to our Lord and his Messiah', if I may be permitted to quote my own translation here.[1] Put Pentecost in the middle of that sequence, and we get the picture. It is not just that some non-Jews might want to avail themselves of a new religious or spiritual opportunity. Nor is it the case, however, that the early Christian message had to be 'translated' away from 'Jewish' thought-forms and into 'non-Jewish' ones in order to be 'relevant' to the wider world. It is, rather, the much more robust claim – one that remains unknown to many modern western Christians! – that Israel's Messiah was supposed to be king over the whole world, and that the resurrection had demonstrated Jesus to be this Messiah, this world king. This is, and remains, a deeply Jewish message, rooted in Israel's scriptures, but it is a Jewish message that in its very nature demands translation. The message of the cross, declares Paul, is 'a scandal to Jews and folly to Greeks'. But the scandal has nothing to do with its being expressed in a different language, and the folly has nothing to do with Greeks having to learn Hebrew to read about their new lord and saviour. This is the primary root-meaning of the title of this paper, [312] 'The Monarchs and the Message'. For the early Christians, Jesus was the monarch, king of all the world; so the message had to be translated.

Translating the message into the world's many languages is therefore organically linked to the central claim of the gospel itself. Not to translate might imply, perhaps, that Jesus belonged, or belonged specially, to one group only – a dangerous idea that some of the earliest New Testament writings strongly opposed. That the New Testament is written in Greek, not Hebrew or Aramaic, tells its own story: this, the early writers were saying by clear implication, is the Jewish message *for the whole world*. To translate is to imply that, just as the gospel of Jesus is for all people, so the early Christian writings that bear witness to Jesus are for all people. No doubt all human languages will find it a challenge, this way or that, to express in their own idiom what the early Christians were trying to say in theirs. Losing things in translation will always be a risk. But it is a risk we recognize. It is the same risk that all Christians face when they try to express their loyalty to Jesus in their own particular lives and situations. Translation is difficult, but it is the same sort of difficulty that we face in discipleship itself.

But once we have the ancient scriptures in English, is not that enough? Should we not be content with the wonderful earlier translations, stretching back in a long and distinguished line through the King James Version of 1611

---

1   Wright 2019b, 554.

to the great pioneer, William Tyndale, and behind him to John Wycliffe? And haven't there been far too many translations even in the last ten or twenty years? Are we not in danger of flooding the market? What about the later monarchs, particularly the two who bookend that great translating century that we might date from 1511 to 1611, from Tyndale to Laud: from Henry VIII, who staunchly opposed translating the Bible, to James I, who commissioned and authorized it?

Monarchs and Messages in the Reformation Era

Throughout my work of translation, I have had in mind the debt we all still owe to William Tyndale. His story has often been told: on the run in a foreign land, in hiding, under pressure from rival Protestants with variant theologies as well as from King Henry's spies and agents. Tyndale has recently caught the public's eye once more through his appearance in Hilary Mantel's award-winning *Wolf Hall*. For some of us, though, he has been a lifelong hero. He was determined to do whatever it would take to break the long centuries of clerical monopoly and manipulation of the [313] sacred text – the long years when, because no new translation was being done, major distortions were happening instead – and to get the Bible into the hands of the ploughboy, the ordinary men and women, where it belonged. He knew it might cost him his life, and it did.

Why was it so difficult? Here we meet the obvious but still interesting point that the political situation of Tyndale and the King James translators could hardly be more different. Tyndale was faced with implacable opposition, because everyone from the king downward knew that a new Bible, one that ordinary people could read for themselves, could and would unleash all kinds of new forces that would be impossible to control. No doubt there was a noble motive alongside that of fear. Ancient and mediaeval political theorists knew just as well as we do that, though social stability is not everything, social instability is normally dangerous – dangerous not only to the wealthy and powerful but also to the 'little people' who are caught up in the middle of it all.

Tyndale's understanding, however, was clear: the social, cultural and political scene needed radical transformation, and a fresh and freshly understood Bible would be a key element in this work. I well remember when I first read Tyndale, looking for good Reformation soteriology, being surprised at how much political argument was there too. It does not surprise me now.

Tyndale's translations, and his wider theological writings, including the prefaces to the individual books, were all aimed at enabling a genuine upward intellectual and spiritual mobility among the ordinary people. A freshly understood Bible, he believed, would not only result from a change in the political climate but would also help to bring that about. Here is the difference. Tyndale was translating with radical intent. King James's appointed scholars were translating – or rather, editing and adapting Tyndale, the Bishops' Bible and the rest – with stabilizing intent. To which of these tasks, they might ask us, is the Bible better suited? It is a good question, and it has been in my mind on and off throughout my own years as a translator, which include the seven years of my active episcopate.

Tyndale, classically, was successful. 'Lord,' he prayed as they strangled him at the stake, 'open the king of England's eyes.'[2] The sign of that prayer being answered came, within a few years of his death, as the moderate Reformation towards which Thomas Cromwell at least had been pushing Henry for some time arrived, and an English Bible was placed in every parish church in the land. The rest – as they often say, but in this case it is true – is history. No less than 87 per cent of the King James Version is pure Tyndale, including some passages for which King James and his transla-[314]-tors are regularly congratulated. But Tyndale's testimony remains exemplary: 'I call God to record against the day we shall appear before our Lord Jesus, to give a reckoning of our doings, that I never altered one syllable of God's word against my conscience.'[3] Oh, he had his theological leanings, of course, as we all do. But he was determined that the message should get out, no matter what the monarch might say; even though he knew that, ultimately, the quickest way to get the message spread across the land was to bring the monarch on side. He was a revolutionary, but a revolutionary with a clear vision of a new, post-revolution stability in which the king would commission and support the work of bringing the Bible to the masses.

Back in the early 1970s when I first made Tyndale's acquaintance, I determined that I should be able to say the same about my own use of scripture as he had done about his. (I did not, at the time, imagine for a moment that I would end up as a translator, but when I did I continued to have him in mind.) When, in the 1990s, I was invited for the first time into Number 10, Downing Street, to discuss the offer of a senior job in the Church of England, I took time beforehand to stop and gaze at Tyndale's statue, a couple of streets

---

2 Daniell 1994, 383.

3 Letter of Tyndale to John Frith, in Wright 1978, 494f.

away. There he stands, looking out across the Thames, with his printing press and his Bibles. We are not worthy to stand in his shadow. I wanted to be sure he would have approved of what I was doing. Would it help to get the Bible into the hands and hearts of the people? That was his goal, and I have tried to make it mine too.

Tyndale's vision, then, was realized, even at the cost of his own life. There then followed, of course, the turbulent period in which many others lost their lives, as monarchs and translations came and went. But, as is now well known, it was with a very different vision that King James, canny Scot that he was, commissioned the translation for which his name would become world-famous. Faced as he was with the two main parties within the church, not to mention with the challenge of holding together two very different countries under the one rule, he hit on the idea of a joint translation project as a way not of bringing about revolution but of preventing one. For him, the monarchical message was that of unity – a theme that could, of course, claim considerable support from the New Testament itself. Unity is not the only virtue enjoined by the early Christian writers – it must, they insist, be balanced with holiness, for a start – but it is one of the great goods for which Christians should strive. So King James's translators, whose story has been told and retold times without number over the last few months, were set to work with a purpose at once very like Tyndale's and very unlike. He was translating in order to stir things up; they were translating in order to quieten things down again. [315]

And where he had succeeded in his aim, they largely failed in theirs. The new Bible did not catch on at once and was powerless, thirty years later, to prevent the outbreak of civil war and the regicide to which it led. The compromise between James's bishops and England's Puritans may have lasted for his own reign, not least because of his strict control over what the Bible was allowed to say about monarchs – a point on which Tyndale had been much more dangerously explicit. But in the next reign, Bible or no Bible, the compromise did not hold. The influence of Geneva on the Puritans was too strong: not for nothing is the English Reformer commemorated on the great Reformation monument in Geneva not Tyndale, not Cranmer or Ridley or Latimer, not even Richard Hooker, but Oliver Cromwell. That too was a shock to me as a young man, indicating the radical difference between what I saw the Reformation as being all about and how people saw things in Switzerland. Although since the Enlightenment we have tended to downplay the political side of theological agendas, there was no such reticence in either the sixteenth or the seventeenth century.

The difference in political context between Tyndale and King James's translators is reflected fairly directly in their words and phrases. No doubt a good deal here depends on other factors as well, not least the explosion of high-calibre English writing that came about in the age of Spenser and Shakespeare. Tyndale was writing before Hooker; James's translators, after him. But we can detect more than just the shifting of language in the contrast between the two. Even though the King James Version employs nearly 90 per cent of Tyndale, the changes are interesting and telling. One of Tyndale's modern editors, David Daniell, puts it like this:

> If 'the former things are passed away' is preferred to 'the old things are gone', then Tyndale will be disliked and there is no way to mend it. Tyndale was writing for ordinary men and women reading the Greek New Testament in English to themselves and to each other, round the table, in the parlour, under the hedges, in the fields; not for those obediently sitting in rows in stone churches being done good to by the squire at the lectern.[4]

No doubt we can detect in Daniell's polemical tone his own dislike of the social and cultural setting of later stolid Anglican worship. King James's translators were not only writing for the squire to read to the peasants, even if by the eighteenth and nineteenth century that was, de facto, quite often the case. But the point is clear, and interesting in one [316] particular. Daniell draws attention to the fact that Tyndale was translating very close to the Greek. Greek often goes quite directly into English, and lends itself far more than Latin to clear, sharp English prose – a point that Tyndale himself put forth in *The Obedience of a Christian Man* (1528). King James's translators were the sort who naturally thought and wrote in Latin, and that may have been part of the point. Though they were, of course, working with the Greek, Hebrew and Aramaic, they were scholars mindful of the dignity of their role, not fugitives desperate to get the message across. Their version, for all its brilliance and its frequent skill in gently polishing Tyndale's rough edges, had the effect – it can hardly have been completely accidental – of making the Bible once more a somewhat elevated book, just a little above the common reader. The difference between the two versions in style thus mirrors the political message. Tyndale seldom missed a chance of cutting princes down to size (though he will not alter what Paul says in Romans 13, or Peter in 1 Peter 2); King James's translators knew that that was what

---

4   Daniell 1989, xxvii.

their master did not want at any price. But, in terms of style, Tyndale had already let the English cat out of the bag. He was responsible almost single-handedly for making the native language, which at the start of the sixteenth century was barely respectable in educated circles, into the supple, powerful, sensitive vehicle it had become by the time of Shakespeare. Thus the implicit message of his translation, as well as the explicit ones, created a world of Englishness the like of which his own monarch, Henry VIII, could never have imagined.

Many passages might make the point about style. Frequently the KJV goes with Tyndale, inch for inch (sometimes indeed into manifest error, as in Romans 6.11, where Paul's declaration that you are dead to sin but alive to God 'in Christ Jesus' has become, in both, 'through Jesus Christ', a significant difference). In the Johannine prologue, often quoted as an example of the wonders of the KJV, the only significant difference is that Tyndale refers to the Word as 'it', where KJV has 'he', until we get to the climax, John 1.14, where for Tyndale's simple word *saw* the KJV has *beheld*: 'we saw the glory of it', says Tyndale; 'we beheld his glory', says the KJV. I wonder if the latter was trying to bring out a possible force of the Greek *etheasametha*. I rather doubt it. I think they were going for sonorous Jacobean prose, which they certainly achieved. Famously the KJV translates *agapē* as 'charity'. Many grumbled when modern translations replaced it with 'love'. Not many realized that the modern translations were simply reverting to what Tyndale had had in the first place. [317]

Not that Tyndale always went for the shorter word. The prodigal son's elder brother, on returning home, hears 'musick and dancing' (Luke 15.25) in the KJV; for Tyndale it was 'minstrelsy and dancing'. (The Greek is *symphōnia*, which implies a plurality of instruments; perhaps one should translate the phrase as a hendiadys, and render it 'a dance band'.) More significantly, in line with his ecclesiology (one of the reasons Henry wanted to suppress him), Tyndale regularly translates *ekklēsia* as 'congregation', whereas the KJV simply says 'church', and renders *presbyteros* as 'elder' rather than 'priest'. (This was the same impulse that made Tyndale insert little jabs into the margin, such as his famous line at 1 Thessalonians 4.11, where Paul exhorts his readers to 'study to be quiet, to meddle with your own business, and to work with your own hands'. Tyndale's comment is pithy: 'A good lesson for monks and idle friars'.[5] Not the sort of thing that King James would have wanted to see.)

---

5 Daniell 1989, 302.

Sometimes, too, Tyndale's language now seems quaintly old-fashioned to us, partly I suspect because the later popularity of the KJV sustained some usages that might otherwise have dropped out, whereas Tyndale's words have moved on. When the holy city comes down from heaven in Revelation 21, we are used to the idea that she is 'prepared as a bride adorned for her husband' (KJV, v. 2); we might raise our eyebrows at Tyndale's word, that she is prepared as a bride 'garnished' for her husband. What King James's translators referred to as 'the days of unleavened bread' (Acts 12.3) were for Tyndale 'the days of sweet bread'; Tyndale clearly saw 'leaven' as making bread sour, so that in 1 Corinthians 5.6 'a little leaven soureth the dough', and the Christian must have 'the sweet bread of pureness and truth' [5.8].

All this merely illustrates T. S. Eliot's sorrowful observation that words will not stay in place: they change their meaning, lose old resonances and pick up new ones. Every serious student of Shakespeare or Milton, George Herbert or John Donne, knows that they used words in ways that do not quite correspond to the ways we use them now. And then there is a real problem, as C. S. Lewis pointed out in *Studies in Words.*[6] Faced with a word we do not know, we may look it up in a dictionary. But when it is a word we use every day, we probably will not look it up – even though it may have changed its meaning since the time the author was writing. Then we are condemned to misread the word, the sentence and the passage.

We can all spot this going on when earlier translations of the Bible refer to sums of money. In the KJV the householder agrees with the day labourers to pay them a penny a day for their work (Matthew 20.2). (Tyndale has a nice note at 22.19, where, explaining the tribute penny, he says, 'A [318] penny is ever taken for that the Jews call a sickle, and is worth 10 pence sterling'.[7]) A 'penny' may have been a day's wage in the early seventeenth century, but it certainly is not in the early twenty-first century. I have tried in my own translation to cope with this in various ways, determined to bring out the flavour of each passage rather than swap a familiar but hopelessly inaccurate term ('penny', 'pound' or 'dollar') for an accurate but hopelessly unfamiliar one ('talent', 'shekel', 'denarius'). But we can see that problem a long way off. It is quite different when we come to a word like *Christ*: what shall we do then? And this brings us to our own day, where the 'monarch' is a benevolent constitutional monarch, and the real power is wielded by the elected dictatorship we call the government. Where does the translator's shoe pinch now?

---

6 Lewis 1960.
7 Daniell 1989, 50.

The Message of the Monarch for Tomorrow's World

For many people in the western world, *Christ* is simply a swearword. Many have forgotten, if they ever knew, that this word has for two thousand years been firmly attached to one human being in particular. Many who have not forgotten that basic point, however, have assumed that 'Christ' is simply the 'surname' or family name of Jesus of Nazareth, so that 'Jesus Christ' corresponds to 'John Smith' or 'Mary Fitzpatrick'. Again, many who have not made *that* mistake have supposed that the word *Christ* conveys, and always did convey, the Christian belief that Jesus was and is the second person of the Trinity, so that 'Jesus' is the 'human' name of the person concerned and 'Christ' is his 'divine' name or title. Books have appeared with titles such as 'Jesus Who Became Christ', hinting that Jesus started off as an ordinary human and was only subsequently elevated to divine status. There we have three quite different meanings of 'Christ' that people today may well 'hear' when they hear the word. And here is the point: *none of these corresponds to what the word conveyed in the first century.* And I believe that none of them makes the point that the New Testament needs to make in our own day. No translation is 'neutral'. Perhaps the biggest difference between the time of the Reformation and our own is that today most people in the western world would simply assume that the New Testament is a 'religious' text that has therefore nothing, or next to nothing, to do with how the world is run, with what we now call social or political issues. That merely shows our own captivity to post-Enlightenment deism or Epicureanism and to the new theories of the state that it produced. What can the translator do – what *must* the [319] conscientious translator do – to enable the New Testament itself to make its proper, and deeply subversive, point?

In the first century the word *Christ*, or rather the Greek word *Christos*, which occurs hundreds of times in the New Testament, was the translation of the Hebrew or Aramaic term *māšîaḥ*, 'Messiah'. 'Messiah' means 'anointed' or 'anointed one'. In ancient Israel various people were anointed as the sign of God's commissioning: prophets, priests and above all kings. But in Jesus' day the various meanings of 'the anointed one' had narrowed down to a single focus: the coming king from the line of David, the one who would rule the whole world and establish God's justice within it. This expectation was popular (though not universally so) in first-century Judaism, and there were various interpretations of who such a 'Messiah' would be, what he would do, and so on. Jesus' followers believed that this range of interpretations had been suddenly and sharply redefined in and around their master, who had proclaimed God's kingdom, who had been executed by the Romans as the would-be 'King of the Jews', but who had been raised from the dead by God and thereby declared to be truly the Messiah, Israel's king, the world's rightful lord.

Comparatively few modern Christians, let alone modern non-Christians, have much inkling of all this. But unless we try to understand it we shall never grasp two-thirds of what they were talking about. The word *Christ*, then, serves both as a central example of the problem of translation, and also as a pointer to the reality (God's claim on the whole world through his anointed servant) that is the ground plan on which the project of biblical translation stands, from which it gains its raison d'être and legitimacy. Jesus' own radical redefinition of what 'lordship' was all about demands it. He will not impose his rule on people from a great height in a language they do not understand. He wants them to know, to love. Biblical translation aims to embody that quite specific aspect of the divine plan and intention.

All right: how then shall we translate *Christos*? No one English word or expression will convey what the Greek word meant to Paul, say, or to Matthew. But to leave it as 'Christ' is, straightforwardly, to falsify it. I have experimented with saying 'King' or 'Messiah' or 'the anointed one' as the different contexts seem to me to demand or at least to permit. Doing that does not solve everything. You cannot capture the full texture of an ancient word with any single, unadorned, unexplained contemporary one. But simply saying 'Christ' does not get us anywhere, except back into multiple misunderstandings. Yes: translating *Christos* as 'King', **[320]** which I have often done, raises all kinds of questions. But not to do so, to leave 'Christ' as either a proper name or a merely 'religious' word, would be to falsify it.

Old words, then, can mislead, or simply go quiet on us. One specific aspect of that problem is that for many centuries in the Christian church the fundamentally Jewish rootedness of early Christianity was screened out and, with it, points like the one I have just made about 'Christ'. This is a problem with the whole tradition from the KJV and, indeed, from Tyndale before it. Faced with this, the translator has to do something (I believe) to joggle the elbow of the reader, to flash a warning light, to signal that things may not mean exactly what has been expected. This corresponds to something Jesus himself did all the time. He told strange, teasing stories about what God's kingdom was really like, to shake his hearers out of their normal assumptions. Perhaps different translations can and should do the same today.

All this may seem disconcerting to 'ordinary' readers, particularly those who themselves speak only a single language. Does this mean we cannot be sure what the Bible actually means? No: for much of the time there is no reasonable doubt. The story of Jesus, and its basic meaning, normally stand out clearly, even through uncertain or distorted translations. (That is not to say that all modern translations are as good as one another, or as good as they should be.) But if we want to get a better idea of why fresh translations are always needed, we have to be clear about rejecting the common idea that each language has a set of words that simply do the same job in that country as their equivalents do in ours. That works all right for 'spoon' and 'fork', for 'mother' and 'father', for 'farm' and 'river' and 'mountain' and 'egg'. And a great deal besides. But there are numerous exceptions. I once received a postcard from a friend in Venice. The picture was of St Mark's Square. Printed on the card was the Italian phrase, Campo S. Marco. But someone had added an English trans-lation, obviously by looking up *campo* in the dictionary. The result: 'St Mark's Playing Fields' – and not a blade of grass, or a goalpost, in sight.

And this is just the beginning. What about a word like *justice*? When ancient Greek speakers used the word *dikaiosynē*, made famous by Plato in the long discussion of 'justice' in his *Republic*, did they mean the same as a mediaeval Latin writer would have meant by *iustitia*, also translated as 'justice'? And when, in late mediaeval English, the word *righteousness* was used to translate those same words and their cognates, was there an inner core of meaning that was simply picked up from the earlier words and [321] deposited in the later, or were other ideas creeping in as well? And when we, today, hear 'justice', 'righteousness' and similar words, do we still hear the nuances and overtones that Paul would have wanted us to hear when he used that language?

Of course not. The English word *righteousness* has had a chequered career over the centuries. For many people it now means 'self-righteousness', a priggish, holier-than-thou attitude that would have horrified Paul himself. But there is more. For Paul, soaked in the Hebrew scriptures both in their original version and in their Greek translation, the word resonated loudly with the hymns and prophecies of ancient Israel, celebrating the fact that Israel's God was faithful to his ancient promises and therefore would deliver his people from their enemies. There is no way that a modern English reader, faced with the word 'righteousness', or for that matter 'justice', will catch any glimpse of that warm-blooded, rich and tender, covenanted love of God for his people. Equally, if we translate the word as 'covenant faithfulness', we will miss the fact that it still carries plenty of meaning to do with 'justice', with things that are wrong being put right at last. We just do not have a single word, or even a single phrase, that will convey all that Paul meant when he wrote *dikaiosynē*. The best the translator can do is to set up signposts pointing in more or less the right direction, and encourage readers to read on and glimpse the larger picture within which the words will flesh themselves out and reveal more of the freight they had all along been carrying. On this point, I am sorry to say, Tyndale was in my view much too enthusiastic a follower of Martin Luther. In the famous passage in Romans 3, he oscillates between 'the righteousness that cometh of God' in 3.21, 'the righteousness which is good before God' in 3.22, 'the righteousness which before him is of valour' in 3.25, and 'the righteousness that is allowed of him' in 3.26: a combination of the genitive of origin and the objective genitive, with no sense (in my view) of what this key technical term is all about.

That is another sharp-edged example of the problem. Translation is bound to distort. But not to translate, and not to upgrade English translations quite frequently, is to collude with a different and perhaps worse kind of distortion. Yesterday's words may sound fine, but they may not say any longer what they used to say.

Another related problem faces the translator of any ancient text: the evidence is thin, and tricky to handle. Someone who compiles a modern English dictionary is swamped with information. Every novel, every newspaper, every political speech may contain either new words or new [322] shades of meaning for existing ones. Keeping track of these, and laying them out clearly, has driven the world-famous *Oxford English Dictionary* away from print altogether and into an online edition capable of being constantly updated. But with the ancient world things are very different. It would be possible for a single-minded scholar to read right through all known ancient Greek literature in a couple of years. One might have to give up watching television or playing golf, but it could be done. And in that entire body of literature, including inscriptions and papyrus fragments, many words occur only once. There are several such in the New Testament. And many others occur so infrequently that trying to catch their precise nuance is delicate, tricky and often quite uncertain. Older attempts to tell you what a word meant by tracking its supposed etymology have some value, but they cannot do the whole job for you. Words are like people: discovering where they have come from does not necessarily tell you where they are now going to. We need etymology, but even more we need comparative studies from every possible angle. A half-hidden inscription here, a half-torn papyrus there, may yield clues and hints as to how an otherwise opaque word was being used in the first century. Work like this is going on all the time, and translators of the New Testament need to keep abreast of it.

Here I gladly acknowledge the contribution of one volume that has been at my elbow throughout my work on this project. I acquired my first copy of W. F. Arndt and F. W. Gingrich's famous *Greek-English Lexicon of the New Testament* when I graduated in theology in 1973. That was actually the second edition of their work, based in turn on the fourth edition of a much older German lexicon by Walter Bauer. Since then, the redoubtable American scholar F. W. Danker has laboured mightily to upgrade 'Arndt and Gingrich', producing a new, third edition so much superior to its predecessors that it is more or less a whole new work. It arrived on my desk early in 2000, when I was about to begin my present translation with a draft of Mark and Luke.[8] The arrival of Danker's new lexicon was providential. Word after word is laid out with its multiple possible meanings, with classical and other references as well as the biblical ones, and with secondary literature. So much new material has been brought together, so many out-of-the-way texts have been located, compared and discussed, the work of so many scholars has been collated to fine-tune our understanding, that in literally hundreds if not thousands of passages we now glimpse, far more accurately than our predecessors, what precisely the New Testament writers intended. The task, like other aspects of this work, [323] remains never-ending, but with Danker it has taken a giant step forward. I and others are privileged to stand on his shoulders.

Or at least to wobble there. There are at least two sorts of accuracy. The first sort, which a good lexicon will assist, is the technical accuracy of making sure that every possible nuance of every word, phrase, sentence and paragraph has been rendered into the new language. But a second sort of accuracy is perhaps deeper than this: the accuracy of flavour and feel. It is possible, in translation as in life, to gain the whole world and lose your own soul – to render everything with a wooden, clunky, lifeless 'accuracy' from which the one thing that really matters has somehow escaped, producing a gilded cage from which the precious bird has flown. Such translations – the remarkable English Revised Version of the 1880s might be one such – are of considerable use to the student who wants to get close to the original words. They are of far less use to the ordinary Bible reader who wants to be

---

8 The reason I undertook this translation in the first place, I should perhaps make clear, was not for its own sake. I had agreed to write a series of guides to the New Testament – the For Everyone series – and one thing I did not want to confuse my readers with was a discussion of differences among translations, or the reasons why I disagreed with one or other version on this or that point. Providing my own translation was the solution.

grasped by the actual message of the text. Ideally, of course, the two would run together. But granted the impossibility (for the reasons already given) of the strictest kind of 'accuracy', it is important from time to time to go for the accuracy of flavour and feel. The whole point of the New Testament, after all, is that it is one of the most dramatic, subversive and life-giving collections of writings ever assembled. Lose that and you have lost the plot.

That, alas, has happened – even in the case of some of the greatest translations ever – even in the KJV itself. Anyone who doubts this should consider Romans 8.19–21:

> For the earnest expectation of the creature waiteth for the manifestation of the sons of God. For the creature was made subject to vanity, not willingly, but by reason of him who hath subjected the same in hope, because the creature itself also shall be delivered from the bondage of corruption into the glorious liberty of the children of God.

In Paul's original Greek, this is one of the most visionary, explosive short passages anywhere in his writings. It offers a bright, clear glimpse not only of humans being rescued from sin and death but of all the world on tiptoe with hope for its own redemption, for the time when God will do for the whole of creation what he did for Jesus at Easter. But for anyone not already in tune with what Paul is saying, the phrase 'the earnest expectation of the creature', offered by the KJV, would be enough to throw them right off the scent. Romans 8 offers plenty of other passages to get one's teeth into; [324] one might be tempted to frown, shrug the shoulders and read on to find something a bit clearer. Cosmic hope, it seems, did not play much of a role in sixteenth-century theology, and King James's translators were not, perhaps, as interested in this passage as they might have been, even though it is arguably the climax of the whole letter to that point. What they wrote was a technically correct reproduction of the Greek. But it failed to catch the exalted and sustained excitement of this decisive passage:

> Yes: creation itself is on tiptoe with expectation, eagerly awaiting the moment when God's children will be revealed. Creation, you see, was subjected to pointless futility, not of its own volition, but because of the one who placed it in this subjection, in the hope that creation itself would be freed from its slavery to decay, to enjoy the freedom that comes when God's children are glorified.
> (Wright 2019b)

I have therefore tried, in my own translation, to go for accuracy of flavour and feel, without sacrificing (I hope) word-by-word linguistic accuracy. I have wanted to catch that sense of explosive and subversive excitement, not only in Romans 8 but in passage after passage and book after book.

No doubt I have failed in all sorts of ways. But I have had to hold my nerve and do things that, if I were teaching a class in New Testament Greek, I would forbid. For instance, Greek regularly connects sentences with 'and', 'but', 'therefore', 'for' and so on. English regularly does not. There are other ways in which Greek and English go more naturally together than either does with Latin; but in this respect they are very different. English speakers leave the logical connections to be made by the reader. Sometimes we can give a nudge this way or that; often we cannot and (in my view) should not. Many times the 'right' translation of such a connecting word, in terms of idiomatic and lively English, may be a comma, semicolon or full stop. The point is this. Paul's letters are highly energetic. Filling translations of his works with stodgy, chewy words and phrases will give the reader indigestion. They may be 'accurate' in one sense, but they are inaccurate in another. Such challenges mean that translation remains exciting, demanding and never-ending.

The same has happened in the gospels. We live in a well-developed novelistic culture where dialogue is presented by means of starting a new paragraph each time a different person speaks. All the writer has to do is to indicate occasionally who is talking, in case the reader has lost the thread. It would be tedious to go on repeating 'he said' and 'she said', still less 'he replied to her' or 'she, by way of answer, said to him'. But [325] the New Testament writers did not have the luxury of our printed layout. Their works were copied out, not only with virtually no paragraph breaks, but with no sentence breaks – *and with no breaks between words, either.* The reader needed a lot more help, and the gospel-writers provided it. But we, who do the same thing by other means, would be frankly pedantic if we constantly said things like 'Jesus answered and said to them'. I have resisted the temptation to omit those connecting phrases altogether. But I have felt free to streamline, knowing that the way a modern English page is laid out will tell the reader exactly the same thing that Matthew and the others were communicating, but without the ponderous little clauses that he needed and we do not.

This leads me to a reflection about what you might call the 'level' of the translation. It has long been reckoned that the KJV employs an 'elevated' English style. It is grand, splendid, magisterial. It strides down the road with measured tread, never in a hurry, looking to right and left and bowing to passers-by. Its cadences roll off the tongue and ring round the rafters, especially when helped on their way by the ample acoustics of an ancient parish church or cathedral. The problem is that most of the New Testament is not like that. Luke and Acts are, up to a point. Hebrews, too. But Mark? Paul?

Mark? Of course not. Mark is always in a hurry, or makes out that everybody else is. His gospel reads as though it were dictated at speed, albeit from a well-stored and much-rehearsed corporate and individual memory. It is more like a scruffy revolutionary tract than a polished, leather-bound treatise. And Paul? Well, was anything less measured, less grand and magisterial, than the letter to the Galatians? Is anything in the New Testament less polished, more jerky and disjointed, torn between anguish and irony, than the second letter to the Corinthians? Granted, Paul gets into a more measured mode in Romans. That all-time masterpiece seems to have been composed with considerable care, so that its main sections and smaller segments balance one another, rising and falling in a flow of argument. The material is every bit as passionate as Galatians or 2 Corinthians; but now it has found a vessel that can contain the passion and sustain it over a longer period. But for the most part Paul's letters are just that: letters, usually in a hurry, often anxious, frequently glancing over the shoulder at the next wave of pagan attack or unjust criticism. Paul could out-think most philosophers; let us be in no doubt. But it would falsify his letters to dress them up as polished philosophical tractates. [326]

I have therefore tried, again no doubt with mixed success, to allow the New Testament to speak with different tones of voice, aiming often for street-level English rather than the somewhat donnish tradition of the King James, the Revised Standard Version and the New Revised Standard Version. That is the tradition on which I was brought up, and which I still use regularly. It is not perfect, but it is a lot better than many of the alternatives. But I do not know many people today who actually talk in the way the Revised Standard Version/New Revised Standard Version tradition writes, and I suspect most of my readers do not know many such people either. (I hasten to add that the same goes for most other modern versions as well.) In my own translation, I have tried to do what I think most of the New Testament is doing: to convey the actual tones of voice of actual people.

One other thing I have had in mind is that, despite the noble vision of King James and his translators, I think it is splendid to have a wide variety of translations on offer. For King James, a single 'Authorized Version' appeared as a political and social necessity. Somehow, it was hoped, this book would hold together the warring factions that threatened to tear apart both church and country. The Civil War in the next generation showed only too clearly how strong the danger was, and how far short the noble aim fell. But the KJV weathered the storm, not least by the strength of its scholarship. People sometimes mock the idea of a committee producing a document, but with the KJV it was not like that. It was an exercise in collaborative scholarship. Many eyes, minds, hearts and voices all contributed, anticipating in a measure the way in which, today, international journals, seminars and conferences enable a rich conversation to take place and, sometimes at least, to produce fresh insight and clarity.

In the first decade of the seventeenth century, then, many translators contributed to one Bible, intending that it should be the only one. I, in the first decade of the twenty-first century, have tried to do the opposite. I have worked alone (except for the remarkable and vital help that I have received, late in the day, from Dr Michael Lakey), intending that this translation should be one of many. When people ask me which version of the Bible they should use, I have for many years told them that I do not much mind as long as they always have at least two open on the desk. It is, of course, better for everyone to learn Greek and Hebrew. The finest translations are still, basically, a matter of trying to play a Beethoven symphony on a mouth organ. But what a new translation can perhaps do today is to jolt people out of the familiar, and open their eyes and imaginations [327] to new possibilities: particularly to the new possibilities that speak of the ultimate monarchy, of Jesus as the king of the world in a way that Paul and Mark understood well but most contemporary readers have hardly begun to imagine.

Like all translations, mine falls well short. It is a signpost, not the reality itself. But I hope it is a true signpost: in particular, that it is a signpost that will alert the reader to what seems to me the forgotten truth of the early Christian message. The American edition of this translation is called *The Kingdom New Testament*, and that makes the point. Most people today have forgotten, if they have ever known, what it might mean to claim, as Jesus did, that God was becoming king on earth as in heaven. Today's ruling powers, whether monarchies or not, need this message, and the church needs to be able to announce and live it. I will be happy if my translation goes even a little way towards bringing about that end.

11

Joy: Some New Testament Perspectives and Questions

Like (I suspect) many scholars, I hadn't thought much about what 'joy' might actually mean until I was put on the spot. The invitation came from Professor Miroslav Volf of Yale University, who with a team of scholars and assistants was launching an innovative project on the subject by getting small groups together for intensive discussions. One does not readily turn down the chance of three days in Tübingen, in lovely summer weather, engaged in detailed study alongside colleagues such as Jürgen Moltmann, Michael Fishbane and Miroslav Volf himself. I learned a lot. The present paper is an edited and expanded version of the one I gave on that occasion.

[39] Every year in the church's calendar we read the story of Jesus' ascension in Acts 1. But we also remind ourselves of the much shorter version of the same story that Luke has placed at the end of his gospel (24.50–53). There we find a phrase that has always puzzled me. Jesus, says Luke, was separated from his disciples and carried up into heaven; whereupon they worshipped him, and returned to Jerusalem 'with great joy'. This seems, to put it mildly, counter-intuitive. Why would they be so joyful if Jesus has been taken from them? Ought they not to be sorrowful? Might not his departure signal the start of danger, of fear, of the loss of a sense of direction? What is this 'joy' that they now have? What is the reason for it – either in the original [40] historical setting, or in Luke's vision, as he writes these books a few decades later?

This problem, to be sure, is noticed in the New Testament itself. The fourth gospel anticipates it in the so-called 'farewell discourses', when Jesus explains that he is going away, and that this will cause his followers great sadness – but that the sadness will be replaced with joy. 'In the same way, you have sorrow now. But I shall see you again, and your hearts will celebrate, and nobody will take your joy away from you' (John 16.22). This finds an obvious echo in the resurrection narrative, when Jesus appears in the upper room, and 'the disciples rejoiced when they saw the Lord' (20.20). And yet in John's gospel, as well as in Luke, the obvious sense of joy at seeing Jesus alive again after his crucifixion does not seem to get to the heart of the 'joy' of which Jesus speaks in the discourses. He speaks of 'this world's ruler' who is 'coming', and who is to be 'thrown out' (12.31; 14.30), and in that light tells his followers that, though they will have trouble in the world, they are to cheer up, because 'I have defeated the world' (16.33). The joy that the disciples have at Jesus' resurrection, and at the prospect of his ascension (14.28), is therefore not simply the human delight at discovering a dead friend and master to be alive again. John is pointing his readers to a deeper meaning, having to do with the world itself. Something is happening – something has happened – as a result of which the world is a different place. That is the ultimate reason for the disciples' joy, a joy resting on a foundation that, it seems, no trouble or sorrow can shake.

It has been easy in modern western Christianity to characterize this 'joy' in terms of human emotions. One might obviously link it either to the 'Romantic' Christian movements that have reacted against rationalism (a notable example being C. S. Lewis's famous autobiography, *Surprised by Joy*), or to the 'charismatic' movements that have brought new energy to staid or static mainline churches, [41] both protestant and catholic. To be sure, it would be bizarre to think or speak of 'joy' while bracketing out the sense of human delight, elation and celebration that for most people is the simple meaning of the word. Yet in the New Testament the 'joy' and 'rejoicing' that forms such a common theme is capable of overlapping with quite different human emotions. Paul can instruct the Philippians to 'celebrate joyfully in the Lord, all the time' while at the same time speaking of the possibility, had his friend Epaphroditus died of his illness, that he himself would have had 'one sorrow piled on top of another' (Philippians 4.4 with 2.27). Something different from 'ordinary' human joy, even exceptional but still 'ordinary' joy, seems to be envisaged here. In Philippians, as in Luke and John, it has to do with 'the lord', who for Paul is the risen and ascended Jesus of Philippians 2.9–11 and 3.20–21. I shall return to this.

But if the 'joy' to which the New Testament summons its readers is of a different order from that of regular, even exceptional, human experience, it is also different – so it seems to me – from the mood of the Jewish world of the second-Temple period. It presents a fresh retrieval of the joy that is a frequent note in Israel's scriptures. To make this point, we need to look briefly at the theme of joy in the scriptures, and then in the world of the second-Temple period.

'Joy' in Israel's Scriptures and Beyond

A quick read through Israel's scriptures would reveal 'joy' as a significant theme with very specific connotations. Sometimes, of course, the reality is present without the word (we must always remind ourselves of the danger of the concordance!): an obvious example is the song of wild delight sung by Miriam and the rest in Exodus 15. It is a celebration of the power and victory of Israel's God. *Something has happened* as a result of which a new world has opened up. The thing that has happened is simultaneously an act of [42] 'judgment' and an act of 'rescue'. God has acted to put things right, to put a stop to evil and to deliver his people from their enslaving enemy. The major festivals, particularly Passover, look back to the same act of judgment and deliverance, and their celebration draws meaning from this original act.

One thinks, in the same way, of David dancing before the Lord as the Philistines are defeated and the ark is brought into Jerusalem (2 Samuel 5; 6). The death of Uzzah prompts a brief pause, but then the celebration begins again (6.6–11, 12–15). David's exuberance draws a sneering rebuke from Saul's daughter (6.16, 20–23), as extravagant celebration often does (compare John 12.1–8!). But the celebration has something of the same flavour as that of Miriam. The enemy has been defeated, a new day is dawning, and Israel's God is showing his powerful presence.

These celebrations also reveal the robustly *physical* nature of 'joy' in the Hebrew scriptures. Celebration will include music, dancing, food and wine, and the giving of presents to one and all (2 Samuel 6.18–19). All are to share in the celebratory feasts, including orphans, widows and foreigners (Deuteronomy 14.29; 16.11, 14; 26.11). Indeed, right through the Bible the idea of a great feast is one of the central ways in which joy is expressed in a family or community. As we think about biblical joy, we are thus led to think about the *reasons for* joy and the *character of* joy. The reasons include a mighty act of God to bring about victory over evil and the rescue of God's people from its grip. The character of joy includes the vigorous and vibrant celebration of the goodness of the created order, expressed through the activities that signal and symbolize human well-being – eating, drinking, the joy of marriage, music and dancing.

Perhaps the most obvious location of 'joy' in the Hebrew (and Aramaic) scriptures is the promise and then the (partial?) reality of the restoration after the Babylonian exile. We think of the mingled joy [43] and weeping as the second Temple was founded (Ezra 3.10–13), and the celebrations when the city wall was dedicated (Nehemiah 12.43, which says, remarkably, that 'the joy of Jerusalem was heard far away'; joy was not simply a shared *feeling*; it was something that could be *heard*, from a long way off). Or, with the psalm:

When YHWH restored the fortunes of Zion,
we were like those who dream.
Then our mouth was filled with laughter,
and our tongue with shouts of joy . . .
YHWH has done great things for us, and we rejoiced.

This note of *retrospective* joy then turns into a prayer for *fresh* acts of deliverance:

May those who sow in tears reap with shouts of joy.
Those who go out weeping, bearing the seed for sowing,
shall come home with shouts of joy,
carrying their sheaves.
(Psalm 126.1–3, 5–6)

This too highlights the close link between national and political fortunes (the main subject of the psalm) and the agricultural basis of national life, with the latter thus serving both as metaphor and as metonymy for the restoration of Israel's fortunes.

We find something similar in Isaiah 9: 'You have multiplied the nation, you have increased its joy; they rejoice before you as with joy at the harvest, as people exult when dividing plunder' (Isaiah 9.3). Here the simile of harvest points on to the new Davidic kingdom of justice and righteousness, in which the animal kingdom will cease from violence and bloodshed (11.1–10). These images are picked up in later portions of the book, as the whole creation celebrates Israel's return from exile: 'You shall go out in joy, and be led back in peace; the mountains and the hills before you shall burst into song, and all the trees of the field shall clap their hands' (55.12). In the great coming restoration, Israel's God himself will be rejoicing (62.5; 65.19; compare Psalm 104.31; Deuteronomy 30.9; Zephaniah 3.17). 'Do not be grieved,' say Ezra and Nehemiah to the returning exiles as they hear the Torah, 'for the joy of YHWH is your strength' (Nehemiah 8.10). They then copy David, feasting and drinking and sending portions to those [44] who have nothing. The end of Isaiah also provides another classic statement of exodus-like joy: 'You shall see, and your heart shall rejoice; your bodies [lit. 'bones'] shall flourish like the grass; and it shall be known that the hand of YHWH is with his servants, and his indignation is against his enemies' (66.14). The great divine action that produces victory over evil and rescue for God's people will be a mixture of new covenant (restoration after exile) and new creation (fresh harvests, producing bodily restoration); and both will cause joy. Indeed – though there are many ways of saying the same thing at this point – one could say that the *covenantal* actions of Israel's God produce *creational* results. History and harvest go closely together. God's actions on behalf of his people will result in the renewal of the good creation. Elements of the latter can serve both as literary metaphors and appropriate celebrations for the former.

All this biblical material remained, of course, very much in the minds of second-Temple Jews. The scriptures, and particularly the Psalms, were the soil in which there grew to full flower all later expectations, aspirations, celebrations and lamentations. The great festivals continued to express and reinforce the celebration of God's powerful deeds in days gone by. But now new elements were added. The 'return from exile' was a mixed blessing. Those who had returned to Jerusalem still had a sense of being 'enslaved'; the full reality promised in Isaiah 40—55 or Ezekiel 36—45 had not come about. Daniel 9, a passage much discussed in the post-Maccabaean period, spoke of the exile lasting not for seventy years but for 490. In particular, though the Temple had been rebuilt, there remained a sense that the promise of glorious divine return (Isaiah 40; 52; Ezekiel 43) had not yet happened. It remained in the future (Haggai 2.7; Zechariah 2.4–5, 10–11; Malachi 3.1). Indeed, when the rabbis, much later, discussed the ways in which the second Temple was deficient when compared with the first, one of the key elements missing from [45] the second Temple was the Shekinah itself (bYom. 21b). The joy of geographical return, and of the restoration of cult, was mixed with a sense that something remained incomplete. (We may exempt Ben-Sirach from this; there, we do seem to find a grand celebration, with the high priest in the Temple and everything seeming to be right with the world. But we have good reason to suppose that this priestly and aristocratic perspective, and such 'joy' as it brought, was not widely shared.)

What we find in the second-Temple period, then, is a rich mixture of celebration and expectation. Joy was still expressed in the traditional ways, and for the traditional reasons – with the added reason of the return itself, such as it was, and then the major new reason of the Maccabaean triumph, resulting in the institution of a new feast, Hanukkah, and the vivid and evocative joy of the ceremony of the light. But the ambiguities of the post-exilic settlement, and the yet more complicated ambiguities of the post-Maccabaean period, meant that the joy itself had an increasingly forward look. The Hasmonean monarchy, the Roman invasion, and the rise of Herod and his family, could not prevent the annual celebrations, the joyful recounting of the kingship of God as expressed in the Psalms and elsewhere. But they ensured that this celebration was inevitably more about expectation than about present triumph. The more Daniel 9 was woven into popular consciousness (and this seems to be what Josephus means when he speaks of 'an oracle in their scriptures' that drove the people to revolt in the reign of Nero (*War* 6.312–15)), the more we must conclude that the dominant note of the second-Temple Jewish worldview was not so much joy as hope. A joyful hope, yes, often; but a hope deferred so long, and dashed so repeatedly, that in many texts we find hope in the form of a gritted-teeth determination to hold on at all costs, rather than an easy or cheerful celebration of the fact that what God [46] did in the past he would soon do once more. And when we reach the post-70 period, in books like *4 Ezra* and *2 Baruch*, hope itself has been under severe threat. It is still there, a function as always of creational monotheism (if there is one God, then despite all appearances he *must* eventually act to set things right); but these books have little of the joy of Isaiah 40—55, or of Psalms 96, 98 and 126.

This is not, of course, a criticism. One might as well criticize a young widow for failing to sing cheerful songs at the funeral of her wise and loving husband. But it poses a sharp question when we remind ourselves that the first followers of Jesus were speaking, at exactly the same period, of a 'joy' that retained the shape and content of the Jewish phenomenon at which we have glanced, but that had sprung to life in a new and unexpected manner.

Joy in the New Testament

Twenty years ago, I conducted a thought-experiment using the worldview model (one particular variation within the contemporary social-scientific study of the New Testament) I had developed in collaboration with others. What would be the defining themes of second-Temple Judaism on the one hand and the first two centuries of Christianity on the other?[9] I came to a conclusion that I had not anticipated. The worldviews are very similar. Both are rooted in the creational monotheism of Israel's scriptures. Both are passionate about the divine faithfulness to the covenant. Both have a measure of joy, and a measure of hope. But the proportions are radically different. For the second-Temple Jews, the dominant note, as I have just said, was hope,

---

9   This study forms the bulk of *The New Testament and the People of God* (Wright 1992).

albeit backed up by the joyful ancient stories of divine faithfulness. For the early Christians, however, the dominant note was clearly joy, albeit still including an ongoing [47] hope. The reasons for this joy, and its character, remain recognizably within the ancient Israelite parameters (the celebrations of exodus and so forth). But the older picture has been brought into new, sharp and startling focus by the events concerning Jesus. Whatever explanation one might give of these events – if, for instance, a sceptic were to say that the whole thing was a fabrication based on wish-fulfilment – one still has to give a historical account of what the early Christians themselves would have said, and indeed did say, about the reasons for and the shape of this joy.

The usual word-studies have been done many times, focusing particularly on the roots *agalliasis* and *chara/chairō* and their cognates. These are frequently combined (for example Matthew 5.12; Luke 1.14; 1 Peter 1.8; 4.13; Revelation 19.7). They occur across the whole range of the New Testament, from the angelic joy (to be shared with 'all people') at the birth of Jesus (Luke 2.10–11) through to the joy when the final kingdom is revealed (Revelation 19.6–7). (It is sometimes claimed that there is theological significance in the etymological proximity between *chara*, 'joy', and *charis*, 'gift'. There may be a grain of truth in this but, since the New Testament writers do not seem to me to make this link explicit, we should be wary of going beyond the usual rule: the meaning of a word is its use in context, not its history or family resemblances.)

In the gospels, references to 'joy' frequently describe the reaction of crowds or individuals at meeting Jesus or experiencing his healing power. But this goes beyond the natural human gladness at healing and hope. There is both a *theological* and an *eschatological* dimension to this joy. This comes out most clearly in Luke 15, where Jesus describes 'joy in heaven' when a sinner repents – in order to explain why he himself is having a celebration with 'sinners'. The point is made explicitly in the first two parables of the collection: the lost sheep and the lost coin (Luke 15.1–10). Then, by strong [48] implication within the narrative itself, the same point is to be understood within the third story, the so-called prodigal son or prodigal father (Luke 15.11–32). Here the verb used is *euphrainō* (four times from vv. 23–32), though the parallel with 15.7, 10 indicates that the meaning is to be understood as close to *chara* there.

The emphasis throughout the chapter is on the *appropriateness* of celebration, of 'joy', *as a result of what has happened and is happening* in the welcome of (repentant) 'sinners' – in other words, as a result of what is happening in the public career of Jesus. And, by implication, as a result of what will happen at its conclusion: 'This son of mine', and then 'this brother of yours' 'was dead and is alive again' (15.24, 32). The public career of Jesus, characterized by (among other things) his celebrations with 'sinners', will reach its appropriate climax in his death and resurrection, and the whole thing together explains why celebration – 'joy' in the form of feasting, music and dancing (15.25) – is not only appropriate in itself but constitutes a sharing of the joy of heaven, that is, of God himself. This is a moment when heaven and earth come together, as in the Temple. And this theological dimension is matched by the eschatological: the story of the son who is lost and found, dead and alive again, reflects the dominant Jewish story of the period, that of shameful exile and rapturous return. It is the story Jesus' contemporaries were eager to experience in full at last. It is the story that, in one way and another, Jesus was telling and enacting wherever he went.

The 'joy' we see in the gospels is thus not simply the natural human delight in times of healing and reconciliation, though it is that as well. It is the fresh instantiation, in a new (messianic) mode, of the joy expressed in Psalm 126 and elsewhere: the joy of discovering that Israel's God was at last doing the thing he had promised, rescuing the people from their 'exile' and providing forgiveness, restoration and new life. And it is the joy to be experienced in the fresh *presence* of [49] God – not now, after all, in a rebuilt Temple, but in the person and the actions of Jesus – and also the fresh *act* of God, rescuing people not now from Egypt or Babylon but from death itself.

John's gospel extends this perspective and, particularly in the farewell discourses of chapters 13—17, speaks repeatedly both of Jesus' own joy and of the disciples' sharing in that joy (for example 14.28; 15.11; 16.20–24; 17.13). This is despite the repeated warnings of suffering to come, of opposition and persecution from 'the world': the world will rejoice at Jesus' demise, but this will be overturned in the events that follow. The context in John indicates that this, too, is not simply the natural human delight at ill fortune suddenly reversed. The whole gospel is about the new creation that comes about through the 'tabernacling' presence of the Word of God (1.14): in other words, the new Temple, from which living water will flow out, as in Ezekiel (John 7.37–39). As with Luke, the reader is meant to detect the theological reason for joy (the presence, and rescuing action, of Israel's God) and the eschato-logical reason (here, the 'new Temple').

The four gospels thus link their narrative, and with it their theme of joy, to the ancient hope of Israel, to the biblical promises and prospects that, so they claim, are now finding a new and different kind of fulfilment. But the difference between, say, what a second-Temple Jew might be hoping for and what a reader of the gospels might be discovering does not consist in the usually imagined distinction between an 'earthly' hope on the one hand and a 'spiritual' hope on the other. Far from it. The reason for the new 'joy' is that certain things are happening 'on earth as in heaven'. The character of the new 'joy', like that of the old, is feasting, a celebration of the goodness of the present creation.

In the letters of Paul, 'joy' takes second place only to 'love', *agapē*. The fact that these, and seven others, are part of 'the fruit of the spirit' (Galatians 5.22–23) does not mean they somehow grow [50] spontaneously without moral or spiritual effort. They are virtues, to be practised. But they are not, of course, self-generated. For Paul, the spirit creates the conditions for the new human characteristics to come to birth. Once again, these conditions have to do with the fulfilment of the ancient expectation of Israel, the fulfilment also of the second-Temple Jewish hope – though not in the form that had been imagined.

In particular, for Paul 'joy' is intimately connected to the resurrection of Jesus on the one hand and to his ascended lordship on the other. This goes wider than mere word-studies. The words for 'joy' or 'rejoicing' do not occur in Romans 8, but one can hardly read that passage without a sense that what is being expressed is joy of the highest quality. There as elsewhere Paul is drawing on the ancient exodus-narrative, seeing it as newly accomplished in the events concerning Jesus (Romans 6: the slaves coming through the water to freedom; Romans 7: arriving at Sinai and the problem of Torah's condemnation; Romans 8: journeying to the 'inheritance'). Romans 8 is thus Paul's own fresh equivalent of the song of Miriam, looking at the defeated forces of sin and death and celebrating the divine victory, the revelation of divine covenant faithfulness. Similar things could be said of the 'apocalyptic' passage in 1 Corinthians 15.20–28, in which Paul draws on Psalms 2, 8 and 110 to claim that Jesus is *already* reigning as Messiah, that he is in the process of completing his victory over all enemies, and that when death itself is finally conquered then this messianic kingdom will give way to the ultimate and final 'kingdom of God'. This same theme is closely cognate with the passages about Jesus' victorious lordship in Philippians 2.6–11 and 3.20–21. This takes us to the letter that is generally acknowledged as the most explicit Pauline statement of 'joy'.

Philippians is both an expression of joy and an invitation to joy. This is not because the circumstances, either of Paul himself or of the [51] Philippian believers, are comfortable. He is in prison; they are suffering for the gospel. But joy abounds in all directions. Paul prays with joy (1.4). He rejoices in his present imprisonment (1.18). He longs for their progress and joy in the faith (1.25). Their loving unity will make his joy complete (2.2). He rejoices with them and wants them to rejoice with him (2.17, 18). The return of Epaphroditus will bring them joy, so they must receive him with joy (2.28, 29). The central command of the second half of the letter is simply that they should rejoice (3.1; 4.4); the second of these passages, uniquely in Paul, involves a repetition ('I'll say it again: celebrate!'). The Philippians themselves are his 'joy and crown' (4.1), an accolade also awarded to the Thessalonians (1 Thessalonians 2.19–20). Paul himself is rejoicing that they have been able to send him practical help (Philippians 4.10). And these verbal occurrences are simply the tip of the iceberg, signs of the larger theme of the letter as a whole. Philippians is itself a celebration, a sustained declaration of joy in God, joy in the gospel, joy in the lord, joy despite adverse circumstances, joy expressed in faith and hope and love and, above all, unity.

Again, we enquire as to the reason for, and the character of, this joy. Why was Paul so particularly joyful in writing this letter? And what exactly did he mean by *rejoice* or *celebrate*?

At one level the answer is obvious. Paul and the Philippians clearly had a deep bond of mutual affection. What's more, as the parallel reference in 1 Thessalonians indicates, Paul regarded the churches of northern Greece with particular delight. They were the proof, the seal, the sign that he really was the apostle to the gentiles, that his work was 'not in vain'. (Why he saw them thus, with the churches of Turkey already established and the church in Corinth yet to come, is another matter.) But there seems to be something more. I believe it is no coincidence that Philippians, as well as being the most explicit letter when it comes to joy, is also the most explicit when it comes [52] to the sovereign lordship of Jesus, and the way in which allegiance to him works out in the wider social and political landscape. This is not the time for a full exploration of these themes, which, like 'joy' itself, permeates much of the letter. But we may at least say this.

The central poem about Jesus in Philippians 2.6–11, now widely recognized to be the theological heart of the letter, has many biblical and theological resonances, but at its centre it is a celebration of *the radically different kind of lordship* attained, and now exercised, by Jesus. It picks up the larger themes of Isaiah 40—55, in which Israel's God triumphs over the pagan gods and lords of Babylon and reveals his royal presence in the strangest of ways, through the work of the 'servant' (Isaiah 52.7–12 with 52.13—53.12; Isaiah 45.23 is quoted explicitly at Philippians 2.10). The joy that suffuses the whole central section of Isaiah is based on this victorious divine sovereignty, revealed in this way, and Paul encapsulates the same quality through his reworking of these themes with Jesus at their heart.

The specific target is, it seems to me, quite obvious (though this remains controversial and has to be stated with care): *Jesus is lord, and Caesar is not.* Caesar offers a 'salvation', of sorts; the followers of Jesus have their own kind of 'salvation', and must work out, with fear and trembling, what this will mean in practice (2.12–13). 'Fear and trembling', in the Bible, are the normal reactions to the divine presence, and Paul makes this explicit (2.13). The Jesus-believers in Philippi lived in a Roman colony where the power and divinity of Rome and the imperial family were all too present and obvious. Paul wants it to be obvious to them that the power and divinity of the one God celebrated by Isaiah – and now revealed in the crucified Jesus! – are also present, and that the 'salvation' they provide is the larger and greater reality. This is the source of, and the reason for, the joy on which he insists. **[53]**

Paul's own example provides a microcosmic vision of the same thing. He is in prison, quite possibly facing death. And the very fact of his being there has meant that the whole imperial guard has come to hear the 'gospel', the royal announcement of Jesus as the crucified and risen lord of the world (1.12–14). The sovereign lordship of the Messiah frames, and renders joyful, his reflections on his likely fate (1.18–26). Then, in offering himself as the model of abandoning privileges in order to 'be discovered in him', Paul expresses his joy at 'the covenant status from God which is given to faith' (3.9), further defined as 'knowing him, knowing the power of his resurrection, and knowing the partnership of his sufferings' (3.10). This is not simply about personal fulfilment and hope. 'The power of his resurrection' points ahead once more – this is where the strands of the whole letter come together – to Philippians 3.20–21, where Paul declares that 'Lord Jesus Messiah' has the *power* to subject all things to himself, and that he will exercise this power in coming from heaven to transform the present world, and with it the bodies of his people. Unlike those in Philippi (perhaps including some of the Christians) whose citizenship is in Rome, the true citizenship of Jesus' followers is in heaven. This does not mean that Paul is here talking about their 'going to heaven' one day, any more than the Roman citizens in Philippi would expect to go to live in Rome one day (as people sometimes mistakenly suppose). Rather, they are part of the extended empire of 'heaven'. The reason why Rome established colonies was partly because central Italy was far too small for all the original military veterans and their families, and partly because Rome was eager to 'Romanize' the major locations of the empire. Jesus' people in Philippi are thus a 'colony of heaven', responsible for bringing heaven's rule to bear in their own sphere. The lord of heaven, on his return, will make their status complete by transforming their bodies to be like his own (compare 1 Corinthians 15.51–54). (We note that the New Testament never uses the word [54] *heaven* for 'the place where God's people go when they die'. Paul can speak about this intermediate state, after bodily death and before bodily resurrection, but he never calls it 'heaven'; here in Philippians (for example 1.23), it simply means being 'with the Messiah', which is far better.)

This, I propose, indicates the source of, and the reason for, the 'joy' of which Paul speaks. It is not simply a spiritual exhilaration, though clearly for Paul it includes that. It is certainly not a sense that though the present world is in bad shape the followers of Jesus will one day leave it behind and go to a better place entirely. Paul has nothing in common with the joy, such as it is, of the Gnostic. No: the source of Paul's joy is that the resurrection and enthronement of Jesus, his 'lordship' over the world, has created a new world, and with it a new worldview. The followers of Jesus understand that the rule of Caesar, and all other pagan powers, is a mere sham, a parody of the truth, and that the truth now revealed in Jesus is the truth glimpsed and celebrated in Isaiah and the Psalms (Paul refers, here as elsewhere, to Psalms 8 and 110). The creator God has announced the verdict; the world has been put right; the trees in the field will clap their hands. A new world has been launched, even in the midst of the present old, corrupt and decaying world. Those who follow Jesus, who are 'found in the Messiah', are already part of it. That is why Paul rejoices, and why he summons the Philippians to rejoice with him. And their joy must express itself in the *unity* of the church as a publicly known fact (1.27—2.4, coupled with 2.12–18).

It would be possible to trace the resonances of this theme through the other Pauline letters. There, as in Philippians, we notice that the usual early Christian 'now and not yet' obtains just as much: 'I'm not implying that I've already received "resurrection", or that I've already become complete and mature', as he says in Philippians 3.12. But – and this is vitally important – the present 'not yet', including suffering, imprisonment and death, is not simply [55] something to be pushed to one side as irrelevant. It too is actually part of the *reason for* the 'joy' of which Paul speaks.

This answers to the famous passage in Romans 5.1–5, where, though the verb *kauchaomai* does not really mean 'rejoice', as in many English translations, the effect is much the same. 'We celebrate the hope of the glory of God', declares Paul, and then immediately adds: 'We also celebrate in our sufferings, because we know that suffering produces patience, patience produces a well-formed character, and a character like that produces hope.' As in Philippians 3.11, so in Romans 8.17–30, which leads to the greatest outburst of joy anywhere in the New Testament (8.31–39), the suffering is part of the hope and hence part of the reason for joy. The suffering of the present time is an indication that the new world and the old are chafing together, and that the followers of Jesus are caught between the two. Paul transposes this into the cosmic context in Romans 8.18–25, interpreting the groaning of all creation as the birth-pangs of the new age. This results not in joy *despite* suffering, but in joy *because of* suffering – not in some masochistic sense (Paul is still quite capable of speaking with horror of the pain and anguish he himself has endured, as in 2 Corinthians), but because Paul insists on seeing the suffering in terms of the crucifixion, resurrection and ascended lordship of Jesus.

With this, we have arrived at an answer to the question with which we began. The disciples returned to Jerusalem after the ascension full of joy because – so the New Testament writers indicate in one way or another – they believed not only that Jesus had been raised from the dead, launching God's new creation, but that he was now enthroned as the world's rightful sovereign. 'Heaven', where the ascended Jesus now resides and reigns, is not (as in the implicit Epicureanism of so much modern culture!) a long way away from 'earth'. The two spheres of the good creation are designed to overlap, to interlock, and eventually to be brought together in perfect harmony for ever in [56] the Messiah (Ephesians 1.10). This has now happened proleptically in the person of Jesus himself.

Thus, even though other powers and dominions would still do cruel and terrible things, the divine verdict longed for in the ancient scriptures had been heard, and would be decisive. God had vindicated Jesus after his crucifixion; at his name every knee would bow; and therefore his followers were to 'rejoice in the lord always'. In terms of theology and ethics, the virtue of 'joy' is inculcated and practised by the celebration of Jesus as the world's true lord, who has revealed the true manner of 'lordship' in his shameful death, and has thus revealed also the way in which that lordship is presently exercised (that is, through the humble, mourning, peace-making, justice-seeking character sketched in the beatitudes). In terms of the history of religions, this vision of 'joy' comes straight from Israel's scriptures, with their vision of the triumph of Israel's God over Pharaoh, over Babylon, over all that corrupts and destroys creation. It is the moment of judgment and rescue spoken of again and again by the Psalms and the prophets. And it confronts the vision of pagan celebration that Paul's readers knew only too well from the daily life of their towns and cities.

This leads to the second question. If this is the reason for joy, the source of joy, what is the content of that joy? It has been all too easy in the modern western world to suppose that *chara* and its cognates refer simply to internal mental or emotional states. Certainly those are involved. It would be farcical to imagine a Christian 'joy' that was purely outward show. But I think that in Philippians at least Paul envisages a 'celebration' that would involve some kind of *activity*. Granted the traditions Paul inherited, and his solidly physical understanding of the new creation, including the resurrection body, it is inconceivable that he would have thought of celebrating Jesus' lordship with a purely mental or emotional happiness, a purely [57] inward sense of well-being. Paul was no hedonist, but as a robust creational monotheist he believed that 'the earth is YHWH's and all that is in it' (Psalm 24.1, quoted in 1 Corinthians 10.26), and that food and drink were good and to be enjoyed. Part of the reason for Paul's anxiety about shared table-fellowship, and shared worship, in Galatians 2 and Romans 14 and 15, was that Christian meals, not least but not only the eucharist, constituted a central part of what he meant by *celebrate, rejoice*. The word *celebration* has become almost a technical term, certainly in my own church and perhaps elsewhere, for 'holding a eucharist'. We must guard against that becoming a dead metaphor.

But I wonder – this is impossible to prove, but I wonder – whether Paul also envisaged something more. The 'celebrations' of Kyrios Caesar took place in public, as whole towns would be given over to days and seasons of festivals involving processions, music and dancing, feasting and drinking, and ultimately sacrifices and prayers at the relevant shrines. Most ancient religions did that kind of thing. Did Paul want to encourage the Christians to do their own public 'rejoicing', perhaps even as a kind of protest? Was their celebration to be only behind closed doors? As I read Philippians 1.27–30 and 4.4–5, I detect at least the possibility that Paul expected the Christians to be known, *in public*, as people who were celebrating the cosmic lordship of Jesus – with a different kind of celebration, to be sure, in which all people would know their *epieikēs*, which perhaps means 'restraint' in contrast to the wild excesses of pagan celebrations. I have argued in chapter 13 of *Paul and the Faithfulness of God* [Wright 2013b] that in many senses, despite protestant fears, Paul's communities did have something that could be called a 'religion' – remembering that in the ancient world 'religion' was something that whole communities *did* as part of their self-definition. A 'religion' in the ancient world, after all, was something that bound together and strengthened the *polis*, [58] the local civic community, through the worship of the local gods. For Paul, there were communal and personal activities that bound together the community of Jesus-followers in worship, united with one another and with the creator God who had made himself known afresh, and decisively, through the gospel. And my suggestion – or at least my question – is whether perhaps 'joy', *chara*, in Philippians and elsewhere, might include this outward, and perhaps public, expression of 'eschatological religion'.

There is no space to pursue the issues raised by 'joy' in other New Testament documents. I note simply a few highlights. The Johannine correspondence speaks of the joy that comes from the mutual relationship of writer and readers (1 John 1.4; 2 John 4, 10, 11, 12). 1 Peter expresses, even more strongly than Paul, the exuberant and unrestrained celebration of joy at believing in the Jesus whose own sufferings have paved the way for those of his followers, transforming them from meaningless agony into the testing of faith and so into the glorious hope (1 Peter 1.6–9). This corresponds, of course, to scenes in Acts and elsewhere, where persecution is hailed and celebrated as a sign that the believers really are the Messiah's people, really are on the right track (Acts 5.41).

Conclusions

I have concentrated on one or two passages rather than attempting to give a full New Testament picture. As I have hinted, and as is the case with many other themes, a *topic* may be present even when the two or three key *words* are not; but I have here focused on passages in which 'joy' is an explicit theme. My basic argument has been that the puzzles we might notice (why do the disciples rejoice when Jesus is taken from them? How can they speak of 'joy' when so much is still so wrong with their lives, with the world and [59] its wicked rulers, and so on?) can find answers when we consider how the whole early Christian worldview actually functions. In the place of the dominant note of 'hope' that we find in second-Temple Judaism, rooted as that was in creational and covenantal monotheism when facing the horrors and perplexities of life under the Romans, we find the dominant note of 'joy', from within the same basic Jewish worldview, and rooted in the same scriptures, but brought into a startling new focus because of Jesus. I have suggested that in the key passages we see the early Christian belief that in Jesus there had come about a new union between heaven and earth, with the celebrations of the one spilling over necessarily into the celebrations of the other. I have pointed out that 'celebrations', within creational monotheism, would naturally involve food and drink, music and dancing, and the other accoutrements of 'joy' as expressed outwardly and publicly. (It was after all the public nature of Jesus' celebrations that caused the angry questions to which Luke 15 was the answer.) And I have suggested that both in the gospels and in the epistles we can trace a link between the sovereignty, the 'lordship', of Jesus and the exhortation to, or expression of, 'joy'.

The *fact* of the resurrection and exaltation of the crucified Jesus opens up a new world, launches the new creation, over which Jesus himself is sovereign; that is the root cause of joy. The *manner* of his coming to that sovereignty – his suffering and shameful death – indicates that when we say 'Jesus is lord, and Caesar is not', we are not (as some anxiously suppose) replacing one oppressive or totalizing system with another. Rather, 'lordship' itself is transformed into the picture we see in the beatitudes, or in Mark 10.35–45, or, of course, supremely in Philippians 2.1–18. In other words – and in terms of our earlier discussion of scriptural *antecedents* – something *has happened* in which the divine judgment on evil, and the divine rescue of the world from its grip, has been unveiled. This is the new exodus, the new 'return from [60] exile'. Yes, the 'second coming' is still to take place. But modern exegesis, reflecting a reticence or outright denial concerning the bodily resurrection and ascension, has put far too much weight instead on the early Christian hope for the *parousia* as the reason for joy. Jesus' first followers did indeed celebrate what was still to come. But they did so because of the physical, creation-renewing events that had already taken place.

Where does this leave contemporary discussion of 'joy'? As with many themes in early Christian thought and life, we see both significant continuities and significant discontinuities. Joy and celebration, within a creational and new-creational monotheism, involve not some superspiritual otherworldly pleasure but the elements of creation itself caught up in new expressions of new creation. This is the birth of sacramental theology within Christianity. Precisely because the early Christians believed, with a faith rooted in Israel's scriptures, that in Jesus they had discerned the human face of Israel's God, the world's creator, their celebrations were bound to express significant continuity both with any and all human celebrations and with the Jewish festivals in particular. Hence the way in which Christian baptism celebrates a new kind of exodus, and the eucharist a new kind of Passover. But at the same time there are radical discontinuities. The Jewish celebrations of the second-Temple period, though rooted in the joy of Exodus 15 and the rest, look on to the future with increasing, and ultimately disappointed, urgency. The disasters of AD 70 and 135 changed the Jewish world for ever. Joy remains within Jewish festivals and Torah study, but it may appear to be shorn of its historical and political elements.

Equally, the pagan celebrations of cult and empire were rooted in a different worldview, a different sort of power, and resulted in a different kind of 'joy'. That is a study worth undertaking in itself. [61] The early Christian celebrations were a reaffirmation of an essentially Jewish vision of the world, over against that pagan vision. They were not an optional extra for the communities generated by the gospel. Not to celebrate, not to express joy in the lordship of the crucified and risen Jesus, would be tacitly to acknowledge that one did not really believe. The human joy of food and drink, of family and civic life, was taken up and transformed, with many paradoxes along the way, into the Jesus-believing joy of eucharist and united fellowship. The deep Jewish roots of early Christian joy enable the church's celebrations to confront the world dominated by Caesar with the news of a different empire, a different *kind* of empire. Like love, peace and the other aspects of the spirit's fruit, joy may be difficult to maintain. But for the early Christians, nothing could take it away. It was, after all, Jesus' own gift to his people, on the night he was betrayed (John 16.20). The many betrayals that Jesus' followers will then face, both personal and political, global and cosmic, cannot ultimately destroy, but will only further contextualize, that joy.

12

Pastoral Theology for Perplexing Topics: Paul and *Adiaphora*

I have been interested in the question of *adiaphora* – 'things indifferent', as expounded by Paul in particular – for many years, both at the historical level (what did Paul mean and why did he take the line he did?) and at the practical level (how does today's church navigate the topics which some today want to treat as *adiaphora* ('let's agree to disagree') and others insist must be regarded as making a real and substantial 'difference' to Christian fellowship?). This essay was requested for a volume attempting to sketch some of the key issues in contentious areas today.

[63] Introduction

Anyone reading swiftly through Paul's letters looking for regularly recurring themes can hardly miss his constant insistence on the unity of the church. Believing Jews and believing gentiles are to worship together, learning to set aside differences of diet and holy days (Romans 14—15). They are to eat together, celebrating their shared membership in Abraham's family in which there is neither Jew nor Greek, slave nor free, no 'male and female' (Galatians 2—4). Together they form the holy Temple where the living God dwells through his spirit (Ephesians 2), and the varied ministries they are given are to serve this unity and the church's resulting growth to maturity (Ephesians 4). Threats from opponents are not to destroy this unity (Philippians 1.27-28); differences of background, ethnic [64] origin, and culture are to count for nothing (Colossians 3); mutual love must bind the disparate membership together (1 Thessalonians 4); the greatest social division of the ancient world (that between master and slave) was to be overcome by the power of shared family life in the Messiah (Philemon). Towering over even these strong passages we find the truly extraordinary exhortation of Philippians 2.2–5:

Bring your thinking into line with one another . . . Hold on to the same love; bring your innermost lives into harmony; fix your minds on the same object . . . Look after each other's best interests, not your own.

How are they to do this? Nothing less than the self-abnegating mind of the Messiah himself must be their model (2.6–11).

Above even this, however, we have 1 Corinthians. In this letter, unity is a main theme from one angle after another. Personality cults must not pull the church apart: that would be to destroy the Temple of God (chs. 1—3). Believers must not take one another to court (ch. 6). Christians who live in a pagan environment (that is, more or less all Paul's churches) are to learn how to navigate the tricky moral challenges of that culture with the paramount task being to remain in fellowship with one another (chs. 8—10). There are to be no divisions at the lord's table (ch. 11): this may indicate the threatening presence of a rich–poor division in the church, but it may go wider as well. The three great chapters 12, 13 and 14 come at the task of unity from numerous angles. There are varieties of gifts, ministries and operations, but a single spirit, lord, and God, and this means that there is one differentiated body of the Messiah, each member of which must respect all the others (ch. 12). When the church meets for worship, all that is done must promote unity and upbuilding (ch. 14). In between these two there is the incomparable poem on love (ch. 13). The long chapter on resurrection (ch. 15) does not contribute overtly to the theme of unity, but a close study of the whole letter indicates that belief in resurrection lies underneath most of the preceding arguments. Thus Paul's letters in general, and 1 Corinthians in particular, insist on a [65] unity in the church which transcends issues of ethnicity, social status and different vocations.

To the modern western mind, all this might speak of a 'tolerance' in which the imperative of unity would push on to the back burner all questions of actual behaviour. Never mind our differences of behaviour; let's simply enjoy fellowship with one another! This might, indeed, seem to be the natural corollary of what Paul says about different views on dietary laws and observance of holy days in Romans 14; and such a conclusion might seem to be reinforced by the doctrine that claims central place in many accounts of Paul's thought, namely justification by faith apart from works of the law. Indeed, Romans 14 might with good reason be seen as the direct outworking of justification: 'justification by faith' in Romans 3 and 4 leads to 'fellowship by faith' in Romans 14 and 15. The shared faith in Jesus as Messiah, and in the fulfilment of the divine purpose through him, overcomes all cultural and ideological differences. Unity is what matters: never mind the varieties of practice.

And yet. Our quick cursory reading indicates just as obviously that this was not how Paul saw things. Romans itself is full of 'ethical' instruction, both in the broad general level of chapters 6 and 8 (where the defeat of the 'power' called 'sin' means that believers are set free and must not re-submit), and in the specifics of chapters 12 and 13 – and also in the way in which, through the logic of the letter as a whole, the catalogue of vicious and dehumanizing behaviour in chapters 1 and 2 is reversed, first in the character of Abraham in chapter 4, then in the life of the spirit in chapter 8, and then in the 'renewal of the mind' – and of the behaviour that results – in chapter 12. The lists, in Galatians 5, of 'the works of the flesh' and 'the fruit of the spirit' are framed with a dire warning: those who do the former 'will not inherit God's kingdom' (a phrase echoed elsewhere too), while those who do the latter 'crucified the flesh with its passions and desires'. Ephesians 4 gives a solemn warning against living in the way ordinary pagans do, going into considerable detail about the styles of behaviour in question. [66] Philippians 3.17–19 gives a tearful warning about those 'who are on the road to destruction, whose god is their stomach, who only ever think about what's on the earth'; the latter phrase is picked up in Colossians 3 in the larger instruction to set the mind on things above. 1 Thessalonians 4 issues clear commandments about the way in which Christian behaviour is not to reflect the pagan world around. Finally, returning to 1 Corinthians, we find clear, strong and detailed instruction both about what to do when people in the church behave as though they are still pagans – or worse than pagans! (chs. 5—6) – and how to prevent pagan-style behaviour creeping into the church in the first place (ch. 10). Clearly, if Paul is keen on unity, he is equally keen on holiness.

Is he thereby being inconsistent? Some might think so. Some might suppose that his sharp moral judgments are simply the hangover from his former culture, not least the moral scruples that he had had as a zealous Pharisee. Some would go further, and insist that if 'justification by faith not law' meant what it said then the whole idea of 'rules', of whatever sort, should be outlawed in a truly Pauline theology. If we believe in grace rather than law, so one hears it said, the kind of definite and specific moral judgments we find in Galatians 5, Colossians 3, or 1 Corinthians 5 and 6 should ultimately have no place.

One kind of answer to this is the theological and philosophical argument we find in a book like Miroslav Volf's *Exclusion and Embrace* (1996). It isn't enough to say 'embrace' (that is, 'include'); there is such a thing as real evil, and if we fail to name it and shame it we are merely incorporating radical dehumanization into the ongoing life of the community. The scandals that have come to light recently in many walks of life show well enough what that dehumanization looks like: in the brave new world of the 1960s and beyond, many treated older moral codes as out of date and irrelevant. As usual, many in the churches went along for the ride, whether in practice or whether, sometimes using apparently Pauline language, in theological theory. The work of Volf and others has shown this up as thoroughly [67] inadequate, the more powerfully in Volf's case because of his own experience in facing, as a Croatian, the question 'How can I love my Serbian neighbour?' Answer: only through the initial 'exclusion' in which evil is recognized for what it is – and which itself always aims at an ultimate, and hard-won, 'embrace'. That kind of theoretical discussion needs to continue.

The present chapter, however, comes at the same questions from the angle of Pauline exegesis. Paul, I shall argue, is not at all inconsistent in his double stress on unity and holiness. Both are functions of his deepest theological insights; both are to be attained through the practical inhabiting of those insights, through their incorporation into the DNA of the Messiah's community and of every spirit-indwelt believer. Properly understood, they do not form a paradox, pulling in opposite directions. They actually reinforce one another.

To understand this, we need to grasp the heart of Paul's vision of the church. That will be my first main section below. To apply it, in my second main section, we need to understand how Paul sees the question of *adiaphora*, 'things indifferent': how do we know which things are 'indifferent' and which are not? How do we tell the difference between the differences which make a difference (for Paul, certain differences of behaviour and lifestyle) and the differences which don't make a difference (for Paul, certain other differences which might equally be seen as 'behaviour' and 'lifestyle')? For Paul, it seems, our modern generalized terms 'behaviour' and 'lifestyle' do not take us to the heart of it! We have to be more specific.

This is where the research of recent generations really helps. A great deal of careful work has been done to locate Paul and his communities within their social and cultural worlds, and to understand how Paul's vision of the church played out in those complex spheres of existence. I am implicitly drawing on this research in what follows. [68]

Paul's Vision of the Church

Every Pauline letter makes its own distinctive contribution to our full understanding of Paul's vision of the church. But it is 1 Corinthians, where the puzzle I have identified finds clearest expression, that arguably offers the richest portrait of his ecclesiology, meshing with strands of thought deployed elsewhere and holding them together within a rich harmony. In 1 Corinthians 10, Paul describes the church as a new kind of people, neither Jewish nor pagan: be blameless, he says, before Jews, before Greeks and before God's church. This fits with the tripartite division that emerges in chapter 1 in people's varied reactions to the gospel: Jews demand signs, Greeks seek wisdom, but we proclaim the crucified Messiah. The gospel is folly to Greeks, scandalous to Jews, but for us who are being saved – a third category! – it is God's wisdom and power.

Something new has happened in the world with the Messiah's death and resurrection and with the sending of the spirit. For Paul, this is a new sort of humanity – indeed, a 'new creation', as in Galatians 6 or 2 Corinthians 5. In 1 Corinthians 15 and Romans 5—8 it is clear that this 'new creation' is the new thing for which the original creation was made in the first place. In the new creation, the original Adamic purpose and destiny is at last fulfilled. But this radical newness does not simply sweep off the board all the signs of divine purpose in the long years of Israelite and Jewish scriptural narrative. At the start of 1 Corinthians 10, Paul identifies the church as the true descendants of the exodus generation, and thereby *narrates the Jew-plus-gentile church into the longer story of Israel.* 'Our ancestors', he says, 'were all baptized into Moses': they were rescued from Egypt, yet with many of them God was not pleased. The force of the ethical warning is missed unless the premise is grasped: those who are now 'in the Messiah' can and must understand themselves as the new representatives of the single great narrative in which the exodus from Egypt was part of the foundation.

Exegetes today struggle to say this accurately and without the appearance of anti-Jewish feeling. Despite the phraseology that [69] used to be employed, Paul never says either 'new Israel' or 'true Israel'; yet he repeatedly implies something like that, not least in 1 Corinthians 10 itself when he compares the church to 'Israel according to the flesh' (10.18, literally translated). His description of 'the Jew' in Romans 2.25–29, and of 'the circumcision' in Philippians 3.2–11, indicates well enough what he is doing. He is casting those 'in the Messiah', Jew and Greek together, as the single family in which the great promises to Israel will be fulfilled, promises that through them the ancient curse of sin and death will be undone and the creator's purposes for the world will be accomplished at last.

One way to get this clear – perhaps the best, or even the only way – is to insist that for Paul *Jesus the Messiah is Israel in person.* God has done for him, in raising him from the dead, what Paul as a Pharisee had supposed God would do for all Israel at the end. He is thereby constituted as Israel's representative. It is not the case, in other words, that Paul thinks in terms of God exchanging a Jewish family for a non-Jewish one (the classic 'supersession' position). Rather, if Jesus is Israel's Messiah then Israel is identified as the people who are now grouped around him. That, after all, was how first-century Jewish thinking would work; there were many would-be messianic movements within a century or so either side of Jesus, and any claim that so-and-so was the Messiah was *ipso facto* a claim that God's people were now to be seen in terms of their allegiance to this figure. Did Paul think that Jesus was the Messiah? Of course. Did recognizing someone as Messiah imply that God's people were regrouped around him? Naturally. Was that a non-Jewish or even anti-Jewish thing to suggest? Of course not.

The point, anyway, is that for Paul the Messiah's people are *both* a 'new creation' *and* the fulfilment of the divine intention for Israel. This chimes with the insistence in Romans 4 and Galatians 3 and 4 that the single messianic family is the true family promised to Abraham in the first place. This family – here is the famous doctrine – is 'justified by faith', since this 'faith', which Paul defines as the belief that God raised Jesus from the dead, and the confession that he is *kyrios*, lord, is the one and only defining mark that the family [70] bears. The resurrection indicates that Jesus' death was indeed 'for our sins' (Galatians 1.4), and part of the meaning of that is that 'gentile sinners' (Galatians 2.15) are 'sinners' no more, and can therefore be full members of the family, whose other members – believing Jews – have themselves 'died to the law through the law, so that [they] might live to God' (Galatians 2.19).

The point of all this for our larger discussion may not be immediately apparent, but it can be drawn out easily in two points.

(1) The divine intention, as Paul saw it unveiled in the messianic events concerning Jesus, was to create a single worldwide family; *and therefore any practices that functioned as symbols dividing different ethnic groups could not be maintained as absolutes within this single family.* Thus the major marks of Israel's ethnic distinctiveness – circumcision, food laws, sabbath and the Jerusalem Temple itself – were to be set aside, not because they were bad, not given by God, or representative of a shabby or second-rate kind of 'religion', but because of 'messianic eschatology', the fact that in Jesus Israel's God had done at last the new thing he had always promised.

(2) This divine intention, glimpsed in scriptures on which Paul drew, and sketched out in much of his teaching, was that this single family would, by the

spirit's work, embody, represent and carry forward the plan of 'new creation', the plan which had been the intention for Israel from the beginning; *and that therefore any practices that belonged to the dehumanizing, anti-creation world of sin and death could likewise not be maintained within this new-creation family.*

The first principle explains why certain things are now 'indifferent'; the second, why certain other things are not. This is the difference between the two kinds of 'difference'. We note that in this double-edged ecclesiology Jewish believers are required to give up the absolutizing of their specific ethnic boundary-markers, and erstwhile pagan believers are required to give up elements of their former life which they have taken for granted. This doesn't mean that Jews are being paganized (though Jewish apologists have frequently charged the church with that, sometimes with good reason), and it doesn't mean that pagans are Judaizing (though from very early on some [71] were tempted to do just that). It means that both are summoned to belong to the family of the crucified and risen Messiah.

This distinction between (1) the differences which don't make a difference, and which one must therefore 'tolerate', and (2) those which do make a difference, and which one must therefore not tolerate, is thus rooted in the twin theological poles around which Paul's thought revolves: creation and new creation on the one hand; covenant and new covenant on the other. In both, there is appropriate continuity and discontinuity, provided repeatedly by the model of cross and resurrection. The old is judged on the cross; the resurrection, ushering in the new, nevertheless is the true retrieval of the created goodness of the old. Without the cross, and its judgment, we are not taking seriously the fact of sin and death. In Volf's terms, we are trying to get 'embrace' without 'exclusion'. Without the resurrection, as the trans-formative re-enlivening of the condemned creation, we have all exclusion and no embrace. In terms of creation and new creation, the new creation retrieves and fulfils the intention for the original creation, in which the coming together of heaven and earth is reflected in the coming together of male and female. This vision of the original creative purpose was retained by Israel, the covenant people, the 'bride' of YHWH, and the strong sexual ethic that resulted formed one noticeable mark of distinction between the Jewish people and the wider world. This was highlighted dramatically in the Torah with the contrast between Judah's 'pagan' behaviour in Genesis 38 and Joseph's rejection of Potiphar's wife's advances in Genesis 39.

Within the Jewish world this sexual ethic was seen as the direct outflow of creational monotheism: the one God had created the world, including the complementary and fruit-bearing differentiation in the animal kingdom. It wasn't just that sexual malpractice happened to take place, often enough, in the precincts of pagan temples. There was an organic connection. If you worship idols, your image-bearing capacity diminishes, and you fail to carry forward the creative purposes of God. That is why, to look at the [72] positive side, when Abraham believes in God's creative and life-giving power, in Romans 4, the corruption of Romans 1 is reversed and he and Sarah conceive a child in their old age. The paradox then becomes clear: *Paul insists that the markers which distinguish Jew from gentile are no longer relevant in the new, messianic dispensation; but the Jewish-style worship of the one God, and the human male–female life which reflects that creational monotheism, is radically reinforced.*

Paul is clear, though many interpreters have not been, how this works out. Circumcision and uncircumcision are nothing; what matters is new creation. Food will not commend us to God; whether we eat or refuse to eat, we glorify God. Keeping this or that holy day, or not keeping any, is not a barrier to fellowship with others who do it differently. In the Messiah, and in the renewed Abrahamic family which is called into being through his death-for-sins and his new-creational resurrection, there is neither Jew nor Greek, slave nor free, and no 'male and female' (in other words, no longer any privileging of the male through the sign of circumcision, since females are baptized, and called to faith, equally with males) because you are 'all one in Messiah Jesus'. All of this means a large area of *adiaphora*, which as we shall presently see needs to be worked out through wise pastoral advice. Equally, the creational and covenantal monotheism that lies at the heart of both Jewish and Christian faith, and is not diluted by Paul's view of Jesus and the spirit but is rather put into dramatic and decisive operation through that view, is radically maintained, and with it the clear, high calling to a sexual and marital standard which, as with Jesus himself in Mark 10, reflects the original creative purpose.

For Paul, as I have just hinted, Jewish-style monotheism was radically reinterpreted through Jesus and the spirit. The hope of Israel – that the divine glory would be revealed for 'all flesh' to see, with Zion's watchmen shouting for joy as the glorious presence returned at last to the city and the Temple – had been radically fulfilled, in a way nobody had anticipated, in the person of Jesus himself and in the presence, power and leading of the spirit. In 2 Corinthians 3 and 4 [73], Paul expounds the story of the coming of the divine presence into the wilderness tabernacle in Exodus 32—34, and explains it in terms both of the transforming presence of the spirit and of 'the light of the knowledge of the glory of God in the face of Jesus the Messiah'. In Galatians 4, the slave-rescuing God is the one who sends the son and then sends the spirit of the son, resulting in the remarkable claim, 'Now that you've come to know God – or, better, to be known by God,' and the very Jewish, anti-pagan challenge, 'how can you turn back again to that weak and poverty-stricken line-up of "elements"?' In Romans 8, the redemptive work accomplished through the sending of God's own son is then applied through the spirit's work, 'leading' the people to their 'inheritance' – in other words, doing in the 'new exodus' what the strange divine presence in cloud and fire had done in the first exodus. For Paul, the events of Messiah and spirit have explicated and shaped afresh what it means to believe in the one God.

Exactly these elements have also contributed directly to the reshaping of the Jewish belief that marital and sexual behaviour is closely allied to belief in the one creator God. Paul's instructions about behaviour in these areas are emphatically 'in the lord', worked out particularly in the remarkable christological analogy for husband and wife in Ephesians 5. The basis for the rejection of pagan sexual behaviour and the embrace of a new way of life (a way which that great pagan, the doctor Galen, recognized as strange to the point of madness in terms of the 'normal' behavioural standards of his world) is that 'you were washed, sanctified and justified in the name of the lord, Messiah Jesus, and in the spirit of our God' (1 Corinthians 6.11). Unity with the Messiah is what matters, and this will be radically compromised by *porneia* (6.15–17). The body that has been 'an expensive purchase' – in other words, that has been redeemed through the blood of the Messiah – is now 'a temple of the holy spirit' (6.19). The closing command of that decisive chapter, 'glorify God in your body' (6.20), is not simply about 'honouring' God in the way one behaves. It is about recognizing, and 'giving glory to', the God who has purchased the body through [74] the person and death of the son, and who now indwells the body through the person and power of the spirit. This is a Trinitarian ethic flowing directly from the Trinitarian reworking of monotheism itself (as in 1 Corinthians 12.4–6 and elsewhere).

For Paul, therefore, there is continuity with the ancient Jewish worship and ethic, and there is also enhancement. The same God; the same standard; but now this God is revealed in radically fresh ways through Jesus and the spirit, and the standard is clarified and energized by that same revelation-in-action. This, for Paul, is foundational.

It ought now to be clear, before we proceed, that we cannot get to the heart of Paul's thinking in these or related areas through the old supposition that he merely opposed 'works of the law' – a category which, for many inter-preters, included circumcision and food taboos on the one hand and matters of personal behaviour on the other in an undifferentiated agglomeration. There was nothing wrong with the Jewish law, as Paul makes clear in various passages. The differentiation he introduces has nothing to do with deciding that some parts of Torah are good and to be retained (sexual ethics) and other parts are bad and to be abolished (food laws, circumcision and so on). That is not the point. The point is, again, *messianic eschatology*: the Messiah has come, and in his death, resurrection and sending of the spirit he has inaugurated the new age, the new covenant, the new creation. Some parts of Torah – the parts that kept Israel separate from the gentile world until the coming of Messiah – have done their work and are now put to one side, not because they were bad but because they were good and have done their work. Other parts of Torah – the parts that pointed to the divine intention to renew the whole creation through Israel – are celebrated as being now at last within reach through Jesus and the spirit. The old has passed away; all things have become new – and the 'new' includes the triumphant and celebratory recovery of the original created intention, not least for male and female in marriage. [75]

Of course, here too (notably in 1 Corinthians 7), Paul introduces a further radical proposal: that, against the assumption and the attempted legislation of the day, widows were free *not* to remarry, and singleness (and hence child-lessness) was a valid and appropriate state for those who were called to it. Marriage thus witnesses to the recovery of the original creative intention; singleness (including staying single after either divorce or widowhood) to the fact that the ultimate 'new creation' is yet to come. There is thus a 'now and not yet' element to Paul's ethic of marriage and singleness, which again is not captured by any suggestion that he is either 'for' or 'against' something called 'the law', seen as a collection of miscellaneous instructions. He has gone far deeper than that. His vision of the church is a vision of the Messiah himself, defeating sin and death and thereby fulfilling Israel's vocation of being the answer to the problems of the wider world. That vision is then implemented through the spirit, calling into being through the gospel a new-covenant, new-creation people. Because this people is the new-*covenant* people, the temporary regulations of the old covenant are set aside as having done their job. Because this people is the new-*creation* people, the creational vision of the one God with his image-bearing male-and-female humans is enhanced, rescued from decay and brought within reach. If we still sense this as a paradox, that may be an indication that we have not yet come to terms with the depths of Paul's reading of scripture in the light of the crucified and risen Messiah and the gift and power of the spirit.

Paul's Vision of Unity and *Adiaphora*

It should by now be clear that when Paul appeals for unity across traditional boundaries, and for the consequent rendering as *adiaphora* of cultural taboos which up to that point have been mandatory, this owes nothing to any sense that, in the new dispensation, one can play fast and loose with fussy old regulations. That is not the point. What we see in the two crucial passages, Romans 14—15 and 1 Corinthians [76] 8—10, is the principled and also pastorally sensitive application of his belief that in the Messiah and by the spirit a new, multi-ethnic people has come into existence in surprising fulfilment of ancient promises.

The two passages are subtly different; we may take Romans 14—15 first. I hold the view that here Paul is addressing the problem that in Rome there are several house-churches, between which there exist significant variations in practice regarding food, drink and holy days. This is only to be expected. There may be some Jewish-Christian groups in Rome who still, like their Jerusalem counterparts, see all of Torah as mandatory, while some gentile-Christian groups have known from the start that their own admission to the Messiah's people is not on the basis of Torah. Equally, there may be Jewish Christians who, like Paul himself (and quite possibly under his teaching), have come to see that Torah, though good and God-given, has in significant ways been set aside as the marker of the eschatologically renewed people. And there may be some gentile Christians who, like some of the ex-pagans in Galatia, have been so delighted with what they have discovered of the Jewish and biblical context of the Messiah's work that they have been eager to embrace even those parts of Jewish tradition that, in Paul's view at least, are no longer relevant now that the Messiah has died and been raised, and that the spirit has been poured out. And this is just a start. There may be many more variations, rooted both in ethnic traditions and identities and in different understandings of the gospel and its significance.

Paul's aim throughout this section of Romans, as becomes clear in 15.7–13, is *united worship*, rooted in mutual respect. He does not here ask the different groups to give up their practices; merely not to judge one another where differences exist. As Paul well knew (though we sometimes forget), this is actually just as large a step, if not larger, than a change in practice itself. *The move from regarding something as mandatory to regarding it as optional is vast,* just as vast in fact as *the move from regarding something as forbidden to regarding it as available.* Even if one is not going to take advantage of the 'optional' clause in the first of these, or the 'available' clause in the second, admitting [77] that it might be so is the main thing. (That, of course, is why the apparently innocuous 'live and let live' proposals for reform are the real crunch, as most reforming groups know well.)

Paul sometimes appears to relish the ironies that result. Neither circumcision nor uncircumcision matters, he says in 1 Corinthians 7.19, since what really matters is *keeping God's commandments* – fully aware, of course, that the command to circumcise was basic in Torah. And here, as the necessary pastoral outworking of this principle, Paul introduces the vital messianic principle: if your brother or sister is being injured by what you eat, you are no longer walking in love; you might, by your exercise of freedom, 'destroy someone for whom the Messiah died' (14.15). This must then be correlated with the principle of conscience: if you have thought through what you are doing, and understand why it is right for you, then go ahead; but to act while doubting, in other words not from faith, is to sin (14.23).

This whole discussion alerts us to the fact that Paul is here applying pastoral wisdom to contentious situations. He knows perfectly well that people cannot change the habits of a lifetime overnight, including the kinds of food they eat or do not eat. He knows that there will therefore be within the church many people living side by side whose 'natural' way of doing things will be different from one another. Here the principles of charity on the one hand (not destroying a sibling for whom the Messiah died) and conscience on the other (acting from thought-out faith) must inform what is done. Messiah-people will make demands on one another's charity; they must not make demands on one another's conscience. This does not, to be sure, produce a fixed and balanced policy that will last a generation. Things will change over time as people think things through afresh, as new members of the body arrive from elsewhere bringing with them their own expectations and sensitivities. The rules of charity and conscience are there, not to nail down a one-size-fits-all rule-book but precisely to enable mutual respect and shared worship in the absence of such a thing. But – and we should note this once again – Paul does *not* apply [78] this to questions of sexual ethics (or for that matter to extortion, murder, violence, lying, mutual lawsuits and so forth). In this passage, he has made that abundantly clear in 13.11–14, before the present discussion can get under way – perhaps deliberately warding off any misunderstandings in advance.

A similar pattern may be observed in 1 Corinthians 8—10, where Paul's dealing with serious sexual misdemeanour in chapter 5 ('Drive out the wicked person from your company') has led to a more general warning against *porneia* in chapter 6, and then the wider instructions about marriage, divorce and singleness in chapter 7. It is as though he needs to get clear on all this before he can begin to address the issues that are to be considered *adiaphora* – though, to be sure, the question of a Christian's relation to idol-temples in a city like Corinth was not detached from questions of *porneia*.

The issue at stake in chapters 8, 9 and 10 is not quite the same as that in Romans 14 and 15. There, Paul was faced with various different groups, most likely in different house-churches, probably reflecting different aspects of their ethnic backgrounds. Here, in 1 Corinthians, there is one church – albeit prone to factionalism! – and the issue is more focused. Granted that virtually all the meat offered for sale in a city like Corinth would have already been offered in an idol-temple, does that mean it is all 'off limits'? Is it irrevocably 'tainted'?

Paul goes right to the heart of the issue, with his christologically redefined Jewish monotheism. There are many so-called 'gods' and 'lords', but they are a sham: for us 'there is one God, the father, from whom are all things and [literally] we to him, and one lord, Jesus the Messiah, through whom are all things and [literally] we through him' [1 Corinthians 8.6]. Paul has reworked the ancient daily Jewish prayer, the *Shema*, and has discerned Jesus at its heart. Monotheism is his main point, here and in the concluding summary when he quotes a similarly emphatic text, Psalm 24.1 ('The earth and its fullness . . . belong to the Lord'). Here too Jesus is at least implied, as it often is when Paul quotes the Septuagint *kyrios* ('lord'). [79]

From this Jewish-style and Jesus-focused monotheism (very different from the pantheistic 'monotheism' of the Stoics) two things follow. First, the idols themselves have no real existence. Zeus, Athene, Mars, Aphrodite and the rest are figments of human imagination. Meat offered to them therefore does not 'belong' to them: a non-existent being cannot own things. It still belongs to the one true God, and it can be eaten if received with thanksgiving. Second, however, when humans worship these non-gods they are actually getting in touch with, and giving power to, the *daimonia* – nasty, shadowy little non-human beings who hang out in the idol-temples like ill-kempt squatters camping in a great mansion. These beings, though in no way 'divine', nevertheless have a power, stolen perhaps from the humans who worship the 'gods' (this is one of the points we wish Paul had made a bit clearer), which can not only mess up human lives but, more importantly, puts them as it were in competition with the lordship of Jesus himself. Someone who belongs to the Messiah but who actually goes into an idol-shrine and eats and drinks there is by strong implication playing off the Messiah against the *daimonia*, and vice versa.

Paul's main point, then, is that to buy the meat in the market, or to eat it when invited to someone's home, is absolutely fine. But to go into an idol-temple and share in the meal on offer there is not. In Ben Witherington's characteristic phrase, 'it is more a matter of venue than menu'.[1] That is the basic framework of his argument, thought out clearly on the basis of the christologically reimagined monotheism.

The key question for Paul is then, 'How does this apply pastorally in a church where many members have in the past frequented idol-temples and shared in the entire way of life that they embody?' For some, we may suppose – reading between Paul's lines, but only a little – the very smell of cooked meat might easily conjure up the sights and sounds, incense wafting around idolatrous statues, boys and girls working the crowd to offer sexual favours, another glass of wine, then another, and then . . . bad memories, a dark mixture of thrill [80] and guilt, a soul steadily eroded, a sense of chaos only warded off by more of the same. That was what the Messiah had rescued them from! Why would they want to have anything to do with it again?

Paul designates these two positions the 'strong' and the 'weak'. The 'strong' know that all meat is available to them; the 'weak' will find that it puts a strain on their conscience. We must remember, reading this terminology, that in writing to the Corinthians in particular he insists that the Messiah's cross has redefined power in terms of 'weakness', so we must not imagine that these terms carry a kind of superiority complex in which the 'strong' (Paul himself included) can look down their noses at the 'weak' who should really, they might think, get their act together. Certainly not. As in Romans 14, these are siblings for whom the Messiah died (1 Corinthians 8.11). And here we come to the heart of Paul's doctrine of *adiaphora*. Meat – in this case, food that has been offered to idols – is not to be a community-divider. It all belongs to the one God. But for that to be a reality – for the community not to be divided – all parties must see that what matters is not the meat itself *but the conscience of the person who might or might not eat*. Paul even, unusually for him, enters into some detailed situational discussion: if a pagan invites you to dinner, go and eat without raising questions, but if someone says 'Don't

---

1 Witherington 2004, 54.

you realize that was offered to an idol?' you should abstain (1 Corinthians 10.27–30), not because of your conscience, but because of theirs.

This, then, is how the *adiaphora* rule works. First, the robust Trinitarian monotheism now made known through Jesus and the spirit is basic, enhancing and explaining further the essential Jewish monotheism in which all creation is good (in other words, Paul is a million miles away from Platonic dualism, still more from Gnosticism). Those who have had scruples about this or that need to think through what this Christ-and-spirit-shaped monotheism means in practice. Second, that will take time, because humans do not always change mental and practical habits overnight, and in this case they should not be forced to do so. But in a mixed community, where people are still 'on the way' in being taught, in prayerfully [81] thinking this through, the 'strong' should defer to the 'weak'. This again neither reflects nor produces a stable situation. Opinions may change, different community members may take different positions, and there is always the awkward moment when, sitting in good conscience at someone's table, a bystander makes a comment that indicates a 'weak' conscience. Paul is not legislating for all situations, nor could he. He is teaching people *to think messianically*, and especially to think through their own faith and practice, and their membership of the community with others on the same journey but at different points along the road, in the light of the Messiah's death and resurrection. He is teaching them to *navigate* through difficult and only partly charted waters, with the Messiah and his saving death as the principal star by which they must steer. And in that situation the subtle rule of *adiaphora* is about as different from a modern doctrine of 'tolerance' as can be imagined. 'Tolerance' is not simply a low-grade version of 'love'; in some senses, it is its opposite, as 'tolerance' can imply a distancing, a wave from the other side of the street, rather than the rich embrace of 'the sibling for whom the Messiah died'.

Conclusion

There is much more, of course, that could and perhaps should be said about Paul and *adiaphora*. What matters is that we grasp as firmly as we can the fundamental principles of ecclesiology which Paul not only articulated as theory but worked out in pastoral and epistolary practice. To understand the church as the Messiah's spirit-filled people and, as such, as the community of new covenant and new creation, is to understand the difference between the matters in relation to which the church can and must live with difference of practice and the matters in relation to which the church has neither right nor mandate to approve or condone such differences. We, of course, live in a world where, in the aftermath of the Enlightenment's watering down of Reformation theology, many have reduced [82] the faith to a set of abstract doctrines and a list of detached and apparently arbitrary rules, which 'conservatives' then insist on and 'radicals' try to bend or merely ignore. It is this framework itself which we have got wrong, resulting in dialogues of the deaf or, worse, the lobbing of angry verbal hand-grenades over walls of incomprehension. Paul's framework was very different. It may be painful for us to learn to think within his framework rather than the one into which we regularly fall. But only if we learn to do so will we understand, and be able to navigate, the real challenges we face today and tomorrow.

13
Apocalyptic and the Sudden Fulfilment of Divine Promise

The question of 'apocalyptic' has continued to challenge scholars in recent decades. I have written at length about this in Part II of *Paul and His Recent Interpreters* (Wright 2015a). The present paper was part of a conference added on to the regular annual meeting of the Society of Biblical Literature in San Diego in 2014. The atmosphere was quite tense, since the popular perception, at least in the USA, is that a good deal is riding on whether or not one accepts some version of the thesis of J. Louis Martyn and his supporters. This debate, like others in the USA, can easily get bundled up within the 'culture wars' that trivialize and distort so many issues. I hope this small contribution, alongside the fuller treatment in the book referred to, will help to keep the discussions on properly historical lines.

[111] The space is too constrained, and the current debates too many-sided and wide-ranging, to allow for detailed interaction with other views. There will, however, be many times when Mark's 'apocalyptic' warning will be appropriate: 'Let the reader understand [Mark 13.14].'

Paul's Setting

Saul of Tarsus lived in a world of intense eschatological expectation, rooted in Israel's scriptures and heated to boiling point by political circumstances. Jewish life since the Babylonian exile was a story of hopes raised and then dashed. The hope was for Israel's ultimate rescue (after an 'extended exile'), and the ultimate glorious return of Israel's [112] God. 'O that you would tear open the heavens and come down'; 'the glory of YHWH shall be revealed, and all flesh shall see it together'; 'Then YHWH my God will come, and all his saints with him'; 'the Lord whom you seek will suddenly come to his temple' (Isaiah 64.1; 40.5; Zechariah 14.5; Malachi 3.1). Israel's God would return in person to sort everything out – to put the world right, and particularly to put Israel right, by dealing with pagan oppression and rescuing God's people from its grip. This powerful strand of Jewish thinking can be seen under the overall heading of 'new exodus'. All this is massively documented and should be uncontroversial.[1] It constituted the 'sudden fulfilment of divine promise'. Saul of Tarsus came to believe that these promises had been fulfilled in the dramatic and unexpected events concerning Jesus and the spirit.

Within this world, the literary form sometimes called 'apocalypse' served a particular purpose. Hope deferred may have sickened the heart, but it sometimes inspired the mind; and one writer after another wrote, whether like Coleridge because of actual dreams or like Bunyan because of literary choice, in a form which declared that, though the coming ultimate revelation was still delayed, a word from beyond, a vision of the heavenly realm and its mysteries, might be given to select mortals to encourage them ahead of the final great day, perhaps even to stir them to new ways of looking at their present circumstances, understanding the dark nature of present oppression, and grasping the sure promise of eventual deliverance. If the longed-for glorious presence of the Shekinah was delayed, and if (in particular) the dark forces of the non-Jewish world seemed to be all-powerful, there might none the less be ways in which, through prayer and study, glimpses might be granted, even in the present time, of heavenly truths, heavenly purposes and perhaps also eventual divine victory. The literary genre we call 'apocalypse' was one way of reflecting or embodying this belief, whether or not, in this or that case, it was intended as a transcript of actual visionary experience. Thus both (what we call) 'mysticism' and (what we call) 'apocalyptic' can be [113] credibly located, within the ancient Jewish world, within the puzzlement, persecution and dogged hope of the second-Temple period.

The genre we have come to know as 'apocalypse' is found in many cultures. But if we are to place Paul in relation to this kind of writing, or its supposedly specific content, we must focus on Jewish sources in particular: on the line from Ezekiel and Daniel through to *4 Ezra* and *2 Baruch*, and within early Christian writing from certain passages in the gospels through to the book of Revelation and second-century texts such as *The Shepherd of Hermas*. When we speak of 'apocalyptic' in relation to a Jewish or early Christian text, we must at the very least indicate that we mean to bring it into this orbit. (How odd it is, in passing, that people discuss 'Paul and apocalyptic' without reference to Revelation or the *Shepherd*! If we want to investigate early Christian apocalyptic, and Paul within it, they might be obvious places

---

1 See e.g. Wright 2013b, ch. 2.

to begin.[2]) The point of introducing 'apocalyptic' as an explanatory or organizing category in New Testament studies, at least since Käsemann, was to locate it within a credible history-of-religions, and perhaps also theological, setting. Whatever form the proposal now takes, it must make sense within that second-Temple Jewish world.

Marking out this *literary* territory does not, of itself, mean highlighting a distinct *theology*. Nor does the theology sometimes expressed in some 'apocalyptic' writings need this particular genre. Most Jews of Paul's day, and on into the high rabbinic period long after 'apocalyptic' had fallen from favour, distinguished 'the present age' from 'the age to come'. Most Jews, then and later, acknowledged the existence of non-human agencies both good and evil. All ancient Jews for whom we have evidence believed that heaven and earth were neither identical nor separated by a vast unbridgeable gulf. Commerce between heaven and earth was thinkable, and the Jerusalem Temple symbolized, and might perhaps actualize, their ideal overlap. (Details of the Temple and its liturgical practices continued, of course, to be [114] discussed for centuries after its destruction.) None of these beliefs is specific either to the literary genre we call 'apocalyptic' or to any 'movement' that might deserve the name 'apocalypticism'. The particular genre we know from Daniel, *4 Ezra* and the rest was one way among others in which these issues could be addressed. In other words, you did not have to write an 'apocalypse' in order to talk about 'the present age and the age to come', or about the baleful influence of hostile non-human powers. Equally, if you *were* writing an 'apocalypse', you didn't have to talk about those themes. Two-age discourse and the narrative of cosmic warfare and victory were neither necessary nor sufficient conditions for the presence of something which can, with historical basis, be called 'apocalyptic', and vice versa. Details about the promised future were naturally an important feature of such writings. But these works were concerned with many other things besides, as Christopher Rowland and others have demonstrated.[3]

Referring to any of these elements as 'apocalyptic', therefore, simply begs the question. To refer (as some do) to suprahuman powers, believed by some to influence the course of this-worldly events, as 'apocalyptic' powers is a combination of muddled thinking about the first century and subtle influence from our own (where the word 'apocalyptic' is used as an arm-waving indicator of the enormous or terrible scale of, say, a natural disaster). Calling

---

2   See Davies 2016.

3   Rowland 1982; Rowland and Morray-Jones 2009. On all this, see further Wright 2015a, Part II.

them 'cosmic' powers may not be much better, since the word 'cosmic' is itself used in a variety of ways, of which 'non-spatio-temporal' or 'supra-human' is only one. Granted, we are here at the borders of language, and we may suspect that first-century Jews were as well. That is why they developed particular genres, to say in symbol and metaphor what ordinary language might struggle with.[4]

One particular problem with our descriptions of ancient Jewish [115] thought, and particularly with 'apocalyptic', centres on the word 'dualism'. That word regularly misleads.[5] There is such a thing as radical ontological dualism, in which the present world of space, time and matter is basically evil and in which another world – without space, time and matter – is basically good. But that is not, so far as we can tell, how most ancient Jews character-istically saw things. There are indeed, within ancient Jewish writings, what may be called 'dualities': between, for instance, 'the present age' and 'the age to come', which (as I noted a moment ago) was a distinction made as much by the rabbis as by the writers of apocalypses. Paul himself, in Galatians 1.4, labels the 'present age' as 'evil'. But to call that statement 'dualistic' (or to regard a belief in the existence of hostile powers as 'dualistic') can mislead us into forgetting that most Jews, Paul included, regarded the present world as, none the less, the good creation of the good creator, and the present time as under the creator's sovereign providence. Part of the point of many actual apocalypses is to affirm this very point, in the teeth of apparently contra-dictory evidence.[6] If we today find it difficult to believe in divine sovereignty at the same time as saying (with, for instance, 1 John 5.19) that the world is 'under the power of the evil one' or of the delegated agents of that dark force, that is our problem. The early Jews, and the early Christians, managed, not perhaps without a struggle, to hold those things in dynamic tension (for example John 19.11).

Nor was the content of 'apocalyptic' writing polarized over against other strands of Jewish culture.[7] People used to play off a supposed 'apocalyptic' Jesus against a supposed 'wisdom' Jesus (this was a favourite ploy of the Jesus Seminar), but this is a false antithesis. Insofar as we can isolate elements characteristic of 'wisdom' or of 'apocalyptic', we find them regularly inter-mingled, as in the Scrolls, the Wisdom of Solomon, the synoptic tradition or

---

4 See Caird 1980. Cf. the defence of this point in Wright 2013b, 163–75.
5 Wright 1992, ch. 10.
6 Among possible exceptions we might include *1 Enoch* 42.
7 This point was already made by Beker 1987, 137. See too Meeks 1983, 179–80.

the book of [116] Revelation. A good deal of ancient Jewish literature, in fact, warns us against confusing genre and content, at this or any other point.

Jewish 'apocalyptic' literature, then, frequently affirms divine sovereignty over the history, not only of Israel, but of the wider world. Such writings often describe the long, dark and puzzling purposes of the one God, purposes that can be mapped through devices like the many-metalled statue in Daniel 2, the four beasts out of the sea in Daniel 7, or the sheep, the bull and so on in *1 Enoch*. The authors of these writings did not envisage the ultimate deliverance, if it were to come, as emerging from a steady crescendo of 'progressive revelation' or immanent development. Any suggestion of such a developmental eschatology, even if dignified with the slippery term 'salvation history', is out of the question; though, as we shall see presently, there *is* something in the texts, both Jewish and Pauline, which can properly be named in that way, as Ernst Käsemann rightly saw. The strange, terrible and often apparently chaotic events of history, into which deliverance would break as a fresh and cataclysmic act, were none the less under some kind of ultimate divine control, and the divine promises of ultimate deliverance, often coming at what seemed like the darkest moments, could be seen at least in retrospect as signs of that control, and of its covenantal focus (see below). Thus 'apocalyptic' texts regularly saw the present state of affairs, not as mere chaos nor, of course, as constituting any kind of 'progress' or 'development' but as a nevertheless divinely ordered sequence of woes or wicked kingdoms, symbolized by metals, animals or monsters. The coming event would be a dramatic reversal in which, suddenly, the long, dark sequence would be over and the ancient promises would be fulfilled. But the sequence itself, though not in any way about 'progress', was all about *providence*. Articulating all this in a balanced way is, to be sure, quite difficult. That, no doubt, is why special literary forms were used for the purpose.

My basic point here concerns false antitheses. Within the literary genre 'apocalypse', and within any putative movement labelled 'apocalypticism', it was normal to *combine* a sense that the present age [117] was evil, dominated by wicked suprahuman forces, with an equal sense that Israel's creator God was working his purpose out, not as a steady evolution, but with an inscru-table justice and timing, and that at the right moment, he would unveil, to an unready world, the shocking and sudden fulfilment of his ancient promises. The underlying doctrine of providence, so prominent in Josephus (to take an example from a quite different genre),[8] did not mean that one could read

---

8   See the account of basic Jewish belief in e.g. Sanders 1992, 247–51.

divine purposes out of observable historical events. When Josephus wanted to explain what God was really up to, he had to invoke his own supposed prophetic powers (for example *War* 3.405–7). Nor did belief in providence imply a steady crescendo leading to a fortissimo fulfilment. The apocalypses affirm a dogged trust that somewhere, somehow, even in the thick darkness, the one God was still in control, and would fulfil his seemingly impossible purposes at the proper time. But the phrase 'at the proper time' was important. Once more, this had nothing to do with a *linear progress*, an evolution or development. On the contrary, it would seem that the night was getting darker. When the dawn came, it would not be heralded by a long, slow twilight, but would burst suddenly on a slumbering, unready world. Here is the first false antithesis to avoid: the idea that because the divine action will come suddenly and unexpectedly, it bears no relation to the ancient promises, or to the ultimate divine overruling of the dark history that precedes it.

Nor do I find a major difference of theology between different putative types of apocalyptic, such that some might be 'cosmic' and others 'forensic'. This is a second false antithesis. The introduction of this supposed distinction (by my fellow essayist Martinus de Boer in his original dissertation) was linked explicitly to the debate between Bultmann and Käsemann, thereby, in my view, foisting an ill-fitting mid-century German polarization on to the ancient material.[9] Quite [118] apart from the slippery and anachronistic nature of both the terms in question, we cannot fail to notice that the texts hailed as 'cosmological' (including *1 Enoch*) also foresaw a great final assize (the 'forensic' idea); while those hailed as 'forensic' (including *4 Ezra*) also foresaw the coming showdown with the forces of evil. (Paul's letters as they stand, of course, include both.) It is not clear that any of the writers invoked on either side were addressing the question which de Boer puts to them – that is, whether the origin of evil lies with non-human evil powers (which must therefore be defeated) or with evil human deeds (which must therefore be atoned for), and hence whether salvation comes through the defeat of evil powers or through the divine dealing with human sin and guilt. Even if there had been any merit in reading back into these ancient texts such a modern polarization (which looks suspiciously similar to that made by Gustav Aulén

---

9 de Boer 1988, 84–8, 182–3; 1989, 180–1; 2011, 31–5, 79–82. In his Hermeneia commentary on *1 Enoch*, George Nickelsburg also makes use of similar categories, but insists they are not antithetical (Nickelsburg 2002, 41). A similar point to mine is made by Meeks 1983, 172: debates about 'apocalyptic' have unfortunately focused on 'the abstractions represented by the terms *anthropology* versus *cosmology*, both of which the discussants use in peculiar senses' (italics original).

in his famous book *Christus Victor*),[10] the subsequent dichotomous use that has been made of de Boer's (initially heuristic) categories[11] has made matters much worse, as we shall see presently.

The third false antithesis which we must avoid – if, that is, we intend to talk about the actual history of belief and practice in the Jewish world of Paul's day, and so to provide a credible historical context – is that between 'apocalyptic' and 'covenant'. The Jewish belief in divine 'providence' went hand in hand with the persistent belief that the creator God was, more specifically, the God of Israel. The word 'covenant' remains an accurate and convenient shorthand for this belief, held by most second-Temple Jews for whom we have evidence, and certainly, more importantly for our topic, by the authors of the actual apocalypses we possess. The 'covenant' hope, allied to the underlying belief in providence, was brought into focus by the scriptural promises to Abraham, Moses and David: the God who was [119] hailed as the world's creator, ultimate ruler and final judge was *Israel's* God. The coming moment when the previously inscrutable providence would suddenly erupt in a fresh act of judgment and mercy would be like the exodus: after long years of unrelieved darkness, God would remember his covenant, and deliverance would appear. Closely allied with all this is 'salvation history', often attacked as radically incompatible with an 'apocalyptic' reading of Paul in particular – though neither Käsemann himself nor, indeed, de Boer drew that conclusion from their more nuanced studies. The idea of 'covenant', and the correlated idea of 'salvation history', have been criticized by those who see them as encapsulating either a private soteriology (the 'covenant' people distinct from the rest of the world) or an automatic or evolutionary revelation or salvation (a steady, linear development leading gradually to the goal). To those, I reply with Latin tags: *abusum non tollit usum*, and *corruptio optimi pessima*. The abuse does not remove the proper use; the worst is the corruption of the best. In fact, Käsemann, to whom appeal is often made in this connection, saw very clearly that there were indeed important strands of covenantal and salvation-historical thinking, both in Israel's scriptures and in Paul's retrieval of them. Whether his description of either, and his attempt to integrate them into his understanding of Paul, really worked is another matter.[12]

Thus to invoke 'covenant', as I have done in my writing on the second-Temple Jewish world, and on Paul in particular, is not to deny the presence

---

10   Aulén 1967 [1931].
11   de Boer 1988, 85.
12   See my article, Wright 2014a.

or importance of 'apocalyptic'. It is rather to contextualize it historically and theologically. In the same way, to invoke 'apocalyptic', as I am happy to do, is not to deny 'covenant' or 'history'. It is, rather, to explain that, in the first century, the covenant hope had been so long deferred that it was natural to choose, for the continued expression of that hope, a genre ideal for articulating secret advance revelations of the divine presence and purpose. Though Paul refers to such revelations, he did not choose that genre to express [120] them. As we shall see, that was at least partly because he believed the decisive unveiling of the long-awaited divine rescue operation had already taken place.

Was there, then, an actual 'movement' which we could call 'apocalypticism'? I doubt it. How many books in a particular genre does it take – spread over several centuries! – to make an 'ism'? Did people think of themselves as belonging to such a body? Did other people speak of them in that way? Did anyone in the ancient world think in terms of different types of movement of which 'apocalypticism' might be one? I am sceptical. When Josephus describes the four 'philosophies' within the Jewish world, he makes no mention of this one (*Ant.* 18.12–25). The real roots of 'apocalypticism', I suggest, lie in the same place as those of many other 'isms': in the world of nineteenth-century idealism (that term being itself an example of its own blessed rage for categorization). But to probe further we must turn from Paul's context to our own.

Our Own Setting

If we are to understand the resonances of the word 'apocalyptic' in today's biblical scholarship, we need at least as much hermeneutical sophistication as when trying to understand the first century. I have written about this elsewhere, so here need only summarize (risky though that is).[13] The relevant parts of the story begin in the German scholarship of the nineteenth century; I still find one of the most helpful accounts to be that of Klaus Koch in his book *The Rediscovery of Apocalyptic*. The original German title, *Ratlos vor der Apokalyptik* ('Clueless in the Face of Apocalyptic') made the point: for much late nineteenth-century German scholarship, 'apocalyptic' was the dark, dangerous mindset at the heart of *Spätjudentum*. Compared with the supposedly earlier 'prophetic' strands of Jewish religion, far more congenial to the optimistic liberal mindset of the day, 'apocalyptic' appeared as a

---

13   See Wright 2015a, Part II.

negative, world-denying religion, abandoning hope for [121] the present world and looking only for divine judgment on the wicked. Books like Daniel and Revelation made little sense in a world which, drawing on Kant and Hegel, believed in social improvement (in some cases, in social Darwinism), and had no historical sense of what the ancient 'apocalyptic' writers were trying to do. Such writing represented, to them, a degenerate and sectarian retreat from the world. One can see a similar reaction among the members of the so-called Jesus Seminar of the 1990s, who saw 'apocalyptic' as the 'bad' side of traditions about Jesus, representing a bombastic, judgmental attitude rather than the wise, savvy 'wisdom' teaching characteristic (so they thought) of Jesus himself. No doubt the bizarre and supposedly 'apocalyptic' teachings in American fundamentalism made such a solution appear all the more attractive.[14] Thus for some in late nineteenth-century Germany, and for some in late twentieth-century America, 'apocalyptic' came to represent the wrong sort of religion, a religion so clearly visible as a separate entity that it could be dignified as an 'ism'. Thus 'apocalyptic*ism*' was born, a hypothetical movement with its own worldview and theology.

The mainstream tradition was therefore horrified at Albert Schweitzer's portrait of Jesus as a first-century apocalyptic Jew. Instead of the wise, loving teacher of 'the fatherhood of God and the brotherhood of Man', Jesus suddenly became remote, unappealing, a first-century fanatic followed by other first-century fanatics, all of them believing that the world was about to end, and all (including Jesus) dying disappointed. Schweitzer represented a would-be Christian version of Nietzsche, warning the upbeat nineteenth century that its easy-going optimism was based on quicksand. Unsurprisingly, most Jesus-scholarship looked the other way, not only for 'religious' reasons (who wanted a 'Jesus' like that?) but for political reasons as well: 'apocalyptic' sounded too like Marxism for comfort.

But the horrific events of the First World War sowed the seeds for the come-back of a post-Schweitzer 'apocalyptic'. Karl Barth's famous *Romans* commentary did not make 'apocalyptic' as such a main theme, [122] but its effect was the same: instead of the liberal belief in 'progress', with humans advancing their own cause and improving their own lot, God had to step in, vertically from above, and denounce the whole plan, breaking in with a fresh Word of judgment and grace. (Barth, himself suspected of being a Marxist, was and remained a sort of Calvinist. Elements in that combination remain powerfully attractive to many.) With the hindsight of nearly a century, we

---

14   On the Jesus Seminar, see Wright 1996a, 29–35.

can see that Schweitzer and Barth were saying something similar, however different their details. Both were protesting in favour of a better understanding of Israel's scriptures. Both were envisaging the gospel as God's sovereign intervention ('invasion'?) into a rebellious and unready world.

By the middle of the twentieth century, the earlier sneers against 'apocalyptic' had given way to a despairing re-embracing. Walter Benjamin, often cited at this point, had developed his own brand of messianic Marxism, a secular version of his native Jewish hope. If there was no divinity, no outside agency to bring the necessary upheaval, revolution would have to emerge instead from the immanent processes of history. But when that hope was thwarted, and with it the parallel (and equally Hegelian and Darwinian) hopes of National Socialism, Benjamin rejected the possibility that 'history' might lead anywhere except wreckage.[15] What Benjamin and others were rejecting, however, as in Käsemann's famous angry response to Stendahl, was the kind of secularized *Heilsgeschichte* which many had embraced, on both sides of the political divide, in the 1930s.[16] There is no sign that either the embracers or the rejecters knew much about the ancient Jewish apocalypses.

Käsemann invoked the category 'apocalyptic' to provide a history-of-religions context for early Christianity, replacing Bultmann's proposal of 'Gnosticism'. He did this partly for historical reasons: he had seen that the gnostic sources did not support the hypothesis. But he also had theological, social and political reasons: Käsemann, like Barth in some ways and Benjamin in others, had seen that immanent [123] historical processes would produce, not utopia, but nightmares. Something quite different had to happen. But what?

Käsemann's placing of 'apocalyptic' as 'the mother of Christian theology', meaning, by that, that the first Christianity focused on 'imminent expectation', was a proposal not only about theology, but about history. The proposal stands or falls by whether or not it can produce a historically credible reconstruction and understanding of first-century Jewish 'apocalyptic'; most specialists would say that, by that test, it falls. Käsemann's view of 'apocalyptic' was still far too coloured by the older German ideas. That, indeed, was why it appealed: the first half of the twentieth century had demonstrated the dismal failure of the old liberal dream, including Bultmann's version. The features that had previously made 'apocalypticism' unattractive were the very things Käsemann wanted to find. But Käsemann, a serious historical

---

15   For this whole subject, see Wright 2013b, 1473–84.
16   On the debate between Käsemann and Stendahl, see Wright 2013c, ch. 1.

critic, was not simply spinning ideas. He was proposing a history-of-religions setting. We can, of course, use words how we like, but we cannot invent a non-historical movement called 'apocalypticism' and expect it to provide a firm historical basis for theories about early Christianity.

That does not mean, of course, that Käsemann was completely wrong, or that we should return (as some now want to do!) to non-Jewish sources as the primary matrix for understanding early Christianity.[17] We need to do history better. But this has been made more difficult by the fact that, in the post-Käsemann flurry of 'apocalyptic' studies, there are almost as many meanings for the word as there are exegetes using it. For Käsemann, it meant simply the imminent *parousia*-expectation.[18] For Martyn, despite his homage to Käsemann, it means something very different: a divine 'invasion' of the world that has *already* taken place in Jesus' crucifixion.[19] For de Boer, on whose work Martyn claimed to rest, the original proposal was [124] a hypothesis about possible tendencies ('cosmic' or 'forensic') *within* Jewish 'apocalyptic eschatology'. De Boer was careful to note that the distinction was not absolute; that many texts contained elements of both; and that both were, in their own way, species of 'apocalyptic'.[20] This fine-grained proposal has been oversimplified and distorted in subsequent discussion, and it has been assumed that an 'apocalyptic' reading of Paul stands over against 'forensic justification', on the one hand, and 'salvation history' or 'covenant' on the other hand.[21] This, as we saw, is strange considering that the writers of actual Jewish apocalypses generally believed in the coming great assize, and also in the providential ordering of history by the God whose covenant with Israel continued to give them grounds for hope. (It also gave them grounds for difficult questions, as with *4 Ezra*; but the questions raised in that work are themselves signs of a strongly implicit covenant theology.) In particular, Douglas Campbell has absolutized the distinction between 'apocalyptic', on the one hand, and Paul's 'forensic' doctrine of justification, on the other. This would have horrified Käsemann, for whom Paul's forensic justification was central.[22]

---

17   See the discussion of van Kooten, Wischmeyer and Wright 2015.

18   I have in my possession a letter from Käsemann in which he says that, for him, 'apocalyptic' simply means *Naherwartung*.

19   Martyn 1997a; 1997b.

20   See e.g. de Boer 1988, 85; 2011, 32.

21   E.g. the dichotomous analyses of Gal. 1.4 offered by de Boer himself (de Boer 2011, 30) and by Martyn (Martyn 1997a, 90).

22   Campbell 2009. See the discussion in Wright 2015a.

It is not always easy to keep one's bearings in this many-sided discussion. The eagerness with which some have heralded and promoted Martyn's version of 'apocalyptic' is an interesting phenomenon in itself. Martyn's polarization of the main alternatives in Pauline interpretation looks remarkably like the either/or proposed, in relation to theories of atonement, by Gustav Aulén, leading one to speculate about hidden but powerful fault-lines within western Protestantism.[23] These are indeed important questions; but invoking 'apocalyptic' in favour of an Aulén-like reading of Paul will not help. Sometimes, this approach merely collapses into a newer, and supposedly historically rooted, version of the debates between [125] Augustine and Pelagius, or between the Reformers and the Arminians (or, even, between Calvin and Luther). Sometimes, the main thing at stake seems to be grace itself, with 'apocalyptic' being invoked as the instrument of that grace (the sovereign divine 'invasion'): at this point, the word 'apocalyptic' can seem, for some at least, to mean merely 'Barthian'.[24] Not for the first time, a supposed technical term can become a blank cheque which those playing theological Monopoly can use as they please. This is precisely why we need history, and historical exegesis: to prevent the whole thing descending into a chaos where the real issues, theological, political or whatever, are hidden behind the outward appearance of historical exegesis. All of which brings us, at last, to Paul.

Paul the Apocalyptist?

If 'apocalyptic' is primarily a literary genre, then Paul is not primarily an 'apocalyptist'. None of his letters looks remotely like Daniel, Revelation or 4 Ezra. Granted, he sometimes employs imagery that reminds us of some of the Jewish 'apocalyptic' works, as in the description of the parousia in 1 Thessalonians 4, of the final judgment in 2 Thessalonians 1 and 2, the victory of the Messiah over all hostile powers in 1 Corinthians 15, or the renewal of all creation in Romans 8. Granted, too, that Paul speaks in 2 Corinthians 12 of being caught up into the third heaven; that he describes his Damascus Road experience in terms of the apokalypsis of God's son; that he speaks of the gospel as the means whereby God's 'righteousness' is 'revealed' (apokalyptetai); that he sees the 'rulers of this age' being thwarted through their own crucifying of the lord of glory; and that he writes of 'new creation' as

---

23 See Aulén 1967 [1931].

24 This was readily admitted by Douglas Campbell in a recent panel discussion at Duke University and, again, at the SBL session at which the present collection of essays [Paul and the Apocalyptic Imagination; see fuller details in Acknowledgments, p. 369] was first presented.

the key not only to Christian ontology but also to Christian epistemology (2 Corinthians 5.16–17). Does this make him an 'apocalyptic' thinker? Does it make him a representative of something called 'apocalypticism'?

No. It simply makes him *Jewish*. Granted that there were many [126] varieties of Jewish thought, life and hope in the period, most Jewish writing of the period might comfortably include most of this list. To categorize such material as 'apocalyptic' *over against* other hypothetical categories is to revert to nineteenth-century constructs, setting 'apocalyptic' against 'legalism' or prophetic insight, or, more recently, against 'wisdom' or 'forensic' categories, or against 'covenant' or 'salvation history'. Just as in Isaiah, Ezekiel, Daniel or the Psalms (all, of course, highly influential in early Christian writing), we find all these things together, not played off against one another. As with the earlier attempts to polarize constructs such as 'Jewish Christianity', 'gentile Christianity', 'early Catholicism' and 'enthusiasm', we should resist such blatant anachronisms, and the projection of modern western antitheses on to ancient texts, as much as we should avoid perpetuating the older, misleading understandings of 'apocalyptic' (even if, now, such views were seen as positive rather than negative!). Jewish thought and life was many-sided. Paul exactly reflects that pluriformity.

However, we must readily acknowledge that much Pauline exegesis has long screened out the supposedly 'apocalyptic' elements in his thought altogether, and that it is important to put them back and, indeed, to give them a central place. For that we must be grateful to Käsemann, Beker, Martyn, de Boer and others. But the challenge of producing a fully rounded account of Paul's thinking and writing, highlighting elements sometimes forgotten, ought not to involve the heavy *Sachkritik* which privileges one 'strand' and relativizes, or even rejects, others that supposedly conflict with the favoured one. The question ought rather to be: how can we give an account of Paul in which previously forgotten themes and emphases, not least those highlighted with the modern label 'apocalyptic', are given their proper place?

Part of the answer to this, which strangely has not featured in the school of supposedly 'apocalyptic' interpretation which draws centrally on the work of J. Louis Martyn, is to recapture the *ancient political* dimension of 'apocalyptic'. Most ancient Jewish apocalypses [127] were decidedly political, offering symbolic narratives about the divine plan which gave coded encouragement to the oppressed, enabling them to see apparently chaotic and horrifying events within a different framework, and predicting the downfall not just of 'cosmic' powers (in the sense of 'suprahuman' entities), but of the actual pagan empires and their rulers. This is so well known in relation (for instance) to the book of Revelation that it is surprising that the study of 'apocalyptic Paul' and the equally vibrant contemporary study of 'political Paul' have not made common cause. Attempts to separate out these two, for instance, by suggesting that Paul's real target was non-human powers and that therefore he was uninterested in earthly ones, have not, in my view, proved successful.[25] Recent major studies of actual Jewish apocalypses, as opposed to hypothetical 'apocalypticism', strongly confirm this.[26]

So to the texts. Obviously, there is no room for detailed exegesis. I simply offer a sketch.

If I had to sum up Galatians in three passages, I would choose the beginning, the end and the middle. Chapter 1 verses 1–5 states that, in fulfilment of the divine purpose, Jesus 'gave himself for our sins, to rescue us from the present evil age'.[27] We cannot de-emphasize the 'giving himself for our sins', or suggest that this is a mere concession on Paul's part to a view he does not completely share, since when Paul reaches the climax of the first two chapters (2.19–20), he makes this central ('the son of God . . . loved me and gave himself for me'). But nor may the 'giving up for sins' obscure the larger purpose – the rescue 'from the present evil age'. For Paul the events concerning Jesus, particularly his death 'for our sins', have launched the long-awaited age to come. These two cannot be played off against one another, as (to be fair) much older Pauline exegesis has done in one direction, and the recent 'apocalyptic' interpretation has done in the other. [128]

The end of the letter makes the same conjunction. 'Circumcision . . . is nothing; neither is uncircumcision' because 'what matters is new creation' (6.15). This means what it means because of 6.14, which highlights the Messiah's cross, through which 'the world has been crucified to me and I to the world'. The cross and the new creation go hand in glove; and the latter inaugurates the 'new age', which supplants 'the present evil age'.

The purpose of new creation, of being rescued by the cross from the present evil age to share in God's new world, is unveiled in the middle of the letter (4.1–11) as the meaning of the exodus-shaped covenantal rescue. Once we were slaves, says Paul, but God acted to redeem us, to make us his children and heirs, so that now, we have a new sort of knowledge, generated by God's knowledge of us, in which we recognize the enslaving powers for what they

---

25 See Wright 2013b. See now Heilig 2015.
26 Portier-Young 2011.
27 For the English translations of scripture in this article, see the note in the preface to the present volume.

are ('now that you've come to know God – or, better, to be known *by* God', how can you turn back to the *stoicheia*?). How, in other words, could you think of going back to 'Egypt'? This (like Romans 8) is an exodus-narrative. At its heart, echoing Genesis 15.16 (from the chapter expounded at length in Galatians 3), Paul says that the redeeming action came 'when the fullness of time arrived', *hote de ēlthen to plērōma tou chronou*. We note that Paul uses *chronos*, not *kairos*. He has in mind a *temporal sequence*, previously invisible. This again, of course, has nothing to do with immanent development or evolution, but rather, as in 1.4–5, with the divine purpose. Thus, as new-exodus people, believers are to understand themselves as *Abraham's family, heirs according to promise* (3.29).

When, therefore, in chapter 1, Paul describes his conversion in terms of God's 'apocalypse' of his son (1.12, 16), this does not mean that we must abandon the ideas of divine promise, of the covenant with Abraham concerning his family and his inheritance. We should not mistake Paul's use of a first-century Greek word for an allusion to a nineteenth-century theory. *The covenant promises have been suddenly and shockingly fulfilled.* Paul believes that this is the way in which the ancient Israelite vision of new creation itself is to come about, and with it, new knowledge, a new mode of knowledge. The Messiah's **[129]** apocalypse unveils the covenant purpose. Isaiah, frequently echoed in Galatians, says as much. Paul's thinking remains Jewish to the core, however much his beliefs about Israel's crucified Messiah have caused radical revisions.

If this is true of Galatians, what of the Corinthian epistles? The whole of 1 Corinthians can be seen in the light of chapter 15, where the thoroughly 'apocalyptic' doctrine of resurrection is expounded at length. In 15.20–28, Paul describes the *inauguration* of the Messiah's rule over all opposing powers: he is *already* reigning, but *not yet* over death itself, the final enemy. This is the stuff of what some today call 'apocalyptic', and Paul expounds it through a complex interwoven exegesis of Psalms 2, 8 and 110: apocalypse, in other words, in service of messianic, and hence covenantal, theology. This produces a new-creational reading of Genesis 1, 2 and 3. The last Adam, the second Man, undoes the fault of the first, and so inaugurates, with his own risen body, the new creation itself. The resurrection of Jesus, symbolizing and embodying the new creation, was not detached from the ancient messianic promises. It was rather to be seen as their fulfilment, however shocking this may have been to Jews who demanded signs and Greeks who sought wisdom.

That, of course, is the point of 1 Corinthians 1—3, one of Paul's central statements of the new mode of knowing brought about by the messianic revelation. God's foolishness and weakness overthrow human wisdom and power, generating a new wisdom. For the ancient philosophers (to speak very broadly), *how* you knew things was a function of *what there was*; that is, *logic* correlated with *physics*.[28] Because Paul believed that in the resurrection God's new world had been launched, there was now *a new mode of knowing*: 'we speak God's hidden wisdom in a mystery . . . the wisdom God prepared ahead of time, before the world began, for our glory' (2.7). The 'rulers of this present age' did not, of course, know about it; otherwise, they wouldn't have crucified the lord of glory. A new kind of wisdom had been let loose in the world, in sudden fulfilment of God's ancient purposes. **[130]** That is why Paul could speak later of the new knowing which was called forth by the divine 'knowing', and which took the form of love (8.2–3, closely parallel to Galatians 4.9; 13.8–13). This knowledge is still 'partial', because the eschatology is inaugurated, not complete. But it looks on to the completion as the fulfilment of what is already begun.

All this points to the classic passage in 2 Corinthians 5 and 6, where Paul explains the nature of his apostolic ministry. He understands this ministry, as in Galatians, in terms of the 'servant' passage in Isaiah 49.8, quoted here at 6.2. When he says, 'The right time is now! . . . The day of salvation is here!', he is interpreting Isaiah: this has been the sudden fulfilment of divine promise. This is the context within which we should understand the statement of new epistemology in 5.16–17:

> From this moment on . . . we don't regard anybody from a merely human point of view. Even if we once regarded the Messiah that way, we don't do so any longer. Thus, if anyone is in the Messiah, there is a new creation! Old things have gone, and look – everything has become new!

One could, of course, take this out of context, as an irruptive invasion of epistemological reflection, without any prior promise. But the wider passage forbids this. The new creation, and with it, the new mode of knowing, have come about – Paul says it four times – through the Messiah's death, which has reconciled people to God by dealing with their sins (5.14, 18, 19, 21). Exactly as in the compressed formula of Galatians 1.4, the Messiah's sin-bearing death brings about new creation. Paul holds together what later traditions divide.

The new creation in 2 Corinthians 5 is, for Paul, directly dependent on the new covenant expounded in 2 Corinthians 3. Some suppose that Paul only discussed Moses and the exodus because his opponents had done so

---

28 For this, and what follows, see esp. Wright 2013b, ch. 14.

first. But the use of related themes elsewhere makes this unlikely. It is better to see the transformation in chapter 3, where the spirit renews the covenant, as supplying the theological energy for chapter 5, since here (5.5), as in chapter 1.22, the spirit is the 'first instalment and guarantee' of what is to come. The new creation, already launched in the Messiah, will be complete when all appear before the Messiah's judgment-seat (5.10). This produces the scandalous message and [131] ministry which remain opaque to the wider world, but which Paul believes to be the appropriate vehicle for (what we might call) the apocalyptic gospel of new creation.

If, then, by 'apocalyptic', we mean the unveiling of things previously hidden, for Paul the gospel was indeed 'apocalyptic'. As we said, he did not express it in the apocalyptic genre; 2 Corinthians 12 hints that he could have gone that route, but chose not to. His message remains that of the crucified and risen Messiah. And that message makes sense, not because of a dualistic 'invasion' of creation, but because of the sudden, shocking fulfilment of ancient covenantal promises.

All of which leads to Romans. It is ironic that, in Douglas Campbell's now famous treatment, Romans 1—4 is relativized in the light, supposedly, of the 'apocalyptic' message of chapters 5—8.[29] But it is in Romans 1.16—2.16 that we find one of the most obviously 'apocalyptic' passages in the whole letter. And the central thing revealed there is *the righteousness of God*, the covenant plan promised ages ago, discussed with such anguish in a genuine 'apocalypse' by Paul's near-contemporary *4 Ezra*. For Paul the 'apocalypse', the decisive divine revelation, *had* taken place in the gospel events, both in themselves and in their apostolic proclamation, and *would be completed* in the final denouement (2.16). The one God had unveiled his age-old purposes in a sudden fulfilment, which was only visible as such in retrospect. The gospel was in this sense 'apocalyptic', not because it represented an invasion without prior warning, but because it was the ultimate revelation to which earlier writings (Torah, Psalms, Prophets) had all looked forward. For Paul the identity and achievement of Jesus was the revelation in action of Israel's returning God. The form and function of second-Temple Jewish apocalypses reflected the belief that God had promised to return in judgment and mercy, but had delayed. The [132] form and function of Paul's letters, and supremely Romans, reflect the belief that God had indeed returned to judge and to save,

---

29 Campbell 2009. I say 'supposedly' because, though Campbell bases his argument on the 'apocalyptic' theology he claims to find in chs. 5—8, he nowhere in this book expounds those chapters or that theology. In Campbell 2012, Campbell promises a detailed engagement with Rom. 5—8, but fails to provide it, as one of his responders in that volume points out (Johnson 2012, 149–52).

but in a way hitherto unsuspected, and that this work would be fulfilled in the events yet to come (8.18–25; 13.11–12).

At the heart of Romans, as with Galatians, there lies the new exodus-narrative: the slaves are set free by coming through the water (ch. 6), the law does its strange God-intended work of allowing sin to grow to its full height (ch. 7), so that Sin (with a capital S) is condemned in the flesh of the Messiah, whereupon the spirit leads the people through the wilderness to their inheritance – which is, of course, the renewed creation. This is the larger narrative matrix that holds together 'apocalyptic' and other elements such as 'covenant' and atonement. New exodus leads directly to new creation. The cross, at its heart, is for Paul both penal in force and cosmic in scope: 'There is no condemnation for those in the Messiah, Jesus', because 'God sent his son . . . and, right there in the flesh, he condemned sin' [Romans 8.1–3]. This is solidly *forensic* language within a larger *apocalyptic* and 'cosmic' setting: no power in earth or heaven can undermine God's Messiah-shaped love (8.31–39), because this 'love' is the *covenant* love spoken of in passages such as Deuteronomy 7 or Jeremiah 31, through which sins have been dealt with. This entire sequence, again, is an expansion of Galatians 1.4. In Romans 8.31–39, themes rush together which both theology and exegesis have held apart: the victory of God over the powers, the forensic dealing with sin, the new creation that follows when death itself is defeated. This is the ultimate horizon of Paul's thought. If it deserves the name 'apocalyptic', despite not belonging to the literary genre, such a label does not rule out, but rather insists on, (1) the covenantal context of ancient scriptural promises, and (2) the dealing with human sin, which has prevented humans taking their intended place within the created order. Of course, there is more to be said; much more. But no less. **[133]**

Conclusion

I have barely scratched the surface of a vital and fascinating topic. Let me, in conclusion, name two related issues.

First, if we are serious about the 'apocalyptic Paul', there is no excuse for not bringing 2 Thessalonians and even Ephesians in from the cold. Ephesians is explicit about the divine plan hidden for ages but now revealed, and about ongoing warfare with the 'powers'.[30] 2 Thessalonians, of course, clearly draws

---

30   Meeks 1983, 90 and 107, stresses the cosmic vision of both Ephesians and Colossians. It is not clear (as in his further comment at 184) that this goes beyond what is both stated and implied in e.g. Rom. 8.18–39; 1 Cor. 10.20; 15.26; or, indeed, Gal. 4.1–11.

on some of the normal apocalyptic tropes. One of the main reasons for its demotion in early scholarship was the anxiety about allowing 'Paul' to be quite so explicitly 'apocalyptic': now that that has changed, why not welcome it on board?

The final point, again very briefly, concerns the Temple. For the devout second-Temple Jew, heaven and earth met in the Temple. That was where one might expect, as with Isaiah, the sudden revelation of things previously hidden. If Paul really had an 'apocalyptic' strand in his theology, as I have argued he did (albeit reworked through the inaugurated eschatology of the crucified and risen Messiah and the gift of the spirit), one might expect his frequent Temple-language to reflect this line of thought. In fact, it does: the spirit who indwells God's people means that, corporately and personally, they are seen in terms of the Temple.[31]

It is therefore no surprise that for Paul the sudden fulfilment of divine promise that has come about through the gospel of Jesus has generated a community which discovers new knowledge, a new *mode* of knowledge. The renewal of the covenant leads directly to the renewal of creation, by the shocking, yet promise-fulfilling, route of cross and resurrection. That is Paul's apocalyptic gospel. It belongs historically on the map of second-Temple Jewish thought, reconceived around Jesus and the spirit. It belongs theologically as an integrated whole, not [134] to be split up into different component strands. If we find ourselves wanting to pry apart what Paul held together, that is our problem. We should not suppose it was his as well.

I am reminded of the lines that T. S. Eliot puts into the mouth of Thomas à Becket as he realizes his assassins have arrived at last:

> However certain our expectation
> The moment foreseen may be unexpected
> When it arrives. It comes when we are
> Engrossed with matters of other urgency.[32]

---

31 See e.g. 1 Cor. 3.16–17; 6.19; 2 Cor. 6.16; and, in the light of these, Rom. 8.9–11; Col. 2.9–10.
32 Eliot 1969, 266.

14
The Bible and Christian Mission

Few scholars and Christian leaders have done as much as Professor Michael Gorman in recent years to remind us all of the importance of reading the Bible 'missionally'. This paper was commissioned for a volume examining the impact of scripture on worldwide culture. The essay, an attempt to say in rather fewer words some things I have tried elsewhere to set out more fully, aims to show the integration, within a missiological reading, of several key biblical themes which, because of their inherent complexity, are often treated separately. If this serves the purpose of alerting readers to the larger integration both of scripture itself and of the Bible with the church's task, it will have achieved its purpose.

[388] Introduction

The Christian Bible hinges on Jesus. It looks forward from his richly complex achievement to the ultimate establishment of his universal lordship, and to the tasks for which, in anticipation of that end, he commissions his followers and equips them by his spirit. It looks back to the biblical narratives of creation and covenant, of Adam and Abraham, of Moses, David and the prophets, seeing there the deep roots both of Jesus' own work, present and future, and of the church's tasks in the interim. The Bible thus constitutes the God-given narrative within which the church discerns its vocation and orders its life. The first Christians did not suppose that their fresh readings of Israel's scriptures were identical to those on offer among their Jewish contemporaries, though there are similarities and analogies. But they claimed that once they saw the events concerning Jesus as the goal towards which the scriptures had been tending, they saw not only a deep coherence in the Bible itself but also a fresh vision of how those same scriptures, with their tantalizing glimpses of a glorious ultimate future, were to be fulfilled.

The events concerning Jesus form a coherent whole, despite modern tendencies to break them up, whether into scattered fragments of early Christian reflection or into the two large (and to modern eyes somewhat contradictory) themes of 'kingdom' and 'cross'. Nevertheless, it will be convenient for [389] clarity's sake to separate here the different strands of kingdom, cross, resurrection, ascension, second coming and the gift of the spirit, concluding with an all-embracing reflection on the underlying theology of Temple and creation. In each case we will see both how the theme in question informed and energized the mission of the early church and how the church read the ancient scriptures as the narrative of God's mission (the *missio Dei*) to the world. Doing so will allow us to read scripture today to help us discern God's ongoing mission and ours within it; that is the task of missional hermeneutics.

Jesus and the Kingdom of God

When the early Christians told the story of Jesus announcing God's kingdom, they were not simply providing historical reminiscences. They were also consciously reinforcing the foundations of their own work. The slogan 'kingdom of God' was itself specific to the first-century Jewish context (where it carried overtones of political revolution), and was not always retained. But when Paul speaks of every knee bowing at the name of Jesus (Philippians 2.6–11), or when John the Seer glimpses the 'lion' who is also the 'lamb' sharing the divine throne (Revelation 4—5), these different expressions and their underlying theology are best understood as the outworking of Jesus' original proclamation. When Acts concludes with Paul in Rome announcing God as king and Jesus as lord 'with all boldness, and with no one stopping him' (Acts 28.31), we are seeing the answer to the disciples' question in Acts 1.6 as to whether this was the time for the kingdom to be restored to Israel. Yes, seems to be the answer, but not in the way you imagine – just as Jesus had corrected the aspirations of James and John in Mark 10.35–45, reframing the notion of kingdom itself around his own cruciform vocation.

That, indeed, characterizes Jesus' entire public career. Jesus' actions and teachings have some things in common with the launching of a revolution (an inner circle, hints of history reaching its climax, a challenge to suffer, and the promise of victory), enough for some to want to hijack his movement for that kind of purpose. But his characteristic public work of healing (especially exorcism) and unorthodox or even scandalous celebration pointed elsewhere: to a sense of creation healed, of covenant renewed, and above all of forgiveness of sins. In Jesus' world, the individual meaning of forgiveness resonated with the larger theme of the undoing of Israel's long exile, as in Isaiah 40 or Daniel 9. Jesus constantly hinted that all this was symptomatic of a revolution deeper than his contemporaries had thought necessary: the breaking of a dark power, more dangerous than any political oppressor. His parables, coming at [390] these themes from many angles, constantly hinted that he was enacting the fulfilment of Israel's hopes, but in a way nobody had previously imagined. The early Christians told and retold these stories to ground their own vocation to be a new sort of kingdom-people. We note, for instance, Jesus' redefinition of kingship in his tense dialogue with Pilate (John 18.33–38).

As the early Christians did so, they were retrieving and re-expressing the scriptural hope that God's kingdom would put the world to rights. The biblical notion of God's kingdom went back at least to the Passover victory over Pharaoh, his armies and his gods (Exodus 15.18). It came to regular expression in psalms such as Psalms 96 and 98; the prophecies of Daniel, especially chapters 2 and 7; and Isaiah, especially the theme of God's return and reign in 52.7–12. Jesus was seen by his first followers to have been claiming that Israel's scriptures constituted a narrative with a goal in mind. God would at last establish his sovereign and rescuing rule over Israel and the world. Jesus' own work was, he hinted, the way in which this was coming true. The early church saw this scripture-fulfilling achievement as the foundation of its own mission. They were Passover-people – but of a new sort.

Jesus and His Death

When Jesus wanted to explain to his followers what his approaching death would mean, enabling them not only to understand it but also to share in its effects, he didn't give them a theory. He gave them a meal, rich in reshaped Jewish symbolism, evoking Israel's ancient traditions and pointing them forward in a fresh direction. Paul taught that this meal looked back to Jesus' death and on to his coming, shaping and energizing the church for its work between those events (1 Corinthians 11.17–34). The Bible thus dovetails with the sacramental dimension of the church's missional vocation, each interpreting and reinforcing the other. And Jesus' final meal, resonating with Passover symbolism but also incorporating the sin-forgiving new covenant of Jeremiah 31, draws together Israel's scriptural traditions into a fresh focus which the first Christians developed in their own work and writings.

The point of it all could be expressed like this. Israel's history was to be seen as the narrative both of divine promise and of human rebellion. Israel's exile in Babylon, the result of idolatry and sin, was the large-scale acting out of the human rebellion and exile catalogued in Genesis 3—11 (also ending in 'Babel'). The call of Abraham's family to reverse and undo this disaster was thus problematic: the people called to bear the promise were themselves radically infected with the disease. The original biblical 'mission' – the commissioning [391] of Abraham and his family, the call of Israel to be the 'nation of priests' (Exodus 19), the vocation of the servant-people to be a light to the nations (Isaiah 49.6; compare 42.6; 60.3) – had thus always been paradoxical, as prophets regularly reminded the people and as the Psalms regularly lamented (a classic example is Psalm 89). The Pentateuch itself, announcing this 'mission' in Genesis and Exodus, warns near its end that Israel, though about to inherit the land and to celebrate divine blessing there, will remain foolish and unfaithful, with disastrous results (Deuteronomy 32).

John the Baptist announced a similar double message of promise and warning. Jesus himself, the greatest prophet of them all, announced not only the arrival of God's kingdom but also God's judgment on his rebellious people, particularly for their refusal to embrace the way of peace (Luke 19.41–44). Jesus seems to have concluded that Israel's own history, and with it the history of God's entire world, was being funnelled down on to one place and one moment in a dark vortex of promise and disaster, of tragedy and triumph. The repeated biblical promises of divine blessing and new creation for the world were to be attained by the obedience of Israel. But, faced with Israel's disobedience, the mission of God could only be accomplished through the single faithful Israelite, the Messiah, coming to the place of rebellion, the place where the world's wickedness would reach its height and the divine love would reach its depth. Jesus saw his forthcoming crucifixion (the four gospels draw this out in various ways) as his messianic enthronement, his missional victory, the overthrowing of the anti-creational powers in the world and hence the revolutionary moment from which the new mission would begin. By dying in the place of sinners, Jesus was robbing the dark powers of their base of operations. Luke especially brings this out: 'the power of darkness' had closed in around Jesus (22.53), but by this means Jesus fulfilled Isaiah 53 in taking the place of the wicked (22.37) and acted this out in submitting to the punishment they deserved (23.2, 25, 30–31, 39–43). That is why, from Easter onwards, 'repentance, for the forgiveness of sins' could be and would be announced to the nations, not simply as a 'religious' option but as the sign that the rule of the powers had been broken (24.47).

The same point comes out forcefully in John 12.20–36. Reflecting on the request of some Greeks for a meeting, Jesus discerns that the moment has come – through his own approaching death! – for the dark power that has ruled the world to be overthrown, so that the nations can be free to come to him, and through him to the father. 'Now comes the judgment of this world! Now this world's ruler is going to be thrown out! And when I've been lifted up from the earth, I will draw all people to myself' (12.31–32). The root of the Jesus-focused mission of the church is the Jesus-shaped victory over the powers. [392]

In all this, and much more, the early church was consciously retrieving, and reading in a fresh way, many strands of Israel's scriptures. Isaiah 40—55 is one obvious source, focusing on the 'servant' songs, particularly the fourth (52.13—53.12). The psalms of suffering, such as Psalms 22 and 69, are another. But it would be a mistake to see these simply as proof-texts. They constitute particular strands, already themselves complex, within the larger narrative. And the narrative was the story of Israel, of the creator's rescue operation in and for his creation. As Jesus' first followers looked back to his death and understood it within its scriptural matrix, they knew that in their own mission they were not simply persuading people to understand and accept a theory. They were summoning them to Jesus himself, the living lord, whose death had dealt with sins and thereby defeated the powers. They were inviting hearers into the new world that had thereby come into existence.

Jesus and His Resurrection

Jesus' resurrection was a shock. Nobody had expected Israel's Messiah to be killed and then to rise from the dead. 'Resurrection', for those (such as the Pharisees) who believed in it, would happen to *all* God's people at the *end* of time, not to one person in the middle (1 Corinthians 15.23). But this unexpected gap, between the Messiah's resurrection and everybody else's, was quickly seen to be the time for mission. What Jesus had accomplished, the church must implement. The energy of Jesus' resurrection was released, through the spirit, into his people, so that they would share in the life of new creation and become its agents in the world (for example Ephesians 1.15–23).

The first Christians thus saw Jesus' resurrection as the beginning of the new creation. From the first their mission was understood in terms of bringing signs of that new creation to birth through the gospel's work of human rescue and renewal. 'We are his *poiēma*', his 'poem', his 'workmanship', wrote Paul (Ephesians 2.10), 'created . . . in King Jesus for the good works that he prepared' – not simply 'good works' of moral behaviour, but the fresh creativity whose rich variety reflects the lavish creativity of God himself, thereby offering a sign to the powers of the world that Jesus is lord and they are not (Ephesians 3.10–11). What has been launched in the resurrection is the new Genesis: heaven and earth are freshly joined in the Messiah (Ephesians 1.10). All this, with its message of 'peace' to those 'far off' and those 'near' (Ephesians 2.13–18), is the context and foundation of the church's mission.

This is well displayed in John 20.19–23. The risen Jesus greets the disciples with the word 'Peace!', resonating backward into the hopes of ancient [393] Israel and forward into the goal and means of their mission. Then he repeats it, making that mission explicit: 'Peace be with you . . . As the father has sent me, so I'm sending you.' That rhythm of 'As . . . so . . . ', in the context of the scripture-fulfilling address 'Peace', says it all. *Jesus' own mission to Israel is the foundation and the shaping of the church's mission to the world.* And for this otherwise impossible task, Jesus' followers are given his own spirit, described here in terms reminiscent of Genesis 2: Jesus breathes on them, as the creator breathed into human nostrils. The ancient promise of life, shimmering like a mirage throughout Torah, now itself comes to life in new creation.

Jesus' resurrection thus looks onwards to the fuller expressions of missional hope throughout the New Testament, especially in Romans 8, where the whole creation will be rescued from its slavery to corruption and decay, and in the 'new heavens and new earth' of Revelation 21 and 2 Peter 3.13. Some might misunderstand this hope as an excuse for doing nothing: God will renew the world, so we can only wait. That was never the early Christian conclusion. Different circumstances allowed for different expressions of new-creational mission, but even martyrdom itself was seen as a paradoxical sign of God's victory. The testimony of the early church was that sharing the Messiah's cruciform path would bear fruit as the watching world came to see death itself as a beaten enemy.

Jesus' resurrection thus compelled a fresh, new-creational and missional reading of Israel's scriptures. In line with some other early Jewish readers, Paul interpreted the land-focused promise to Abraham in terms of the worldwide extension celebrated in the Psalms (Genesis 15 with Psalms 2; 72; see Romans 4.13). The whole world is now, in that sense, God's holy land. The notion of a total renewal of heaven and earth looks back to Isaiah 65 and 66, reflecting the growing awareness both that the creator God has ongoing plans for the entire creation and that those plans must include rescue and healing from decay and death. All these strands of hope, retrieved by the early Christians in terms of their own mission, looked back to the good creation itself, to Genesis 1 and 2, where heaven and earth were designed as a single though differentiated whole – as, in fact, a *temple*, with the human pair as the 'image' reflecting God to the world and the world back to God.

The resurrectional renewal of humans in God's image (Colossians 3.10, applying the christological 'image' of 1.15) was the sign and means of the reconciliation and renewal of all creation (Colossians 1.18–20). The 'renewal of all things' (Acts 3.21) was the goal, and the life and mission of the church was the path towards that goal. The final overthrow of death itself, and with it the promise that God would be 'all in all' (1 Corinthians 15.28), remained firmly [394] in God's own hands. In other words, in the present we do not 'build the kingdom' by our own work, even by our own spirit-driven work. We build '*for* God's kingdom' (emphasis added), as Paul puts it in Colossians 4.11. Paul's last word in his long exposition of resurrection in 1 Corinthians 15 is to insist (v. 58) that 'in the Lord . . . the work you're doing will not be worthless'. This is the assurance of mission: all work done in the lord and in the power of the spirit will somehow be taken up, enhanced and transformed no doubt, when God finally renews all things.

Jesus and His Ascension

The ascension of Jesus has sometimes been misunderstood in terms of Jesus' *absence*. By itself, this would either undermine mission ('What shall we do, now that Jesus has gone?') or reduce it to merely human effort ('We'll have to get on with it by ourselves'). This is a mistake. The Bible can use 'up' and 'down' language for heaven and earth, but this natural metaphor ought not to disguise the underlying biblical cosmology, which is of heaven and earth being made for each other, with 'heaven' being in effect the 'control-room' for 'earth'. Heaven, God's space, is the sphere from which the whole world is run. The point of the ascension is that Jesus is now in control: 'He has to go on ruling', writes Paul, 'until "he has put all his enemies under his feet"' (1 Corinthians 15.25). That is why Matthew has the risen Jesus declaring, 'All authority in heaven and on earth . . . has been given to me' (Matthew 28.18); this is then the context for the disciples' missional task: 'Go and make all the nations into disciples. Baptize them . . . Teach them . . . ' (28.19–20). This again is consonant with the idea of Jesus' reign in Philippians 2.9–11, and with the victory shout in Revelation 11.15: 'Now the kingdom of the world has passed to our Lord and his Messiah . . . and he will reign for ever and ever.' That is the biblical framework for mission.

Like every other aspect of the early church's missional vocation, this too is rooted in Israel's scriptures. The Psalms speak repeatedly of a coming time when God will be exalted as king and the nations will be brought into his realm:

God is king over the nations;
God sits on his holy throne.
The princes of the peoples gather
as the people of the God of Abraham.
For the shields of the earth belong to God;
he is highly exalted.
(Psalm 47.8–9)

Paul, summing up the entire message of Romans with its emphasis on mission and unity (Romans 15.7–13), quotes the Psalms (18.49; 117.1), the Torah (Deuteronomy 32.43) and the Prophets (Isaiah 11.1): 'There shall be the root of Jesse, the one who rises up to rule the nations; the nations shall hope in him' (Romans 15.12). That scripture-rooted celebration of Israel's Messiah as lord of the whole world is, then, the basis [395] not only for the ultimate hope but also for the mission in which signs of that future hope are brought forward into the present time.

Jesus and His Spirit

We have already spoken of the spirit breathed by Jesus on his followers, equipping them so that their peaceful kingdom-mission will be both their own work and that of Jesus himself. The classic statement of this comes in Acts 2, with the wind and fire of Pentecost coming upon the disciples. This is not primarily about a new 'religious experience'. It is the further joining of heaven and earth: the powerful energy of heaven coming to reside in, and to operate through, Jesus' followers. The church quickly anchored this experience and energy in readings of scripture, going back to passages like Joel 2.28–32 and Ezekiel 37.9–10 to explain that this was the effective sign of the new creation, happening both in the disciples and through them in the wider world. Here again, Romans 8 takes centre stage, as Paul unfolds his vision of God's rescuing and restorative justice and love. This is a new exodus; and Paul envisages the spirit performing the work which, in the first exodus, was done by the divine presence in the pillar of cloud and fire. The spirit, in other words, is 'leading' God's people to their 'inheritance'; and in the process the spirit is enabling them, as the deep heart of their mission, to be intercessors for the world, sharing and bearing the suffering and inarticulate groanings of all creation so that the father's love may come to birth in the darkest places of the world (Romans 8.26–27).

This chimes in with the 'farewell discourses' in John, where the disciples are commissioned for their own mission and assured that their prayers will be answered. That is the context for the promise that the spirit will call the world to account: the spirit 'will prove the world to be in the wrong on three counts: sin, justice and judgment' (16.8). This difficult but important passage offers a blueprint for the church's mission, rooted in Jesus' confrontation with Pontius Pilate in John 18 and 19. This spirit-led mission will involve speaking the truth to power, holding up a mirror to the ways in which God's world is still rebelling against his rescuing rule. Here too we sense the scriptural rootedness: when the servant is exalted, 'he shall startle many nations; kings shall shut their mouths because of him' (Isaiah 52.15). This theme looks back to Abraham's victory over the kings in Genesis 14, and also to the exaltation of the 'son of man' and the destruction of the [396] 'beasts' in Daniel 7. That missional vision of the overthrow of the powers which oppose God's good creation and then restoration of creation requires the church to look to the spirit for the power, the words and the effective result (Mark 13.11).

Jesus and His Coming

Properly speaking, the 'second coming' (*parousia*) lies beyond the mission of the church. Once Jesus returns, the church's present work will be complete. To be sure, there will be new tasks in God's new world; we are rescued in order to be 'kings and priests', and this will be as true in the new Jerusalem as in the present (Revelation 5.9–10; 20.4; 22.5). But from the first the early church understood the promise of Jesus' 'coming' or 'appearing' (Colossians 3.4; 1 John 3.2) as colouring their work in the present time. The glorious future, which every generation must anticipate, is not to mean laziness now (2 Thessalonians 3.6–13). 'Don't get tired of doing what is right!' (3.13).

New Temple, New Creation

In and through the whole story of Jesus, the early Christians discerned the coming-true of ancient scriptural promises and hence the renewal of their scripture-based mission. The powers had been overcome, so that the good news could make its way into the wider world. Heaven and earth had come together. In all this we detect, in repeated patterns, a central feature of the exodus-story. The construction of the wilderness tabernacle brings to a preliminary conclusion the story that begins with Genesis 1 and goes horribly wrong in Genesis 3. Heaven and earth are made for each other, with the human pair as the 'image' in the original creational 'temple': that image-bearing vocation is the foundation of all other missions, human in general and Israel-shaped in particular. The tabernacle was designed as a 'little world', a symbolic representation of the heaven-and-earth creation. There was, of course, no human-made 'image' of the divinity. In the place of the original image-bearing humans there was Aaron the high priest, representing Israel. And there was, above all, the clouded presence of Israel's God himself, coming to dwell with his people.

This was not an end in itself. The scriptures regularly hint that what was true in the tabernacle, and then in Solomon's Temple, was a long-range signpost to God's intention for creation as a whole. The whole world, in other words, was to be filled with the divine glory, with God's people – represented by the [397] priest, the king, or both, or even a prophet – functioning as the representative of God himself and thus as the image-bearer. That, from one angle or another, is what is said in Numbers 14.21; Psalm 72.19; Isaiah 6.3; 11.9; 35.2; 40.5; Habakkuk 2.14; and elsewhere. In particular, this is the vision of the End held out at the close of Ezekiel, where in chapter 43 the glorious divine presence comes to fill the newly rebuilt Temple.

All of this comes to its biblical climax in the arrival of Jesus himself. 'The Word became flesh, and lived among us. We gazed upon his glory, glory like that of the father's only son, full of grace and truth' (John 1.14). God's project for the world is focused on the incarnate son, and then on the worldwide, spirit-led implementation of the son's work. What John says explicitly, evoking both Genesis and Exodus, the other biblical writers hint at from several angles. The promised divine glory has returned, in the person and work of Jesus; and God will do for the whole creation at the end what he did in Jesus, bringing it through death to a new life, a new world. The picture of the new Jerusalem in Revelation 21 and 22 is of a structure like an enormous version of the Holy of Holies in the Jerusalem Temple; and the redeemed humans are there as the royal priesthood, as a result of the royal and priestly work of Jesus himself. The present life of the church, energized for mission by the spirit, is thus the anticipation of the eventual filling of all creation: the Messiah 'living within you [plural] as the hope of glory!' (Colossians 1.27). This is the biblical narrative, from Genesis to Revelation, which sets the terms and the context for the church's mission.

That mission, then, is not about rescuing people *from* the world. It is about rescuing humans *for* the world, for new-creation tasks of every kind in the present, pointing on to the eventual new creation, a fresh gift from the creator. Mission is not something added on to 'biblical theology', as though one first had to discover the content of scripture and then, by 'mission', had to teach or preach that content. The story of scripture, focused in the gospel-events concerning Jesus, is about mission from start to finish:

- God's mission in creation, with his image-bearing humans charged with bringing creation to full flourishing;
- God's mission in redemption and covenant, calling Abraham and his family to be the means of rescuing and restoring humans and therefore creation;
- God's strange mission in Jesus, coming to the place where Israel and all creation had plunged into the darkness of death, defeating all the powers that had opposed and corrupted humans and the world, and thence launching new creation in resurrection, ascension and spirit. [398]

The church's mission is not something other than this story. It *is* this story, seen from the point of view of those who hear Jesus' call, 'As the father has sent me, so I'm sending you' (John 20.21). The Bible provides a real-life, real-time drama. It hands us the script and bids us play our part.

15
Wouldn't You Love to Know?
Towards a Christian View of Reality

This essay, in a somewhat different register from many of the others, was requested as a lecture for a meeting of church and community leaders in Glasgow in September 2016. The invitation came from the Most Reverend Angus Morrison, who was then the Moderator of the Church of Scotland, and was determinedly trying to put theological thinking at the heart of the church's mission. Having discovered that I was due to give the Gifford Lectures in Aberdeen in 2018, Angus sat me down to enquire what themes I would be exploring, and when I spoke of the 'epistemology of love' he insisted that this was what he wanted me to expound in Glasgow. What I had not quite bargained for was that the lecture was to be given as the final item in a rather full evening whose main feature was a very good dinner. How much of what I had to say was missed in the relaxed post-prandial atmosphere it is hard to say. But I am glad that it can now be read at leisure, and perhaps – for those interested in such things – compared with the lines of thought I then developed in the Giffords eighteen months later, which have been refined and (I hope) clarified still further in the published version (Wright 2019a). I have left the present piece in the form in which it was delivered.

We live in a strange world, and things one group of people take for granted can be quite opaque to another. I've heard it said that in Germany everything is forbidden except that which is permitted, while in Russia everything is forbidden *including* that which is permitted; meanwhile in France everything is permitted except that which is forbidden, while in Italy everything is permitted *including* that which is forbidden. In the UK, of course, we know that everything is either forbidden or permitted, but we're not sure which is which because we are waiting to be disentangled from *the European Court*. (There has to be a whole raft of similar reflections in the midst of our puzzles about Brexit and, indeed, about the UK, but I leave those to your imagination.)

I have been asked to talk this evening about how we know things and, more specifically, about our present confusions on what we know and how we know it, and particularly about the continuing stand-off between supposedly *scientific* ways of knowing things and *faith-based* ways of knowing things. My title reflects my underlying argument, which is that beyond the split world of supposedly objective and supposedly subjective 'knowing', there is a deeper mode of knowing which has to do with that vital but elusive quality we can call 'love'. Thus, 'Wouldn't You *Love* to *Know*?' (a title kindly supplied by the former moderator, Angus Morrison).

A friend asked me what on earth I was going to be speaking about at nine o'clock on a Thursday evening after my hearers had eaten a good dinner, and I replied 'comparative epistemology'; to which the only reply was that he hoped the hotel would be paying me a royalty on all the extra whisky that would be consumed as a result. Well, as A. E. Housman put it in *A Shropshire Lad*, 'Malt does more than Milton can to justify God's ways to man'; so if such extra justification be required I'm sure our hosts can rise to the challenge. But my own less liquid contribution is to sketch where our present confusions have come from and to suggest how we might not just avoid them but use the present moment as a springboard to fresh insight, fresh teaching, fresh wisdom. That is my prayer for the splendid 'Grasping the Nettle' project to which these reflections are a small contribution.

I confess that when I heard about this project I was surprised. Hadn't we got beyond the old stand-off I remember from my schooldays? Wasn't it C. P. Snow in the 1950s who named and shamed the 'two cultures' divide? Had we learned nothing? Well, many voices in the last generation have shown that, in the words of Jonathan Sacks, religion and science ought to be a 'great partnership', in which 'science takes things apart to see how they work, while religion puts things together to see what they mean'. Many leading scientists, such as John Polkinghorne in this country and Francis Collins in the USA, have articulated not only their well-thought-out Christian faith but also their views on how science and faith belong firmly together. One might have supposed those battles had been won.

But, it seems, this ain't necessarily so. Earlier this week I received two unsolicited emails within a few hours of each other. One was from a zealous 'new atheist', urging me to inspect a website which showed that God was a delusion, a book which proved that Jesus never existed and an article which demonstrated that religion was bad for your health. The other was from a zealous American fundamentalist railing against the compromises of people like myself who believe in evolution though not evolutionism (I'll explain that later), in science but not scientism, and insisting that when Genesis said six days it meant six days. If anything, I fear that the tone of both my uninvited correspondents was more shrill than it might have been in the days of my youth. In today's culture wars, electronic road-rage is, well, all the rage. People rant at their computer screens in ways they might not do if their target were sitting there beside them.

Both approaches are, of course, highly rationalistic. Fundamentalism, whether supposedly scientific or supposedly Christian, is a rationalist parody of what true science and true faith might look like. Just as Maggie Thatcher declared that the Socialist Workers' Party on the one hand and the National Front on the other were actually 'the left and right boots of fascism', so the ranting atheists and the ranting six-day creationists are the left and right boots of a fundamentalism which is, ironically, more about the subjective quest for certainty in a confusing world than about any actual objective truth. And the question for us is: how can we leave behind these sterile antitheses and reach out towards fresh, creative and reconciling wisdom?

At this point people often say three things which are important but which I think don't go far enough.

First, as I've already said, many world-class scientists not only believe and practise Christian faith but also articulate sophisticated accounts of how science and faith actually go together. One might couple this with the reflection that modern science has deeply Christian origins, and that for many generations science and faith were seen as complementary.

Second, people often point out that science is never simply the objective collection of neutral data. It always involves imaginative leaps to hypotheses and the quest for an elegance of explanation which goes beyond the normal rationalistic assumptions by involving the knowing subject as a subject. Conversely, Christian faith is never simply believing a bunch of impossible things on no real evidence. It involves hard-nosed engagement with the world of history, specifically the history of Jesus, and with the real and often perplexing world of one's own day. Real science and real Christian faith are much more like one another than many people suspect. Again, fair enough but not far enough.

Third, people often point out that science can neither generate nor measure many of the most important things in the world – justice, spirituality, relationships, beauty, freedom, truth. All these contain deep paradoxes. Wise human flourishing means wrestling with those paradoxes rather than sweeping them aside in favour of this or that type of fundamentalism.

In fact, the wisest of scientists will draw lines and insist that their discipline will take them thus far and no further. Once when I was in debate with an agnostic Australian astrophysicist – now there's a good phrase to try after a couple of shots of Talisker – he quite properly insisted that his brief did not extend to questions of morality or spirituality. I am reminded of a dinner years ago in Downing College, Cambridge, where we were served small roast guinea-fowl. One of the guests turned to the Master of the College, Professor Sir John Butterfield.

'Master,' he said, 'you're a medic: how do I begin to cut into this?'

'You're asking the wrong person,' replied the Master. 'I'm not a surgeon; I'm a physician. I can tell you what it died of!'

And, of course, there would be other questions too, such as why we eat some birds and animals and not others . . . which might call for different specializations. Life is highly complicated. Any attempt to reduce it to things you can measure in a test tube or a bank balance or, indeed, to a few shibboleths of faith, however true in themselves, is bound to fail. So how can we proceed? How can we get beyond the false 'either/or's that trip us up in the media, in education, in public policy?

I have two answers for you tonight. The first is that we must understand more clearly where our present dilemmas have come from. The second is that there are resources within the Christian tradition itself through which we can articulate a better way, a better way of *knowing*, the 'more excellent way' of love itself. I turn at once to the first of these: how did we get into this odd position?

I have discussed elsewhere the brilliant recent account by Iain McGilchrist in his famous book *The Master and His Emissary*. McGilchrist, both a brain scientist and a literary critic and hence straddling the 'two cultures' divide, argues that modern western culture has exhibited large-scale symptoms that correspond to the type of schizophrenia in which the brain's left hemisphere dominates and the right hemisphere is underused or screened out altogether. He insists that this is deeply unhealthy, since the right hemisphere, which handles metaphor, music, imagination, poetry and indeed faith, is designed to take the lead (as 'the master'), and the left hemisphere, which crunches the numbers and works out the details, is designed to back it up (as 'the emissary'). The take-over bid by the left brain produces, in a culture, the same effect as when the bean-counters take over the business. That's not their job. The beans need to be counted, of course. But that must serve the larger purpose, which can never be glimpsed by merely counting beans.

I take McGilchrist's analysis for granted and move to a different though related point, central to all my reflection on how we've got where we've got as a culture. We have inherited the Enlightenment's assumption of a split world which has produced new definitions of the key terms 'science', 'faith' and 'religion' themselves. This split-world assumption, though, is itself rooted neither in science nor in faith. It is a philosophical take-over bid which has distorted each element in the picture, and has deliberately generated the false either/or of which we have spoken. The split world in question comes partly from deism, but more particularly from its older and more rigorous cousin Epicureanism, an elite philosophy in the ancient world which taught that even if the gods exist they are a long way away and never concern themselves with our world, and that our world simply makes itself up as it goes along, evolving under its own steam. Ancient Epicureanism was a protest against ancient paganism; fifteenth-century Epicureanism was a protest against western mediaeval theology; Enlightenment Epicureanism was a protest against the perceived errors of the ongoing western church. Here is the joke at the heart of our problem: that people imagine that we in the 'modern' world have suddenly discovered 'evolution', and that this has suddenly made life awkward for believers. What actually happened was that some seminal eighteenth- and nineteenth-century thinkers believed passionately in Epicureanism for quite other reasons, and seized on the signs of biological evolution as apparent evidence for it, producing what I've called 'evolution*ism*'. This is a classic 'enlightenment' project, resulting in the implicit belief of western Europe and North America that we are the world's elite, the enlightened ones, able to look down on all other civilizations from the supposed height of our new wisdom. We had 'discovered' that a sharp division existed between the hard facts of this world, which does its own thing without divine intervention, and the vague fantasies of 'religion', which were unprovable, unreliable, intolerant and unhealthy.

In part this was, as I said, a reaction to a church that had become dogmatic and out of touch. But the Epicurean revival of the Enlightenment was, more importantly, in the service of political agendas. It produced, of course, the French Revolution; but, more insidiously perhaps, by kicking God upstairs and insisting that the downstairs world of 'facts' could get on by itself, it paved the way for massive exploitation both of natural resources and of the conquered lands and peoples of the European empires. *The split between science and religion is one aspect of a larger split between God and the world, affecting equally the question of faith and public life.* We can't understand the roots of the science–religion split unless we map it on to the much larger split and take into account the other areas where the same problem has taken hold, particularly in the political sphere. That is why the same rhetoric that Richard Dawkins uses about science and faith is found in those who are desperate to keep the church out of public life. And the language of this movement has been, again and again, about *modes of knowing*: the science studied, and the technology developed, were about 'objective' knowledge, whereas the world of faith and religion was seen as quintessentially 'subjective' ('true for you but not for me' and so on). And since the western world had all these 'facts', including, of course, better weapons of war, it made sense to create new facts on the ground that would serve the interests of that same western world. And my case to you tonight is that this objective–subjective split must be, and can be, transcended when we realize that the highest form of knowledge is love.

There's another aspect to this which we must put on the table, though there isn't time to develop it. Once you have separated God and the world, then miracles naturally become problematic. Indeed, the way we now hear the word 'miracle' itself is conditioned by these Enlightenment perspectives, so it now *sounds* as though it refers to a distant God, normally outside the world's processes, but just occasionally reaching in to do something bizarre and then going away again. The fact that many devout Christians think they have to defend just this shows how great a victory the Enlightenment has won. But the supreme 'miracle' is, of course, the incarnation and resurrection of Jesus; and the reason why the Enlightenment passionately rejects this is clear. It isn't just that Hume had declared that miracles don't happen. It is that if there is a living God who became human and was raised from the dead, then that must be, cannot escape being, the climax and turning-point of history. *And the whole point of the Enlightenment was that history reached its climax and turning-point in – the Enlightenment itself.* There cannot be two decisive moments. What we today perceive as the science–religion split, or the faith-and-public-life split, is the long outworking of the Enlightenment's self-serving and elitist claim that world history had turned its decisive corner, that humankind had come of age, when Europe and America suddenly opened their eyes. Subsequent history shows what this has meant: wonderful advances in medicine, technology and travel; terrible disasters in warfare, genocide and new forms of slavery. I do not want to be operated on by a pre-modern dentist (or a postmodern one, for that matter); but I do not trust world leaders who have swallowed the Enlightenment's agendas wholesale, as most of them have.

Such a historical moment deserves a myth, and there are two which sharpen up the story: the myth of Faust and the myth of Frankenstein.

The mediaeval legend of Faust, re-used by writers like Marlowe, Goethe and Thomas Mann, has Faust making a pact with the devil. Faust will have limitless knowledge and boundless pleasures, but the devil will have his soul in the end. There is one condition: Faust must not love. His heart and soul belong to Mephistopheles; true, deep love would be a sign that the world is after all the good creation of a good God. In Goethe's *Faust*, the crucial point is that Faust must never say, on pain of instant death, *Verweile doch, du bist so schön*, 'Stay a while, you are so beautiful.'

The legend remains popular, in theatre, cinema and elsewhere. It isn't just a good story. It is *our* story. Western culture has flirted with playing Faust: has banished God to a distant 'heaven' and has grasped at success, technological advancement, untrammelled pleasure, exploitation of the world's natural resources and its defenceless peoples. But there is a day of reckoning. For Thomas Mann, the astonishing success and the horrible downfall of Nazi Germany was such a moment. There might be others. And part of the point is that, as we saw earlier, godless culture-making, particularly godless science, cannot explain or contain love or, indeed, justice or freedom or beauty. Take the latter: 'aesthetics' only became a distinct 'subject' in the eighteenth century. The word 'beauty' hardly occurs in the Bible, not because the biblical authors didn't believe in it or delight in it but because the beauty of creation is an integral part of everything else. The psalmist says, 'You make the outgoings of the morning and evening to praise you', referring to the evocative beauty of dawn and dusk, but for him this is not something other than the ceaseless worship offered by the glad creation to the good creator, and celebrated as such by God's people. That is the kind of epistemic unity which the Faustian pact carefully picks apart and must not reassemble. The Romantic movement was in part a protest against this but, though Coleridge and others did their best, its main thrust was to highlight the world of human feeling and emotion, not to join that back into the worship of the one God. There is much more we could say about that, but not here.

The other myth that has haunted our culture, and still reappears in movies, is Frankenstein. Once you cut science loose from its earlier context within faith and culture, it can and will produce rampaging monsters. If ever there was a story for the twentieth century, there it is; and our question, a question even more urgent for western governments than that of Brexit or the refugee crisis, is: how to stop our home-made monsters pulling down the house on top of us. Once again there's more that could be said about that, but let me just comment that if I were devising an education programme for teenagers, trying to get them to think into our current global dilemmas, I would love to show them Faust and Frankenstein in the movies and get them to discuss not only the Holocaust but 9/11, nuclear weapons, multi-national tax arrangements and so on with those myths in their minds. And then, with all those questions and resources still resonating, I would have them read the stories that have a radically different twist: Joseph in Egypt; Daniel in Babylon; and on to plays like *Measure for Measure*, poems like Eliot's *The Waste Land* or, indeed, Coleridge's *The Ancient Mariner*; always circling back, with all aesthetic antennae fully operative, to the book of Revelation and, ultimately, to the gospels themselves. (We have allowed the Bible to be locked into a sanitized space called 'religious studies'; that is a classic post-Enlightenment way of making sure they can't come out and challenge the received folly.) There is a different story. We do not have to stay trapped in the Faust and Frankenstein myths. Once we realize how deeply we have sunk into the split-level universe, so that our current surface noise about science and religion is seen to be part of a much larger problem, we might be able to see ways in which the next generation may find its way into a wiser, more complete way of being human.

Of course, it should also go without saying that there are equally important mythological dramas about the way in which faith and religion have gone sour. The media and the movies can never get enough of ecclesial scandals. We in the church must acknowledge them with shame. I suspect I don't need to say more about that just now, but it has contributed to our current problem.

But here is the challenge of our times. When I became Bishop of Durham in 2003 somebody asked me at the opening press conference to summarize the task facing the church in our day, and I said, perhaps assuming too much, that our task was in prayer and faith to lead the way through postmodernity and out into the as yet undiscovered world of post-postmodernity. One of the journalists present, reporting this, commented that 'They talk of nothing else in South Shields'. It was a friendly tease and, indeed, he became a good friend; but I stand by the summary, even though, of course, it needed spelling out. Postmodernity, from Nietzsche to Derrida and beyond, has blown the whistle on modernist arrogance, but it can't stop it in its tracks. Politicians and journalists still go round the same, tired old loops of unresolved pragmatic secularism, assuming (as we all did with the so-called 'Arab Spring'!) that all you have to do is topple a few tyrants and freedom, flower-power and western-style democracy will automatically emerge. Half the population of Syria is today paying the price for our failed narrative, washing up quite literally on our shores. The horror of 9/11 was one dramatic actualization of the failure of arrogant modernity; the present refugee crisis is another. We have no idea what to do because the Enlightenment worldview gave us no story, no script, for such a moment. We make things, we sell things, we vote every so often, but we have forgotten how to love. The scientists can make very clever weapons for destroying cities but they can't make any to put communities back together again. The questions of science and religion are symptoms of a much larger problem. But the good news is that, though there is a long way to go, the gospel of Jesus, once liberated from its cultural captivity, from the exile of 'private religion' to which secularism has tried to banish it, has unparalleled power to transform the world. That is why the secularists, not least the eager advocates of atheist scientism, are so keen to keep it out of sight. Our job is to bring it back again. When we really grasp this nettle, we'll find that its roots go right down to the heart of our present dilemmas.

And now the question of knowledge finally comes into focus. The secular revolution has separated out knowledge into objective and subjective. The scientist, in this paradigm, has 'objective' knowledge, tested in laboratories, universally true. The artist, the poet, the theologian, has 'subjective' knowledge – dreams, fantasies, unprovable ideas, which are to be set aside when we (metaphorically and literally) get 'down to business'. You can see this in education: when the school budget is stretched, the head teacher is tempted to cut down on music, drama, art and so on. They are 'the pretty bit around the edge', a luxury we may not be able to afford. That is dangerous nonsense. Look at the Venezuelan Children's Orchestra. Look what happens when people take drama into prisons. Look at the way J. K. Rowling has taught a generation to read, to imagine, to dream. If you want true knowledge you have to love. And to learn about true love you have to hear, to smell, to imagine the story of the crucified Nazarene.

The point about love, at this level, is that it transcends the object–subject distinction. Of course it does: when I truly love, whether the object of my love is a planet or a person, a symphony or a sunset, I am celebrating the *otherness* of the beloved, wanting the beloved to be what it really is, greater than my imagining or perception, stranger, more mysterious. Love celebrates that mystery: in that sense, it is truly 'objective'; but it is also, of course, delightedly 'subjective'. Without the subjective pole, it becomes mere cool appraisal or 'tolerance'. Without the objective pole, the celebration of the other *as* other, it is simply lust, cutting the beloved down to the size of my desires and projects, whether it be sexual lust exploiting another human being or industrial lust exploiting raw materials for profit despite the consequences. A colleague of mine put his finger on the first of these, speaking of 'the decline of sex', and explaining, 'We all know how to do it but we've all forgotten why.' That is exactly the same as the second, the Frankensteinian scientism of our day: we *can* do it, so why not and who's to stop us? And this is where Jonathan Sacks's aphorism comes in again: science takes things apart to see how they work; religion puts things together to see what they mean. And sometimes the meaning tells you to stop pulling them apart. It's a crisis of *meaning* that we face in our day, and a crisis of *knowledge* that brings that into focus; and the answer to the false antithesis of objective and subjective, which has been throttling our culture for too long, is a full-on reawakening of *an epistemology of love*. We have had enough of the Faustian pact in which we merely 'tolerate' one another; 'toleration' is an Enlightenment parody of love. It is time for the dangerous gospel notion of love to make a come-back in our culture.

Once we glimpse this possibility we discover that it is written all through scripture, emerging at key points but bubbling along under the rest. Paul challenges the Galatians: what matters is not your knowledge of God but God's knowledge of you, and that knowledge is revealed in God sending the son and the spirit. He challenges the Corinthians: if you think you 'know' something in your own way, you are merely puffed up and don't really 'know' at all; but if you love God, you are known by God – once again the God revealed in the crucified Jesus. Paul was addressing the 'knowledge' systems of his day with a new kind of knowing, a knowing rooted in the love of God. How does this work?

It works because humans are made to reflect the wise, loving creator into his world. Our knowledge and speech are designed vocationally to do two things which reinforce one another: to worship him by telling the story of creation and covenant, of new creation and new covenant, and then to bring his wonderful purposes to fruition in the world. That is what it means to be made in God's image; we are angled mirrors, designed to reflect creation's praises to the creator and the creator's wisdom into his creation. The science-religion split is a symptom of the distortion that comes about when the mirror gets twisted so that it simply reflects the world back into the world, generating idolatry instead of true worship and a false, Faustian 'success' instead of genuine human flourishing. We all know 1 Corinthians 13: love is patient and kind; if I don't have love, I am nothing; and alongside faith and hope the greatest of these is love. But the fact that we often read it at weddings lures us into hearing those great words as a recipe for a detached Romanticism which leaves the wider world untouched. (That reaction means we are also belittling weddings, but that's another story, though closely related.) For Paul, all this is explosive: we know in part, we prophesy in part, but with love we are already engaging in the mode of knowing that will last into God's new creation, when we shall know as we are known.

Where do we start with this? In worship, of course – a worship constantly renewed through fresh scriptural reading, prayer, good liturgy of whatever kind. A worship consciously and conscientiously bringing the praises of the whole creation before the creator, articulating in human speech the powerful allegiance of the farthest planet and the smallest particle and everything in between. (When I was Dean of Lichfield we hosted a West Midlands 'Industrial Harvest Festival', encouraging local industries to display their products, and their craftsmanship, in the cathedral for a week and ending with a great service.) But then we need preaching and teaching, with the teaching flowing out quickly into public discourse whether broadcast, journalistic, parliamentary or in schools, in which we challenge the latent Epicureanism of western culture at its root by speaking of – and particularly by living out – the powerful healing and recreative love of the creator God, who is not the deist's distant faceless bureaucrat, nor yet the Epicurean's totally detached being, but is known, and is dangerously present, in Jesus and in the spirit.

The 'Jesus' bit of that demands that we do history. A central part of Christian discipleship is that we constantly go back to the first century and discover more and more what was actually going on in that explosive and world-changing moment, refusing to be fobbed off with the pseudo-history which tried to fit Jesus on to the eighteenth-century Procrustean bed. History itself, especially the history of Jesus, is in fact one of the theatres in which the epistemology of love matters most, paying absolute attention to every scrap of evidence as it is in itself and at the same time constantly delighting in the play of explanatory hypotheses in which we glimpse more and more of the actual motivations of Peter, of Pontius Pilate, of Jesus himself. The more we realize just how mysterious the whole world is, just how puzzling justice and beauty and love itself really are, the more we should delight in seeing the puzzles and paradoxes rushing together in the story of Jesus, and supremely in his death and resurrection. I deeply regret that these historical questions are usually relegated to a sub-sub-branch of curricula in schools and colleges, a small corner of a 'religious studies' syllabus which then is itself played off against 'science', rather than finding their way into the heart of literature, drama and global history itself.

Historians have focused on the so-called 'axial age' of the last centuries BC, but the truly remarkable story is not about the pre-Christian trans-formation of ideas but the Christian-initiated transformation of society in the first centuries AD. Against much misinformation, we must tell and teach that story as if our lives depend on it, because actually they do. It is not simply a knowledge-story, a history-of-ideas project. It is a love-story, the story of ordinary, often frightened, but faithful men and women who went out to bring healing, education, freedom and hope to a world where such things had before only been available to a tiny minority, and who did so because they were following Jesus. And in that love-story new knowledge emerged, not simply because of the great thinkers, though they matter as well, but because the followers of Jesus were opening up new ways to be human, were *loving* in order to *know* and then finding that deeper knowledge led to deeper love. What we are about, after all, is *new creation*. Nietzsche derided Christianity as 'Platonism for the masses', but that's because he was looking at the Platonized western church which had downgraded the resurrection and with it the whole biblical project of new creation. Fascinatingly, it was Ludwig Wittgenstein who said 'It is *love* that believes the resurrection'; and that works both ways. A spurious pseudo-objectivity looks at the world and says 'Resurrection is impossible', and mocks as fantasy any attempt to reimagine it. Love looks at the God revealed in Jesus and says 'Yes'; and believing in the resurrection, as has been shown time and again, awakens a love which is not simply the romantic antithesis of rationalism but which frames and energizes an integrated project of knowledge in every sphere.

I've had to compress the big picture into a very small frame for this evening. But I hope I have at least stimulated you to realize that the presenting issue for 'Grasping the Nettle' takes us right to the heart of the gospel challenge to our culture. I am very much aware at this time of night of the old Anglican line about the priest who dreamt he was preaching a sermon and woke up to find it was true, and I hope that you, having done me the honour of staying awake, will sleep all the sounder as a result. Let me leave you with three very quick 'so what' suggestions. I have already mentioned new possibilities in the teaching of culture and of history: we need fresh integration and the schools are a vital place to start. In churches too, however, we need to ratchet up our teaching ambitions, for adults as well as young people, to set out the Christian worldview in terms of creation and covenant, of new covenant and new creation, in such a way that the Bible isn't just a strange vaguely Christian version of Aesop's Fables but rather tells the story which the western world has all but forgotten, the story of an integrated world in which science and music and history and art and politics and philosophy come rushing together into new syntheses under the impetus not of a detached 'knowledge' but of a delighted 'love'. That is a teaching agenda we could all pursue in our own contexts.

Second, we might try the experiment I played out once or twice in Durham. I used to get local churches to host meetings to ask the question: what would this town look like if God was in charge? People find that question scary because it conjures up visions of mad theocratic clergy bossing people around. That image has been central to the secular resistance to the gospel-message of the kingdom of God – a resistance with which the churches themselves have often colluded. In places like Darlington we invited the mayor and the council, the prison workers, hospital administrators, social workers and the like, and addressed this question head on – what would Darlington look like if God was in charge? – in a cheerful atmosphere with drinks and nibbles and no holds barred in questions. It opens up new discussions and in my experience can facilitate new partnerships, and in such work completely outflanks the silly secularism of the science–religion divide.

Third, we need to explore new ways of praying. Many spiritual guides have gone further down this road than I have, and there is always the danger that if we simply try to bolt on some spirituality to the outside of the present scientific or, indeed, political world it looks just like that – something incongruous stuck on the outside, easily detached again. For those with the opportunity, however, I think it would do us all good to wonder what it would look like to celebrate the kingdom of God in the world of the laboratory, the observatory or the council chamber. Partly, of course, it would be by doing well, faithfully and lovingly, what we are called to do as scientists, as government officials, as teachers or journalists or whatever. But there are ways of interweaving patterns of prayer into all of life which go much deeper than the bolt-on kind, and I would love to see us develop those as central to the whole strategy.

And so, 'The greatest of these is love.' We have lived for too long in the split-level world of Enlightenment fantasy. The voices from left and right that want to keep us there must be answered. This is a big nettle to grasp, and I'm glad we are taking our courage in both hands to do it. Where will it take us? How will we do it? I answer with my title, as a question for all of us tonight: 'Wouldn't you love to know?'

16
Sign and Means of New Creation: Public Worship and the Creative Reading of Scripture

One of the quiet scandals of much modern church life is the poor quality of public reading of scripture. This applies as much, if not more, in churches that think of themselves as 'biblical' as in the so-called 'mainstream' denominations. There are many notable exceptions, of course, but since more or less all churches profess in theory to base themselves on scripture it is hardly a strange or outlandish request that scripture itself should be read and heard, enjoyed and understood, in order that it may be lived out in mission and transformed lives. To that end, I have given different versions of this lecture in various locations, including Calvin College, Grand Rapids, Michigan, in January 2017 (the version reproduced in this chapter) and the Anglican Cathedral in Hong Kong in March 2019. The enthusiastic response I have received has encouraged me to think that there are many clergy and laity who agree that something has gone wrong and are eager for fresh ways forward.

At the start of the First World War, the young Karl Barth was a parish minister in Safenwil in Switzerland. At this moment of crisis, Barth and his friend Eduard Thurneysen plunged deeply into the Bible, which they had begun to read not simply as a record of other people's religious awareness but as a living word from God. The point that emerged with devastating clarity was what Barth sometimes spoke of as the 'new world in the Bible'. I think he meant 'new' in two ways: it was new to him, but it was also the world of God's new creation. It was a world where God was sovereign and called nations and individuals to account. If the Bible opens up a world which is the new creation accomplished by Jesus Christ in his death and resurrection and now energized by the spirit, there can be few tasks more important, for us as for Barth, than engaging appropriately with this book, challenging though that has always been.

Now obviously this must be done through study and teaching, through the preaching and pastoral work for which ministers are, supposedly at least, specially trained. But I have in mind today particularly the challenge of reading the Bible within public worship; and to contextualize that I want to say a few things first about public worship itself, public worship as the sign and the means of new creation. The underlying problem of the world is not sin, but idolatry; not that sin doesn't matter, but that sin is what happens *because of* the root cause, which is idolatry. When we worship the false gods of this world – the many gods and lords of which Paul spoke in 1 Corinthians – we hand over to them the power that is ours by virtue of our creation as image-bearing human beings, designed (according to Genesis and Psalm 8) to be set in authority over the whole world. False worship gives up that vocation and submits to slavery instead. And the Bible tells the story of creation and new creation, exodus and new exodus, the freeing of the slaves under Moses and the freeing of the world from its deepest slaveries through the death and resurrection of Jesus. It tells the story of the ultimate new creation. And when we worship the God of whom this story speaks – and retelling the story is central to that as I shall be explaining – then this worship, and this biblical storytelling, become both a *sign* and a *means* of that new creation.

It is a 'sign', in that this very act points forward. The story only makes sense if it is leading to that conclusion, to the renewal of creation. But it is also a 'means', because when this story is told, and when men and women are worshipping this God in this way, then they are as Paul says 'renewed in knowledge according to the image of [their] creator' (Colossians 3.10 NRSV). The reason we can reassume that status of image-bearers, of the 'royal priesthood', is because the forgiveness of our sins means that the grip of the 'powers' on us is broken. Thus, when the church is being the church, and nowhere more than in scripture-focused worship, the church itself is also the sign and means of the manifold wisdom of God being made known to the principalities and powers in the heavenly places. And, as Paul stresses in Romans 8, the renewal of human beings is God's means towards the renewal of the whole creation. When, therefore, we worship the living God, using for that purpose the great story of scripture, we are celebrating in advance, and thereby materially contributing to, the ultimate new heavens and new earth. This is particularly and critically so in sacramental worship, where elements of the present creation are taken up to become foretastes of the world to come. But the burden of my song today is that this is especially the case with the use of scripture in worship. And this raises a problem to which the rest of this lecture is offered as a solution.

Here's the problem. Our use of scripture in worship strikes me – to put it mildly – as impoverished. This is related to the other obvious problem about scripture in church life. Every church I know claims in some way or other to be based on scripture; to be in some sense 'living under the authority of scripture'. But what does this actually look like? If we walked into a room and saw people living under the authority of scripture, what would we see going on?

Without being cynical, it seems normally to mean some people quoting a few texts this way or that, or someone recalling what they learned in seminary. Few clergy have the time, it seems, for serious and sustained Bible study of a sort that might freshly inform and undergird creative and formative ministry. Few laity have the tools even to start (though in the USA far more seem to make a stab at this than in the UK). And this wider problem is umbilically related to how we use scripture in worship. I believe that if we understood what it means to use scripture in worship, in worship that is both sign and means of new creation, we might thereby bring the Bible back into the life of the church as a rich, deep, positive presence, rather than an occasional and contested footnote.

What I now offer you is a set of proposals in this direction. I have three notes about the problem as I see it, four starting-points towards a fresh approach, five creative proposals and six classic examples. Obviously these will all be brief, and all could be expanded considerably.

Three Notes about the Problem

My first note is that the older I get, the more I see the larger story of scripture as a whole: of the gospels as wholes, of the Pentateuch as a whole, and so on. It's then all the more frustrating when I realize that few churches see this; few in their worship consciously find themselves within this larger narrative. Instead it seems as though western Christianity as a whole lives within its own narrative, either the regular going-to-heaven narrative or the 'Jesus-the-social-worker' narrative, or something in between, rather than the full-on, full-blooded heaven-and-earth narrative of scripture. When I talk to individuals and groups, I find that people are fascinated and excited by the larger scriptural narratives. They want to know more; but it's not easy to see how to achieve this in church and study groups. The Bible is a large and complex collection of mostly large and complex books, and seeing it whole is difficult. At the same time, I have been rebuked this last year by watching my own grandchildren, at quite an early age, wrestling with the large issues of Tolkein's *The Lord of the Rings* or with the seven Harry Potter books, and I realize that actually we humans are hard-wired, from an early age, not only to 'get' what a large and complex story is about, but also to be able to think through its characters and its plot, its twists and turns, with considerable sophistication. Why shouldn't we do that with the Bible, starting as young as we can?

My second note about the problem is that this is partly practical – because within regular worship there's not very much time to read very much scripture out loud – but more particularly theological. The Christian churches in general have always been subject to the temptation to use the Bible to annotate the story we want to tell for ourselves, rather than allow the Bible to tell its own story and invite us to join in. Instead of really grasping what it means that 'the Messiah died for our sins and rose again according to the scriptures', we have actually meant 'the Messiah died and rose again according to our narrative of sin and salvation, for which we can find some biblical proof-texts'. Our theology has often been *dualistic*, rejecting the biblical heaven-and-earth interpenetration and then wondering why so much of the Bible has to be allegorized in order to fit with the story we want to tell; or it has been *Marcionite*, rejecting or distorting the Israel-focus of scripture. Then either the Old Testament falls off the back, or we effectively teach that the God of the Old Testament is different from the God of the New.

My third note is that when we therefore use scripture in little bits, cut off from their proper context and made to dance to our tunes instead, all sorts of doubts can creep in, like weeds among the wheat. Did Jesus really say this? Did Paul really mean that? Wasn't this bit of teaching just a quirk of first-century culture which we can leave behind? If we reject Leviticus by not offering animal sacrifice any longer, why should we accept what it says about sexual behaviour? And so on. Our liturgical practice thus first reflects and then reinforces a sense both of holding scripture at arm's length and then also of making it hard to hear what those individual snippets were actually all about in the first place.

In these three ways and many others, I think it's time for a fresh look at how we use the Bible in church: how we can ourselves, in planning and leading worship, make sure we are doing justice and honour to scripture itself, rather than simply using it within schemes of our own making. And I believe that every step we take in this direction will be a move towards making our worship more clearly and obviously the sign and means of new creation.

Four Starting-Points towards a Fresh Approach

My first starting-point is that we need a fresh grasp, at least in outline, of how the larger story of scripture actually works. I have often seen eyes opening wide and jaws dropping when I have sketched, even briefly, the great sweep of scripture from Genesis to Revelation, from the creation of the garden with image-bearing and community-building humans to the garden city with humans as the royal priesthood. This framework is vital. We need that whole-Bible sweep if we're to make proper sense of all the bits in between.

This applies especially to the four gospels. I have written elsewhere about the way in which, in both popular and scholarly readings, the gospels have tended to fall apart with Jesus' preaching of the kingdom on the one hand and his going to the cross on the other. Western theology has found it hard to hold these together, and that problem is reflected both in academic discussions of the gospels and their traditions and in popular imaginings of Jesus the miracle-worker or social revolutionary on the one hand and Jesus the suffering saviour on the other. We have failed to realize that the four canonical gospels (as opposed to the non-canonical ones) see Jesus' kingdom-work as completed on the cross and see the cross as the ultimate kingdom-bringing moment. The two are mutually defining and, of course, the resurrection vindicates and validates that combination rather than one or other of the detached and distorted themes. (It is noticeable, though, that when people concentrate on the kingdom rather than the cross they often downplay or deny the resurrection, and when people concentrate on cross rather than kingdom they reinterpret the resurrection in terms of 'going to heaven' rather than 'new creation'.)

In particular – still within my first starting-point – we need to recapture the biblical Temple-theology. Huge strides have been made in this area over the last generation or two by Jewish and Old Testament scholars, and New Testament scholars are at last catching up. Genesis 1 and 2 are about the construction of a *temple*, namely, the heaven-and-earth creation in which God wants to dwell, with humans as the 'image' in the temple. The first great narrative arc within the Pentateuch runs from there to Exodus 40 when the wilderness tabernacle is constructed and the divine presence comes to dwell in it. The tabernacle, and then the Temple in Jerusalem, are designed as a *microcosmos*, a little creation, a small working-model of creation as a whole which functions as a signpost to YHWH's intention to renew the whole world.

The New Testament declares in a hundred different ways that this is precisely what's happened in and through Jesus: Ephesians 1.10 declares that God's plan from the start was to sum up all things in the Messiah, things in heaven and things on earth, and it goes on to explain that if Jesus is the heaven-and-earth person, the ultimate human *microcosmos*, then the church, indwelt by the spirit and uniting Jew and gentile together, is the new Temple, the sign to the powers of the world that God is God and Jesus is lord and that they are not. All of this big-picture biblical reading needs to be in place as the starting-point if the practical proposals I'm going to offer are to make the sense they ought to.

The second starting-point I propose is to reflect on how a big picture of scripture makes sense within public worship. My fear is that in most churches, including those which use a lectionary to help the congregation move slowly but surely through quite a lot of scripture, the public reading of scripture on a Sunday morning has become perfunctory. We assume that more or less anyone can read in public and that church members don't need a lot of rehearsal or encouragement. Their names are put down on a rota and they turn up and do it. Of course, if the choir were to do that – just anybody turning up and singing without practising and direction – people would soon complain; but we've got used to poor reading, partly I think because we haven't stopped to think what the public reading of scripture is *for*. Often it seems that it's simply there as the text, or the pretext, for a sermon which may end up being about something quite different: a jumping-off point rather than the foundation for what the preacher wants to say. That's not a good way to go.

Actually, the public reading of scripture in the course of the church's worship is not about 'teaching'; it's not there to impart information. It is part of the worship and praise of God; it is a way, a central way, a more central way even than the best hymns and worship songs, of *praising God for his mighty acts*. We rehearse the *story* of what God has done, not primarily to remind ourselves of it (though that happens as it's done, of course), but so that we can acclaim and celebrate God's mighty acts. We praise him for creation itself, and within creation for his acts through Israel and in Jesus and the spirit in rescuing and renewing his world. You see this focused sharply in Revelation 4, where all creation praises God as the creator, and Revelation 5, where all creation praises God as the redeemer – with the human voices joining the non-human ones to add the word 'because' – we praise God *because* of who he is and what he's done. And this sense of worshipping God by reciting his mighty acts belongs closely with the Temple-theology I have just mentioned.

We by the spirit form the new Temple, and this new Temple is to be filled with the praise which is the sign of the spirit's presence. And that in turn is both sign and means of new creation.

Recitation of scripture is the Christian equivalent of the pillar of cloud and fire in the desert, the very presence of the covenant God standing there with his people in awe and intimacy and leading them to their inheritance. This sense of the spirit-filled, praise-filled community is the sign to the world – and to us as still part of that world – that one day the whole earth will be filled with the divine glory as the waters cover the sea. And, by celebrating Jesus' lordship and renouncing the otherwise powerful idols, this worship becomes also a means towards that end. That is what our public worship ought to be saying. Those who join in with that worship ought to be able to sense that living rhythm, that longer vision, that larger horizon of promise.

All this depends on grasping the third of my four starting-points. Unless our services are to take a very long time indeed, we choose short readings for our public worship. In my Anglican tradition the staple daily diet of morning and evening prayer always includes two: one from the Old Testament, of course, and one from the New. Having that rhythm is important because it reminds us that our scripture readings are extracts from a *narrative*. If we just have one reading, whatever it is, we can easily imagine that it is just a piece of wisdom or learning which we meet straight on, rather than a part of the larger story into which we ourselves are caught up. The two or more readings make sure that in principle we are sensing that narrative movement, which opens up at least the chance that the worshippers will find themselves caught up in the story which then points on to the new creation.

This leads to the centre of this third starting-point: that our scripture readings, however short they are, are designed to function as small windows on the larger narrative. We may only be reading fifteen verses from 1 Kings, but like children pressing their noses against a small window high up in the house we find we can see, through that small window, the whole landscape, the distant mountains of Genesis and Isaiah, the fields and woods of Numbers and Nehemiah, the little streams of the minor prophets. We may only be reading from the New Testament one paragraph of Paul, but as we get close to that reading and look not only *at* it but *through* it we can see the entire sweep of Paul's vision, of the biblical narrative focused now on Jesus and his messianic death and resurrection.

Of course, in order to be able to see these larger wholes we need to be acquainted with them. Equally, as we look *through* these windows we mustn't neglect to look *at* them, to take stock of, and take delight in, the particular and specific things this particular passage has to teach. And one of the ways we do this – I am again thinking of the way the ancient daily offices are constructed – is to flank these readings, however large or small, with psalmody, with the Psalms themselves to which I shall come presently and with the poems and prayers of the New Testament and the early church, poems like the Magnificat and the Benedictus, or in many traditions the Te Deum and the Benedicite. These are in a sense obvious, but I worry that many traditions, particularly the newer charismatic and free-church worship traditions, have never reflected on how liturgy actually works and particularly on how the liturgical reading of scripture actually works – what it's there for. So they assume that it's simply part of the teaching ministry, and therefore they content themselves with a perfunctory reading on Sunday morning and they hope that the midweek Bible study will make up the deficiency. Well, I'd much rather people did at least read out part of the Bible on Sunday and go to some kind of Bible study midweek. But there is so much more going on here; and the new generation badly needs it.

My fourth starting-point towards a fresh approach is to insist on some kind of *lectio continua*, both personally and publicly. There are, to be sure, many times and occasions when we need to choose special readings to suit a particular moment or challenge. But the church's staple diet ought to be to work through the books of the Bible on a more or less continuous loop. There is an oddity about this, of course. Paul didn't write Galatians expecting the church to read, or hear, the first ten verses one week and the next ten verses the next week, and so on. None of the biblical books was written with that kind of reading in mind, though the early church, following the example of the ancient Jewish lectionaries, found itself quite soon dividing the New Testament up like that. And this is particularly acute when it comes to the gospels because again and again you only really get the point of a particular story when you see it in its larger context. *Lectio continua* does give you the chance of that, for all its problems.

These, then, are my four starting-points. Let me now move to five creative proposals: and, as I do, let me say a word about translations. Because of my professional work I naturally normally read the Bible in Greek and Hebrew, but I know very well that many even of those who want to do this really can't. You need to start young, ideally, and many just didn't have or didn't take that opportunity. But if you don't have the original languages you need to read, regularly, from more than one modern translation; preferably from two or three at least, and in quite different idioms. It's hard for me to comment on particular translations because they are all, including my own *New*

Testament for Everyone (known in the USA as the *Kingdom New Testament*), a mixed bag, with some bits that 'work' better than others. Translation is not an exact science at the best of times, and translating scripture, though a wonderful challenge, is also frustrating as the rich meanings seldom if ever come through unscathed. In the mercy of God, however, Christianity has been a translating religion from the first, with the New Testament written in Greek, not Aramaic, and the gift of tongues symbolizing God's desire that comprehensible praise should arise from every language under heaven.

Five Creative Proposals

As I launch into five creative proposals, let me say that all this could work really well ecumenically. We all know we ought to get together with Christians of other traditions but we're all so busy we're not quite sure how to do it. The Bible is one of the great ecumenical instruments and we should seek out ways, whether in ministers' meetings or in house-groups, for studying the Bible together across our various traditions. You learn far more from and with one another when you do it together. That thought could be developed further, but not here.

My first proposal is obvious but it needs saying. We need whole-book readings and whole-Bible readings. How are you going to do that? We need to encourage one another that, in addition to whatever Bible-reading scheme we use for our daily devotions (and if we're not doing daily Bible-reading we should start at once), we should take time, perhaps once a week or once a month, to set aside an hour or two and read right through a book at a sitting. That is what they were designed for, after all. And actually with some of the harder books – I think of Leviticus as an obvious example – it's much easier to read them straight through at a run. If you do half a chapter a day it'll take you a couple of weeks just to get through the daily sacrifices, and unless you are a real geek for that stuff you will get bored; whereas to read the whole thing through at a run is to realize that the book works like a song, with the rhythms and repetitions coming round in an almost incantatory fashion. I had a friend whose spiritual director once advised him to read Romans every day for a month. 'What,' he said, 'a chapter a day?' 'No,' said the director, 'the whole book, every day.' And so he did – coming home from work, getting a cup of tea, sitting down and reading Romans one more time. He said it was a life-changing month. But most Christians, including highly intelligent Christians, have not only never done that; they've never even *thought* of doing that, or anything like it. What an impoverishment.

When it comes to the whole Bible, I believe we should not only be reading right through the Bible individually at least once a year – for clergy I'd say twice a year at least, and perhaps the gospels four times a year, and if this means reworking your personal schedules then fine, do it – but that we should make it possible for our congregations to try creative experiments for how to experience the whole Bible. I know some churches and some cathedrals that have done sponsored whole-Bible readings, on a 24/7 basis, with people signing up to do the 3 a.m. slot on Numbers or the midnight ride through Revelation. If the church is open and people are invited in to hear, well of course that makes sense and you never know what will come as a result, as people are suddenly struck by this or that passage or, indeed, by the larger sense of narrative flowing through it all. And whatever we do down these lines we ought also to have proper follow-up in terms of seminars or discussion groups, to enable people to catch the fleeting impressions and, not least, to pray them in, to turn curiosity into learning, learning into prayer, and prayer into the fabric of our lives. I would love to see Isaiah 40—55 done like that, or the book of Revelation. What a challenge.

My second creative proposal is for actual performance of individual books or long passages. This can be spectacular. The actor Alec McCowen famously put on Mark's gospel, from the King James Version, night after night in London's West End, with minimal staging and props, and people came and found it utterly compelling. I have seen the actor Paul Alexander do John in the same way, and you'll never read John the same after living through it like that for a couple of hours. I once saw a New Testament scholar who was also an actor doing Galatians, at a conference of Bible scholars, and when the scholars came back to a seminar-style discussion of the letter immediately afterwards we had a whole different angle on the entire text. Most congregations have one or two or more actors who would probably love to be asked to do that, perhaps on a Sunday evening as part of an alternative worship service. In my experience it's probably better with just one or at most two voices, otherwise it becomes more of a staged play – though that can be brilliant as well, but it's, of course, much harder and more time-consuming to do and demands all kinds of extra production elements. But the important thing is for people to experience the books of the Bible as wholes, to be shaped by them so that when they come back to read particular parts they will be returning to an old friend for a particular conversation. And this, even if it's not in a church and not on a Sunday, is bound to be an act of worship, of praising God for his great story; an act of worship which points once more towards new creation.

There is a particular variation on this kind of performance which can be very powerful. In my tradition some churches and cathedrals on Palm Sunday sing the entire Passion narrative from one of the gospels. This takes the place of *both* the gospel reading *and* the sermon. I have known people who, when they discover that there isn't going to be a sermon, are shocked; but then, when they have lived through the whole story in a simple musical setting, they realize. This is more powerful than any sermon. We are now part of the story. That is what music can do.

My third creative proposal is quite simply for *lectio divina*. This is the practice, whether individually or in smallish groups, for spending prayerful time with a particular passage. There are many ways of doing it, but one simple one is that, in the course of morning or evening prayer, one should pause for several minutes – say, five or ten – after each reading; then perhaps go round the group, and each person can say one short thing that has struck him or her; then read it again, and again a time of silence and again a short comment from everyone; then read it again (and it might help if the different readings were from different translations), and this time have a free-for-all about what you as a group are hearing. You can, of course, do this by yourself, but it's exciting and challenging to do it together. When I was Bishop of Durham we did this every month as we began an all-day staff meeting; and again and again we found that our sitting silently, and then sharing what we were hearing, shaped our discussions on all sorts of matters during the rest of the day. There are many ways of inhabiting that ancient tradition of *lectio divina*; I have described one, but there are others and, of course, there are no strict rules, only good practice, and each group will find that out by trial and error. The important thing is that symbolically and practically what this says is that we are trying to be still before the word of God, to listen to what the spirit is saying to the church and to ourselves, and not least to listen for what the spirit may be saying through one another. And in all this we are embodying and celebrating in advance the new creation to which scripture points and which the spirit brings into reality.

My fourth creative proposal comes from an enterprising church in Durham. In 2010 we had a Lenten project, ecumenically, across the whole of the north-east of England. We called it the Big Read, where churches and small groups right across the region got together to read Luke, which was the gospel in the lectionary that year. The members of one church had the brilliant idea that instead of inserting long passages of Luke into the liturgy at the weekly eucharist they would insert the weekly eucharist into Luke. The first Sunday in Lent they began the service by reading the opening of Luke, then singing the first hymn, then reading the next passage, then doing the confession and absolution, and so on. They worked it all out so that it covered Lent and arrived at Holy Week as Luke arrived at the cross – and then, of course, did Easter with Luke 24 as the framework. Their testimony was that it worked like a charm – that all sorts of things fitted together helpfully, with great resonances this way and that from the text into the liturgy, and vice versa. I suspect that all those who worshipped through those services will never forget it, and that whenever they read Luke they will have been permanently transformed in their reading by that experience. Now imagine extrapolating from that up into other possibilities. The sky's the limit . . . or perhaps I should say the new creation, to which this obviously points.

My fifth creative proposal concerns the sermon. Once you realize that the readings in the liturgy are a small window on the larger biblical story, it ought to be natural to draw that out in the sermon. Faced with any biblical passage, a careful preacher will often go looking for particular points of theological detail or pastoral application. Commentaries will often steer you in that direction. But, again and again, the passages we read are themselves opening up and pointing to larger themes. Obviously, if you preach about the larger themes all the time, the congregation might get tired of hearing the same big picture week after week – though to be honest the big picture has so many fascinating details, so many twists and turns, that it would be quite a few weeks before you were in any danger of repeating yourself. But my sense is that most congregations in the western church – and for all I know in other churches as well – simply don't know the big story, and left to themselves they will flick back into the natural default position of thinking that the whole Bible is about how to believe in Jesus so you can go to heaven. They will need constant reinforcement of the larger scriptural story if that is to become the new default mode. We need to be soaked in the story if we are to become wise, worshipping Christians for the next generation and beyond; if, in particular, we are to worship in a way which is both sign and means of new creation.

All this leads me to my final point, the six classic examples of what I'm talking about.

Six Classic Examples

I choose my examples almost at random and there could have been literally dozens of others. I begin with Psalm 2. It's well known both in itself and in its fresh uses in the New Testament. You know it well, I hope: the nations rage and threaten, but God laughs and declares that he has set up his king on Mount Zion. Then the king himself speaks, announcing that God has decreed: 'You are my son; today I have begotten you. Ask of me, and I will make the nations your heritage, and the ends of the earth your possession.' The king will establish his rule over the whole world, and the nations will be humbled and have to learn wisdom by submitting to his rule. Now this psalm obviously goes with several others, like Psalm 72, in which the coming rule of God's chosen king will bring a new situation to birth in the world as a whole. But it might be all too easy to focus simply on the christological application – what it means to say that these words were spoken to Jesus himself. A high Christology – there we are, job done, sermon complete. Or one could imagine a pastoral homily in which these words are spoken to each of us at our baptism: you are my beloved child, and I have a glorious inheritance for you. Great sermon in its way; but the psalm looks so much wider. In this psalm, as we press our noses up against it, we see the story of Genesis: here are the nations raging and eventually building the Tower of Babel, but God laughs and calls Abraham and promises him a worldwide inheritance. Or we look through this window in the other direction and we see Israel in exile, clinging to hope despite the oppression of the nations. Or we look again, with the disciples in Acts 4, and we see the early church invoking this psalm to explain the meaning of the cross, that when the world's rulers did their worst, God raised Jesus and exalted him to be ruler of all. We look outwards to the church's political task: 'Now therefore, O kings, be wise!' The members of that church, those to whom in Christ God says 'You are my child, and the world is your inheritance', have the God-given responsibility to speak that truth to power and to remind the nations, as Jesus reminded Pilate, where their limited authority comes from and how that responsibility is to be exercised. Plenty there to occupy several sermons, to help people worship by reading or singing that psalm and looking *through* it at the larger biblical picture, and so celebrating that larger picture and the God of whom it speaks.

My second example is another psalm, or rather a pair of psalms: 105 and 106. These psalms tell the story of Israel – from two very different angles. Some of you may recall that, about thirty years ago, there was a movie made of Charles Dickens's book *Little Dorritt*. Actually it was two movies, and you had to go on successive nights to the two showings. And here's the thing: the first film covered the whole plot, but from the angle of the heroine; you saw her scenes, you went with her when she left the room, and so on. Then the second film covered the whole of the same plot but from the angle of the hero. Some of the scenes were identical, but then we were taken back with the hero to see what was happening to him at the same time. It was a wonderfully bifocal experience. Well, Psalms 105 and 106 are a bit like that, and together they provide the clue to what is sometimes misleadingly called 'salvation history'. Psalm 105 tells the story of Israel as a success: God calls the people of Israel, rescues them from Egypt, takes them home to the promised land so they can obey his laws. Result! But Psalm 106 tells the *same* story *from the other point of view*. The people of Israel rebel, twist and turn, and try to do anything but go the way their rescuing God wants. Things go from bad to worse; utter disaster threatens; but time and again God finds a way to redeem the situation and to start up again, whereupon they go ahead and worship idols once more. And so on. Now it's unlikely that with quite long psalms like these the congregation is going to sing them both, but that's a pity because we need them both. We need them both to understand the story of Israel in its two-sided puzzlement; and we need them both to understand the story of the church, which even though it's on the nearer side of Jesus' death and resurrection, and even though we are promised and given the spirit, will still get it wrong again and again. Psalm 106 warns against triumphalism, Psalm 105 against despair; and we need them both, and in proper balance. Together they form the darkly textured story of God and Israel, and we rightly worship God by holding them together.

Moving to the New Testament, my third example is the collection of worship songs in Revelation 4 and 5. These are some of the most glorious poems in the Bible, and they illustrate perfectly the point I'm making: that through poetry the biblical writers enable us to glimpse in a vivid little frame the entire narrative of creation and covenant. Revelation 4 has the non-human creation praising God, and the humans (if that's what they are) joining in with an explanation: God is worthy to be praised *because* he created all things. Then Revelation 5 begins with the challenge: who can open the seal? Nobody, it seems: all humans have failed to be image-bearers. But the 'lion' of Judah, who is also the 'lamb', has conquered: *he* is the true image-bearer, the one through whom God's plan of salvation can now go forward. So the new song arises: he, the lamb, is worthy of all praise, because by his blood he ransomed humans for God, to make them kings and priests on the earth. Here in these two chapters, we have the entire story from Genesis to Revelation, focused on Jesus and opening up with a welcome for all and sundry, sinners though we be; and the welcome is not into 'heaven' – the chapters have often been misread as though that's what it was about – but into the new vocation, the Israel-vocation, the challenge to be the royal priesthood, the redeemed human family through whom God will bring about his new creation.

My fourth passage is Colossians 1.15–20. Once again early Christian poetry is brilliant in drawing together strands of biblical thought and weaving a dense and complex tapestry as a song of praise. Indeed, this poem symbolizes for me everything I've been talking about: one small gem which we can look *at* to see a distilled statement of who Jesus is and who we are in him, and which we can look *through* to see the whole story from Genesis to Revelation. I won't take time just now to explain it in detail, since I've done that in various places in my writings. Just to say that here we have one of two Pauline examples of a fascinating phenomenon: that it really looks as though the earliest Christology was accomplished in poetry, and that the discursive theological statements had to come later. It is as though what had just happened in Jesus was so rich that only poetry would do; and perhaps that tells us something about theology and worship. Paul here takes themes from Genesis 1, from Proverbs 8, and from many other biblical sources, and turns them into a song of praise. Augustine said that to sing was to pray twice, and if you were to sing this passage you would be praising three times; once because the poem as it stands is a hymn of praise to Jesus himself, the image, the head, the firstborn, the first-fruits, the redeemer; second because singing brings your whole body into play so that you, as a temple of the spirit, are resonating with this act of praise; but third – and this is my main point here – because as you pray this poem you are actually reciting the whole of God's mighty acts from beginning to end with Jesus in the middle, an effective sign and means of new creation. This is Christian worship at one of its highest early points.

The fifth example is the other obvious Pauline one: Philippians 2.6–11. This is an extraordinary poem, simple in structure with the two halves meeting in the middle in the little phrase *thanatou de staurou*, 'the death of the cross'. And here again the whole story is present before us in these short poetic stanzas which, so far as we know, predate any detailed formulation of the extraordinary doctrine that they embody. Poetry first, then theology; worship first, then thinking in the light of that, which is why Paul says 'Have this mind among you which is yours in the Messiah Jesus . . .' – in other words, take this poem and use it to reshape your thinking. Take this act of worship and use it to pray your way into the mind of the Messiah, in which humility and wisdom and unity and love are stitched together so tightly. Here we have the great biblical story again, but this time seen with special reference to Isaiah, to the promise of the 'servant' through whose ministry

God will be glorified – only now the God who will not share his glory with another has shared it with Jesus. Once again we can press our noses up against this tiny but complete example of early Christian poetry and through it we can see clearly the whole sweep of the narrative, from the rebellion of Adam to the restoration of creation under Jesus' lordship. This is a small but powerful example of how reading scripture means both praising God for his mighty acts and retelling, through one short sample, the whole story of those saving events.

My sixth and final example is, as you may have guessed, the prologue to John's gospel. This again is the story of Genesis and Exodus told eschatologically, that is, told so that the narrative reaches forward into the promised future and declares that it has arrived in Jesus. Not for nothing is this passage read – though sadly often stopping at verse 14 – in Christmas carol services. Not for nothing, in some catholic traditions, is this passage prayed as a prayer by the celebrant after the administration of the bread and the wine. *'The Word became flesh and tabernacled in our midst, and we gazed upon his glory . . .'*: there really isn't much more to be said. Genesis begins with the creation 'in the beginning', the creation of the heaven-and-earth reality of God's whole world where God wanted to dwell, to 'take his rest'. The rebellion of the image-bearing humans hasn't thwarted that desire and design, but has merely determined the shape and the specific content of that intention. Exodus 40 describes the new creation in the form of the wilderness tabernacle into which the divine glory will come as the sign that God's glory will one day fill the whole of creation. Yes, says John, the Word is the true tabernacle – the normal translation of 'dwelt among us' hides the more precise meaning of the Greek, which is that the Word became flesh and 'pitched his tent' in our midst, with the verb *eskēnōsen* using the root *skēnē* which is, remarkably, the same word etymologically as the later Hebrew term for the indwelling glorious divine presence, the Shekinah. Etymology doesn't solve all problems but it certainly helps here. We gazed, says John, upon the divine glory *as we were looking at Jesus*, at the Word made flesh. And we deduced that, though nobody has ever actually seen God, the only-begotten God who is by the father's heart, he has made him known. Once again, a small poetic passage through which we can see the full sweep of the biblical revelation. When you read or pray John 1 you are reading and praying the whole story of creation and covenant, of creation to new creation, of revelation and redemption; and you are doing so in an act of praise, celebrating God's mighty acts in this miniature but majestic paragraph. Using this passage in worship catches us up within God's story and points ahead unerringly to the ultimate new creation.

I hope you see the point, and I don't need to labour it further. I simply wanted to hold out before you the possibility of seeing the public reading of scripture in fresh ways, and to urge you to use every opportunity to teach this way of reading and understanding scripture to those in your care. We live in turbulent times – as, of course, did many of the biblical writers. And if in these times we can draw in fresh ways on the insights and liturgical wisdom which are hidden deep within this old book, there is at least a chance, in the mercy of God, that we will train up the next generation to think and pray and act in the church and the world with the wisdom that is shaped by the entire biblical gospel.

There are, of course, many other points one could make. I look forward to your questions. But for me the focus remains on worship. Worship of the God revealed in Jesus Christ is what makes us human; it renews us in our image-bearing vocation. It points ahead to God's new world, and summons us to play our parts within that purpose. And if worship is to do all this, it is vital that we use the book God has given us. Scripture, after all, is not simply there to provide us with true information about God, the gospel and the world. It is there to be the central focus and vehicle of Christian worship, to provide fuel for the sacrificial flame that burns in our hearts, to bring us into the true Temple; to point ahead to God's new world and, by anticipating that new world in the present, actually to contribute by the spirit to its effective realization. The Bible comes to us from God's mighty acts in the past and points powerfully forward to God's mighty purposes for the future. In worship, we are refreshing our roots in that past in order to bear fruit for that future.

17
The Powerful Breath of the New Creation

The University of Fribourg in Switzerland was the first to host a conference on my book *Paul and the Faithfulness of God* (Wright 2013b); and the moving spirits behind that proposal were the university rector, Professor Guido Vergauwen, and the professor of theology, Dr Barbara Hallensleben. It was a delight to discover, in a Dominican university, such enthusiasm both for Paul and for the exposition of his thought which I, as an Anglican, was offering. Since then, my wife and I have enjoyed several subsequent visits to Fribourg, and Barbara Hallensleben has always been most hospitable in her welcome and stimulating in our conversations. So when I was asked to another conference, on the understanding that the papers were to form the basis of a Festschrift (*Veni, Sancte Spiritus!*; see fuller details in Acknowledgments) for our friend, I was naturally delighted; and I was honoured to be able to present my reflections alongside no less than the Archbishop of Canterbury and the Cardinal Archbishop of Vienna. Though I have written a fair amount about 'new creation' as a biblical theme, I had not, to that point, explored so much the particular role of the holy spirit within that promised new reality. This essay gave me that opportunity.

[I] 1 Introduction

It is a delight to be able to contribute to this congratulatory volume for Professor Barbara Hallensleben. Her creative academic contributions have been formative; her ecumenical enthusiasm is infectious and exciting; her friendship has been a delightful gift to my wife and myself. I offer her these reflections with gratitude and admiration.[1]

If it has sometimes been true that the holy spirit has been 'the forgotten member of the Trinity', that is not because the Bible fails to provide a rich

---

1 I am grateful to Simon Dürr, who, in addition to producing his own article for this volume [*Veni, Sancte Spiritus!*], has been very helpful in the preparation of this one.

variety of images to help us think about this extraordinary, powerful reality. When we think of the spirit in biblical terms we think of the wind, with the Hebrew *rûaḥ* and the Greek *pneuma* both meaning 'wind' and 'spirit'. And then we think of the fire at Pentecost, echoing the pillar of fire in the desert or Elijah's fire coming down from heaven. Then there is the dove at Jesus' baptism, sending our minds back to the dove sent out by Noah to see whether new creation was yet happening after the mega-'baptism' of the flood. And we think of the water itself, the baptismal water but also the rivers of living water that Jesus promises will flow out of the believer's heart.[2]

We can often be dazzled by this wealth of biblical imagery, and in our daze we reach out for a familiar narrative and try to make it work. But at this point it is easy for devout Christians to say the right things but join them up in the wrong way. I have in my mind the child's game in which you connect a number of dots on the page by following a numbered sequence. If you follow the numbers correctly, you get the right picture; but it's always possible to join up the dots some other way, with more or less ingenuity, to draw a different picture you may have had in mind from the start. You might end [2] up, perhaps, drawing a giraffe rather than a lion. The point I want to make is that this is what we have done, often enough, with the biblical language about the spirit. Western Christianity has often lived in a radically split world of nature and supernature, and has often imagined that the point of it all is to leave 'earth' and go to 'heaven', while, in the meantime, a normally rather distant God sometimes reaches in, stirs the pot, and goes away again. People describe this 'intervention from outside' by talking of the spirit; but they are joining up the dots in the wrong way. The spirit is then imagined in terms of an occasional 'invasion' of God into our lives or our world from the 'outside'. People talk on occasion about 'having a holy spirit moment'; I know what that means, but in scripture the sovereign holy spirit, as well as doing one-off things which surprise us, is at work in a much deeper and more consistent way as the energy which drives new creation itself.

My argument, then, is that scripture presents the spirit as *the powerful breath of new creation*. When the new creation finally arrives, the new

---

2 For *rûaḥ* and *pneuma* as 'wind', see e.g. Gen. 8.1; Ex. 10.19; as 'spirit', see e.g. Gen. 6.3; Ex. 31.3; Dt. 34.9. Fire at Pentecost: Ac. 2.1–4; pillar of fire: Ex. 13.21–22; Num. 14.14; Neh. 9.12, 19; cf. also Wis. 18.3; Elijah's fire: 1 Kgs. 18.20–40, esp. vv. 37–39; but cf. also 2 Kgs. 1.9–14. Spirit like a dove at Jesus' baptism: Mt. 3.16; Mk. 1.10; Lk. 3.22; Jn. 1.32. Noah's dove: Gen. 8.6–12. Water at baptism: Mt. 3.11 (note also the fire!); Mk. 1.8; Lk. 3.16; Jn. 1.26–27; Ac. 1.5; cf. e.g. Ac. 8.36; 10.47. For the rivers of living water, see Jn. 7.38–39.

heavens and new earth that we are promised, this will be the work of the spirit, the spirit by whose power Jesus was raised from the dead, the spirit who is doing new creation right now both *in* us – painful and costly as this is – and *through* us in our mission in the world. My proposal is that we conceive of that mission, energized by the spirit, on the much larger canvas of the biblical theology of creation and new creation, and that we will get the New Testament missional theology right when we revisit the ancient Old Testament roots and allow them to refresh our understanding. So I shall begin by going back to the first creation, and to the wilderness tabernacle. From that vantage point, we will see how the scriptural promise of new creation, and the spirit-driven missional impulse towards it, make the sense they make because of the creator's plan from the beginning.

2 Creation and Tabernacle

We begin with the original creation, the world of heaven and earth, the twin halves of God's good creation, brought to birth by the mighty wind, the wind of God, the *rûaḥ 'ĕlōhîm*, the 'spirit' or 'wind' or 'breath' of God, seen as the mothering bird, brooding over the waters of chaos.[3] This heaven-and-earth reality is described in the way you'd describe the construction of a *temple*: the sevenfold sequence, after which the architect would take up resi-[3]-dence, to 'take his rest', in the new dwelling.[4] When you build a temple in the ancient world, the final thing you put into it is the *image* of the god, so that the god may be present to and powerful within the wider world, and so that the wider world may see and do homage to this god. So in Genesis the creator God puts into this temple the creature we call human, male and female together in and as his image. And the human vocation is then to be the *royal priesthood*, to stand at the borders of heaven and earth, to sum up the praises of earth before the throne of heaven and to be the means by which the loving wisdom of heaven may flow out into the earth. *All the mission of the people of God is the specific application, in new circumstances, of this primal human vocation.* Genesis 1 and 2 are not about God setting humans a moral examination and watching them fail it. Genesis 1 and 2 are about God giving humans a *vocation*, the royal-priestly, image-bearing vocation, to be the *angled mirrors* reflecting the wisdom of the creator into the world.[5] Worship and mission

---

3   Gen. 1.2. For *rûaḥ* as breath, cf. e.g. Gen. 6.17.

4   See e.g. the work of Beale 2004; Walton 2009; and the very suggestive articles in Morales 2014.

5   I draw at this point on Middleton 2005, e.g. 90: 'The human vocation as *imago Dei* in God's world

are the bidirectional image-bearing vocation, the two-way flow of the love of God.

For this purpose, in Genesis 2, God breathes into human nostrils the breath of life, the *nišmat ḥayyîm*, the gift that enables the image to come to life, to be in itself a link between heaven and earth, the breath of heaven in the dusty life of earth. Here again, already our ears ought to be attuned to the missional import of this powerful idea. But at this point the stories western Christianity has told are creating a giraffe where we ought to be creating a lion: a giraffe as a symbol of the Platonic worldview, stretching its neck higher and higher away from ground level and into a supposedly 'supernatural' world. That is not the way the Bible sees things. In the Old Testament, the places where the Adam-and-Eve vocation is retrieved include particularly passages that were taken as royal, like Psalm 8, which spells out the human vocation in terms of being given dominion over the world and particularly [4] the animals, the birds and the fish.[6] As in the ancient world in general, where it was the king, the lion of Judah, who was the true image of the god, ruling the world on his behalf, so Genesis both democratizes that vocation – we are *all* image-bearers – and uses it to shape the theology of the monarchy.[7]

Now, of course, the kings of Israel and Judah did (more or less) what Adam and Eve did. David and the subsequent psalmists celebrated God's vocation, although they knew they were also getting it wrong. Nevertheless, Genesis 1 and 2 remain there, like a shimmering mirage, reminding God's people not only of what their true vocation was but of how it was to be put into effect. This is the point that has been so difficult for generations of western theologians, labouring under the legacy of Plato, to get their heads around. God's mission in the world is not a matter of God doing everything and us just watching from the sidelines. But nor is it a matter of us doing it 'in our own strength', with God in the background as a mere spectator. The powerful breath of the spirit means *both* that God is doing it *and* that we are doing it, precisely because as God's image-bearers there is a natural fit between what God wants to do in and through us and what, when we are in tune with God, we ourselves want to do and find we can at least start to do. That is one of the major themes of the farewell discourses in John (chs. 13—17), though that would take us beyond the limits of the present argument.

---

thus corresponds in important respects to Israel's vocation as a "royal priesthood" among the nations (Exodus 19.6).' Middleton, however, prefers the metaphor of a 'prism' to that of a 'mirror' (p. 90 n. 119).

6 On the retrieval of Ps. 8 in the gospels, see Wright 2018b.

7 See Middleton 2005, 207.

However, when I say 'when we are in tune with God' we all recognize a problem. The Bible assumes on every page that humans have turned their back on their vocation, have listened to the voice of the snake, have been kicked out of the garden . . . and that Israel, and Israel's kings and priests, have likewise forsaken their true vocation and have likewise been exiled. What does the Bible have to say to this condition? The answer is not that it describes a way by which we can escape the world and go to heaven instead. The answer is that the kingdom of God has been launched 'on earth as in heaven', and that, by the Messiah and the spirit, the creator God has renewed the original image-bearing vocation. [5]

3 The Powerful Divine Presence in the Tabernacle

But this is to run ahead of ourselves. Very briefly, let us look at the initial plan of redemption and what that tells us about the biblical roots of new creation and the work of the spirit. Abraham is called to reverse the sin of Adam and its effects.[8] Abraham, a childless nomad, is promised a family and a land. But, from the start, the point of this double promise is not for the sake of Abraham, his descendants and their small territory. The point is that through *this* family God will create a vast, worldwide family – that's what is promised to Abraham, over and over again – and that through *this* land God will stake his claim on the entire created world.[9] Abraham's family and Abraham's land are signposts pointing forward to the creator's intention to flood and transform the creation with his powerful love, so that the earth may be full of the knowledge of the glory of the Lord as the waters cover the sea.[10] But Abraham and his family – here is the problem! – Abraham and his family are themselves Adamic. The people who are called to provide the solution are themselves carriers of the problem. The chosen doctors are themselves carriers of the disease. So Abraham's family has to learn the painful lessons of exile and restoration. The point of the exodus is to create the people of Israel as the rescued people, the people then of *promise* and *presence*: the promise of the land, the presence of the divine glory. Both of these are vital for understanding the spirit.

---

8   See the full discussion of this widespread theme in Wright 2013b, 783–95.

9   Promise of a family: Gen. 12.2–3; 15.5; 17.2, 6; 22.16–18. Promise of the land: Gen. 12.1, 7; 13.15; 15.18; 17.8; 24.7; 26.4; 28.13; 35.12. The promise is extended in Pss. 2.8–9; 22.27; 72.8–11; 89.25; 105.44; 111.6; Isa. 9.7; 11.1–10; 42.1–4, 6, 10–12; 49.6–7; 52.10, 15; 55.1–5; 60.1–16; 61.1–7; 66.18–21.

10   Isa. 11.9; Hab. 2.14.

See how it works. The people are led through the Red Sea and off to Mount Sinai by the divine presence, by the pillar of cloud by day and the pillar of fire by night. Torah is given in Exodus 20 to prepare the people for what is to happen next. Again, as with Genesis, this is not about God setting the people a moral examination which they will then fail, but about God calling them to their vocation, reiterated in Exodus 19.6 (the royal priesthood), and about God equipping them for that dangerous vocation. And the point is this. *God the creator wants to renew heaven and earth from top to bottom; but since from the start he has chosen to make a world where the central elements of his purpose are to come about through human image-[6]-bearing agency, he has called a people to be the heaven-and-earth people; so he is preparing them for the tabernacle, where his presence will dwell with them, in their midst, to lead them to the land of promise.* The presence *and* the promise. And so the tabernacle gets built, despite the sin of the golden calf.

Here is the point. The tabernacle is a small working-model of the cosmos, as its decoration indicates by symbol and narrative.[11] In Exodus 40 the divine presence comes to dwell in it, so that when Moses goes in he comes out with his face shining. God has already promised to Moses: 'my presence will go with you, and I will give you rest' – and the 'rest' there corresponds to the 'rest' in Genesis 1 and 2, the creation of a building where God and his people will enter and be at home.[12] And as the later prophets look back on this promise of God's presence in the tabernacle, leading and guiding the people to the promised land, they speak of that divine presence and promise in terms of God's own spirit. In Isaiah 63 the prophet looks back to the exodus and speaks of God's powerful spirit coming to dwell with them and lead them home. In Haggai 2 we find the same thing: God's spirit is at work as the returning exiles build the Temple.[13] [7]

---

11 Construction of the tabernacle commanded: Ex. 25.1—27.21; 30.1—31.18. Ex. 31.1–5 relates how Bezalel, the master craftsman for the construction of the tabernacle, is filled with divine spirit. A report of how it is carried out: Ex. 35.1—40.33. The glory filling the tabernacle: Ex. 40.34–38. For a cosmological interpretation of the symbolism of the tabernacle, see Jos. *Ant.* 3.179–83. For a parallelization of the tabernacle with the cosmos, see Philo, *Vit. Mos.* 2.71–108, esp. 73 (portable sanctuary), 81 (tabernacle's twofold structure corresponds to realm of mind and realm of sense), 88 (four materials and the four elements of the cosmos; rationale: 'For it was necessary that in framing a temple of man's making, dedicated to the Father and Ruler of All, he should take substances like those with which that Ruler made the All' (tr. Colson)), 89 (tabernacle resembling a temple), 99 (the cherubim correspond to the creative and kingly potencies), 101 (altar of incense and earth, water, as centrally placed in the cosmos), 103 (menorah symbol of planets), 105 (heaven and earth correspond to candlestick and altar of incense), 106–8 (construction stands for the right intention of the worshipping soul, which participates in the whole universe); Aaron's sacred garments also represent the universe (Philo, *Vit. Mos.* 2.143). Cf. also *Somn.* 1.201–7.

12 Ex. 33.14; cf. also Ex. 20.11; Gen. 2.2–3.

13 Isa. 63.7–14, esp. 11 (put his spirit within them), 13–14 (led them), 14 (spirit gave rest). Hag. 2.2–9,

Between these two events, Solomon built the original Jerusalem Temple.[14] This too was a working-model of creation, and hence – granted the strong sense of a purposive narrative throughout so much ancient Israelite tradition – a signpost towards the intended new world. The king was the image at the heart of that model of creation, as Aaron the priest had been the image at the heart of the tabernacle.[15] But Solomon and his successors, and Aaron's sons and their successors, rebelled and failed in their respective vocations, despite the prophetic words summoning them back. And the worst thing about exile was the withdrawal of the divine presence. As in Ezekiel, YHWH abandoned the Temple, leaving it wide open to Babylonian attack.[16] The consequent sense of divine absence is not so much a philosophical speculation about where God was in some abstract sense.[17] It was, rather, a *historical* sense that – to put it colloquially – he used to live here but now he's gone. That sense of divine absence haunts the second-Temple period. Malachi, at its heart, scolds the priests because they are bored and bringing polluted sacrifices; he warns them that one day the Lord whom they seek *will* suddenly come back.[18] The promises of Ezekiel will be fulfilled: the new Temple will arise, and the divine glory will return to it.[19] The promises of Isaiah will be fulfilled: the glory of YHWH shall be revealed, and all flesh shall see it together; the watchmen will shout for joy as in plain sight they see him returning.[20] The people of Israel and their leaders remained puzzled, throughout the second-Temple period, as to what that would look like when he did. That is the world within [8] which new modes of enquiry and prophecy became popular, in the mode we loosely

---

esp. 5 (exodus promise recalled, presence of spirit assured), 7 (promise of filling the Temple with splendour; cf. also 9). On the assurance of the presence of the spirit for the building project of the Temple in Hag. 2.5, cf. Leuenberger 2015, 166: '[D]ie partizipial formulierte Präsenz [ist] statisch gedacht, [besagt] also nunmehr einen stabilen Dauerzustand der heilvollen, "begeisternden" Gegenwart des Gottesgeistes . . . der sich im vorliegenden Kontext wiederum günstig auf das Tempelneubauprojekt auswirkt.'

14 Preparation for the Temple: 1 Kgs. 5 (cf. 2 Chr. 2.1–18); building of the Temple: 1 Kgs. 6.1–22 (cf. 2 Chr. 3.1–14); ark brought to Solomon's Temple: 1 Kgs. 8.1–11, esp. 10–11 (glory fills Temple); cf. also 2 Chr. 5.2—6.2, esp. 13–14 (glory fills Temple).

15 Note the central role of Solomon in the dedication ceremony: his address to the people, the prayer and the sacrifices (1 Kgs. 8.12–66; 2 Chr. 6.3—7.11). On Aaron's role in the tabernacle, and the symbolism of his vestments, see Ex. 28; 39.

16 Ezek. 10, esp. vv. 4, 18, 19, 22–23. Babylon attacks Jerusalem: Ezek. 17.12; 24.2.

17 For a discussion of the conceptions of divine presence and absence in ancient Judaism, cf. the contributions in MacDonald and de Hulster 2013.

18 Priests criticized for the way their sacrifices are offered: Mal. 1.6–8, 12–13 (priests unwilling to serve). The Lord suddenly appears at his Temple: Mal. 3.1.

19 New Temple: Ezek. 40—42. Glory returns to the new Temple: Ezek. 43.1–5.

20 Isa. 40.5 (glory revealed; all see it together); 52.8 (watchmen see YHWH return).

know as 'apocalyptic': was there ever to be a fresh revelation from heaven, and if so might that be anticipated in the present?

Despite this puzzlement, at several points the Old Testament insists that what God had done with the tabernacle and the Temple was what he intended to do for the whole creation. 'May his glory fill the whole earth', prayed the psalmist.[21] The Temple was not a retreat from the world. It was the sign of what God intended to do in and for the whole creation: the earth shall be filled with the knowledge of the glory of the Lord, as the waters cover the sea.[22] That is the promise which the early Christians believed had been fulfilled in Jesus and was being fulfilled by the powerful breath of the spirit. The narrative of early Christian mission is deeply rooted in biblical imagery; and the images in question are not a random collection of miscellaneous illustrations, but form part of a deep, coherent if perplexing biblical narrative.

4 John and Paul: Spirit and New Creation

The centre of early Christian belief was that in Jesus the divine presence had returned at last. This is a theme for another occasion, but I believe that all four gospels in their different ways make this point.[23] We see it most graphically in John 1.14, where the Word becomes flesh and *tabernacles* in our midst; the Greek word, echoing the biblical tabernacle-language, indicates the meaning 'pitched his tent'. John's prologue is a new Exodus as well as a new Genesis. Paul says the same thing in his own way in Colossians 2.9: in him (that is, in the Messiah) all the divine fullness came to dwell bodily. This is Temple-language, indicating that in the very person of Jesus himself the new creation was beginning. And this shapes the way the story of the cross and resurrection are then told: the new creation can only make its way by overcoming all the powers of evil and death that are ranged against it.

But what God does uniquely *in* Jesus he then does *through* Jesus, by his powerful breath, for Jesus' followers. So in John's gospel in particular we find the promise of the spirit, the spirit that will effect new birth, generating a new, renewed form of human existence, and commissioning Jesus' followers [9] for the mission which is precisely the new-creation mission in the world. That is how the sequence of thought works in John 7 through to John 20 where

---

21 Ps. 72.19.

22 Isa. 11.9; Hab. 2.14.

23 For such an argument on the basis of the various ways in which the gospel-writers retrieve scripture, see now Hays 2016.

the powerful breath of Jesus himself is given to the disciples. In John 7 the image is of water, like the rivers flowing out of Eden (in Genesis) or the rivers flowing out of the Temple (in Ezekiel) or out of Jerusalem (in Zechariah).[24] Jesus is the new Temple in person, from whose heart flow rivers of living water; and once his death has cleansed them from defilement, Jesus' followers are to be the same, people from whose heart there flow rivers of living water.[25] So in John 20, when the new creation has begun with Jesus' resurrection on the first day of the new week – John is still thinking in terms of Genesis and Exodus – we find Jesus coming to the disciples and, somewhat as with God and the first humans in the gardens, breathing into their nostrils the breath of life.[26] Only now it is the life of the new creation, the life through which the original project of creation, thwarted by human idolatry and sin, can get on track at last. When Jesus says to them, 'As the father has sent me, so I'm sending you', and when he equips them with his own spirit so they are able to shoulder this responsibility, he is saying that they are to be for the whole world what he, Jesus, had been for Israel.[27] They are to be the [10] new-Temple people, the new-exodus people. They are to be a kind of dispersed Temple, no longer a building in one place but a people spread across the whole world, a people in whose heart and lungs there blows the powerful breath of new creation. That is why their solemn task of forgiving and retaining sin is so important [see John 20.23]. If this is really new creation, then there can be no question of being deceived once more by the voice of the snake.

We find the same picture, though in a very different mode, in the writings of Paul. In Ephesians 1 we have a great hymn of praise, a Passover hymn reworked around Jesus himself.[28] At the end of that hymn, in verses 13

24 Gen. 2.10–14; Ezek. 47.1–12; Zech. 14.8.

25 Jn. 7.37–39. The passage admits of two different punctuations, so that 'out of his heart' in 7.38 could refer either to Jesus or to the believer; the former might be supported by Jn. 19.34 and the latter by 4.10–14. Perhaps an overlap is intended: through the event of the cross, where Jesus is the source, and through the reception of the spirit, a believer can become in turn a source for others. So e.g.Westcott 1903 [1881], 123: 'He who drinks of the Spiritual Rock becomes in turn himself a rock from within which the waters flow to slake the thirst of others.' For detailed discussion, see Keener 2003, 728–30; and, especially with regard to the motif of living water (Zech. 14.8), Hübenthal 2006, 282–94. She concludes with regards to Jn. 4.10, 14; 7.38; and 19.34: 'Am Kreuz ist Jesus der Spender des (lebendigen) Wassers. Im Kreuzesereignis und in der Übergabe des Geistes kann der oder die Glaubende das lebendige Wasser empfangen, das späterhin auch in ihm oder ihr zur sprudelnden Quelle wird. Es spricht nichts dagegen, dass in der nachösterlichen Zeit im Rahmen der Mission . . . jeder Glaubende selbst durch die Weitergabe der Botschaft Jesu für andere zur Quelle wird, weist doch sein Wort hin auf die wahre Quelle, den Erhöhten und Auferstandenen' (pp. 289–90).

26 Jn. 20.19–24; the 'first day of the week' in 20.1; 20.19.

27 Jn. 20.21. I explore this further in Wright 1999a, ch. 8.

28 Eph. 1.3–14; the Passover-motif is clear in e.g. 1.7 and in the whole sweep of the prayer from divine election to promised inheritance via 'redemption'.

and 14, we celebrate the fact that when the word of truth has done its work in people's hearts they find that they have been sealed with the holy spirit of promise, because the spirit is the guarantee, the 'down-payment', of the future inheritance until we finally possess it. But what is that inheritance? Generations of Christians, at least in the west, have assumed that the 'inheritance' is 'heaven'. But Ephesians 1.10 insists that this is wrong. That is a form of Platonism or even Gnosticism. It is choosing the giraffe instead of the lion. The 'inheritance' is God's original intention: 'to sum up all things in the Messiah, things in heaven and things on earth'. Heaven and earth are not to be split apart; they are to be brought together; *and the spirit is the sign and means in the present by which that future becomes real in advance*. The spirit is the powerful breath of that new creation, bringing signs and foretastes of the heaven-and-earth reality to birth here and now.

Once again, if this is new creation it will mean a joyful embrace of the holiness that constitutes genuine God-reflecting human identity. If we are to be people in whose lives heaven and earth are coming together, we can expect nothing less as the spirit *anticipates* that eventual new world. That is the message of Ephesians 4—6, and we note that it comes with a warning: if you sign up for this bracing agenda, be prepared for spiritual warfare (6.10–20). But the point for our present purposes comes particularly at the end of Ephesians 2. What does it mean in the present that by the spirit the new creation is already starting to be visible? It means *church unity* – a cause dear to the heart of the addressee of the present volume. Jews and gentiles come together into a single body; and the single body is then to be thought of, exactly in line with the ancient biblical logic, as the new Temple. Just as the tabernacle and then the Temple were the signs and foretastes of God's desire to fill the whole world with his glory, so the coming together of different [11] cultures and ethnicities in the Messiah, forming (2.22) a building in which God comes to dwell by the spirit, are the sign to the world of God's eventual purposes. That is why he says, in Ephesians 3.10, that the church is to be a sign to the principalities and powers of the world that Jesus is lord and that they are not. When the powerful breath of new creation brings together Jesus-followers of all sorts into a single family, then the rulers of the world, both spiritual and political, are confronted with a reality to which they have no answer. New creation speaks for itself. The language it speaks is the many-tongued language inspired by the spirit who dwells in the community; and the community is to be understood as the new Temple, the sign and foretaste of the ultimate new creation, the promised heaven-and-earth reality.

294

All this points us now to Romans 8, one of the most magnificent chapters in the whole Bible. Paul here draws on the exodus-story in a fresh way, using the language of the children of Israel wandering in the desert and the pillar of cloud and fire leading them to their 'inheritance'.[29] Here, as in Ephesians, the Christian's 'promised land' is not 'heaven', despite a thousand hymns and prayers which tell the story that way. This is to make once more the giraffe, stretching up towards a Platonic 'heaven', instead of the lion of Judah. The 'inheritance' is the whole world promised to the Messiah in the Psalms, as the radical extension of the promise to Abraham.[30]

So what is the spirit doing in this chapter? The powerful breath of the spirit in Romans 8 is playing the same role that the pillar of cloud and fire played in the story of the exodus. There, the divine splendour came to live in the tabernacle to lead the people to their inheritance, as a sign of the long-term divine intention to fill the whole world with glory. So here Paul envisages the church as the community of the new Exodus and hence of the new Genesis, the new creation in which creation itself will be set free from its slavery to decay and receive the freedom that comes when God's children are glorified. We ourselves are promised bodily resurrection in the glorious rebirth of creation itself; and by the spirit we are to be signs and foretastes of that here and now. We need that long and winding biblical story, the story of ancient Israel, to prevent this New Testament story from collapsing into mere religious experience (as has happened with spirit-language in some circles in my lifetime) or into an invocation of the spirit which is aimed solely at opening people's hearts to God so that their souls will go to heaven [12] after their body has died. Of course, the spirit works through the gospel to open people's hearts to God's love in Christ, but the aim is then ultimately *the renewal of the world through the renewal of humans.*

Just as in Ephesians, then, the spirit is the guarantee of the promise, the down-payment, the 'first-fruits' that assures us of the full new creation to come.[31] Here is the foundation of the spirit-driven Pauline vision of mission. Romans 8 focuses on Jesus as Israel's Messiah and the world's true lord; Paul insists that he already rules over the whole creation. He does so, we note, as the heaven-and-earth person, the new-Temple person, in whom God becomes king *in the person of the man who becomes king.* The two vocations, divine and human, are made for one another. Paul here draws on Psalm 8:

---

29   On the exodus-motif in Romans, see Wright 2002b, 511–13; 2013c, ch. 11.
30   See n. 6 above.
31   On the *arrabōn*, see 2 Cor. 1.22; 5.5; Eph. 1.14; and cf. Rom. 8.23.

what are human beings, the 'son of man'? 'You made them a little lower than the angels, to crown them with glory and honour, putting all things in subjection under their feet.' God always intended to rule his world through wise humanity. The 'glory' here is the renewed dominion, the renewal of the image-bearing vocation, as Paul says in Romans 8.29: conformed to the image of the son. We are to be the royal priesthood at last, sharing in creation's worship of God and sharing also in God's sovereign rule over creation. This is the spirit-generated life of mission, the true vocation of the church – not to snatch people out of this world for a Platonic heaven, but by the spirit's breath to be agents of the renewal of human lives and of the whole creation, right here and now.

So what does this look like in practice? The spirit leads us as the new-tabernacle people to the new creation – but at the moment creation is groaning in travail. It is in the midst of severe birth-pangs. We see it and know it all around us and in our hearts and homes as well. And we share this image-bearing, spirit-driven, new-creational mission primarily in ways which many mission-minded Christians would not expect: suffering and prayer. We are to share Jesus' glory if we suffer with him. And – as with the central gospel-events themselves – this suffering is not simply a nasty side-issue we have to endure as a prelude to the real task. As with Jesus, the suffering is the way in which the pain and shame and sorrow of the world is once again concentrated on the Temple-in-person, or rather the Temple-in-people, the spirit-filled community, so that the new world can be born. This is what is going on right now in Cairo and Damascus, in parts of China and South East Asia, and in many other places where our brothers and sisters are being conformed to the image of the suffering Messiah. Think of Jesus-followers bend-[13]-ing their necks for beheading on a beach in Libya and shouting out Jesus' name with their last breaths. If Paul saw that he would say, 'Yes, that's what I was talking about in Romans 8.'

Because the vocation is to be the royal *priesthood*, and the priestly vocation is to sum up the prayers and praises of creation before the throne of the creator. This is the missional vocation. But if the creation is in sorrow and lament, what does that mean? It means that the church will also be in sorrow and lament at the heart of the pain of the world. And, because we are the new-tabernacle people, the people in whom the divine glory has returned in the form of the spirit, *the spirit groans within us* as we await our adoption, the redemption of our bodies, and with that the renewal of all creation. Groaning and lament are the central mode of the way in which the vocation spoken of in Psalm 8 is now to be lived out in the life of the church. This is not the only thing that spirit-led mission means, but if it is not centred here it is not being true to the gospel itself. Jesus' cry from the cross ('My God, why did you abandon me?'[32]) is worked out in the church by the spirit, in the groaning of the spirit from the heart of the church at the heart of the pain of the world. Yes, says Paul, God the heart-searcher knows what is the mind of the spirit – because the spirit intercedes for God's people according to God's will.[33]

This priestly vocation, to sum up in prayer not only the glad praises of all creation but also and particularly the tortured groaning of all creation, is part of the intercession of the Messiah himself. Without his prayer, and our prayer joined through the spirit with his, there is no mission. A few verses later Paul talks about Jesus himself interceding for us, and here, at the heart of the New Testament's theology of mission, we find the spirit uniting us to the Messiah, conformed to his image, his cruciform image. Paul's primary missional concern is to ground the vocation of the church in Messiah and spirit, in cruciform and resurrectional reality, and in being the new-exodus people who are led by the spirit into the new creation. As such, therefore, we are called to share and bear the pain of the world in agonized and often wordless prayer.

This seems to me a vital part of what it means to pray for the holy spirit to come upon us afresh. People sometimes speak as if the spirit were given to make us happy and relaxed. Well, that may sometimes happen, but this expectation looks suspiciously like an attempt to get the spirit to endorse [14] our modern western aspirations. In the New Testament, the spirit drove Jesus into the wilderness after his baptism,[34] and the spirit drives the church into the places of pain and danger so that new creation may happen right there, where it is most needed. Again and again, as I have seen the church struggling with various issues over recent decades, I have realized that these struggles and puzzles, and the times when we really don't know where to turn, do not necessarily mean that we have taken a wrong turning somewhere. Of course, we may have done so. That will have to be faced. But we should not be surprised when the spirit leads us into this place of birth-pangs and wordless groanings. *The church is called to stand at the place where the world is in pain precisely in order that the spirit, the living presence of the loving God, may be there, groaning to the father from within the depths of the world's pain, of our own pain, of the puzzles of the birth-pangs of the new world.* This is what it

---

32   Mt. 27.46; Mk. 15.34; cf., of course, Ps. 22.1.
33   Rom. 8.27.
34   Mt. 4.1; Mk. 1.12; Lk. 4.1.

looks and feels like when the powerful breath of new creation is given to us by the father of Jesus the crucified Messiah and risen lord.

We are thus called to be now-and-not-yet people: not the cheap-and-cheerful type of charismatics who can call on the spirit for instant solutions in all situations (think of Jesus refusing to call for angelic help in Gethsemane[35]), but the wise, mature charismatics who use their gifts of tongues and prophecy and whatever else comes from the spirit's breath as part of the larger royal-priestly task of praying in lament at the heart of the world's lament. The aim of it all, to repeat, is not so that we can then leave this world and go off to a safe place somewhere else. The aim is so that the new world may come to birth from the agonized womb of the old.

Out of that place of darkness, of Messiah-shaped and spirit-led lament, that mission will always grow. It must. It will take many forms. Its primary form may well be a ministry to those places in the world where the groaning is most obvious and most intense. The spirit will lead us to *do* things – signs of new creation – which will produce the question, as did the actions of Jesus himself, 'Why are you doing that?' As the Messiah-shaped and spirit-led new-creational missional community – as the royal priesthood, in other words – we have to be equally prepared for the inconvenient vocation of bringing the love of Jesus to the places that need it most, the places that often polite society doesn't want us to go because it's embarrassing and awkward, because it upsets our easy social categories. There are many in our churches [15] who are already doing exactly this. We must thank God for the powerful breath of the spirit in and through all such, leading them to actions and words of hope and new life.

That, then, is how it happens. We are called by the spirit to be new-Exodus people, new-Genesis people. We are to be the worldwide community whose very life together, whose prayer and holiness and suffering, are the sign to the world that new creation has been launched in Jesus, and that this divine project will continue until heaven and earth are one. Every single one of us is called to be a person in whom that is coming true already in the present time. And that can only happen through the powerful breath of new creation. Likewise, all those who name the name of Jesus, from whatever ecclesial tradition we may come, are called to be a single community in whom that is already coming true by the same powerful spirit, and which therefore constitutes the sign to the world that God is God, that Jesus is lord, and that his kingdom has come and will come on earth as in heaven.

---

35   Mt. 26.53.

18
Sacred Space in the City

In recent years, my wife and I have been privileged to be part of the extended family of Central Presbyterian Church in Park Avenue, New York City. This itself is a sign of happier ecumenical times. A hundred years ago, an Anglican bishop would never have been invited to speak in such a place and, if invited, would certainly have refused. But the regeneration and rejuvenation of that church has been exciting to watch. Thus, though my first visits there took place simply because the building offered a central location for book-launch events and broadcast interviews, the hospitality of the church, and of its senior pastor, Jason Harris, has drawn us back many times. So when Jason was launching his campaign to renew and restore the remarkable historic building, it was exciting to be invited to offer some reflections on the notion of 'sacred space', a topic to which, as we both suspected, few Presbyterians had given much attention. The only other place where I recall addressing the subject is in my little book on pilgrimage, *The Way of the Lord* (Wright 1999e), and in private memoranda during my time as Bishop of Durham. There is, of course, a much larger literature on the theological significance of both 'space' and 'place', and this essay makes no attempt to engage with it. But I hope it will contribute, as a fresh and biblically rooted reflection, to the further discussions that are certainly needed as many historic churches face the cultural, theological and practical challenges of announcing and living the gospel in symbol and sign as well as word and action.

Introduction

If you knew my background you might suppose that I grew up familiar with the idea of sacred space, but actually I didn't. My family worshipped in a church built in the eighth or ninth century, but nobody ever drew my attention to the spiritual significance of that. My grandfather was Archdeacon of Lindisfarne, 'Holy Island', where Aidan and Cuthbert had launched the ancient Celtic church; but I just took this for granted as part of history, not a sign of sacred turf. When, in my teens, my faith came alive in new ways through the evangelical message of Scripture Union, I was drawn into an implicitly protestant world where you could pray to God anywhere at any time. The idea of some places or times being special would have appeared to threaten the much-cherished intimacy and immediacy of practising God's presence in every place. I went on to study the Bible, and was ordained in the glorious mediaeval chapel of Merton College, Oxford; but I still had no idea of sacred space. I had an aunt who was an Anglican nun, and when we visited her we always commented on the sense of peace and calm we found on going through the gate in the high convent wall; but I never figured out why that was, or why it mattered. I would have thought that any suggestion that one place might be more 'sacred' than another was ruled out by Jesus' words in John 4: neither on Jerusalem nor on this mountain will you worship God, because the father seeks people to worship him in spirit and in truth. And, he implies, you can do that anywhere.

So how did I change my mind? In the 1980s I began to realize that my faith had been strongly dualistic. This was challenged head-on when I wrote the Tyndale Commentary on Colossians in the early 1980s, coming to grips with the fact of Jesus as lord of the whole world, not just the 'heavenly' bit. Around the same time, I had sudden experiences of sacred space in unexpected places, rather like Lucy's first stumble through the wardrobe into Narnia. I'll just describe one. My oldest son went to a school in Montreal which had earlier expanded its premises by purchasing a redundant United church across the street. The building wasn't used as a chapel; it functioned as an assembly hall, a space for music, theatre, graduations and so on. There was no sign of its former use. One evening my son, aged about ten, was playing the clarinet in a cheerfully chaotic jazz concert. We trooped in with a hundred or two other parents and supporters, all chatty and jolly for a very secular evening out. And as I walked in – I don't really know how to put this – I was greeted by Jesus. I felt his presence. He was there. We took our seats and the music began: a bit raucous, nothing spiritual or religious about it. And all the time I sat there looking around and thinking: am I the only one who's realized? Doesn't everybody else feel it too? The joke at the time for me was that this had been a *United* church, which in Canada then, and I fear still, was something of a byword for liberal revisionism. But clearly, though I didn't have language for it or a theological explanation, Jesus had been invoked there, worshipped there, adored there. And there he still was. Make of it what you will.

Life was busy and I didn't have time to think it through or read books about a theology of place. But this and other occasions prepared me for the more predictable experience I had on Good Friday 1989 when I went for the first time into the Church of the Holy Sepulchre. There, and in Galilee a few weeks later, there was no question: whether or not you have a theory of sacred space, the sense of Jesus' presence was palpable, to me at least. In that place, it suddenly makes sense to suppose that the hopes and fears of all the world – and particularly the pain and tears of all the world – might actually be concentrated on one spot, on the one Man who lived and died and rose again there. That's a whole other story.

And there in Jerusalem, too, I was first struck by the biblical clue that I would now regard as the intellectual starting-point for a true understanding of holy places. You might begin way back with Moses being told to take his shoes off because he was standing on holy ground; then, after the exodus, that is where the tabernacle is constructed. But coming forward into the later period, you have the Temple and the Psalms. When you pray the Psalms in Jerusalem, you can't easily escape into metaphor. You say and sing that the creator of the universe, for reasons best known to himself, has decided to take up permanent residence on the little hill just down the road. All our western post-Enlightenment instincts – and the protestant instincts that surreptitiously fund them – rebel against any such idea. Surely all that stopped when the Temple was destroyed? Surely to go back there would lead to idolatry – or even to something like Roman Catholicism?

Not so fast. As many scholars, both Jewish and Christian, have been exploring in recent years, the whole biblical narrative is not about how humans can leave the world of space, time and matter and go off to a supposedly 'spiritual' heaven. That is the view of Plutarch, not Paul. It's Platonism. The Bible story is about how the creator makes a world, a heaven-and-earth reality, *in order that he may dwell there with his human creatures.* Genesis 1 is a statement of intent, and that statement is Temple-shaped: heaven plus earth with an 'image' at its heart. By the end of Exodus, we get the point. Even though humans have messed up, God calls a people and gives them the highly dangerous vocation of hosting the world's creator in their midst. The tabernacle evokes Genesis 1, just as Genesis 2 anticipates the promised land. The tabernacle is the *microcosm*, the 'little world', the small working-model of the whole creation, God's statement of future intent, as in Ephesians 1.10 where the divine plan is to sum up in the Messiah all things in heaven and on earth. The tabernacle is saying, 'This is what God wants to do with the whole creation.' Israel is called to live with the hope that one day not only the tabernacle or Temple but the whole creation will be full of the divine power and glory as the waters cover the sea. Holy places are not a retreat from the world; they are the beginning of God's advance into the world.

From the tabernacle we then find a straight line not only to Solomon's Temple – with all its ambiguity and tragedy – but also to John 1.14, where the Word becomes flesh and *tabernacles* in our midst; and ultimately to Revelation 21, where scripture's story reaches its climax in the dwelling of God with humans. John's theology rather obviously, and Paul's less obviously but just as powerfully, is *Temple*-theology. The tabernacle, and then the Temple, *and then Jesus himself, and then those in whom the spirit dwells*, are all about inaugurated eschatology, about God doing, close up and personal, what he intends to do in and for the whole creation. I have often summarized the doctrine of justification by saying that God intends to put the whole world right in the end, and having launched that project in Jesus he puts people right in the present so that they can be models and agents of his putting-right project for the world. You could equally say that God intends to renew the whole creation and fill it with his loving presence, and that having launched *that* project in Jesus he fills people with his spirit in the present, not so that they can escape the world but so that they can be models and agents of God's plan for all creation.

One of my favourite passages for this, as I was saying yesterday, is Psalm 72. This psalm highlights the vocation of Israel's coming king: to do justice and mercy, to care for the widow and the oppressed, to set right what has gone wrong in the world. And the psalm ends with the prayer: 'Let the whole earth be filled with his glory, amen, amen.' Do you see what's happening? The other obvious vocation of Israel's king was to be the Temple-builder: David planned the Temple, Solomon built it, Hezekiah and Josiah restored it, and one of the problems after the exile was that even Judas Maccabaeus didn't really get it right. The point of building the Temple was *so that the glorious divine presence would come and dwell there.* The king builds the Temple so that God's glory will fill it; the king does justice in the world, putting everything right in society, so that God's glory may fill the whole earth. Heaven and earth are the true and ultimate Temple, with humans as the 'image', dwelling in the holy, hallowed place. All that is at the heart of biblical theology. The great climactic moments of the New Testament – obvious passages like John 20, Romans 8, or Revelation 21 and 22 – are soaked in these themes.

So where might this take us in terms of a theology of sacred space in general, and the possibility and challenge of sacred space in the world today – in a great modern city today?

The overall point I want to make – and it's exciting to be able to make it in a place like this – is that church buildings, though they can sometimes be idolized and treated as though they were the reality to which they point, nevertheless do point to that reality. It's easy for us Platonized westerners to imagine that a church building is meant as an escape-hatch from the world, a place you go to forget the world for a while. Absolutely wrong. A church building is an anticipation, an ambiguous anticipation but an anticipation none the less, of God's desire to be known and loved on every square inch of the world. A church building is a *bridgehead* into the world, not an escape-hatch away from the world. And therefore the more it can point to the eventual goal of filling the whole creation with God's glory, the better.

That's why the great traditions of church-building have been what they have been. Take, first, the early practice of building churches on top of pagan shrines. People are often startled by that. Our western dualism shies away from the idea of worshipping Jesus on ground where Mithras, or Caesar himself, had been worshipped. But that misses the point (a Colossians-style point, I think). All pagan worship is a *parody* of the truth, taking some element in the good creation and absolutizing it. To worship Jesus instead is to celebrate the goodness of creation. In every eucharist, we are trumping the old corn-kings, and Bacchus the wine-god too, with the self-giving life and love of creation's true lord. By building a substantial church at a strategic point on a famous street like this, the builders, and you the restorers, are saying that Jesus belongs on the high street, not just down some dark back alley. There are new challenges on the high street and we must be prepared to meet them. Indeed, staking a claim to such a place is to invite such challenges. But this is where the gospel belongs.

This is why church buildings have traditionally symbolized the joining of heaven and earth. And it brings us from the question of *place* to the question of *sacred space* as a sub-category of how we understand the theology, the sociology and the cultural significance of buildings in general. When you visit eastern Europe to this day you see the Brutalist housing into which people were put as so many dehumanized units. The buildings people live in, work in and visit say a great deal not only *about* them but also *to* them about the sort of people they are and are to become. Churches have always done this, often with great sophistication, which today's casual functionalism ignores at its peril.

So how do buildings speak of heaven and earth coming together? The Eastern Orthodox do it horizontally: earth is where the people stand, and then, behind a screen covered with icons of the saints, heaven is at the altar where the priests celebrate the liturgy. The two are joined as first the gospel-book, and then the sacramental bread, are brought out from heaven to earth, and in other ways as well which symbolize the easy though scary commerce between God's space and ours. In the western churches we have often built Gothic masterpieces, of which this church is a modern variant. The point here is vertical: the building is far too high to make sense as a place of human activity, but we humans find ourselves then sharing the space with the angels and archangels. (That idea of sharing the angelic liturgy goes right back to ancient Judaism and remains central to many eucharistic liturgies.) And the way we do that in particular is through music. One of the things that has always excited me about Central is its vibrant music ministry. When you make music, and especially when you sing – perhaps I should say especially when you sing the Psalms – or when you use the music designed for these great buildings, like Tallis and the other masters of the high English Renaissance, you are physically inhabiting the upper spaces, joining with the angels. Of course, it may not always feel like that, but that is the theory, the framework for what we believe we are doing. That's why I'm excited about the developments here, not least the organ.

Another thing that great churches have done down the centuries is to ring bells. Sometimes newcomers to English towns and villages complain about the noise of the bells, but that's like buying a house beside a farm and then complaining that the cows moo too loudly. The bells offer an ancient, haunting message, and even when people can't put into words what that message is they often find it evocative. Simply chiming the hours and the quarters can be important: one of the church's primary roles is to remind the world what time it is, and the striking clock keeps that vocation symbolically alive. Sacred space, properly used, creates contexts for the gospel in the heart of the world that is supposedly secular but actually often ready for something deeper. A colleague of mine once worked in a village parish in the west of England in which the tower of the ancient little church stood on a prominent hill, where you could see it from a major highway. He used to get letters and other messages from people who had driven by – families, truck drivers, whatever – who said that just seeing the church there had reminded them of deep truths to which they needed to pay attention. Now you could, of course, explain that as a kind of atavistic folk-memory in the culture. Perhaps that is indeed part of how it 'works'. But once you get to grips with the biblical theology of sacred space I think there's much more going on.

So here, on a world-famous avenue in a world-famous city, a great cathedral-like building like this is a gift to be cherished, a sign to the world around, so that the casual shopper, the cab-driver doing a quick U-turn, the homeless man wandering by, the young executive on the way to the office, may all be reminded of the truth that nobody ever totally forgets: that we humans are called to bear God's image, that heaven and earth are made for one another, and that one day this will become reality. We often say in the UK that our cathedrals function like the Athenian altar to the unknown God: many people walk by and wonder, many come in to look around, frequently with an inarticulate sense that something is going on here that might just offer hope and healing, solace and a sense of direction.

In our often over-rationalized world, some people want to put up little signs in churches and cathedrals with biblical verses or helpful truths. But actually that's often a mistake. It ignores how sacred space actually *works*. The building itself will speak to people, as architects will tell you. Actually, any building that becomes a house of prayer may well have the capacity to speak like this; a Christian home which has been a place of love and prayer and welcome can do it too. But buildings that are designed prayerfully and consecrated prayerfully to embody and symbolize the truth of the gospel, of the coming together of heaven and earth through the redeeming love of God in Jesus his son, can and will do it in the way great art always does it, in its own language and with its own profound effect.

There are, of course, buildings, including alas some churches, whose architecture has a negative impact. I think of one where I was told in advance that the outside of the church says to you 'I wouldn't come in here if I was you', and when you go inside it says 'There, I told you so!' But I know of many others, thank God, which mysteriously draw you in, which welcome you, and which gently suggest at certain points, without any fussy people or little signs badgering you, that you might want to stop and pray. That is how, quite often, sacred space actually works. If you've ever been to the island of Iona, you'll know that the great abbey there does that amazingly. Every stone seems to say, 'Why not just stop here a moment and pray?'

It does depend in part, of course, on the building being open. That depends in turn on having properly trained people to staff it, appropriate security systems in place and so on. The practicalities of this will vary from one place and time to another. In some city churches I know, there is a rota of trained volunteers available so that people can find someone to talk to if that's what they want and need; though again often it's the building that does the talking.

It is only fair that I should also say what sacred space is *not*. It is not a bit of sympathetic magic. I have taken part in the consecration of churches and other buildings, and I believe there is wisdom and good practice in that kind of thing. But it doesn't, so to speak, work automatically. Like the children in C. S. Lewis's story, it's always possible to blunder into the wardrobe and find that it is only a wardrobe after all. Many will look and look but never see. But I have observed down the years that sacred space still works like the wardrobe, not least for people who aren't expecting it. I recall a young man with no overt faith who spoke of sneaking into a Midlands cathedral while other members of his family were playing in the park nearby and just sitting there enjoying something he couldn't explain. I remember a highly secularized young woman walking into another cathedral and, hearing the choir practising for evensong, suddenly dissolving into floods of tears without knowing why. These stories could be multiplied many times – and, of course, we remind ourselves, they could be matched by stories of many other people who go into the same buildings and come out with no apparent effect; or, worse, those who go in as professionals, even religious professionals, and allow familiarity to breed contempt. That's another warning: don't expect that the work we're doing, which is a real sign of God's coming kingdom, will go ahead without attacks. From the senior leadership down, we need to be prepared for that, and those of us who care about what's going on here need to be committed to praying for the safety and wisdom of all. Sacred space, to repeat, doesn't work automatically. And there are real tragedies when people who have loved a particular building come to love it above the truth it was meant to embody. There are temptations to idolatry at every level, and the greater the good the greater the temptation. There have always been seasons in the church's life when iconoclasm has seemed the only way, though often, as in England's Puritan period, this picked up a darker energy from existing social and cultural tensions.

The antidote to idolatry, then, is not to escape the world; that merely leaves the pagan deities ruling the roost while we escape. The antidote is sacred space of all kinds: the sacred space that we make in our homes when we pray and love and welcome strangers and celebrate God's goodness; the sacred space we make in our cities when we put the vision of Psalm 72 into practice at every level; the sacred space we make with our art and our music when we use our creative talents, and encourage others to do so, to the glory of God. And when families and justice-makers and culture-makers and beauty-creators come together to worship in a place they bring that sacredness with them, and the place itself, this place itself, becomes sacred too: not as a cold, detached shrine, but as a place where, in Eliot's words, 'prayer has been valid'.[1] I remember when I first read that being shocked; surely prayer is 'valid' wherever it is offered? Yes indeed, of course; but as we live between Easter and the final new creation it seems to be the case that when God's

---

1 From 'Little Gidding', in Eliot 2001 [1979], 36.

people have prayed in a particular place for many years there is an ease, a naturalness, about prayer in that place which you don't find in many others.

All this is to say that church buildings ought to be modelling and proclaiming the fact that the gospel of Jesus Christ is *public truth*. We have been browbeaten by secularism for quite long enough, and many Christians have retreated into the private world where the secularists want us to stay, the world in which we might indeed build prayer spaces but we would see them simply as places of escape. They are not. They are signs of hope and outward-looking theology and mission. They belong on the theological map which Paul draws in Romans 8 where he speaks of the Christians' 'inheritance' in terms of the renewal of the whole creation. Part of our problem has been that we have seen the 'inheritance' as 'heaven', and so have imagined a world in which buildings are merely functional. That, actually, plays right into the secular post-Enlightenment narrative in which the older implicit theology of place was ousted, so that – as native Americans and many others found out to their cost! – 'place' simply becomes a commodity or investment, a merely pragmatic convenience. No: the whole world is God's world; actually, if Paul is right, *the whole world is now God's holy land*, claimed by Jesus and by the promise that one day it will be filled with his glory. And every place of prayer, not least when that prayer is the inarticulate groaning of which Paul speaks, from the place where the world is in pain – every place of prayer is a sign that every place will finally be claimed as God's promised domain.

So to conclude. The biblical theme of tabernacle and Temple points forward to Jesus and the spirit in the New Testament, but we cannot infer from that that the idea of holy place and sacred space is now abolished. No: it is fulfilled. We are creational monotheists, not Platonic dualists. That's why, unlike the single shrine in the Old Testament, we have built more and more places of worship around the world: to declare to the whole world that Jesus is lord, to encourage more and more communities and individuals to pray and praise and worship and witness. Thank God for the holistic vision of scripture; for the holistic salvation of Jesus and the spirit; for the holistic hope of new creation; for the holistic ministry of strategic churches, holy places to symbolize God's claim on entire cities, and sacred spaces to symbolize and embody God's desire to fill all creation with his glory.

19

Foreword to *The Church and Its Vocation: Lesslie Newbigin's Missionary Ecclesiology* by Michael Goheen

I have been delighted by the renewed and now continuing interest in Lesslie Newbigin's theological and practical teaching. My own debts to him personally are recorded in this piece. Looking back at his life and work, I am struck by the reflection that our academic sub-disciplines have become so stuck in their own small circles that unless someone 'belongs' in that particular group – turns up at the relevant conferences, publishes in the relevant journals – he or she is likely to be ignored. It's only in retrospect that people may see, as they are now seeing in Lesslie's case, that a truly creative mind and spirit were at work, schooled in the practical life of a hands-on missionary and thus able, by instinct, to envisage situations quite different from those encountered by the ordinary desk-bound western scholar. I hope and pray that there will be room in tomorrow's church for people like Lesslie to flourish; though I have a sense that Lesslie was one of those who quietly made his own room, his own space. His mixture of alpha-plus intelligence, real humility, gentle humour and quiet determination combined into the gift from God of 'a man truly alive'.

[ix] Like many, I have personal reasons to be grateful to God for Lesslie Newbigin. I don't remember which occasion it was when I first met him, but he was already a legend in his own lifetime; I was like a teenager suddenly meeting a rock star. He had, after all, been a missionary in India, working through all the issues of missionary theology and praxis, and had been secretary of the body that drew up the founding charters of the famous ecumenical experiment we know as the Church of South India. I think Lesslie quietly relished the fact that he, a lifelong Presbyterian, was called to

be a bishop: God's sense of humour, he might have said, or (perhaps better) the way in which the sovereign grace of God overrules our small human attempts at organization. He had been involved in the founding of the World Council of Churches (in the heady days after the Second World War when people were looking for signs of new hope) and had sat around the table with Karl Barth and others. And, being Lesslie, he was completely unaffected by it all. Quite short in stature, but with a strikingly handsome face and a quiet composure and poise, he was the very antithesis of the highly strung, self-promoting rock star. He gave every impression, not that he had got life figured out, but that he knew God had it figured out and he was totally content just to trust him.

Mike Goheen, in this fine study that opens up the heart and breadth of Lesslie's thought, has told the story of how I had invited Lesslie to preach in Worcester College Chapel, Oxford, and how his mere arrival that evening [x] transformed my mood from one of nervous anticipation of the new academic term to one of readiness for the challenges and possibilities that would come. I remember telling that story to a friend who had worked in India, in the area where Lesslie had served as bishop. My friend at once told me that, in that part of India, one could go from town to town and admire a school, a hospital, a church building, only to be told, 'Bishop Newbigin encouraged us to build this, and told us who we should employ to get it done.' Lesslie was, in other words, a walking model of the theological truth that lay behind all that he did: a quiet confidence in the sovereignty and loving purposes of God, not such as might make you sit back and shrug your shoulders, but such as would make you think that it was therefore going to be a good idea to discern your own vocation within that purpose and steadily set about whatever tasks such a vocation might entail.

This same doctrine of divine sovereignty undergirded Lesslie's sense (strongly reinforced by his reading of Michael Polanyi) that if all truth was God's truth, then there was no area of life over which human research could claim absolute rights; in other words, there was no such thing as neutrality or 'objectivity', no such thing as a God's-eye view of reality available to us. All the truth we see, in whatever sphere, comes with strings attached: worldview-strings having to do with our own motivations and mindsets, and not least with our wider culture. In the wrong hands, this might have meant the collapse of all truth-statements into a subjective morass. But with Lesslie's strong view of the world as God's creation and all human vocations as located within God's purposes, it meant that all human research would ultimately belong within the celebration of God's good creation and the humble obedience to his redeeming purposes. I well remember the anger expressed by one Chemistry professor who heard Lesslie preach on that occasion in Worcester College Chapel and felt that his own professional integrity as an 'objective' scientist was being undermined. Interestingly, it was his fellow scientists, atheists all, who put him right. Yes, the experiments can be repeated on the other side of the world; but, excuse me, why were we doing *these* experiments in the first place? It doesn't take long to get back to the culture-conditioned human motivations behind all our apparently 'neutral' observations. That is important, as Lesslie saw very well, for our reading of the gospels as history, as part of God's true history: sceptical historiography put on a pose of neutral objectivity that needed to be unmasked. Lesslie helped many of us not only to glimpse a bigger vision of God and God's creation but also to reflect on the epistemology required for that glimpse to become a grasp.

Within all that, Lesslie taught a generation of us that a primary task of the Christian in any culture was *engagement*. He had, after all, sat on the floor of [xi] his local ashram with Hindu teachers, getting inside their worldview, not in order to work towards some fashionable relativistic synthesis, but to discern (much like Paul in Athens) points of contact and points of radical disagreement. If all truth was God's truth, then one might well expect many happy surprises as well as many moments of courteous challenge. This was quite different, in the 1980s, from what many Christians (British Christians at least) had supposed, poised as we were between a liberal 'affirmation' and a conservative 'rejection' of this or that aspect of 'culture'. Indeed, Lesslie taught us what he himself had discovered on his return to live in the UK after so many years in India: to look at British culture itself with a critical discernment, to stop taking things for granted, and to enquire of this or that cultural development whether it was honouring to God the creator. Lesslie, after all, had not come back to the UK to retire: he just translated his missionary vocation into a sequence of different modes.

What was more, Lesslie had been through a period of radical exploration and had come out the other side. He had, by his own admission, walked down the path towards a more liberal or relativisitic view of gospel and culture, had seen where it had led, and had firmly turned round again – not, being Lesslie, to any kind of closed-in conservatism, but to the larger world, the fresh outside air, the fully biblical vision of the creation and redemption of the world. I remember being at one or two conferences with him in the early 1990s where some young would-be radicals were trying to argue for relativistic positions and Lesslie, kindly and courteously, would argue a biblical case for the massive and all-embracing truth of the gospel: for, in the phrase he made his own, the gospel as 'public truth'. (This is all the more important given the way in which some followers of Karl Barth appear to argue for a distinct sphere of Christian 'truth'.) He carried conviction as few others could have done. This was reinforced, in terms of his rhetorical style, by his unnerving ability, being almost totally blind, to give a perfect lecture, laying out a large theme with its many interlocking parts and bringing it all in to land just under the hour without a glance at notes or a watch. He was the kind of consummate professional who made it all look easy.

I was especially fortunate to have met Lesslie and been captivated by his vision of Jesus and the kingdom just before I set about writing up my own big book *Jesus and the Victory of God* [Wright 1996a]. Many strands come together in a project like that, but Lesslie's vision, expounded and also exemplified, helped give me the courage to shape the argument. But that wasn't the end of it. The year after it was published I was startled to pick up the phone one day and hear Lesslie's voice on the other end. Being far too blind to be able to read for himself, he made a virtue of necessity – perhaps I should say a seminar [xii] of necessity – by calling a team of students from King's College in London to come and read to him. They had been reading *Jesus and the Victory of God* out loud, footnotes and all; and he was phoning to tell me which chapter they had just finished and how excited they had been by it. I was overwhelmed with gratitude, especially since the debt was much more in the other direction. Lesslie was, after all – as Mike's book bears out again and again – a *biblical* theologian of the church's mission. It was that deep, lifelong engagement with scripture that undergirded all he did. The phone call was then followed up with letters; unable to see, Lesslie would use an old typewriter and bash away at where he remembered the keys ought to be, producing masterpieces of impressionistic writing whose overall impact was of the excitement still motivating this old man, increasingly frail in physique, to relish scripture, to celebrate God's kingdom and to encourage relative youngsters like myself in our work.

It was only later, after Lesslie's death, that I began to discover more of his earlier writings. We had all read *Foolishness to the Greeks*; indeed, it was like a second Bible to some of us. But there was so much more. Lesslie had thought his way into, and then through, most if not all of the great theological issues of the day, reflecting on them with his own mixture of prayerful humility and missionary strategy. Because his life didn't fit into the normal academic pattern, I suspect that many of his profound and original books have mostly been ignored by professors who review books by other professors and engage with them in their footnotes. I hope that this book will go a long way towards turning that round. I have often reflected that, like some musical composers, Lesslie may in fact have his greatest impact generations after his death, and my prayer is that Mike's work will play a role in that process. Certainly, as I reflect on the beliefs about the church's vocation that I have come to hold over the years, and then as I look at the vast sweep of Lesslie's work surveyed here in *The Church and Its Vocation*, I begin to realize that, at my best, I have simply been thinking Lesslie's thoughts after him. I thank God for Lesslie Newbigin and for books like this present one that introduce him powerfully to a new generation.

20
The *Honest to God* Controversy*

A more unlikely episcopal pair than Lesslie Newbigin, the subject of the previous essay, and John Robinson, the subject of this one, it would be hard to find. Both were creative and inquisitive scholarly readers of the Bible; both had worked for the church in areas where the challenge of the gospel in the modern world seemed particularly acute. Both were kind to me, as a young scholar and churchman. But there, it seems to me, the similarities end. Robinson was shy and could be awkward socially; with Newbigin everyone was at their ease. Robinson had grown up in a cathedral close and the conventional world of public school and Cambridge, leaving to become Bishop of Woolwich and write the famous book discussed in this essay, before returning to Cambridge as Dean of Trinity College, where he stayed until his early death. Newbigin, originally from rural Northumberland and familiar with working conditions on Tyneside, attended a Quaker school, only became a Christian while a Cambridge undergraduate, and was at first ordained in the Church of Scotland, serving for many years as a missionary in India, being made bishop after the Presbyterians had united with Anglicans and others in the Church of South India. Both Newbigin and Robinson were greatly exercised with the challenges of communicating the gospel in the secularized modern western world; but they went about it in dramatically different ways. I know of people whose faith was restored by reading *Honest to God*; the book clearly scratched where some were itching. Whether now, in retrospect, it can be seen as anything other than a period piece is the underlying question of the following fortieth-anniversary review.

* An earlier version of this essay is published as 'Doubts about Doubt: *Honest to God* Forty Years On' in the *Journal of Anglican Studies* 3.2 (2005): 181–96, which is a revision of a paper delivered in November 2003, at the annual SBL meeting which celebrated the publication of a new fortieth-anniversary edition of *Honest to God* with concluding essays by Douglas John Hall and Rowan Williams. The present version of this chapter is edited for this publication. Reprinted by permission from Palgrave Macmillan, 'The *Honest to God* Controversy' in *The Palgrave Handbook of Radical Theology*, edited by Christopher D. Rodkey and Jordan E. Miller. Copyright © 2018.

[621] John A. T. Robinson was a New Testament scholar who was plucked from academic work to serve the Anglican church as a bishop. Despite his popular image as a man who had questioned and doubted the essentials of the Christian faith, his Johannine emphasis on entering into 'eternal life' in the present, so that physical death becomes less relevant, shone through his unsuccessful battle with cancer, and won the admiration of all who witnessed it. Like his beloved John himself, his work and its contribution is yet to be truly felt in the world of Johannine scholarship, which has been concentrating on quite different questions. But, of course, it was *Honest to God* (1963), not New Testament scholarship, that made Robinson world-famous, and one of the hardest questions to address is, 'Why?'

Apparently Robinson first conceived of this book in a period of forced inactivity during an illness for which he was hospitalized. He worked through a number of versions of the manuscript before it was published by SCM Press in 1963.[1] He had taught New Testament at Cambridge, and he wrote the book [622] after he had moved to the inner-city responsibilities of being Bishop of Woolwich in London. He identifies his position as a bishop with a responsibility to be a guardian and defender of the faith, but he says that he is also writing at a time 'when it is going to become increasingly difficult to know what the true defence of the Christian faith requires'. He goes on to say that he believes Christians at this time were being called to a radical 'restating of traditional orthodoxy in modern terms' (7).

The overall structure of the book is relatively simple. The first three chapters deal with what he sees as the present dis-ease with traditional notions of God and suggest the end of that kind of theism and a new notion of the 'ground of our being' as a way of speaking about God. There is a single chapter about Jesus as the paradigmatic 'man for others', and then two chapters on recasting the mould in terms of our understanding of worship in that it must be in the world as 'worldly holiness'. A chapter on the new morality of 'love alone' follows naturally from this, and the last chapter returns to the general theme of recasting the mould. Not many concessions are made for the reader in terms of difficult technical language or ideas. Yet the book turned out, to the surprise of the publisher and many others, to be a popular best-seller, aided in the UK by being serialized in a national paper.

But I do not want to start there. Nor, at the moment, do I want to refer to the many other aspects of Robinson's biography which shed light from

---

1 References to *Honest to God* are taken from the original edition and are given in parentheses in the text.

various and sometimes confusing angles on the mind behind the book. Rather, I want to raise seven substantial questions which I regard as damaging to the book's overall argument. Only then will I come back and, in acknowledging not only that the book obviously struck a deep chord with its generation but that its central thesis seems to me of abiding importance, I shall ask how we might retrieve that thesis, in a revised form no doubt, for today and tomorrow.

Foundations

What is Robinson's starting-point and authority for the many claims he makes? He draws on Tillich, Bonhoeffer, and to a lesser degree Bultmann and others, but that selection is the result of, not the reason for, his thesis, which seems to be that fewer and fewer people are able to believe in Christianity in anything like its traditional form. More especially, Robinson finds that he himself is, partly at least, unable to believe in the traditional expressions of Christianity. He also, in this book, found it hard to say how far he could and could not do so, though he followed *Honest to God* with a popular-level work entitled *But That I Can't Believe*, which made it a little clearer.[2]

But there are all sorts of problems with this. For a start, the decline of belief was not a post-war phenomenon; it had been going on in one shape or another from at least the eighteenth century. When A. N. Wilson wrote his book *God's Funeral*, it was about the nineteenth, not the twentieth, century.[3] Equally, at the same time as Robinson was writing, C. S. Lewis, Dorothy Sayers and other [623] apologists had an enormous following; Billy Graham was at the height of his popularity, with frequent visits to the UK; many churches were growing, not shrinking.

To all this *Honest to God* remains impervious – except to say that for many Christians the traditional ways of expressing belief appear still to be working, but none the less generally to comment that for most people these traditional ways did not work.[4] I suspect Robinson's real starting-point was in fact a combination of his own inner questionings, coming suddenly from a sheltered and traditional Anglican background into the hurly-burly of south London, and his belonging, as an erstwhile Cambridge don, to the liberal

2 Robinson 1967.
3 Wilson 1999.
4 See e.g. Robinson 1963, 15, 138–9.

intelligentsia of the time. I doubt if it was anything more substantial. At no point does such a thing as a sociological survey, an index of changes in belief over time, make any appearance.

On Tillich and Bonhoeffer

Has Robinson got Tillich and Bonhoeffer right and do they prove his point? We leave to one side the questions raised about Tillich by his biographers and by, for instance, Donald MacKinnon: to try to build a new morality of Robinson's kind, in which men will respect women sexually, on a Tillichian foundation, looks a decidedly shaky prospect. I am more interested in Bonhoeffer, and in the context of Bonhoeffer's embracing of the 'weakness and suffering of God' (39). Nowhere does Robinson acknowledge that Bonhoeffer's theological exploration was heavily conditioned by his situation as a pastor of the Confessing Church in Hitler's Third Reich – indeed, granted that Robinson had lived as a young man through the 1930s and 1940s, it is strange that his context-driven theology does not do explicit business with the questions raised by this period. Bonhoeffer's protest against 'religion', like that of Barth and Käsemann, had a very different meaning, within the Germany of the 1930s and 1940s, with its *Kulturprotestantismus* and its *Deutsche Christen*, than it did in the UK in the 1960s.

In fact, here Bonhoeffer was not saying that a new species had arrived, *homo nonreligiosus*, for whom allowance and accommodation had to be made, but rather that *homo religiosus* was a dangerous species which had to be resisted – a very different case. Robinson was arguing that one should go with the flow; Bonhoeffer, that one should stand out against it. Similarly, Bonhoeffer's insistence on God's weakness seems to me very different from Robinson's stress on God's virtual absence. But then, 'religion' itself has always meant subtly different things in Germany and the UK, and this alone makes it problematic to follow Robinson's too-easy translation from one to the other.[5]

Whether or not Robinson got Tillich and Bonhoeffer right, does his thesis make sense? I am aware that various sytematicians found it at the time confused and confusing, and today it's easy to see why. In particular, it strikes me as woefully incomplete and lopsided, not so much in that it fails to balance [624] immanence with transcendence – I shall come back to this point – but in that, though Robinson acknowledges the problem he finds himself in, of

---

5   See too MacIntyre's remarks about Bonhoeffer, quoted by Williams in Robinson 2002, 165.

a naturalism which appears simply reductionist, he does not seem to me to have found any answer, any way out. His wrestlings at this point, interesting though they are in themselves, do not seem to me to constitute one (50–61). Tillich's 'self-transcending and ecstatic naturalism' does not address the real question, which emerges when we look back at the twentieth century with its wars and human suffering (56 n. 2).

I find it quite shocking that Robinson has no account to give of evil, either its existence, its analysis, or the solution offered to it in either traditional or revisionist Christianity. He recognizes that the normal liberal analysis is shallow and inadequate, but has nothing to offer in its place. How a theology rooted and born in the twentieth century could do justice to that twentieth century without a serious account of evil simply defeats me. Alternatively, if awareness of serious evil in the world is at the root of the secularism to which Robinson is reacting sympathetically, we would have expected that to have been highlighted. There are from time to time apologists for secularism or atheism who cite as their main argument the difficulty of believing in God, granted all the evil in the world – as though the main argument for belief were a kind of pre-Enlightenment natural theology such as we find in Butler. Small wonder that Robinson finds it urgently necessary to demythologize the atonement (78–9).

This is directly cognate with Robinson's impossibly naive attempt at restating ethics. The thought that anyone in the 1960s was likely to be checked from sexually exploitative behaviour by being told that the only rule was love was ludicrous then and appears tragic in hindsight. And it left, and leaves, the way open for the Nietzschean response that has once more come to the fore in our own day: who needs love when you can have power? Any attempt to 'follow and find the workings of God' within the 'exhilarating, and dangerous, secular strategies of our day' (139), must, it seems to me, come equipped with the means to analyse and critique evil and proclaim and explain the way in which the Christian gospel addresses it. Otherwise, the scheme collapses back into the kind of thing which Barth, Bonhoeffer and others denounced in the 1930s – and which, from its very different standpoint and by its very different methods, postmodernity has been denouncing in our own day.

The Bible

Why is there no real role for the Bible in the book? Robinson was basically a biblical scholar: he was described on the cover of the early editions of the book as 'one of Britain's most brilliant New Testament scholars'.[6] How is it, then, that the Bible appears to play no role in the foundations of his thinking? The Bible appears at the start of the book, and frequently thereafter, as part of the problem rather than part of the solution. When it is the latter, it is mostly detached snippets rather than either sustained exegesis or a large-scale overview of books or themes. Granted Robinson's overall thesis, he could so easily have [625] drawn on the exilic texts, or Job, or Lamentations – or, if he wanted to be more robust, he could have gone to Exodus to sustain the idea of humankind set free from slavery, a motif that could have been applied to modern superstition. He calls on Tillich to expound Psalm 139 for him (57–9), which in my view adds nothing to his case.

Or, coming to the New Testament, Robinson could have explored Pilate's famous 'What is truth?' when faced with Jesus; or Paul's subversion of the *religion* of his Jewish contemporaries, a point which was made precisely by some of Bultmann's German followers at just this time. But all Robinson gleans from Bultmann, again without recognizing its context in Bultmann's own theological and pastoral concerns, is demythologization. Or he could have turned to Jesus' attack on the Temple; or the scene in Gethsemane. As a result of this remarkable lacuna, we are left wondering whether biblical scholarship has anything to do with helping people understand and integrate their faith and questioning. There seems to be, in fact, no theology of revelation at all in the book, except in the most downgraded sense of natural theology – 'what people today find credible'; 'the exhilarating and dangerous secular strivings of our day'. Similarly, Robinson offers no theology, or even account, of resurrection, not even an attempt to explain Easter away in a naturalistic fashion. Robinson had already suggested in *The Body* that the church itself is the real resurrection body of Jesus; perhaps his experience as a bishop had rendered this proposal problematic.[7]

Robinson seems to assume, in fact, that theism begins, not with the Bible or human awareness of God, but with the classic intellectual proofs (29). His attempt to substitute for these his own kind of natural theology – both the discovery of God in the ground of our being and the discovery of criteria for acceptable belief in the unsorted opinions of 'modern man' – carries, to my mind, no conviction.

---

6 Though one might have supposed that a person so described would recall that in Greek the complement does not take the definite article, so that in 'the word was God' we would expect what John wrote, i.e. *theos* rather than *ho theos* (Robinson 1963, 71).

7 Robinson 1952.

Contemporary Culture

Why, in particular, did Robinson so readily acquiesce in the then current theses about where western culture had got to? He accepts without demur the Enlightenment rhetoric of 'man come of age' – a claim which should have appeared threadbare already in the 1960s, in the light of two world wars, the Jewish Holocaust, and other genocidal acts, and looks even thinner now when confronted with the full range of the postmodern critique. Like Bultmann, Robinson relies on generalized language about outdated world-views, without asking whether the difference between a Christian worldview and a post-Enlightenment one is really one of chronology or one of ideology, a point I return to later.

Like Harvey Cox, Norman Pittenger and others, Robinson relies on a thesis about secularization which has now been shown to be very time-limited; his chapter on 'worldly holiness', and his assumption that fewer and fewer people would understand or want the mysterious dimensions of an older [626] religion, look frankly comic in our world of New Age mysticism, of a burgeoning 'retreat' movement, of Taizé, and of a renewed interest in Eastern Orthodoxy, not least its icons and incense. But even at this level, it isn't clear that Robinson had really plugged in to the serious thinkers of his time. Had he read, for instance, A. J. Ayer's *Language, Truth and Logic*? Was his charge of 'meaninglessness' related to Ayer's dismissal of theology and metaphysics, and if so, how (40–1)? It is no real charge, of course, to say that Robinson used some ideas fashionable then but discredited now – as Ayer admitted that his philosophy had been, and as Harvey Cox has admitted that the secularist thesis has been. Rather, the issue is that, given there were many voices to the contrary in the UK at the time when he wrote, why did he feel free to paint such a monochrome picture?

Omissions

Why did Robinson not consider other great theologians? In particular – this is perhaps the most serious question of all – why did Robinson not enquire whether there were other great theologians, alongside Tillich, Bonhoeffer and Bultmann, on whom he could call for help, or to whom he might look for alternative viewpoints on the central questions that exercised him? How, in particular, could he simply ignore Barth, whose whole project so directly addressed Robinson's questions and who could hardly be dismissed in the way Robinson dismisses so much traditional Christian conceptuality?[8] Robinson, in fact, never takes any specific writers as representative of the viewpoint he chips away at, leaving one with a sense of caricature, of straw men being set up and knocked down.

The best we can guess is that what Robinson is attacking is the implicit religion and theology of the cathedral close of his Canterbury boyhood, of the public school and university of his youth, of the cloistered college of his training, and of the Cambridge of his earlier career. Though I am not a twentieth-century historian, I know enough about these worlds to reckon that their faith was oblique, mysterious to the point of dryness, understated, a mixture of devotion and duty to a distant God, based on unquestioning assumptions of a fixed, static order in church and world, on earth and in heaven. I would not wish, in turn, to descend into caricature. But since Robinson has not engaged with any actual opponents, it is hard to do other than speculate like this – and to enquire, once more, why he did not go looking for the substantial help that not only Barth but many others could have given him in addressing the precise questions he was raising.

Honesty

My final question returns to the matter of Robinson's biography, and asks: in what sense is the book truly 'honest'? The word 'honest' seems to me multiply contested and even abused today, often being used to mean 'reductionist'. [627] As with Alasdair MacIntyre's book *Whose Justice? Which Rationality?*, we are compelled today to ask, 'Whose Honesty?', and to suspect all claims to absolutize the concept of honesty and thereby to claim an apparent moral high ground.[9] In particular, Robinson himself seems to me to protest too much when he declares again and again that for the most part he remains a traditional Christian – yet says in the preface, revealingly, that he finds less and less of himself to what he calls the right side of the line that runs through the middle of himself. He was, of course, a complex character.[10] But how he kept the two sides of himself integrated, if he did, has never been clear to me. Maybe it was honesty that compelled this disunity, but the sense of 'owning

---

8 See Douglas Hall's comments and references in Robinson 2002, 146.

9 MacIntyre 1988.

10 In later life, he edited and republished, movingly, his father's devotional book *The Personal Life of the Clergy* under the title *The Personal Life of the Christian*, reaffirming warmly the central disciplines and habits of Christian devotion (Robinson 1980).

up', of 'coming clean', which the title implies is not, I think, borne out by the apparent confusion of the author.

And Yet . . .

These seven questions press themselves on me as I read the book today, but as I stop and reflect, there is another one, to which the answer is resoundingly positive. Granted the book made an enormous splash, being gobbled up by an eager public in a manner which befell no other post-war books of theology, it is hard to say that Robinson did not have his finger on something. What was it? What felt need did he meet? Did he describe adequately what it was that he had rightly spotted? If not, can we go beyond him?

It would be easy, of course, to try to explain the book's impact in as reductionist a fashion as Robinson himself employs from time to time. In a sense the book was *addressing* the 1960s, but in another sense it was *expressing* where the culture already was, and thus helping to *sustain* a mood already present – with the doubtful legitimacy of endorsement from a liberal churchman called in to give permission for trends in the culture, many of which Robinson himself would not have welcomed. 'People always like being given permission for what they want to think and do,' we might say, and leave it at that. But apart from the dubious nature of such an analysis even in its own terms, I believe there is a lot more going on, which we still need to attend to quite carefully, though I find Robinson's expression of it frequently unhelpful and misleading for the reasons given above.[11]

The problem focuses easily on the word 'supranaturalism' and its cognates, which Robinson regularly uses, not least in drawing on Tillich.[12] I think it is important to sketch what I take to be the English story behind this idea and its problems, which is perhaps not quite the same as either the continental or the American story. In the USA, for instance, it gets ensnared in the Darwinian controversies, which in turn carry both continuing sociological freight and also memories, and caricatures, of the Civil War, with the liberal Yankees pitted against the redneck South, overtones quite absent from English discussion.

---

11   Here, I invoke the fact that my background is very similar to Robinson's (albeit a generation later) as an excuse for claiming to see into what he was trying to do. After all, despite all my criticisms, I find myself insisting in my own work on some of the very same things as Robinson did, some of the same central points, though because of what I perceive as weaknesses in Robinson's position I try to do it in different ways.

12   It is not clear to me, I might add, whether either of them intends to distinguish this from 'supernaturalism', and if so in what way, but I will assume that the two words mean more or less the same thing.

In English theology, the easy-going pre-Enlightenment assumption that the world of creation gave reliably straightforward witness to a good creator (I cited Bishop Butler above; we might include writers like Joseph Addison, [628] too) had been shaken to the core by the Lisbon earthquake of 1755, which as Susan Neiman has argued must be seen as one of the proximate causes at least of the Enlightenment revolution.[13] That revolution attempted to solve the problem, as well as several others, by cutting God loose from the world, drawing on the old upstairs–downstairs world of English deism. Religion became the thing that people did with their solitude, a private, inner activity, a secret way of gaining access to the divine rather than either an invocation of the God within nature or a celebration of the kingdom coming on earth as in heaven. God became an absentee landlord who allowed the tenants pretty much free rein to explore and run the house the way they wanted, provided they checked in with him from time to time to pay the rent (in much middle Anglican worship until the last generation, taking up the collection has been the most overtly sacramental act) and reinforce some basic ground-rules (the Ten Commandments, prominently displayed on church walls, and the expectation that bishops and clergy will 'give a moral lead' to society). As we know, the absentee landlord quite quickly became an absentee, as in Feuerbach, whom Robinson quotes to this effect without any sense that Feuerbach himself has been subjected to damaging critique (50).

But whereas liberal continental theology developed ways of coping with this problem, many in the UK carried on as though nothing much had happened, or as though by preaching in a louder voice one could reassure people that all was well.[14] Continental liberal theology was confronted by its own bankruptcy in the early years of the century, producing Barth's dramatic reassertion in the *Romans* commentary of the transcendence and holiness of God and his stout resistance to the politically freighted natural theology of the 1930s.[15] Bultmann also attempted to reread the gospels as though they were basically about the faith of *die Gemeinde* rather than about Jesus, dovetailing nicely with Germany's Weimar emphasis on *die Gemeinde* having got rid of the Kaiser – another point most UK readers of Bultmann missed. But UK theology carried on for the most part without getting to grips with the malaise.

---

13 Neiman 2002.
14 I am reminded of J. B. Priestley's play *An Inspector Calls*, in which upper-middle-class UK society tried to carry on after the First World War as though everything was just the same (Priestley 2009).
15 Barth 1933.

Instead, Anglican theology, piety and preaching oscillated uneasily and inarticulately between a firm reassertion of the old truths, as though they were unproblematic and a kind of *enfant terrible* flirtation with questionings of the virgin birth and bodily resurrection, and attempts to naturalize German theology and exegesis (such as R. H. Lightfoot's Bampton Lectures), without regard for the close integration of philosophy, politics and sociology in which that exegesis had its natural habitat. The great German ocean-going whales were thus housed in small freshwater tanks and made to do tricks to delight or shock (according to taste) the surprised UK public.

This was the climate in which Robinson was nurtured; and the religion of the middle Anglican at the time carried a certain mark of devotion, a certain tone of voice even, which betrayed its sense of the still-existing gulf between humans and God. The gap between being heavenly-minded and being of earthly use was wide, and there was a certain embarrassment at trying to [629] straddle it, an embarrassment conveniently hidden behind the understated but powerful Anglican liturgy. We might compare and contrast the Eastern Orthodox worldview where, precisely in liturgy, God is richly present albeit shrouded in mystery.

This inadequate and impressionistic sketch of Robinson's context suggests at least some of the reasons for his protest. If you meet the question of God within a framework which demands that you straddle that large gap, a gap moreover which seems too wide for your friends and neighbours, you will perceive the problem as one of an unbelievable supra- or supernaturalism; and you will turn, like Feuerbach a century earlier, to an attempt at a restated naturalism. Hence Robinson's feeling for Bultmann, who was explicitly applying Feuerbach to gospel studies in his insistence that theology is really anthropology. Granted that the problem is perceived in these terms, there was perhaps little else that he could do.

My sympathy for his plight has grown over the years as I have lived within the continuing split-level world of much English piety. The word 'miracle' is a case in point. Most people, not least in the media, still think of it as meaning an action performed by a distant, remote deity reaching in to the world from outside – just as to many people, still, the word 'God' itself conjures up a basically deist image of that kind of a being. I know that in fact that word 'supernatural' has a longer history than this and that, for instance, mediaeval theologians were able to use it in such a way that it did not carry the baggage of an implied deism or semi-deism (by which I mean the view which, while sharing deism's gap between God and the world, holds that from time to time this 'God' can and does 'intervene'). But I continue to find that this model dominates UK theological discourse, particularly among those of, or near, Robinson's generation.

Is there an alternative, then? In company with many of the post-Robinson generation of systematicians in the UK – people like Rowan Williams, David Ford, Oliver O'Donovan, Trevor Hart, Alan Torrance, and the late Colin Gunton and John Webster, and many others – I am struggling to express what seems to me a more biblical perspective: that God's sphere and our sphere, 'heaven' and 'earth' in biblical language, intersect and overlap in many and various ways, so that God remains present to the world while simultaneously over against it as sovereign, lover, lord and judge. In particular, the *mode* of God's presence, within the world as it is, seems to me to combine laughter and tears, joy and sorrow; we cannot say automatically that a particular state of affairs must be God's will because it is simply what we find in creation (think of the protests of Barth and Käsemann against this kind of thing!), or that a particular state of affairs must be displeasing to God because it shares the life, and the corruptibility, of the present old creation. We cannot read off God's presence or absence, God's pleasure or displeasure, in any straightforward way from the surface of the created order (or the opinions of humans within it). We must rely on some kind of revelation (this is the move, of course, which [630] Robinson never made, and which still remains unmade by, and worrying to, many of his generation); *not* to leap over the ontological or moral gap between a remote deist God and ourselves, but to enable us rightly to recognize the laughter and the tears, the celebration and the judgment, of the true God.[16]

And, of course, at the heart of all this, we find Jesus: not just the 'Man for Others', true and powerful though that remains, but the flesh-and-blood Jesus of Nazareth, who fed the hungry, celebrated with the outcasts, grieved over Jerusalem, struggled with messianic vocation, cried out in anguish in Gethsemane, died God-forsaken on the cross, rose again in surprising bodily triumph, and, in and through all this, believed that he was thus and thereby embodying the long-awaited return of Israel's God to Zion. I have argued elsewhere that we discover the divinity of Jesus, not (as much post- Enlightenment theology has tried to do) as an extra quality or add-on over and above this humanity, but precisely within it. I see my historical investigations into what it meant to be Jesus (if I can put it like that) as contributing centrally to this task of reconceiving the ways in which we talk of God in

---

16 I find Robinson's brief remarks about revelation (1963, 128) – Christ as the disclosure of ultimate truth – at best inadequate for anything like this task.

the postmodern culture which has shaken to the foundations the modernist framework on which Robinson relied and which seemed to him set in stone for ever. I thus find myself sharing, at a deep and sympathetic level, Robinson's unease at the supernaturalist language and frame of reference about which he spoke. But instead of accepting that framework and setting about a kind of naturalism instead, albeit one with a bad conscience, I want to suggest that the framework itself needs dismantling and replacing with something else.

An obvious objection to this proposal might come in the form: does this new framework not simply rehabilitate a biblical worldview, which is one manifestation of an ancient worldview we can no longer share? Here, sticking my neck out, I protest. The idea of ancient worldviews being set aside by modern ones – the point is often couched in terms of pre-scientific and scientific worldviews – likewise comes to us with all kinds of Enlightenment baggage.[17] Of course, there are differences in worldviews over time; but the most significant differences between worldviews are not those between 'ancient' and 'modern', but those which occur in philosophical assumptions that cut across chronological divides. What post-Enlightenment thought has offered us, in fact, is more or less exactly the same choice as outlined by Cicero in the first century BC in his *De Natura Deorum*: either a pantheism which is some sort of Stoicism, or a deism which is more or less Epicureanism, or a scepticism or agnosticism which is a variant of the ancient Academic view. Either God and the world are pretty nearly the same thing, or they are ontological light-years apart, or the evidence is confused and we cannot really tell.[18]

Each of these worldviews, with its attendant philosophy, survives quite well the transition from pre-scientific to scientific. But the worldview we find in the Hebrew and Aramaic scriptures, and its fresh mutation in early Christianity, always did cut across those ancient non-Jewish worldviews with a fresh challenge, however humbling it may have been: the challenge that there is after all a creator God, who, having made the world, remains in dynamic though [631] puzzling relationship with it, especially with the human race, and more especially with Israel; the challenge of revelatory events, revelatory scriptures and, in Christianity, a supremely revelatory person.

---

17 I am reminded of C. S. Lewis's pantomime figure of Mr Enlightenment in *The Pilgrim's Regress*: on being asked how he knows there is no God, he exclaims 'Christopher Columbus, Galileo, the earth is round, invention of printing, gunpowder!' (Lewis 1933, 35).

18 Cicero took the last view, but believed it was important for social and cultural reasons to keep public religion going anyway, a position familiar to many Anglicans.

Second-Temple Judaism developed sophisticated ways of speaking about God's dynamic relationship with the world, with humans and with Israel. Significantly it was exactly those forms of speaking – not least word, wisdom, Torah, Shekinah and spirit – that the early Christians drew on when trying to explain the significance of Jesus and the freshly outpoured holy spirit. This Jewish and Christian challenge offers a new and startling alternative to Cicero's three options, which, like them, can move quite easily from the so-called pre-scientific period to that of modern science.[19]

A particularly sharp edge of this has been the claim, repeated over and over, that the early Christians and their Jewish counterparts lived in an *apocalyptic* worldview, meaning by that that they believed the space–time universe was about to come to an end. This claim has been a central part of the kind of problem Robinson faced in *Honest to God* as in his other writings. But it is demonstrably false. That reading of apocalyptic does no historical justice to the actual beliefs of second-Temple Jews and early Christians. This is not demythologizing; it is historical investigation. Indeed, part of the demythologization programme can be seen to be a stripping away, not of parts of actual first-century belief (though no doubt some of that was envisaged as well), but of ways in which first-century belief had been falsely described precisely by those post-Enlightenment sceptics eager to rubbish early Christianity and reinscribe their own variation on Cicero's alternatives. Until the rise of contemporary studies of apocalyptic which have revealed its true subtlety and political sensitivity, most writers remained content to describe it in ways designed to assist in the Enlightenment's portrayal of first-century people as flat-earth ignoramuses.

Let me sum up my alternative proposal. Robinson had his finger on a real problem in post-war UK church life and, in a measure, theology. I believe the problem was mostly or largely caused not by the New Testament and historic Christianity itself, but by the way in which the post-Enlightenment world had assimilated and re-expressed the Christian faith. What Robinson referred to when speaking of supra- or supernaturalism belonged within an essentially deist or Epicurean framework, and he was struggling with the unwelcome consequences of people being unable to relate to their absentee landlord, and simultaneously puzzling over the fact that some people did not find this a

---

19 I say 'so-called' because many post-Enlightenment thinkers like to portray all who went before them as stupid and ignorant, a claim challenged by a reading of, say, Ptolemy or Pliny, or by the contemplation of the Parthenon, or the acoustics of the great ancient theatres.

problem. The huge popularity of his book shows that he struck a chord with a great many people.

The tragedy of *Honest to God*, as I perceive it, is that Robinson did not see that what he was rejecting was a form of supernaturalism pressed on Christianity by the Enlightenment; that he did not therefore go looking for help in finding other ways of holding together what the classic Christian tradition has claimed about God, the world, and Jesus; that in addressing these ontological questions, he never laid out the parallel moral ones or explored the [632] ways in which, centrally, the Christian scriptures and tradition address them; and that, in consequence, his high modernist construct now looks very shaky in the cold light of a postmodern dawn, as well as in the warmer light of the mainstream Christian alternative. The good news is that, precisely once the postmodern critique has done its work, we can see that there are other ways of retrieving the ancient Jewish and early Christian witness and faith – a daunting and difficult task, no doubt, but one still full of promise and possibility.

21

Christ and the Cosmos: Kingdom and Creation in Gospel Perspective

I was delighted to work with the Biologos Foundation in the USA on several occasions, and the present paper was delivered at their 2017 conference in Houston, Texas. It gave me the opportunity to point forward to the Gifford Lectures, which were very much 'work in progress' at the time, while cautiously pointing to some potential areas of convergence between the larger world of scientific research and my own world of biblical exegesis. As with my other Biologos work, it was a delight to team up with Professor Francis Collins. (Two earlier Biologos papers were published in *Surprised by Scripture*, Wright 2014b.)

Introduction

[97] A biblical scholar reflecting on the questions that animate many of the contemporary debates on science and religion (debates that originated in the early modern period) will often be struck by the sense in which, despite sometimes vociferous disagreements, the many sides of a pluriform discussion often share a set of basic assumptions. These assumptions, though quite foreign to the world of the biblical texts, strongly influence many scholars' approach to these same texts. The creation of the cosmos, celebrated in the vivid imagery and multi-layered stories of the biblical texts, and especially the New Testament's vision of Christ as an agent of that creation, seem a far cry from the picture of 'nature' against 'supernature' over which cultural wars are still waged. The public mood on both sides of the Atlantic may be shifting on many of these issues, as on much else. Such shifts often go hand in hand with social, cultural and political turbulence. This is the complex context within which I offer the following reflections on the New Testament vision of 'Christ and the Cosmos'. This has the nature of a preliminary exploration; I hope to develop this line of thought elsewhere in due course.

The problem I shall address here comes in three stages. First, the New Testament affirms that the whole creation was made in, through and for the Messiah, the Christ, Jesus. In saying this, the writers seem to be echoing the ancient Jewish belief that the one God made the world through his 'wisdom' or his 'word'; but this 'wisdom' or 'word' has now become human, and we see and know who he is. But what exactly does this mean?

Second, many orthodox theologians have been happy to embrace the main [98] findings of modern science, not least a belief that the world we live in has evolved in significant ways over 14 billion years or so. But some have questioned whether a consistent belief in evolution might actually undermine orthodoxy, leading to a loss of a Trinitarian theology and a collapse back into the deism of earlier centuries. I can see why some might think that, but I want to suggest that this would be a wrong implication.

Third, the question of science and religion has long been associated with the question of natural theology: can we start with observation of the world and argue up to Christian truth without an appeal to some kind of revelation? Again, I want to suggest that putting 'Christ and the Cosmos' at the centre of the argument shifts and clarifies this important but complex discussion. Here again, the present study is a preliminary reflection in advance of fuller study elsewhere.

All Things Were Made through Him

First, then, to the New Testament. The prologue to John's gospel takes us back to 'the beginning', but 'the beginning' is now explicitly about the 'Word', the *Logos*, the one through whom all things were made. John is echoing the Psalms: by the word of the Lord were the heavens made, and all the host of them by the breath of his mouth (33.6). He is also echoing Proverbs 8 (which itself echoes Genesis), and its retrieval in later Jewish writings: 'Lady Wisdom' was God's handmaid in planning and making the world. The question of whether *Sophia* in this passage was simply one metaphor among other possible ones, and to what extent pre-Christian Jews saw 'wisdom' as a second quasi-divine figure, is important, but not within my present argument.[1] What matters for the moment is that the New Testament retrieves this tradition, not least in John 1, and declares that any such ideas

---

1   Cf. my discussion in Wright 2013b, 670–7. For a discussion of second-Temple ways of speaking about God acting through his wisdom and how this relates to Jewish monotheism, cf. the work of Richard Bauckham, for instance in Bauckham 2009, 217 and elsewhere.

are in fact to be predicated on Jesus himself, the Messiah. The climax of John's prologue is, of course, the moment when 'the Word became flesh and dwelt in our midst', with the word 'dwelt' evoking, in the Greek, the notion of the Temple or tabernacle: the Word 'pitched his tent', 'tabernacled' among us. As many studies have insisted, Genesis 1 [99] describes the creation of the world in terms of a *temple*, a heaven-and-earth reality, with humans as the 'image' within the temple. John is working with that theme: the divine Word, through whom the creation-Temple itself was made, himself became the Image within the Temple, the personal presence of the creator. In the second-Temple period, many saw the Temple, and its ancestor the tabernacle, as a *microcosmos*, a 'little world', a small working-model of the new creation that was yet to be, with kings and priests at its heart. Now, in the New Testament, Jesus is the 'royal priest', the truly human one, who is *both* the true image-bearer, the genuine human, *and* the Temple in person. So what might it mean to say that all things were made through him?

Two Pauline passages echo the same theme. 1 Corinthians 8.6, in what looks like a formulaic prayer developing the Jewish *Shema* prayer, declares that there is one God, the father *from* whom all things come, and one lord, Jesus the Messiah, *through* whom all things come. The father is the origin; the son is the agent. This develops into the extraordinary poem of Colossians 1.15–20, which echoes Genesis 1.1 and Proverbs 8.22.[2] The Messiah is 'the image of God, the invisible one, the firstborn of all creation; for in him and through him and for him all things were created . . .' and then, in the second half of the poem, all things are *reconciled* in and through and for him. Hebrews 1 likewise echoes the Psalms and the wisdom tradition, stressing up front that in the last days God has spoken through a son, whom he made the heir of all things, *through whom also he made the worlds* (1.2). All this is well known, though its interpretation is inevitably contested.

What are we to make of all this? Here is my proposal. Most theologians and exegetes, reading passages like this, have assumed that what is going on is (1) an affirmation of the one God as the creator of all, and then (2) a kind of honorific exaltation of Jesus, so that somehow we are now to associate Jesus with this initial act of creation. We *first* get a picture of creation, and of God the creator; *then* we fit Jesus, or at least the pre-incarnate Word, into that picture. But that's not actually how these passages work. The New Testament insists that the epistemological track runs in the opposite direction. It isn't that we know who God is – in this case, the creator – and somehow fit Jesus,

---

2   On some of these echoes, see Wright 2013b, 673, esp. n. 172.

or the pre-incarnate Word, into that. These passages stress that we don't actually know that much about who or what God is, but that Jesus reveals him. Nobody [100] has ever seen God, insists John; the only begotten God, the one close to the father's heart, has made him known, has (in the Greek) *exegeted* him. In Colossians 1.15, God himself is invisible, but Jesus is the visible 'image', where 'image', of course, insists on the *humanity* of Jesus. It is by looking at the humanity of Jesus that we discover who the invisible God really is. That is how the 'image' works.

This means, I suggest, that the more we discover about Jesus himself, the more we find out about, not simply about God in the abstract, but about *the means of creation itself*; and that when we explore this line of thought all sorts of things look differently from how they look when we come at things the other way round. The four gospels tell us, after all, what Jesus did and how he did it.[3] Jesus of Nazareth went about announcing that *this was the time for God to become king* and that *this was what it looked like when he did.* His whole project was about the rescue of creation and the launching, from within that creation, of 'new creation'. The gospel-writers, like Paul and the author of Hebrews, make it clear that 'new creation' is *the renewal of creation itself.* It is not, in other words, a matter of scrapping the original creation and replacing it with something else. (The assumption that 'the kingdom of God' would involve the latter kind of move is at the heart of the century-old idea that Jesus and his first followers expected the literal end of the world.[4])

But, if this is so, we know – because Jesus makes it abundantly clear – how 'new creation' happens. This is what several of the parables are about, and it's no accident that Jesus takes imagery from the first creation to make the point. His fellow Jews were thinking of 'the kingdom of God' as a new social and political state of affairs which would come in with a bang, with a sudden revolution, quite possibly with a Messiah driving out the Romans and establishing a new, free [101] Jewish state that would last for ever. A similar

---

3   Part of the trouble here is that we read the evidence wrongly, based on various pressures to make Jesus conform to different expectations arising from within our modern framework. Conservative western Christianity has often tended to be docetic (emphasizing the divinity of a 'Jesus' figure who performs 'supernatural' miracles over against his humanity, which receives a more perfunctory acknowledgment), and Platonic, in carving up creation into an earthly, sensible sphere and a spiritual, heavenly sphere, where the whole point of Jesus' ministry seems to be to provide a means of escape from the former to the latter. Liberal western Christianity has often tended to be sceptical and to deny that we can know that much about what Jesus did in the first place, let alone what he meant by it. This is where history really matters. For methodological reflections on history and the first century, in particular with reference to pressures arising from within a late modern horizon, see Wright 1992, 81–120.

4   See my article, Wright 2018a.

revolution had taken place two hundred years earlier, against the Syrians, and it partially succeeded but then went bad. They tried it again a hundred years after Jesus, in the famous Bar-Kochba Rebellion; it worked for three dangerous years, and was then crushed for good.[5] Jesus stands between these two; he is saying 'Yes' to the kingdom but 'No' to the way his contemporaries were imagining its arrival. It will be, he said, like a seed growing secretly; like a small mustard seed that grows into a great plant; like someone sowing seed all over the place, some of which goes to waste but some of which bears a crop out of all proportion to what was sown – thirtyfold, sixtyfold, a hundredfold. The new creation comes through a strange and slow process of sowing, with an eventual harvest in mind but not by the means Jesus' contemporaries suppose.

But that's not all. Some of Jesus' kingdom-stories are about remarkable acts of rescue despite the odds. The parables of the prodigal son and the good Samaritan are obvious examples. Here it isn't just a strange and slow process; it's a work against all probabilities, in the first case of the father welcoming back the prodigal, in the second case of an outsider turning out to be the true neighbour. There are paradoxical twists and turns; unexpected outcomes. This is how the kingdom comes.

When we reflect on all this, and put it together into a historical narrative, we realize that all the kingdom-stories in the gospels are designed to lead the eye up to the moment when Jesus is actually enthroned – on the cross. It was not, after all, such a silly idea to think that there might be a single moment which would change the world for ever.[6] To summarize a long, complex story: [102] the four gospels present Jesus' death in converging ways, and through them all we find the imagery of creation and new creation. Jesus goes to the heart of the darkness in order to take the full weight of that darkness on to himself and so to exhaust it. He submits to the forces of chaos so that there

---

5   For an overview of the historical background, see Wright 1992, 157–66. For a summary of the present point, see Wright 2011d, esp. 104–16.

6   See Wright 2016a. This is the idea behind the word 'apocalyptic' – a sudden revelatory moment when God reveals himself in decisive action. God reveals himself to Moses in Ex. 3.14 and this initiates the saving action of God, liberating his people from the oppression of their slavery in Egypt. The dramatic event of the crossing of the Red Sea becomes, in the tradition and memory of Israel, a moment of the self-disclosure of Israel's God in his decisive rescue (see Ex. 15.1–21). The visions in Dan. 7 are at the same time disclosures of the God of Israel in his confrontation of the empires as they focus on the critical moment of the vindication of those who belong to him. That the gospel-writers, in different ways, retrieve both the exodus-narratives and Dan. 7 should come as no surprise. For a discussion of some of the complexities involved in the use of the term 'apocalyptic', especially in Pauline scholarship, see Wright 2015a, 135–44. An earlier discussion of 'apocalyptic', including a discussion of Dan. 7, can be found in Wright 1992, 280–99. See now the collection of essays in Reynolds and Stuckenbruck 2017.

may be new order. He tastes death itself in order to bring new life. And all the gospels, and Paul as well, of course, insist that this was an act of utter self-giving love.

In and through it all, the gospels make it clear – we should say, the Jesus of the gospels makes it clear – that his kingdom-project constituted a radical redefinition of what the world means by power. In Mark 10.35–45, Jesus is faced with James and John wanting the best seats in the kingdom. He tells them sternly that while the high-and-mighty power-brokers in the pagan world get their way by bossing and bullying, 'We're going to do it the other way.' The one who wants to be great must be the servant, the slave of all. Ultimately, Jesus himself expresses this in matchless acted symbolism by washing the feet of the disciples at the supper (John 13.1–20).

This is the New Testament's picture of how the kingdom comes. The same point is picked up in Acts, and particularly in Paul's discussions of 'power'. We might instance 2 Corinthians 12.9, where Paul insists that God's power is made perfect in weakness. We could develop this theme much further, but we must hurry on to the point, which should be obvious but I think is not usually made. *When we say that 'all things were made in and through and for Jesus the Messiah', this is the Jesus we must be talking about.* There is no other. He is the same yesterday, today and for ever. And this means that we should at least try to think what it might mean to say that *this* Jesus, and this vision of the kingdom, is the lens through which we might understand creation. Instead of starting with a great act of creation and then fitting Jesus into it, simply declaring in general terms that somehow he was involved in it all, we ought to start with what we know of Jesus' own vision of kingdom, truth and power (think of Jesus' conversation on these topics with Pontius Pilate in John 18 and 19!), and ask what that might mean about creation itself.

The results are striking. To begin with, if creation comes through the kingdom-bringing Jesus, we ought to *expect* that it would often be like a seed growing secretly; that it would involve seed being sown which went to waste and other seed being sown which produced a great crop. We ought to *expect* that it would be a strange, slow process which might suddenly reach some kind of a harvest. And we ought to expect that it would involve some kind of [103] overcoming of chaos. Above all, we ought to expect that it would be a work of utter self-giving love; that the power which made the world, like the power which ultimately rescued the world, would be the power, not of brute force, nor of some vast robotic machinery controlled by a distant bureaucrat, but of radical outpoured generosity.

We ought to expect, in other words, that creation would not look like an oriental despot deciding to build a palace and throwing it up at speed with his architects and builders cowering before him. We ought to have anticipated that the deist models of creation, conceived I think on the analogy of the early industrial successes, might in fact be misleading, and that they would need correcting in the light either of a better picture of the one through whom creation was accomplished or in the light of fresh scientific research.[7] And what do we find? Very few people in the late eighteenth or early nineteenth century were doing the kind of fresh work on Jesus and the gospels that would lead us to this picture. But various scientists, not least the Darwin family, *motivated by a quite different worldview, namely that of a developmental Epicureanism*, none the less came up with a picture of 'origins' that looks remarkably like Jesus' parables of the kingdom. Some seeds go to waste; others bear remarkable fruit. Some projects start tiny and take for ever but suddenly produce a great crop. Some false starts are wonderfully rescued; others are forgotten. Chaos is astonishingly overcome. This says nothing about generosity, since that word only makes sense in terms of a personal creator, which the Epicureans like Erasmus Darwin had ruled out. But the evolutionists have been driven again and again to speak of the prodigality of the natural world. And the theologians can pick that up and say 'Yes: and this is precisely what you might expect if there is a God of boundless, generous love behind it all. The prodigal father. The God we know in and as Jesus the Messiah.'

This proposal could be developed in all sorts of directions, for which there is unfortunately no space here. I will restrict myself to two points that follow from an attempt to look at creation through the lens of the kingdom of God as portrayed in Jesus' parables. [104]

Evolution and Orthodox Theology

A good deal of our trouble to this day stems, I think, from the way in which the controversies of the eighteenth and nineteenth centuries were set up. These controversies took place in a wide cultural and political context, not

---

7 We recall that the deists were keen to get Jesus out of the picture or at least relegated to the margins of the merely exemplary. If creation appears to an age fond of mechanics as a clockwork machine, which God winds up at the beginning and which is then supposed to run on its own, then Jesus must seem at best an interruption of the established order. Jesus might be allowed to exemplify the virtue of punctuality, but he should really not interfere with the productive schedule of bourgeois society. For the influence of deism on Reimarus, for example, see Wright 1996a, 16–18.

always taken fully into account in the well-publicized debates over science and religion. There are several interesting parallels between nineteenth-century attempts to get rid of a creator in what was then claimed to be the domain for the various independent actors and forces of nature, on the one hand, and the revolutions of the late eighteenth century, getting rid of monarchy and of the very idea of the divine right of kings, on the other. Epicurean science, in other words, was making essentially the same move as the French and American Revolutionaries; in other spheres, similar things were happening with economics (as in Adam Smith's *The Wealth of Nations*) and, of course, with studies of Jesus, as in the work of Reimarus and its propagation by Lessing.[8] In the political sphere, the replacement of divine right with an evolving society of democratic elections resulted in what some have called 'the biopolitical'.[9] Elections function as evolutionary triggers of natural selection within a political system which is self-created by voluntary agreement, owing nothing to a higher purpose beyond the self-serving preservation of power. The operative assumption is that the natural world and the political sphere work in the same way: only the fittest survive. The best physical specimens, and the best political proposals, will win out in the long run. Looking at the last two centuries in the western world, it would be difficult to maintain that this biopolitical process has done what it said on the tin. But, as with evolution, the theorists might reply that these things take time – that, indeed, lots of seed will be wasted before one will produce good fruit. To change the metaphor, you may have to break a lot of eggs before you create an omelette. And the problem is that breaking eggs by itself gets you nowhere. You have to turn the stove on, for a start.

To be sure, these things may only pan out in the long run. But from the position of biblical theology it is precisely at this point that the analogy between politics and the natural world breaks down. The political process involves humans, and (according to scripture) humans have a God-given responsibility [105] and vocation to rule wisely. A blind evolutionary process – which is indeed how democracy does sometimes seem to work, rejecting the paths of wisdom and embracing the wrong sorts of power – may never of itself 'evolve' into wise and peaceful governance. But that is for another time.[10] My point at the moment is that the development, not just of 'evolution' – a hypothesis about

---

8 On Reimarus and Lessing, see Wright 2019a, 20–1.

9 On John Milbank's stimulating essay 'Paul against biopolitics' (in Milbank, Žižek and Davis 2010, 21–73), see Wright 2015a, 323–8.

10 For some initial reflections, see Wright 2016b.

biology and then the wider world, with data to match – but of evolution*ism*, the necessary correlate of an Epicurean worldview which is a very different thing, came not least as a response to an older would-be Christian but in fact semi-deist position.[11] In this framework, 'creation' was not about seeds being sown slowly and secretly, not about a creation that was the work of a generous self-giving love. It was about raw, hands-on power. As we saw a moment ago, the would-be orthodox Christianity of the day had often tended to a docetic view of a divine Jesus whose humanity was necessary for what had to be done but otherwise largely irrelevant. A false stand-off was thus generated between the kind of would-be Christian view that went with the divine right of kings, a quasi-docetic Jesus, and a 'creation' accomplished by naked divine power, and the kind of reaction that was agitating for popular rule, for evolutionary biology and for a 'quest for the historical Jesus' which would find out that he was just a deluded religious or political teacher. The Bible itself speaks against this entire construct. So, interestingly, does evolution itself, once we eliminate the Epicureanism at the heart of it. The charge of implicit deism ('Go with "evolution" and you'll end up with deism') rebounds on the accusers. A fully Trinitarian vision of God, Jesus and the spirit goes with the vision of a theistic, that is, a non-Epicurean, evolution.[12] And this leads to my final point.

Science, Jesus and 'Natural Theology'

The project of 'natural theology', as conceived in the early eighteenth century, belongs with this older model. Few today would argue that we can straight-forwardly begin with the natural world and argue our way up to a view of God that corresponds more or less to the Christian one. But if I'm right in what I've said above, then a more interesting and complex possibility opens out before [106] us. 'Natural theology' as popularly conceived, that is, the attempt to reason up to God without the use of revelation, was always a strange and culturally conditioned thought-experiment. Most humans do not work like that most of the time. I think – though a forceful presentation of this argument would take many more words than I have space for here – that this contrast of two types of knowledge, that which we have by revelation and that which we have by unaided observation and reason, makes two mistakes.[13]

---

11 I have developed related ideas further in the first two essays in Wright 2014b.
12 I have not been able here to comment on the role of the spirit in creation and new creation, but passages like Rom. 8 offer a powerful starting-point for such reflections.
13 For a preliminary statement on types of epistemology, see Wright 1992, 31–46. I have expanded the point considerably in Wright 2019a.

First, it flattens out what actually happens in revelation, and for that matter what actually happens in observation and the use of reason. For a start, the Bible is not, as it were, naked 'revelation'. Precisely because of the sort of book it is, it invites and, indeed, demands reflective reading. It means what it means as the book that a community reads to give direction and order to its common life, hope to its common sorrow. The Bible demands that people live within its teasing and troubling narrative and try to make sense of it, or perhaps to let it make sense of them. The Bible should not be treated as, so to speak, a list of naked truths given on a take-it-or-leave-it basis. That is a rationalist parody (a trap into which many would-be orthodox Christians have fallen). In the same way, observation and reasoning never take place in a vacuum (unless you artificially create such an epistemological vacuum and demand that everyone live inside it).[14] When we observe the natural world, we are *involved observers*, trying to make sense at the same time of what that involvement might mean, including the question of what 'observation' itself consists of and how it affects the observers, in this case ourselves. This will then naturally involve a critical awareness of our own context, cultural encyclopaedia and so forth. So the idea of 'natural theology' as often imagined creates an artificial disjunction. It colludes with the trivial idea that scientific knowledge is somehow 'objective' and faith-knowledge is somehow 'subjective'. Things are more complex, and interesting, than that. This is where the theme of an epistemology of love would help, though there is no space here to develop that important notion.[15] [107]

Second, this false antithesis then gets bundled up with the regular antithesis between induction and deduction. Scientific knowledge is thought to be inductive, starting with raw data and working up without a big overarching narrative, whereas theological knowledge is supposed to be deductive, starting with divine revelation and working downwards. The western world has privileged the former ever since Descartes. Many theologians are currently hurrying back to the latter, looking for a 'perfect' vision of God from which everything else might be deduced. Both of these models are oversimplifications.[16] They have bedevilled the debate between exegesis and theology as well as between science and faith. It's time to think more clearly

---

14 For a dense and multifaceted description of the cultural, historical, experiential and epistemical factors involved in the shift of the default approach to the world for many people in the west, from an always already meaning-endowed cosmos to a physical world devoid of moral meanings, which requires our constructive efforts, see Taylor 2007, esp. 25–35.

15 For a short preliminary statement, see Wright 1999a, 134–52.

16 Cf. the discussion in Wright 2015b, 100–7.

about how all knowledge actually happens and to see the larger integration, held as I believe it must be within a Trinitarian (that is, Jesus-shaped and spirit-animated) ontology and expressed in an epistemology of love.[17]

At the heart of all this stands the story of Jesus. That has been the problem as well as the promise. How 'scientific' is history, not least the history of Jesus? But without knowing for sure about Jesus, how can any of this be anchored? What use might it be to say that looking at Jesus will give us the clue as to how creation, as well as new creation, came about or comes about, if 'looking at Jesus' turns out to be a complex series of 'ifs' and 'buts' in which all chance of historical knowledge seems to recede like a rainbow's end?

There are many problems, of course, about making any claim about past events. The practice of history is not like the practice of the so-called 'hard sciences', in that the experiment cannot be repeated. But there are nevertheless rules of procedure which correspond to scientific enquiry, namely the method of hypothesis and verification with the aim of getting in the data (in the historian's case the source material of whatever kind), doing so with appropriate simplicity or elegance, and shedding light on other areas.[18] History is, in other words, a form of *knowledge*, not merely of opinion.[19] Disputes continue both at the level of method and at the level of specific application to Jesus, as they would to the detailed interpretation of any figure of the past; some theologians may well worry about whether this leaves their Christology, and with it their whole [108] construction of the faith and, in our present case, their whole view of creation and new creation, without proper anchorage. It is incumbent on those who study Jesus as Christian historians both to present the history as what it is, a publicly available argument and narrative, and to insist that, despite the questions which attend all historical accounts, this is more than sufficient for Christian faith.[20]

One could say much more here, but that is for another occasion. I conclude with the following reflection.

Jesus himself, and the first Christians, used Psalm 8 as one of their key texts. The psalmist praises God for his wonderful name in all the world; then, looking at the moon and the stars, doesn't ask 'So who is God?' but 'So what is a "human being", what is "man", or the "son of man"?' That is the challenge and the clue: and the answer, reflecting Genesis, is that God

---

17 For further reflections on a hermeneutic of love, see Wright 1999a, 194–6.

18 See Wright 1992, 81–120.

19 Still helpful on this is Meyer 1979, 87–92 (see my remarks in the introduction to the 2nd edn., 2002).

20 My own major attempt in this direction is Wright 1996a (see n. 7 above).

has made humans in his image, a little lower than the angels, and crowned them with glory and honour, putting all things under their feet. The gospels and Paul link this with Psalms 2 and 110, and particularly with Daniel 7, and insist that this has come true in a new way in Jesus, and in his humiliation and exaltation.

In other words, if you want to know the meaning of creation, look at humans, but if you want to know the meaning of being human, look at Jesus. From Genesis 1 onwards, the story of humans is told as the focal point of the story of creation, just as from Genesis 12 onwards the story of Israel is told as the focal point of the story of humans; then, in the gospels, the story of Jesus is told as the focal point of the story of Israel, then also of humanity and therefore also of creation. We learn about creation, in other words, by reflecting on the claim that God made humans to stand at the metaphysical bridge, the dangerous interface between heaven and earth; and we learn what that human role itself meant when we reflect on Jesus himself, what he was, what he did and what he accomplished. When we look at new creation, we look back and reflect on the meaning of creation itself. When the New Testament says that 'all things were made through him', we don't start with a view of 'how God made the world' and insert Jesus into that. We start with Jesus himself, as I have tried to do in this essay, and we therefore reflect on creation itself not as a mechanistic or rationalistic event, process or 'fact', not as the blind operation of impersonal forces, but as the wise, generous outpouring of the [109] same creative love that we see throughout Jesus' kingdom-work, and supremely on the cross. This, I think, is part of what Paul meant when he wrote that 'He is the image of God, the invisible one, the firstborn of all creation' [Colossians 1.15]. This is why historical-Jesus work is so hard but also so necessary: necessary for understanding Christian origins, of course, but necessary too if we are to understand creation and new creation, and, indeed, our own place and vocation within that narrative. There is more to the theme of 'Christ and the Cosmos' than normally meets the eye.

22

Get the Story Right and the Models Will Fit: Victory through Substitution in 'Atonement Theology'

The meaning of Jesus' crucifixion has continued to be a storm centre, both in itself and as a central topic in the dialogue (more often implicit than explicit, alas) between exegetes and systematic theologians. I regard this as a classic example of later theologians trying to reassemble the bits and pieces of biblical reflection on a topic without fully grasping the narratives which the biblical writers had in their heads and hearts. My overall case, here as elsewhere, is that the different 'models' of atonement (and, indeed, of other topics) all reflect various themes which are found in the Bible, but that, by detatching them from the implicit narratives where they originally made sense, they then force them into apparent opposition rather than recognizing their underlying coherence. This paper thus follows on from *The Day the Revolution Began* (Wright 2016a), and reflects some of the discussions which have been stirred up by that book.

[112] It has become increasingly clear to me that in discussions between exegetes and theologians the latter regularly approach theological topics by means of the different 'models' which they see being explored. This at least has the benefit of allowing different emphases to be put on the table rather than trying to pretend that one of the 'models' is the 'correct' one and that all the others must be subsumed within it. But I frequently find myself reflecting that the 'model' which is absent from such discussions is the biblical one itself, which is always couched in terms of a *story*. I know that some theologians are allergic to this suggestion, but anyone who professes to regard the Bible as in some way the ultimate source, or even *an* ultimate source, for theological knowledge and understanding, cannot ignore the fact that the Bible – both the

Jewish Bible, in its way, and the Christian Bible, in its subtly different way – presents an overarching narrative which is more than simply a loose frame in which abstract theological teaching happens to be embedded. Israel's scriptures in themselves, and the Christian scriptures which (because of their view that Jesus was and is Israel's long-awaited Messiah) saw Israel's scriptures as the necessary foundation for the story they now had to tell, had to do with the creator God and his people, and with the story of creation and covenant which that involved. This is not an incidental framework. It is what the story is about.

Within that story, the question of 'atonement' has routinely loomed large. I have addressed this in various places over the years, particularly in a recent book [113] and one or two related articles.[1] The present essay continues the discussion, going beyond my earlier attempts not least by trying to integrate into the same picture the themes of Temple and cosmology which have occupied me more recently.[2]

Introduction: The Distorted Story

I begin with an analogy. When Albert Schweitzer, aged twenty-three, was studying the organ in Paris with Charles-Marie Widor in 1899 (between writing his first two books on Jesus, and for that matter between his first two hearings of Wagner's Ring Cycle at Bayreuth), Widor asked him to explain the Chorale Preludes of J. S. Bach.[3] Widor could play them, of course, but he didn't understand why Bach had written them or what they were really about. Schweitzer replied that this was because Widor and his French Catholic tradition didn't know the words of the Lutheran chorales for which these were the music, and Schweitzer illustrated the point by quoting the texts and translating them into French. Widor was fascinated, and asked Schweitzer to write a little essay explaining all this for other French pupils. Schweitzer did so – and the pamphlet grew into his famous two-volume work on Bach, which he published in 1904, between his second and third books on Jesus (and for that matter during his early medical studies). The reason Widor

---

1 See Wright 2016a; 'Redemption from the new perspective? Towards a multi-layered Pauline theology of the cross' and 'Reading Paul, thinking scripture: "atonement" as a special study' in Wright 2013c, chs. 19, 22.

2 See particularly my Gifford Lectures, *History and Eschatology: Jesus and the promise of natural theology* (Wright 2019a), ch. 5. I am grateful to Simon Dürr for his help in editing this essay for publication.

3 On Schweitzer and Wagner, see Wright 2019a, ch. 2. Widor himself tells the story of his conversation with Schweitzer in his Preface to the German edition (1908) of Schweitzer's two-volume book on Bach (in English translation, Schweitzer 1923 [1911], vii–xii). See too Oermann 2016, 46–59.

couldn't quite understand the Chorale Preludes was because he didn't know the words, the underlying narrative that made sense of the music.

My proposal in the present article is that something similar has happened within what we think of as western atonement-theology as a whole. We have forgotten the story that makes sense of the music. When we play the music, [114] repeating words like 'redemption', 'sacrifice', 'reconciliation' and, indeed, 'atonement' itself, we hear them (as speakers have already noted) as basically saying the same thing, reducing their specific content to the status of metaphors or models which can be explored or even played off against one another; distant and somewhat vague gestures to a single but fuzzy reality.

Actually, it's worse than that. The analogy doesn't go far enough. In the case of western atonement-theology, we are more in the position Widor would have been had some French theologian written different words to the chorale, words that didn't quite fit either metrically or theologically, thus making it look as though Bach hadn't quite written the right music. We have got the story wrong, and so have reduced its various themes to a miscellany of motifs or 'models' or metaphors.[4] While, of course, every language-field is planted thick with bushy metaphors, in biblical atonement-theology they mean what they mean within the story: the story to which they belong.

How does this work out? In *The Day the Revolution Began* I have outlined three wrong moves in the dominant western atonement-narrative. First, we have *Platonized our eschatology*; second, we have *moralized our anthropology*; third, we have *paganized our soteriology*.[5]

First, most western theology (and particularly popular preaching) has taught that we humans have souls which are exiled from their true home, which is heaven, and that we are looking forward to going back there one day, leaving behind this shabby and shadowy old world. But in the first century this is precisely the teaching of the Middle Platonist Plutarch; not of Jesus, or Paul, or the early Christians.[6] The early Christians were robust creational monotheists who, like the Psalms and Isaiah, were looking for the renewal, not the abandonment, of heaven and earth.[7]

Second, if our 'souls' are the key thing, and getting them into heaven the key challenge, the problem is sin. This is not to say that 'sin' is unimportant. But western theology both in the academy and the church has moralized our

---

4   See Wright 2016a, 93f.

5   Wright 2016a: eschatology, 28–34; moralizing, 74–87; paganized soteriology, 38–46; summarized at e.g. 94.

6   See e.g. Plutarch, *On Exile* 607A–F.

7   See Wright 2013b, ch. 9.

anthropology, supposing that the *only* thing that matters is whether or not we have kept the rules (or, if not, how we can get round the problem). The early Christians, however, retrieving all sorts of bits of classic Israelite thinking, saw the human vocation as far more than merely rule-keeping. Being made 'in the image of [115] God' had to do with the purpose for which humans were made, which cannot be reduced to 'fellowship with God', vital though that remains. The 'rules' matter; the 'role' matters far more. The creator had a purpose for his whole creation, and image-bearing humans had a vital part to play within that creation.

Third, if the problem is getting sinful souls into heaven, the solution has been to take certain key passages, particularly in Paul, and to construct from them a form of penal substitution in which God so hated the world that he killed Jesus. No preacher ever says it like that, of course, but that is what many generations, of Catholics as well as Protestants, have heard; and many have rejected it. Once more it is important not to misunderstand. There *is* such a thing as a biblical doctrine of penal substitution. I'll come to that. But it doesn't function within that narrative, and the key texts normally invoked in its support do not say exactly what the theory demands. (A good example would be Galatians 3.10–14, where Paul doesn't say that Christ became a curse for us to free us from the guilt, penalty and power of sin but that he became a curse so that the blessing of Abraham might come on the gentiles and that 'we' – Jewish Jesus-believers, it seems – might receive the promised spirit through faith.[8]) We have forgotten the true biblical story; we have substituted a different (albeit distantly related) story instead; and we have then had to cope with the key strands in the true story collapsing into a disparate little heap of models or themes, all appearing to be imprecise ways of saying the same thing, that sinners can go to heaven after all.

I Contours of the Biblical Narrative

The Unfinished Project

So what is the true story? No doubt we all have our own ways of answering that question; here is mine. There are five interlocking strands to this narrative, which then set the scene for what I take to be the New Testament's theological portrayal of the significance of Jesus' death. There are, of course, many differences of emphases and imagery, particularly relating to this

---

8   See the discussions in Wright 2013b, 863–8 and elsewhere.

theme, among the early Christian writings. The narrative strands I present here underlie not only the Pauline letters but also, in various different ways, all four gospels. This seems to be a good start. The exercise I am undertaking here is a form of 'biblical theology', though that phrase means many different things to many different people.[9] My [116] construct here depends at every point on the detailed exegesis of many texts which I have offered elsewhere and now am pulling together as best I can into a larger picture. This is an explicitly Jesus-based reading of Israel's scriptures, following the New Testament writers in their retrieval of many ancient themes, some of which were prominent in some second-Temple circles and some of which – so far as our evidence allows – seem not to have been.

It should be noted that I am not saying that 'all Jews of the time' believed this or that.[10] Rather, the story the early Christians tell is emphatically a story of *how the creation-project was reaching its goal*. It is, to repeat, the story of creational monotheism: of how the good and wise creator God made a world, how this God made it to work and move forward in a particular way, namely through the work of his image-bearing humans, and how this project, through tragically derailed by human non-cooperation, was to be put back on track.[11] The Psalms, and many passages in Isaiah, speak not of humans rescued from creation but of creation itself restored, often under the rule of the ultimate human being, the Davidic king.[12] The puzzle that the early Christians thought had been solved by the events concerning Jesus, including centrally though not exclusively his death, was the puzzle of how the divine project would reach its goal.

The Unquiet Sea

This puzzle was given depth, in Israel's scriptures, by a second theme, going back all the way to Genesis 1 verse 2 but emerging in the Psalms, Isaiah and notoriously Daniel 7: *the unquiet sea*.[13] Woven into many biblical texts is a theme familiar from wider cultures: that within creation as it stands, albeit for Genesis 1 tamed by the creator's act of making heaven and earth, there

---

9   See e.g. Hafemann 2002.

10 I have sketched something of the diversity of Jewish views in the period in Wright 1992, Part III. It is now commonplace to make sharp distinctions between the contexts and contents of different Jewish traditions, e.g. Ben-Sirach from Qumran, *4 Ezra* from the rabbis, etc.

11 See Gen. 1.26–28; Ps. 8; for a study of 'image' in its ancient context, see e.g. Middleton 2005; in the first-century Jewish world, van Kooten 2008, 1–91.

12 See e.g. Pss. 2; 72; 89; 96; 98; Isa. 11.1–10; 35; 55.12–13; 65—66.

13 See, for a start, Alster 1999.

is a dark, wild force of chaos that might threaten to destroy it all – and that, indeed, under severe provocation in Noah's day, was used by the creator himself to destroy all but [117] a tiny remnant.[14] The question of responsibility, as between Adam, Eve and the serpent, is not resolved; all are implicated. The ancient world, whether of Moses' day or Jesus' day, doesn't seem to have had very good language for the dark forces of evil and chaos, any more than we do. But to suggest that such ideas are therefore outdated or dispensable is dangerously naive. Jesus, making the vindication of the 'son of man' thematic for his own vocation, certainly saw the dark powers, operating through political powers but not reducible to them alone, as a vital element in a cosmos yet to be rescued.[15] Paul saw the present creation as still enslaved to corruption and decay.[16] He used language for its coming liberation which borrows rather obviously from the foundational narrative of Passover and exodus, to which I shall soon return. This ties together my first two strands of forgotten narrative: as at the Red Sea, when the chaos-monsters thwart the creator's purposes by enslaving and destroying his creation, they will themselves be defeated and destroyed. Once we put the creator's purpose at the top of the narrative line, though we must recognize the vital positive role humans are called to play as image-bearers within that purpose, we must fully take into account the role of the powers of chaos. When Jesus, in the parable, says 'an enemy has done this', he is gesturing towards the same overall theme.[17]

The Idolatrous Humans

Once we have done this, however, human responsibility comes back with a bang. But the human failure cannot be reduced simply to 'sin', as though the point of Genesis 1 and 2 were that the creator was setting humans a moral examination to see if they were fit for his presence or if he would have to kill them after all. No: the point, again, is *image-bearing*, which I like others have expounded in terms of the 'royal priesthood': humans are to reflect the wise stewardship of the creator into his world, and they are to do this not least by summing up the worship of all creation.[18] The 'image' is like an angled mirror; not simply reflecting the creator back to the creator, but reflecting

---

14 Gen. 7.7.

15 On the question of the 'powers' in relation to human vocation, see Wright 2016a, ch. 4. For Jesus' view, see e.g. Lk. 10.18; 22.53.

16 Rom. 8.19–22.

17 Mt. 13.28.

18 The 'royal priesthood' is reflected explicitly in Ex. 19.6; 1 Pet. 2.9; Rev. 1.6; 5.10. One might compare the royal motif in Rom. 5.21.

God into the world and the world, in [118] worship, back to God.[19] The human problem is then to be seen in terms, not simply of moral failure, but of *idolatry*. If you worship anything other than the one true God, your image-bearing humanness will deconstruct, and will drag down with it all those bits of the world into which you ought to be reflecting God's love and creative purposes but into which you will reflect instead whatever aspect of creation you have chosen as your alternative object of worship.[20] *Hinc illae lacrimae*, as Terence put it.[21] Idolatry results directly in sin; or, if you like, sin is the outward and visible sign of the inward and spiritual false worship. That is the ultimate human problem to which the gospel, if it is to be gospel, must be the solution. But we must never forget that the problem about dysfunctional humans isn't just that they are in danger of self-destruction. The problem is that humans were assigned a central role in God's purposes for creation. The purpose of putting humans right is so that, as restored image-bearers, they can take up that vocation once more.

The Unrealized Hope

The combination of the dark forces of chaos and human idolatry means that not only is the creational project unfinished; the hope at its heart remains unrealized. As many writers have stressed, Genesis 1 echoes the theme of Temple-building, reaching its climax with the insertion into this new heaven-and-earth reality of the 'image' of the creator; and, when all is done, God comes to dwell in this new 'house', to take his rest, his ease, in the house which he has built and which he wishes to share with his human creatures. I have explored this theme at much more length, noting its turns and twists and the range of scholarship that has taken different sides on the relevant issues, in the fifth chapter of *History and Eschatology*. Rather than repeat the arguments, I am here cutting long corners and will simply say that I see an initial narrative arc running from Genesis 1 to Exodus 40: with the construction of the tabernacle, a small working-model of heaven and earth has come into being, with Aaron the priest standing in for the purpose of the exodus. It is a sign of the creator's intention for [119] the whole cosmos; Israel is to be the bearer of this purpose. One might think, reading Moses' repeated request to Pharaoh that he should let the Israelites go so that they

---

19 I first employed this image in my interpretation of 2 Cor. 3.18: see Wright 1991, 185.

20 G. K. Beale explores this theme in Beale 2008.

21 Cf. *Andria* 126, though the text there reads *lacrumae*; in allusions to this by Cicero (*Pro Caelio* 61.12) and Horace (*Epistulae* 1.19.41) it is spelled *lacrimae*.

might serve their God in the desert, that this was just a ruse, covering up the ultimate intention, which was to reach the promised land.[22] But the purpose seems to be, rather, rooted in the belief that Israel would not be able to worship the covenant God in Egypt, a country full of idolatry and – as it later appeared, for instance in some psalms – guarded by the watery chaos-monster in the form of the Red Sea, which had to be overcome by superior divine force before Israel could escape.[23] Likewise, if one reads through the book of Exodus quickly, it is easy to feel that the story runs out of steam after chapter 20 (with the giving of Torah). But the detailed commandments in the chapters immediately following constitute only a momentary pause. It soon becomes clear that the purpose of the plagues in Egypt, of Passover itself, of freeing the slaves, of overcoming the Red Sea, and even of giving Torah, was to prepare Israel to be the 'tent-bearers', the people in whose midst the living God would come to dwell. And if that was to become a reality, there would need to be a stringent theological health-and-safety code, which is what Leviticus then supplies. (As it turned out, of course, the making of the golden calf in Exodus 32 meant a further hiatus, after which, as a compromise, the tabernacle was placed, not in the middle of the camp, but just outside the gate.)

But this purpose – for God to dwell in the midst of his people, or at least alongside them – is more complicated than just setting up the taber-nacle and watching it be filled with the glorious divine presence. Whoever edited the Pentateuch was, we assume, very much aware that the golden calf had been just the start of a long history of rebellion on Israel's part. Deuteronomy, particularly chapters 28, 29 and 32, says just this. Despite great and glorious days, particularly under David and Solomon, and particularly with Solomon's Temple, the tabernacle's replacement, similarly filled with glory (1 Kings 8), Israel had failed again and again, from David's adultery to Solomon's corrupted heart to the calves at Bethel and Dan, to the multiple idolatries even in the Temple itself, as in the great indictment in Ezekiel 8. Exile was a new slavery, requiring a new exodus. And as Ezekiel insists, in parallel with Isaiah 40 and 52, and picked up by Zechariah and Malachi even after the return from Babylon, the new exodus, the real return from exile, would not have happened, would not be complete, however much the Temple might be cleansed by the Maccabees or [120] rebuilt by Herod, until Israel's God returned in power and glory, with Jerusalem's watchmen shouting with

---

22   On the request, see Ex. 3.12; 4.23; 7.16, 26; 8.16; 9.1, 13; 10.3, 7, 8, 11, 24, 26; 12.31. See too Ex. 20.5.
23   E.g. Pss. 77.16, 19; 106.9; 114.3, 5; Isa. 43.16; 51.9–11. For the story: Ex. 14.21f.; 15.7f.

joy and all enemies being put to flight.[24] The theme of the divine return to Zion has been downplayed or even ignored in much scholarship, and I think it's time to put it back where it belongs. I have become increasingly convinced that it is central to New Testament Christology.[25] I believe it is also vital for both eschatology and (our present theme) 'atonement'-theology itself. The New Testament writers, in different ways, tell the story of Jesus' crucifixion as the story of how Israel's God came back in person to do for Israel and the world what Israel and the world could not do for themselves. Up to that point, so Jesus' followers believed, the hope had remained unrealized.

The Unkept Covenant

All this was taken by many to indicate that the covenant God had made with Abraham, the promises of family and land, remained unkept on Israel's side and therefore unfulfilled on God's side. We may assume that almost all first-century Jews, except perhaps the Sadducees, would have agreed on this point. In particular, some of the great promises of an extension to the family and the land – we may think of psalms like 2 and 72, where the 'inheritance' is spread out widely to reach to the ends of the earth, or Psalm 87, where the other great nations are included in the divine blessing, or 47, where the princes of the people are joined to the people of the God of Abraham – had likewise remained unfulfilled. There was no Davidic king ruling over the world from a high throne in Jerusalem. There is a reason why Jesus, using the shepherd-imagery associated with royalty, said cryptically that all who came before him were thieves and brigands.[26] So much the worse, his hearers might have thought, for the Maccabees,[27] for the Hasmoneans and for the Herodians. Jesus has in mind a different kind of victory, one which will fulfil Psalm 2 at last: when the Greeks come to the feast and ask to see him, he declares (John 12.23) that now is the time for the son of man to be glorified; that now is the moment of victory when 'this world's ruler' is to be cast out (12.31), so that then he, Jesus, [121] will draw all people to himself. At the centre of John's theology of the cross is the victory through which the dark power is overthrown and the nations of the world are summoned to give allegiance to Israel's Messiah. John's reader knows that this is because he

---

24 See e.g. Isa. 40.3–11; 52.7–12; Ezek. 43; Zech. 1.16f.; 8.3; Mal. 3.1. For the larger issue of an extended 'exile' and a long-awaited 'return', see now Scott 2017.

25 See Wright 2013b, ch. 9.

26 Jn. 10.1, 8.

27 The Maccabees will have been in mind in Jn. 10 because the scene is dated to Hanukkah (10.23).

is the Word made flesh, the new and ultimate 'tabernacle' where the divine glory is displayed at last (1.14).

These five narrative strands – the unfinished project of creation, the unquiet sea which is the source of chaos and all evils that lead to it, the idolatrous humans who have failed as image-bearers, the unrealized hope of the creator coming to dwell in the midst of his people, and the unkept covenant which meant that the promises associated with Abraham and David had yet to be realized – these strands are brought together in many rich and mutually illuminating ways as the New Testament writers tell, or allude to, or evoke, the story of Jesus and particularly his death.

2 Contours of Jesus' Saving Death

Jesus' Chosen Symbol

As is well known, the New Testament and the Christian tradition developed many ways of speaking about the meaning and effects of Jesus' death. It is equally common knowledge that, unlike doctrines such as the Trinity and Incarnation, the 'atonement' (as some though not all Christians refer to it) has never officially been defined – until, that is, the sixteenth-century controversies made it important for various protestant groups to do so. Among many reasons for this there is one which sometimes gets overlooked, and which I wish to highlight: that the central point of it all for Jesus was not a *theory* but an *action*. When Jesus wanted to explain to his disciples what his forthcoming death was all about, he didn't give them a set of ideas. He gave them a meal. And the meal is more than a mere visual aid, because the reality to which it points (and in which it partakes rather as the grapes brought back from the promised land in Numbers 13 partook of the reality which they symbolized) is not a set of true beliefs or – back to Plato again! – an abstract 'spiritual' reality. The reality to which the eucharistic bread and wine point is the reality of *new creation*, creation set free from its slavery to decay.

This is where the Platonizing of our eschatology has led not only to bad atonement-theology but to the twin dangers of rationalism (imagining that being Christian is a matter of figuring out and then believing a true set of ideas) and romanticism (supposing that being a Christian is about people [122] having their hearts strangely warmed). I have nothing against figuring out true ideas; and I am certainly in favour of the strange warming of the heart. But in the New Testament these are in service to the larger goal of new creation, the new creation that is launched in the resurrection of Jesus

349

after the defeat of all hostile powers, including death itself. This new creation will finally include the resurrection of all Jesus' people. In the meantime, it already includes their revivification by the power of the spirit.

But this is to run somewhat ahead of ourselves. We may display the point in a sequence of three further features of the New Testament, before then summing it up in five complex but coherent propositions which correspond to the puzzles of my earlier section.

Jesus Chose Passover as the Kingdom-Moment

First, Jesus chose Passover to do what had to be done. He did not choose the Day of Atonement. It is striking, indeed, that though the gospels, particularly John, mention many of the Jewish holy days, Yom Kippur is conspicuously absent. This relates to something my colleague David Moffitt has stressed in various places: when in the grip of exile – as many Jews believed they still were – what is required is not another regular sacrifice, but a fresh rescuing divine action. And the obvious model for that is not the Day of Atonement but the rescue from Egypt: Passover, in other words.

For Jesus, the final Passover was the kingdom-moment, the royal moment par excellence. Remarkably, the four gospels are normally all but ignored in discussions of 'atonement', precisely because they don't fit the normal, and I have suggested inappropriate, narrative that western theology has wanted to tell. They are simply not about how sinful souls go to heaven when they die – though some people still try to squash them into that thoroughly inappropriate mould. They are about God's kingdom coming on earth as in heaven. Here we meet the well-known problem, which I have seen all over the place in church life as well as theology: what has Jesus' kingdom-proclamation got to do with his cross, and vice versa? In the gospels, the two are intricately bound up together. If that is hard for us to grasp, it shows how deeply we have misread the whole tradition. God's kingdom (according to Isaiah 52 and many psalms, and also, of course, Daniel, which are all invoked in this sense in the New Testament) means that God is returning at last to take charge, to put things right, to make all things new. As we might have anticipated, the gospels tell the story of how, when Jesus announced God's kingdom, at once the forces of chaos seemed to strike back: shrieking demons in the synagogue, plotting [123] Pharisees in the cornfields, malicious accusations from detractors, malevolent despots in the background, treachery among his own followers, and finally the symbolic and actual power of Rome. The gospels describe how, after his initial victory over the satan, Jesus drew all these strands of evil on to himself in order to exhaust them in his own death.

The dominant note of the gospels at this point is that of victory. That is where you arrive if you take the gospels' kingdom-theme seriously all the way to the cross. That is why, when I have highlighted it, those who see things through the lens of Gustav Aulén's famous book assume that I am playing his game, which is to oppose a supposed *Christus Victor* motif to that of 'substitution' or some equivalent.[28] That, I might add, is exactly the same spurious theological either/or as the one advanced by J. Louis Martyn and his followers; but I have dealt with that elsewhere.[29] The point is that, for the gospel-writers, the cross is seen as the moment when Israel's God, in and through the Emmanuel, the Word made flesh, wins the victory over all the forces of evil. This victory does not mean that saved souls can now ascend to a Platonic heaven. It means that new creation can at last be launched.

The means by which the victory is won (as indicated in the subtitle to this paper) is through substitution: through Jesus *taking the place of sinners*, dying in their stead. This is woven into the gospel narratives at point after point, without any statement of a grand theory but simply in the course of events. Jesus identifies with the tax-collectors and sinners; he is betrayed; he is handed over to sinners.[30] Barabbas is guilty, but Jesus dies in his place.[31] The brigands crucified beside him are guilty, but he has done nothing wrong.[32] He was officially condemned, but he was in fact innocent.[33] Thus, whether on the large scale – where Jesus as Messiah stands in for Israel, and hence (because of Israel's representative status in God's purposes) for the world – or on the small scale, with individual moments, the point is rammed home by all four gospels. It is not *either* 'victory' *or* 'substitution'. The victory is won by Jesus dying the death of the unrighteous.

How does this 'work' theologically? When you worship an idol, you give **[124]** that idol power over you; and the idol's grip is tightened by the sin which you commit as a result. Thus, if God is to win the victory over the idols that have usurped his rightful rule over his creation, he must deal with the human sins through which the idols consolidate and maintain their power. *Victory through substitution* is thus the name of the game; just as substitution itself is based on Jesus' representative Messiahship, as he stands in for Israel and thence for the whole world. That is how Jesus' Passover-project,

---

28 Aulén 1967 [1931].

29 See Wright 2015a, 135–218.

30 E.g. Lk. 5.30; 7.34; Mk. 14.41; Lk. 24.7.

31 Mk. 15.6–15 and parallels.

32 Lk. 23.39–43.

33 Lk. 23.47.

his kingdom-project, is implemented. All this, of course, needs much more filling in, as I've tried to do in *The Day the Revolution Began*; but this must suffice for now.

Paul Saw Jesus' Death as the Defeat of the Powers through Messianic Substitution

The second point about the New Testament is that for Paul all the lines of gospel narrative run through the cross, but those lines can by no means be reduced to the normal formulae of protestant dogma or preaching. We are not talking about how sinful souls go to heaven. Again and again – not least in Galatians 3 which I mentioned before – the death of Jesus is for Paul the means by which the divine purposes for the world can go forward. Abraham's promise-bearing family were stuck in the Deuteronomic curse because of sin, so that the promise could not get out to the nations; now, with the curse borne, the gentiles can come in. This applies particularly to the great scene in Galatians 2, with Paul's confrontation with Peter at Antioch. Perhaps the main reason why Jews wouldn't share table-fellowship with gentiles was because all pagans were assumed to be fatally tainted with idolatry.[34] But Paul insists that with the death of the Messiah the grip of the pagan idols has been broken. When someone is in the Messiah, as evidenced by faith, then he or she can and must be treated as a full member of the messianic family, because the Messiah's death has dealt precisely with the power of the idols. Not to welcome gentile Jesus-believers is thus to deny the victory of the cross.

So too, in 2 Corinthians 5.21, Paul's famous statement about God making the Messiah to be sin is part of his long discussion of his own apostolic ministry, which had been challenged by the Corinthians. Paul applies to himself what he would say of every Christian, that God made the Messiah, who knew no sin, to be sin for us; but the specific purpose is not the normal forensic one of protestant dogma (that we might have something called 'the righteousness of God' imputed to us), but rather that we – apostles in particular, though [125] no doubt others as well if we'd asked Paul that – might *embody* the divine covenant faithfulness. That is why he goes on at once to quote Isaiah 49, where the servant is given as the covenant to the peoples. The death of Jesus wins the victory that enables the gospel to go out and fulfil the Isaianic as well as the Abrahamic promises.[35]

---

34 Cf. e.g. *Jub*. 22.16–17.

35 See the discussion of the passage, with other references, in Wright 2013b, 881–5.

We could follow this up in Romans in particular, where the cultic imagery of Romans 3, with the glory and the mercy-seat, needs to be brought to the fore instead of being displaced by the heavy-handed post-Anselmic attempts at an imputed legalism.[36] And in Romans 8 we find, at last, the true location of something we can properly call 'penal substitution', where there is 'no condemnation for those in Messiah Jesus', since God has, on the cross, condemned sin in the flesh of the Messiah, so that the spirit may do in and through the Messiah's people the life-giving work which the law had all along wanted to do but could not.

That is the point, too – though there is no space here to develop this – where Paul gives his own version of the narrative of the gospels. Torah was given, he says in Romans 5 and develops in Romans 7, in order 'that sin might be exceedingly sinful': in other words, Torah was given paradoxically in order to draw 'sin', the dark power that had enslaved the world, on to the one place, the single spot, where it could at last be condemned. Sin did its worst in Israel, in the idolatry and rebellion even among those who officially delighted in Torah, leading to the extended exile of Deuteronomy and Daniel, alluded to here in the image of imprisonment.[37] But this was all in the service of the divine purpose in which the Messiah would come, as the focal point of Israel, to take on himself the weight of Israel's rebellion and with it the idolatry and catastrophe of the whole human race. That is the overall argument of Romans 7 and 8, summed up densely already in Romans 5.20–21.[38]

All this, once more, is in the service, not of a Platonic gospel in which souls make their way to heaven, but of the biblical gospel in which the new-Temple people (those in whom the spirit dwells) are on their way to the 'promised in-[126]-heritance' that is now the whole redeemed creation. The spirit here plays the role of the glorious divine presence in the exodus-narrative. The whole world is now God's holy land; Romans 8 celebrates the paradoxical arrival, through suffering and prayer, of the long-awaited kingdom of God on earth as in heaven. There is no time to look wider, except to note that in the climactic passage in 1 Corinthians 15.20–28 Paul offers his own 'apocalyptic' scenario of the divine victory, through the Messiah, over all forces of evil, in

36 See Wright 2016c.

37 See Rom. 7.23: the root *aichmalōtizein* resonates with the regular term for 'exile', particularly that in Babylon, in e.g. Pss. 13.7; 125.1 (both LXX); Neh. 1.2f. [= 2 Esdr. 11.2f.]; Jer. 1.3; Ezek. 1.1f.; 3.11, 15.

38 I have discussed this in considerable detail in various places, including my commentary on Romans in *The New Interpreter's Bible*, vol. 10 (Wright 2002b).

order that, exactly in line with scriptural promise, the cosmic Temple might be filled with divine presence: so that God may be 'all in all'.[39]

Thus, exactly as in the gospels, Paul holds together what many have wanted to split apart. The Messiah, he says at the start of what I take to be his earliest letter, 'gave himself for our sins in order to set us free from the present evil age'.[40] Victory through substitution. These are not alternative models or schemes, though people have tried to make them so. They are interlocking features of the one story.

Revelation Highlights the Victory of the Lamb

The third point, more briefly, is found in Revelation. There, as in John's gospel (1.29, 36), Jesus is the lamb who was slain (Revelation 5.11). That Passover-motif resonates through much of the complex symbolic narrative, as the plagues mirror those in Egypt, as the monster comes up out of the sea but is defeated, as the people sing the song of Moses and the 'lamb', and as – the equivalent of Exodus 40! – the new Jerusalem comes down from heaven as a bride adorned for her husband.[41] The dimensions of the new Jerusalem mark it out as the great Holy of Holies in a new creation which, holding heaven and earth together, is the new Temple itself.[42] There is no more sea, because in the new creation there is no threat of a resurgent evil. There is no snake in the garden city. And all is achieved through the victory of the lamb: the scene in chapter 5 says it all. The creator's purposes, the scroll waiting to be unrolled, cannot be taken forward because no human is capable of it – except the lamb himself, and then only by virtue of his victorious death. But with that death humans are rescued from their plight of sin and death, not so that they may 'go to heaven', but so that, when heaven comes to earth, and even in advance of that ultimate promised reality, they may be the 'royal priesthood', the kings and priests in the new Temple, the genuine humans in the ultimate heaven-and-earth creation. [127]

3 The Cross in Its Narrative Framework

We may now draw the threads together in five propositions, working back up the five points with which I began and showing how the different 'models' or

---

39   1 Cor. 15.28.

40   Gal. 1.4.

41   Rev. 8—9 (plagues); 13 (beast); 15.3–4 (song); 21.1–5 (new Jerusalem).

42   See e.g. Beale 1999, 1075f.

'metaphors' or 'images' cohere within the larger narrative framework we find in the New Testament – but only once we give up the Platonic hope, and the false trains of thought into which it has led us.

Covenant Renewed

First, the covenant has been renewed. Jesus' words at the Last Supper, however tricky they are to reconstruct exactly, are clearly meant to carry the connotations, within the carefully staged quasi-Passover celebration, of Moses' inauguration of the original covenant and Jeremiah's prophecy of its renewal. The creator God has been faithful to his promises to Abraham and David. That faithfulness, embodied in the faithfulness of the Messiah, becomes the badge which distinguishes the Messiah's people, whatever their ancestry. *God is faithful to the covenant, renewing it through Jesus' death and resurrection and the gift of the spirit, so that those who come to belong to the renewed family may be faithful stewards of the covenant purposes.*

Hope Realized

Second, what Paul calls 'the hope of the glory of God' has been realized. That hope, as in Isaiah 40 and 52, was for the divine glory to return to Zion in public, visible, redeeming action. That action, in Isaiah 40—55, was focused poetically and theologically on the work of the 'servant', which, when complete, issued precisely in the renewal of the covenant (Isaiah 54) and the renewal of creation (Isaiah 55). All four gospels, albeit in very different ways, indicate clearly that they see Jesus as the fulfilment of this hope for the victorious and liberating return of Israel's God.[43] Paul develops the same point in various ways. Thus, as in Exodus, God always intended to dwell with his people, and he does this in Jesus, the Emmanuel, the Word who tabernacles in the midst but who, like the original tabernacle, is placed outside the camp.[44] If the God of life is to dwell with humans, this can [128] only be through the removal of the pollution which would prevent his being there, and the New Testament, at precisely this point in the argument, draws on Israel's sacrificial traditions to explain how that has now happened. I did not develop the sacrificial theme in *The Day the Revolution Began*, but this is where I think it belongs. *God intends to dwell with his people, and he does this in and as Jesus the Emmanuel, thereby also dealing with the problem of*

---

43   See Hays 2016; and my discussion in Wright 2017.
44   Mt. 1.23 (Emmanuel); Heb. 13.12 (outside the camp).

pollution; he now dwells in his people by his spirit so that they can be both the foretaste and the agents of his plan to fill the whole creation with his glory.

The Royal Priesthood

Third, formerly idolatrous humans are transformed by the gospel into the 'royal priesthood' – the ancient Israelite designation of God's people, indicating their vocation to be genuine humans, image-bearers, idolaters no longer. It is striking that in Revelation 5 this is seen as the aim and the result of the lamb's victorious death: 'You were slaughtered and with your own blood you purchased a people for God, from every tribe and tongue, from every people and nation and made them a kingdom and priests to our God and they will reign on the earth.'[45] As such, the ransomed – the people of the new exodus, in other words – are to be people of prayer and worship, as well as people who bear witness to the gospel with their own suffering and testimony. Their worship, exactly in line with the democratization of the sacrificial system which was taking place in the Jewish world already in the synagogue communities and then much more after the destruction of the Temple, was expressed in sacrificial terms, as in Hebrews 13 or Romans 12. No doubt this sounded strange to pagan neighbours for whom life without animal sacrifice was unusual to say the least. And to get to this point these renewed humans must be liberated from the sins because of which they have been in thrall to the idols they have worshipped, a situation which has allowed the idols to gain a wrongful power not only *over* them but *through* them in the wider world. That is where all the usual questions about God dealing with human sin on the cross come in, as I have already indicated. But as in Revelation, so in Paul and the gospels, sinners are forgiven not simply so that they can 'go to heaven' or have 'restored fellowship with God', but so that they can be part of his ongoing purposes as genuine humans. Thus in Romans 8 sinners are to be 'glorified' in the sense of Psalm 8, that is, set in authority over the world and thereby renewing it into its original purpose.[46] And in the resurrection narratives in the gospels, particu-[129]-larly in Luke and John, the result of Jesus' crucifixion and resurrection is that the disciples are commissioned to be for the world what Jesus was for Israel.[47] *God intends to work, as from the start, through obedient, worshipping, image-bearing*

---

45 Rev. 5.9–10.

46 See Jacob 2018, esp. 233–51.

47 See esp. Jn. 20.19–23, focusing on v. 21: 'As the father has sent me, so I'm sending you.'

humans; so he deals with their sin to liberate them from idols and set them free for his service once more.

No More Sea

The last two points can be made more briefly. Fourth, in the new creation there is 'no more sea'; that is, no more dark chaos-monster threatening to rise up again and attack the fulfilled new creation.[48] Once sins are dealt with, the idols have lost their power. *God intends to overthrow the power of chaos and evil, in order to establish the new world as the ultimate 'house' where he will live. He does this in the death of Jesus, establishing his new house through the resurrection and the spirit. Now, in the lives of those who believe, he defeats chaos and evil through their mortification, suffering and obedience, so that they may be part of his defeating-evil plan for the world.*

New Heavens, New Earth

Fifth and finally, God has always intended to put the world right. This is what is meant by 'justice' or 'justification'; in the Psalms and Isaiah the 'justice' of God is God's determination, like a good judge, to put right what has gone wrong. But this is far wider than simply the 'putting right' or 'justification' of individuals, though that remains vital.[49] We could say it like this: *God intends to put the whole world right at last; he accomplished this through the death and resurrection of Jesus, and will complete it at Jesus' return; and, in the meantime, he puts people right through the gospel and spirit, so that they can themselves be part of his putting-right project for the world.*

Conclusion

Thus at every point the larger, more complex but still rigorously coherent biblical narrative finds its dramatic focus on the crucifixion of Jesus. Once that is put at the centre, however, it works its way out into the areas of creation and **[130]** new creation, covenant and renewed covenant, the defeat and overthrow of evil, the rescue of idolaters from the grip and consequence of their sin, and the establishment of the new heaven and new earth in which 'the dwelling of God is with humans'. That, after all, is the ultimate biblical goal, and it is brought about by the victory of the lamb. The final scene in the Bible is not of saved souls going up to heaven – that would make no sense in

---

48 Rev. 21.1.
49 See Wright 2013b, ch. 10.

terms of Israel's scriptures, either – but of God's kingship expressed in his rescuing sovereignty, of the great cosmic Holy of Holies established 'on earth as in heaven'. The narrative arc from Genesis 1 to Exodus 40 is the foretaste of the larger arc that reaches all the way to Revelation 21. And in the centre, presented in the New Testament as the shocking but authentic fulfilment of the scriptures of Israel, is Israel's Messiah doing what (according to Psalm 72) Israel's king should do – rescuing the helpless, so that the world might be filled with the glory of God. The early Christians, then, were not merely ransacking miscellaneous metaphors or models, throwing random items like the lawcourt, the slave-market, human relationships and the sacrificial cult into a melting-pot where they would all end up meaning more or less the same thing. They were reflecting the coherent interlocking themes of the biblical narrative and affirming their fulfilment in Jesus and the spirit. If we get the story right, the models will fit.

Ironically perhaps, the word 'atonement' has not featured very much in this presentation. It has become, as has often been said, too awkwardly polyvalent, too redolent of narratives that have slipped their biblical moorings and drifted off on other philosophical or cultural tides. But if we may use the word heuristically, so that 'atonement' in a Christian context simply means 'what the death of Jesus achieves so that the creator's purposes may be accomplished through the rescue of humans', then it should be clear that this essay has been about nothing else. Perhaps the best reason for not defining what we mean by 'atonement' in one quick formula is that, when rightly understood, the word points to the entire biblical narrative, without losing the centrality of the cross; it points, too, to the real world, the world of creation renewed; of flesh and blood, of laughter and tears, of bread and wine.

Bibliography

Adams, E. 1997. 'Abraham's faith and gentile disobedience: textual links between Romans 1 and 4.' *Journal for the Study of the New Testament* 65:47–66.

Allison, D. C. Jr. 1998. *Jesus of Nazareth: Millenarian prophet.* Minneapolis, MN: Fortress Press.

Alster, B. 1999. 'Tiamat.' Pages 867–9 in *Dictionary of Deities and Demons,* ed. K. van der Toorn. 2nd edn. Leiden: Brill.

Aulén, G. 1967 [1931]. *Christus Victor: An historical study of the three main types of the idea of atonement.* London: Macmillan.

Barclay, J. M. G. 1996. *Jews in the Mediterranean Diaspora: From Alexander to Trajan (323 BCE – 117 CE).* Edinburgh: T&T Clark.

Barth, K. 1933. *The Epistle to the Romans,* tr. E. C. Hoskyns. London: Oxford University Press. Translation of Barth, Karl. 1921. *Der Römerbrief.* 2nd edn. Zollikon-Zürich: Evangelischer Verlag.

Bauckham, R. J., ed. 1998. *The Gospels for All Christians: Rethinking the gospel audiences.* Grand Rapids, MI: Eerdmans.

——. 2006. *Jesus and the Eyewitnesses: The gospels as eyewitness testimony.* Grand Rapids, MI: Eerdmans.

——. 2009. *Jesus and the God of Israel: 'God Crucified' and other studies on the New Testament's Christology of divine identity.* Grand Rapids, MI: Eerdmans.

Beale, G. K. 1999. *The Book of Revelation: A commentary on the Greek text.* Grand Rapids, MI: Eerdmans.

——. 2004. *The Temple and the Church's Mission: A biblical theology of the dwelling place of God.* Downers Grove, IL: InterVarsity Press.

——. 2008. *We Become What We Worship: A biblical theology of idolatry.* Downers Grove, IL: IVP Academic.

Beckwith, R. T. 1996. *Calendar and Chronology, Jewish and Christian: Biblical, intertestamental and patristic studies.* Leiden: Brill.

Beker, J. C. 1987. *Paul the Apostle: The triumph of God in life and thought.* Philadelphia, PA: Fortress Press.

Bockmuehl, M. 2006. *Seeing the Word: Refocusing New Testament study.* Grand Rapids, MI: Baker Academic.

Boer, M. de 1988. *The Defeat of Death: Apocalyptic eschatology in 1 Corinthians 15 and Romans 5*. JSNTSup 22. Sheffield: JSOT Press.

———. 1989. 'Paul and Jewish apocalyptic eschatology.' Pages 169–90 in *Apocalyptic and the New Testament: Essays in honor of J. Louis Martyn*, ed. J. Marcus and M. L. Soards. JSNTSup 24. Sheffield: JSOT Press.

———. 2011. *Galatians: A commentary*. Louisville, KY: Westminster John Knox Press.

Borg, M., and J. D. Crossan. 2007. *The Last Week: What the gospels really teach about Jesus' final days in Jerusalem*. New York, NY: HarperCollins (UK edn. London: SPCK, 2008).

Borst, G., W. M. Thompson and S. L. Kosslyn. 2011. 'Understanding the dorsal and ventral systems of the human cerebral cortex: beyond dichotomies.' *American Psychologist* 66(7):624–32.

Bradley, I. 2002. *God Save the Queen: The spiritual dimension of monarchy*. London: Darton, Longman and Todd.

Briggs, A. 2011. *Secret Days: Code-breaking in Bletchley Park*. London: Frontline.

Bultmann, R. 1964. 'πιστεύω κτλ.' *TDNT* 6:174–228.

Burridge, R. J. 2004. *What Are the Gospels? A comparison with Graeco-Roman biography*. 2nd edn. Grand Rapids, MI: Eerdmans.

Caird, G. B. 1980. *The Language and Imagery of the Bible*. London: Duckworth.

Campbell, D. A. 2009. *The Deliverance of God: An apocalyptic rereading of justification in Paul*. Grand Rapids, MI: Eerdmans.

———. 2012. 'Christ and the church in Paul: a 'post-new perspective' account.' Pages 113–43 in *Four Views on the Apostle Paul*, ed. M. Bird et al. Grand Rapids, MI: Zondervan.

Daniell, D. 1989. *Tyndale's New Testament*. New Haven, CT: Yale University Press.

———. 1994. *William Tyndale: A biography*. New Haven, CT: Yale University Press.

Davies, J. P. 2016. *Paul among the Apocalypses? An evaluation of the 'apocalyptic Paul' in the context of Jewish and Christian apocalyptic literature*. LNTS 562. London: Bloomsbury/T&T Clark.

Dodd, C. H. 1959 [1932]. *The Epistle of Paul to the Romans*. London: Fontana.

Dunn, J. D. G. 1988. *Romans 1—8*. WBC 38A. Dallas: Word.

Eliot, T. S. 1969. 'Murder in the Cathedral.' Part II in *The Complete Poems and Plays*. London: Faber & Faber.

———. 2001 [1979]. *Four Quartets*. London: Faber & Faber.

Ferguson, N. 2004. *Empire: How Britain made the modern world*. Harmondsworth: Penguin.

——. 2005. *Colossus: The rise and fall of the American empire.* Harmondsworth: Penguin.

Fowler, D. P., and P. G. Fowler. 2012. 'Virgil.' In *Oxford Classical Dictionary,* ed. S. Hornblower and A. Spawforth. 4th edn. Oxford: Oxford University Press.

Frei, H. W. 1974. *The Eclipse of Biblical Narrative: A study in eighteenth and nineteenth century hermeneutics.* New Haven, CT: Yale University Press.

Gay, P. 1966. *The Rise of Modern Paganism. Vol. 1: The Enlightenment: An interpretation.* New York, NY: Alfred A. Knopf.

Gibson, J. 1998. 'Testing temptation: the meaning of Q 11:4b.' Paper presented at the meeting of the Society of Biblical Literature. Orlando, FL.

Goldingay, J. 2003. *Israel's Gospel. Vol. 1: Old Testament Theology.* Downers Grove, IL: InterVarsity Press.

Grayling, A. C. 2011. *The Good Book: A secular bible.* London: Bloomsbury.

Greenblatt, S. 2011. *The Swerve: How the Renaissance began.* London: Bodley Head.

Hafemann, S., ed. 2002. *Biblical Theology: Retrospect and prospect.* Downers Grove, IL: InterVarsity Press.

Hauerwas, S., and C. Pinches. 1997. *Christians among the Virtues: Theological conversations with ancient and modern ethics.* Notre Dame, IN: University of Notre Dame Press.

Hays, R. B. 1985. 'Have we found Abraham to be our forefather according to the flesh? A reconsideration of Rom 4:1.' *Novum Testamentum* 27:76–98.

——. 2002 [1983]. *The Faith of Jesus Christ: The narrative substructure of Galatians 3:1—4:11.* 2nd edn. Grand Rapids, MI: Eerdmans.

——. 2005. 'The conversion of the imagination: scripture and eschatology in 1 Corinthians.' Pages 1–24 in *The Conversion of the Imagination: Paul as interpreter of Israel's scripture.* Grand Rapids, MI: Eerdmans.

——. 2016. *Echoes of Scripture in the Gospels.* Waco, TX: Baylor University Press.

Heilig, C. 2015. *Hidden Criticism? The methodology and plausibility of the search for a counter-imperial subtext in Paul.* WUNT 2.392. Tübingen: Mohr Siebeck.

Hornblower, S., and A. Spawforth, eds. 2012. *Oxford Classical Dictionary.* 4th edn. Oxford: Oxford University Press.

Horsley, R. A., ed. 1997. *Paul and Empire: Religion and power in Roman imperial society.* Harrisburg, PA: Trinity Press International.

——, ed. 2000. *Paul and Politics: Ekklesia, Israel, imperium, interpretation.*

Essays in honor of Krister Stendahl. Harrisburg, PA: Trinity Press International.

Hübenthal, S. 2006. *Transformation und Aktualisierung: Zur Rezeption von Sach 9—14 im Neuen Testament.* Stuttgart: Katholisches Bibelwerk.

Hurtado, L. 2003. *Lord Jesus Christ: Devotion to Jesus in earliest Christianity.* Grand Rapids, MI: Eerdmans.

Jacob, H. G. 2018. *Conformed to the Image of His Son: Reconsidering Paul's theology of glory in Romans.* Downers Grove, IL: InterVarsity Press.

Johnson, L. T. 2012. 'The Paul of the letters: a catholic perspective.' Pages 65–96 in *Four Views on the Apostle Paul,* ed. M. Bird.

Jones, G. L. 1995. *Embodying Forgiveness: A theological analysis.* Grand Rapids, MI: Eerdmans.

Keener, C. 2003. *The Gospel of John: A commentary.* Peabody, MA: Hendrickson.

Keesmaat, S. C. 1999. *Paul and His Story: (Re)interpreting the exodus tradition.* Sheffield: Sheffield Academic Press.

Kinman, B. 1994. 'Jesus' "triumphal entry" in the light of Pilate's.' *New Testament Studies* 40(3):442–8.

Kittel, G., and G. Friedrich, eds. 1964–1976. *Theological Dictionary of the New Testament,* tr. G. W. Bromiley. 10 vols. Grand Rapids, MI: Eerdmans.

Koch, K. 1972 [1970]. The Rediscovery of the Apocalyptic: A polemical work on a neglected area of biblical studies and its damaging effects on theology and philosophy, tr. M. Kohl. SBT 2.22. London: SCM Press.

Koenig, J. 1998. *Rediscovering New Testament Prayer: Boldness and blessing in the name of Jesus.* San Francisco, CA: Harper. Repr., Harrisburg, PA: Morehouse.

Kooten, G. van 2008. *Paul's Anthropology in Context: The image of God, assimilation to God, and tripartite man in ancient Judaism.* Tübingen: Mohr Siebeck.

Kooten, G. van, O. Wischmeyer and N. T. Wright. 2015. 'How Greek was Paul's eschatology?' *New Testament Studies* 61(2): 239–53.

Leuenberger, M. 2015. *Haggai.* Freiburg im Breisgau: Herder.

Lewis, C. S. 1933. *The Pilgrim's Regress.* London: J. M. Dent & Sons.

———. 1960. *Studies in Words.* Cambridge: Cambridge University Press.

MacDonald, N., and I. J. de Hulster, eds. 2013. *Divine Presence and Absence in Exilic and Post-Exilic Judaism.* Tübingen: Mohr Siebeck.

McGilchrist, I. 2009. *The Master and His Emissary: The divided brain and the making of the western world.* New Haven, CT: Yale University Press.

Bibliography

MacIntyre, A. 1985 [1981]. *After Virtue: A study in moral theory.* 2nd edn. London: Duckworth.

——. 1988. *Whose Justice? Which Rationality?* Notre Dame, IN: University of Notre Dame Press.

Martin, D. 2011. 'Heapeth Up Riches.' Review of A. C. Grayling, *The Good Book: A secular bible. Times Literary Supplement* 3 June: 25–6.

Martyn, J. L. 1997a. *Galatians: A new translation with introduction and commentary.* AB 33a. New York, NY: Doubleday.

——. 1997b. *Theological Issues in the Letters of Paul.* Nashville, TN: Abingdon Press.

Meeks, W. 1983. *The First Urban Christians.* New Haven, CT: Yale University Press.

Meyer, B. F. 1979. *The Aims of Jesus.* London: SCM Press (2nd edn. San Jose, CA: Pickwick, 2002).

Middleton, J. R. 2005. *The Liberating Image: The imago Dei in Genesis 1.* Grand Rapids, MI: Brazos Press.

Milbank, J., S. Žižek and C. Davis, eds. 2010. *Paul's New Moment: Continental philosophy and the future of Christian theology.* Grand Rapids, MI: Brazos Press.

Morales, L. M., ed. 2014. *Cult and Cosmos: Tilting towards a Temple-centred theology.* Leuven: Peeters.

Myers, C. 1990. *Binding the Strong Man: A political reading of Mark's story of Jesus.* Maryknoll, NY: Orbis.

Neiman, S. 2002. *Evil in Modern Thought: An alternative history of philosophy.* Princeton, NJ: Princeton University Press.

Nickelsburg, G. 2002. *1 Enoch 1.* Minneapolis, MN: Fortress Press.

Niebuhr, R. H. 1952. *Christ and Culture.* London: Faber & Faber.

O'Donovan, O. 1996. *The Desire of the Nations.* Cambridge: Cambridge University Press.

——. 2005. *The Ways of Judgment.* Grand Rapids, MI: Eerdmans.

O'Donovan, O., and J. L. O'Donovan. 1999. *From Irenaeus to Grotius: A sourcebook in Christian political thought.* Grand Rapids, MI: Eerdmans.

Oermann, N. O. 2016. *Albert Schweitzer: A biography.* Oxford: Oxford University Press.

Peppard, M. 2010. 'The eagle and the dove: Roman imperial sonship and the baptism of Jesus (Mark 1.9–11).' *New Testament Studies* 56(4):431–51.

Pinches, C. 2000. 'Virtue.' Pages 741–3 in *The Oxford Companion to Christian Thought,* ed. A. Hastings. Oxford: Oxford University Press.

Porter, J. 2001. 'Virtue ethics.' Pages 96–111 in *The Cambridge Companion to Christian Ethics,* ed. R. Gill. Cambridge: Cambridge University Press.

Bibliography

Portier-Young. A. 2011. *Apocalypse against Empire: Theologies of resistance in early Judaism*. Grand Rapids, MI: Eerdmans.

Priestley, J. B. 2009. *An Inspector Calls*. Stuttgart: Klett Sprachen.

Reynolds, B. E., and L. T. Stuckenbruck, eds. 2017. *The Jewish Apocalyptic Tradition and the Shaping of New Testament Thought*. Minneapolis, MN: Fortress Press.

Robinson, J. A. T. 1952. *The Body*. London: SCM Press.

——. 1963. *Honest to God*. London: SCM Press.

——. 1967. *But That I Can't Believe*. London: HarperCollins.

——. 1980. *The Personal Life of the Christian*. Oxford: Oxford University Press.

——. 2002. *Honest to God*. 40th anniversary edn. Louisville, KY: Westminster John Knox Press.

Rowland, C. 1982. *The Open Heaven*. London: SPCK.

Rowland C., and C. R. A. Morray-Jones. 2009. *The Mystery of God: Early Jewish mysticism and the New Testament*. Leiden: Brill.

Sacks, J. 2008. 'Credo: the right hemisphere of the brain knits it all tgthr.' *The Times* 4 July, available at <http://rabbisacks.org/right-hemisphere-brain-knits-tgthr/>.

Sanders, E. P. 1992. *Judaism: Practice and belief 63 BCE – 66CE*. London: SCM Press.

Schweitzer, A. 1923 [1911]. *J. S. Bach*. London: A&C Black.

Scott, J. M., ed. 2017. *Exile: A conversation with N. T. Wright*. Downers Grove, IL: IVP Academic.

Sherwin-White, A. N. 1963. *Roman Society and Roman Law in the New Testament*. Oxford: Oxford University Press.

Stanton, G. N. 2004. *Jesus and Gospel*. Cambridge: Cambridge University Press.

Taylor, C. 2007. *A Secular Age*. Cambridge, MA: Belknap, 2007.

Volf, M. 1996. *Exclusion and Embrace: A theological exploration of identity, otherness, and reconciliation*. Nashville, TN: Abingdon Press.

Wallace, D. R. 2008. *The Gospel of God: Romans as Paul's Aeneid*. Eugene, OR: Pickwick.

Wallis, J. 2006. *God's Politics: Why the American Right gets it wrong and the Left doesn't get it*. Oxford: Lion.

Walsh, B., and R. Middleton. 1998. *Truth Is Stranger than It Used to Be*. London: SPCK.

Walton, J. H. 2009. *The Lost World of Genesis 1*. Downers Grove, IL: InterVarsity Press.

Wells, S. 2004. *Improvisation: The drama of Christian ethics*. Grand Rapids, MI: Brazos Press.

Westcott, B. F. 1903 [1881]. *The Gospel according to St. John*. London: John Murray.

Wilson, A. N. 1999. *God's Funeral*. London: John Murray.

Wilson, C. 2008. *Epicureanism at the Origins of Modernity*. Oxford: Oxford University Press.

Wise, M. O. 1999. *The First Messiah: Investigating the savior before Christ*. San Francisco, CA: Harper.

Witherington, B. 2004. *The New Testament Story*. Grand Rapids, MI: Eerdmans.

Wright, N. T., ed. 1978. *The Work of John Frith*. Courtenay Library of Reformation Classics 7. Appleford: The Sutton Courtenay Press.

———. 1991. *The Climax of the Covenant: Christ and the law in Pauline theology*. Edinburgh: T&T Clark.

———. 1992. *The New Testament and the People of God*. COQG 1. London: SPCK; Minneapolis, MN: Fortress Press.

———. 1996a. *Jesus and the Victory of God*. COQG 2. London: SPCK; Minneapolis, MN: Fortress Press.

———. 1996b. *The Lord and His Prayer*. Grand Rapids, MI: Eerdmans.

———. 1999a. *The Challenge of Jesus*. London: SPCK; Downers Grove, IL: InterVarsity Press.

———. 1999b. 'In grateful dialogue.' Pages 244–77 in *Jesus and the Restoration of Israel*, ed. C. C. Newman. Downers Grove, IL: InterVarsity Press.

———. 1999c. *The Myth of the Millennium*. London: SPCK.

———. 1999d. 'New exodus, new inheritance: the narrative structure of Romans 3—8.' Pages 26–35 in *Romans and the People of God: Essays in honor of Gordon D. Fee on the occasion of his sixty-fifth birthday*, ed. S. K. Soderlund and N. T. Wright. Grand Rapids, MI: Eerdmans.

———. 1999e. *The Way of the Lord*. London: SPCK; Grand Rapids, MI: Eerdmans.

———. 2000a. *The Challenge of Jesus: Rediscovering who Jesus was and is*. London: SPCK.

———. 2000b. 'Paul's gospel and Caesar's empire.' Pages 160–83 in *Paul and Politics: Ekklesia, Israel, imperium, interpretation. Essays in honor of Krister Stendahl*, ed. R. A. Horsley. Harrisburg, PA: Trinity Press International.

———. 2001. 'A fresh perspective on Paul?' *Bulletin of the John Rylands University Library of Manchester* 83(1):21–39.

———. 2002a. 'Paul and Caesar: a new reading of Romans.' Pages 173–93 in

A Royal Priesthood: The use of the Bible ethically and politically, ed. C. Bartholomew. Carlisle: Paternoster.

———. 2002b. 'Romans.' Pages 393–770 in *The New Interpreter's Bible*, vol. 10, ed. L. E. Keck et al. Nashville, TN: Abingdon Press.

———. 2003. *The Resurrection of the Son of God.* COQG 3. London: SPCK; Minneapolis, MN: Fortress Press.

———. 2004. 'Redemption from the new perspective?' Pages 69–100 in *The Redemption*, ed. S. T. Davis, D. Kendall and G. O'Collins. Oxford: Oxford University Press.

———. 2005a. *Paul: Fresh Perspectives.* London: SPCK.

———. 2005b. *Scripture and the Authority of God* (US title *The Last Word: Beyond the Bible wars to a new understanding of scripture*). London: SPCK; New York, NY: HarperCollins.

———. 2006a. *Evil and the Justice of God.* London: SPCK.

———. 2006b. 'New perspectives on Paul.' Pages 243–64 in *Justification in Perspective: Historical developments and contemporary challenges*, ed. B. L. McCormack. Grand Rapids, MI: Baker Academic.

———. 2008. *Surprised by Hope.* London: SPCK.

———. 2009. *Paul in Fresh Perspective.* London: SPCK.

———. 2010. *Virtue Reborn* (US title *After You Believe*). London: SPCK; San Francisco, CA: HarperOne.

———. 2011b. *Revelation for Everyone.* London: SPCK.

———. 2011c [2005]. *Scripture and the Authority of God: How to read the Bible today.* 2nd edn. San Francisco, CA: HarperOne (UK edn. London: SPCK, 2013).

———. 2011d. *Simply Jesus: Who he was, what he did, why it matters.* San Francisco, CA: HarperOne; London: SPCK.

———. 2012. *How God Became King.* San Francisco, CA: HarperOne; London: SPCK.

———. 2013a. *Creation, Power and Truth.* London: SPCK.

———. 2013b. *Paul and the Faithfulness of God.* COQG 4. London: SPCK; Minneapolis, MN: Fortress Press.

———. 2013c. *Pauline Perspectives: Essays on Paul 1978–2013.* London: SPCK; Minneapolis, MN: Fortress Press.

———. 2014a. 'A new perspective on Käsemann? Apocalyptic, covenant, and the righteousness of God.' Pages 243–58 in *Studies in the Pauline Epistles: Essays in honor of Douglas J. Moo*, ed. M. S. Harmon and J. E. Smith. Grand Rapids, MI: Zondervan.

———. 2014b. *Surprised by Scripture.* San Francisco, CA: HarperOne (UK edn. London: SPCK, 2015).

——. 2015a. *Paul and His Recent Interpreters*. London: SPCK; Minneapolis, MN: Fortress Press.

——. 2015b. *The Paul Debate*. Waco, TX; Baylor University Press.

——. 2016a. *The Day the Revolution Began: Reconsidering the meaning of Jesus' crucifixion*. San Francisco, CA: HarperOne; London: SPCK.

——. 2016b. *God in Public: How the Bible speaks truth to power today*. London: SPCK.

——. 2016c. 'God put Jesus forth: reflections on Romans 3:24–26.' Pages 135–61 in *In the Fullness of Time: Essays in honor of Richard Bauckham*, ed. D. Gurtner, G. Macaskill and J. T. Pennington. Grand Rapids, MI: Eerdmans.

——. 2017. 'Pictures, stories, and the cross: where do the echoes lead?' *Journal of Theological Interpretation* 11(1):53–73.

——. 2018a. 'Hope deferred? Against the dogma of delay.' *Early Christianity* 9(1):37–82.

——. 2018b. 'Son of man – lord of the Temple? Gospel echoes of Psalm 8 and the ongoing christological challenge.' Pages 77–96 in *The Earliest Perceptions of Jesus in Context: Essays in honour of John Nolland on his seventieth birthday*, ed. A. W. White, D. Wenham and C. A. Evans. London: Bloomsbury/T&T Clark.

——. 2019a. *History and Eschatology: Jesus and the promise of natural theology*. London: SPCK; Waco, TX: Baylor University Press.

——. 2019b. *The New Testament for Everyone* (US title *The Kingdom New Testament*). London: SPCK; San Francisco, CA: HarperOne.

Acknowledgments

The author and publisher are grateful for permission to reproduce the material listed below in this volume.

Chapter 1: 'Introduction to *The Language and Imagery of the Bible* by G. B. Caird.' Grand Rapids, MI: Eerdmans, 1997, pp. xi–xviii. Reprinted by permission of the publisher.

Chapter 2: 'The Lord's Prayer as a Paradigm of Christian Prayer.' In, *Into God's Presence: Prayer in the New Testament*, ed. R. L. Longenecker. Grand Rapids, MI: Eerdmans, 2001, pp. 132–54. Reprinted by permission of the publisher.

Chapter 4: 'Christian Origins and the Question of God.' Excerpt from *Engaging the Doctrine of God: Contemporary Protestant Perspectives*, pp. 21–36, ed. Bruce McCormack, copyright © 2008. Used by permission of Baker Academic, a division of Baker Publishing Group.

Chapter 5: 'Faith, Virtue, Justification, and the Journey to Freedom.' In, *The Word Leaps the Gap: Essays on Scripture and Theology in Honor of Richard B. Hays*. ed. J. R. Wagner, C. K. Rowe, and A. K. Grieb. Grand Rapids, MI: Eerdmans, 2008, pp. 472–97. Reprinted by permission of the publisher.

Extracts from 'Little Gidding' and 'East Coker' by T. S. Eliot, in *Four Quartets*. London: Faber & Faber, 2001 [1979]; Orlando, FL: Harcourt, 1943. Copyright © UK, Faber & Faber; USA, Houghton Mifflin Harcourt. Reprinted with permission from Faber & Faber and Houghton Mifflin Harcourt.

Chapter 6: 'Neither Anarchy nor Tyranny: Government and the New Testament.' In, *God and Government*, ed. Nick Spencer and Jonathan Chaplin. London: SPCK, 2009, pp. 61–79. Reprinted by permission of the publisher.

Chapter 7: 'The Bishop and Living under Scripture.' In, *Christ and Culture: Communion after Lambeth*, ed. M. Percy, M. Chapman, I. Markham and B. Hawkins. Norwich: Canterbury Press, 2010, pp. 144–66. Reprinted by permission of the publisher.

Song lyrics by Phil Ochs from 'Flower Lady', on his album Pleasures of the Harbour, 1967. Copyright © Universal Music Publishing Group. Reprinted by permission of the record company.

Acknowledgments

Chapter 8: 'Imagining the Kingdom: Mission and Theology in Early Christianity.' *Scottish Journal of Theology* 65.04 (2012): 379–401. Copyright © Scottish Journal of Theology Ltd 2012. Reproduced with permission of the Licensor through PLSclear.

Chapter 9: 'Revelation and Christian Hope: Political Implications of the Revelation to John.' In, *Revelation and the Politics of Apocalyptic Interpretation*, eds. Richard B. Hays and S. Alkier. Waco, TX: Baylor University Press, 2012, pp. 105–24. Reprinted by permission of the publisher.

Chapter 10: 'The Monarchs and the Message: Reflections on Bible Translation from the Sixteenth to the Twenty-First Century.' In, *The King James Version at 400*, eds. David G. Burke, John F. Kutsko and Philip H. Towner. Atlanta, GA: SBL Press, 2013, pp. 309–27. Reprinted by permission of the publisher.

Chapter 11: 'Joy: Some New Testament Perspectives and Questions.' In, *Joy and Human Flourishing: Essays on Theology, Culture, and the Good Life*, eds. M. Volf and J. E. Crisp. Minneapolis, MN: Fortress Press, 2015, pp. 39–61. Reprinted by permission of the publisher.

Chapter 12: 'Pastoral Theology for Perplexing Topics: Paul and *Adiaphora*.' In, *Good Disagreement? Grace and Truth in a Divided Church*, eds. Andrew Atherstone and Andrew Goddard. Oxford: Lion Hudson, 2015, pp. 63–83. Reprinted by permission of the publisher.

Chapter 13: 'Apocalyptic and the Sudden Fulfilment of Divine Promise.' In, *Paul and the Apocalyptic Imagination*, eds. J. K. Goodrich, B. Blackwell and J. Mastin. Minneapolis, MN: Fortress Press, 2016, pp. 111–34. Reprinted by permission of the publisher.

Extract from 'Murder in the Cathedral', in T. S. Eliot, *The Complete Poems and Plays*. London: Faber & Faber, 1969. Copyright © UK, Faber & Faber; USA, Houghton Mifflin Harcourt. Reprinted with permission from Faber & Faber and Houghton Mifflin Harcourt.

Chapter 14: 'The Bible and Christian Mission.' Excerpt from *Scripture and Its Interpretation: A Global, Ecumenical Introduction to the Bible*, pp. 388–400, ed. Michael Gorman, copyright © 2017. Used by permission of Baker Academic, a division of Baker Publishing Group.

Chapter 15: 'Wouldn't You Love to Know? Towards a Christian View of Reality.' Grasping the Nettle, Glasgow, 1 September 2016. (Previously unpublished.)

Chapter 16: 'Sign and Means of New Creation: Public Worship and the Creative Reading of Scripture.' Symposium on Worship, Calvin College, Grand Rapids, Michigan, 27–28 January 2017. (Previously unpublished.)

Chapter 17: 'The Powerful Breath of the New Creation.' *Veni, Sancte Spiritus! Festschrift für Barbara Hallensleben zum 60. Geburtstag.Theologische Beiträge zur Sendung des Geistes.* Münster: Aschendorff Verlag, 2018, pp. 1–15. Reprinted by permission of the publisher.

Chapter 18: 'Sacred Space in the City.' A lecture at Central Presbyterian Church, Park Avenue, New York, 22 April 2018. (Previously unpublished.) Extract from 'Little Gidding' by T. S. Eliot, in *Four Quartets.* London: Faber & Faber, 2001 [1979]; Orlando, FL: Harcourt, 1943. Copyright © UK, Faber & Faber; USA, Houghton Mifflin Harcourt. Reprinted with permission from Faber & Faber and Houghton Mifflin Harcourt.

Chapter 19: 'Foreword to *The Church and Its Vocation: Lesslie Newbigin's Missionary Ecclesiology* by Michael Goheen.' Excerpt from Michael Goheen, *The Church and Its Vocation: Lesslie Newbigin's Missionary Ecclesiology,* pp. ix–xii, copyright © 2018. Used by permission of Baker Academic, a division of Baker Publishing Group.

Chapter 21: 'Christ and the Cosmos: Kingdom and Creation in Gospel Perspective.' In, *Christ and the Created Order: Perspectives from Theology, Philosophy and Science,* ed. A. B. Torrance and T. McCall. Grand Rapids, MI: Zondervan Academic, 2018, pp. 97–109. Reprinted by permission of the publisher.

Chapter 22: 'Get the Story Right and the Models Will Fit: Victory through Substitution in "Atonement Theology".' In, *Atonement: Jewish and Christian Origins,* eds. M. Botner, J. H. Duff, and S. Dürr. Grand Rapids, MI: Eerdmans, 2020, pp. 112–30. Reprinted by permission of the publisher.

Index of Ancient Sources

Index of Modern Authors

The New Testament in Its World

An Introduction to the History, Literature, and Theology of the First Christians

N. T. Wright and Michael F. Bird

The New Testament in Its World is your passageway from the twenty-first century to the era of Jesus and the first Christians. In short, it brings together decades of ground-breaking research, writing, and teaching into one volume that will open your eyes to the larger world of the New Testament. It presents the New Testament books as historical, literary, and social phenomena located in the world of Second Temple Judaism, amidst Greco-Roman politics and culture, and within early Christianity. Book, workbook, and video/audio resources are available.

Available in stores and online!

ZONDERVAN®
.com